D0992511

The Eastern Fleet and the Indian Ocean 1942–1944

The Eastern Fleet and the Indian Ocean 1942–1944

The Fleet that Had to Hide

Charles Stephenson

Pen & Sword
MILITARY

An imprint of
Pen & Sword Books Ltd
Yorkshire – Philadelphia

First published in Great Britain in 2020 and reprinted in 2021 by
PEN & SWORD MARITIME

An imprint of
Pen & Sword Books Ltd
Yorkshire – Philadelphia

Copyright © Charles Stephenson 2020, 2021

ISBN 978-1-52678-361-5

The right of Charles Stephenson to be identified as Author of this work has been asserted by him
in accordance with the Copyright, Designs and Patents Act 1988.

A CIP catalogue record for this book is available from the British Library

All rights reserved. No part of this book may be reproduced or transmitted in any form or by
any means, electronic or mechanical including photocopying, recording or by any information
storage and retrieval system, without permission from the Publisher in writing.

Typeset in 11/13 by Ehrhardt

Printed and bound in the UK by CPI Group (UK) Ltd, Croydon, CRO 4YY

Pen & Sword Books Ltd incorporates the imprints of Pen & Sword Archaeology, Atlas,
Aviation, Battleground, Discovery, Family History, History, Maritime, Military, Naval,
Politics, Social History, Transport, True Crime, Claymore Press, Frontline Books,
Praetorian Press, Seaforth Publishing and White Owl

For a complete list of Pen & Sword titles please contact

PEN & SWORD BOOKS LTD
47 Church Street, Barnsley, South Yorkshire, S70 2AS, England
E-mail: enquiries@pen-and-sword.co.uk
Website: www.pen-and-sword.co.uk

Or

PEN AND SWORD BOOKS
1950 Lawrence Rd, Havertown, PA 19083, USA
E-mail: Uspen-and-sword@casematepublishers.com
Website: www.penandswordbooks.com

Contents

In memory of
Harriet Elizabeth 'Peggy' Evans
17 November 1934–21 July 2019
'Goodbye always makes my throat hurt'

List of Illustrations

1. The British Aviation Mission to Japan.
2. An Italian Sound Locator.
3. The German ships at Mormugao (Marmagoa) Harbour, Goa.
4. The Officers of the Calcutta Light Horse in 1944.
5. HMS *Cornwall*
6. HMS *Dorsetshire*
7. HMS *Erebus*
8. HMS *Glorious*
9. HMS *Hermes*
10. *Hosho*
11. *Indomitable*
12. Japanese and Germans at Penang
13. HMS *Ramillies*
14. HMS *Renown*
15. HMS *Repulse*
16. HMS *Richelieu*
17. *Shokaku*
18. HMS *Warspite*
19. Admiral Sir James Somerville
20. The Combined Chiefs of Staff with Roosevelt and Churchill at Quebec 1944.

Foreword by
Commander Daniel Clarke OBE RN (Retd.)

Though I am delighted to have been asked to contribute this foreword to it, Charles Stephenson's book is, in one sense, a rather depressing read. It charts the relegation of the service from pre-eminence following the First World War, to the realisation that in battle-fleet terms it had fallen to second, or even third, place during the Second. Stephenson chronicles the several strands, political, technological and doctrinal, that led to this decline, which only became fully revealed in 1942. Then the Eastern Fleet, the largest fleet deployed by the Navy during the Second World War up to 1945, was compelled to decline battle with its enemy, the Imperial Japanese Navy, and 'hide, more or less'.

This course was forced upon the Fleet because it couldn't compete with the enemy tactically. Since strategic success depends upon achieving operational successes, which in turn result from tactical successes, this had the potential for disaster. That this potential was mitigated to a large extent was due to the 'strategic imbecility', as Samuel Eliot Morison put it, of Japan simultaneously deciding to make an enemy of the United States of America. Because of this incalculable error, the Eastern Fleet was able to survive as a 'fleet in being'. As the author states it, however, 'whilst discretion may well be the better part of valour, it rarely brings victory, and though it may exercise a deterrent, neither does a "fleet in being"'.

On the other hand, the story is ultimately a stirring one. Despite the incredible disadvantages and difficulties under which they laboured, the officers and men of the Eastern Fleet under the inspiring command of Admiral Somerville not only survived but sprang back. Indeed, they held in check an enemy submarine campaign before, in 1944, being able to take large-scale offensive action against the enemy.

Ultimately, the Eastern Fleet segued into the British Pacific Fleet and successfully participated in the final actions against Japan alongside the, by now much larger, American Fleet. Stephenson's tale thus provides a happy ending – more or less. As he puts it: 'In the league table of offensive naval power the

British now came a definite second, and that only because the new holder of the top spot had destroyed the only other contender.' Quite so.

There are, I think, larger lessons to be learned from this relatively little-known story. Politicians and, yes, senior service commanders need to ensure that they match means with ends. Indeed they have a bounden duty to do so. Even the best-crafted strategy will end up trashed unless those sent into harm's way to deliver it have a reasonable chance of dealing with whatever they might encounter. Neglecting this timeless principle inevitably results in failure and the expenditure of much blood. And the latter, particularly, is unforgiveable. Sadly, as any study of relatively recent events will serve to demonstrate, it is a principle more often honoured in the breach than the observance.

Dan Clarke attended Britannia Royal Naval College (1994–6) and was Officer Commanding Royal Navy Submarine School (Jan 2015–Jul 2015), Commander Sea Training (Submarines) (Aug 2014–Jan 2015), and Commanding Officer (Aug 2012–Aug 2014) of the *Trafalgar* class nuclear submarine HMS *Triumph*. He was awarded the OBE in 2015 'in recognition of gallant and distinguished services in the field during the period 1 October 2013 to 30 June 2014'.

Introduction

'Fast bound in misery and iron'

The autumnal North Sea is notoriously dreich, to appropriate the (highly appropriate) Scottish term, so the sunny and only intermittently misty conditions pertaining on 21 November 1918 were perhaps a trifle out of the ordinary. Certainly, the melancholy call of the foghorn was missing that morning, which was fortunate for those who wished to appreciate a sight that would, and indeed could, never be repeated. At daybreak the Royal Navy's mighty Grand Fleet, under the command of Admiral Sir David Beatty, had begun to steam from its base at Rosyth, initially under the great, red-lead shaded cantilever rail-bridge opened in 1890, and then out of the mouth of the Firth of Forth. At first arrayed in line ahead, once clear of the coast it deployed into two columns some six miles apart heading directly eastwards.

The northernmost column comprised no fewer than nineteen battleships, including five belonging to Battleship Division Nine of the United States Atlantic Fleet under the command of Rear Admiral Rodman (attached as the 6th Battle Squadron), four battlecruisers (battleships and battlecruisers being designated Capital Ships; the contemporaneous currency in which naval power was weighed), two cruisers and thirteen light cruisers. Its southern counterpart totalled fourteen battleships, four battlecruisers, the 'Flying Squadron' including the aircraft carriers *Furious* and *Vindictive*, one French cruiser (*Amiral Aube*), and twelve light cruisers. It was easily the largest conglomeration of naval power yet seen anywhere on the planet. Ever. This mighty fleet, escorted by scores of destroyers (two of which were French), was ready for battle. Indeed all hands were at action stations, as per Beatty's orders:

> Turrets and guns are to be kept in the securing positions, but free. Guns are to be empty with cages up and loaded ready for ramming home. Directors and armoured towers are to be trained on. Correct range and deflection are to be kept set continuously on the sights.[1]

The Grand Fleet was fully prepared for a sea-fight, but it did not expect one. It was known that the fleet they were going to meet was largely disarmed, both by armistice terms and by the Red revolution that had eaten up the crews whilst in their home-ports. Nevertheless, there was to be no taking chances; all was ready to open a deadly cannonade should any trick be attempted.

Just before 10:00 hours, it met a substantial portion of the *Hochseeflotte*, the German High Seas Fleet, under the command of Rear Admiral Ludwig von Reuter, heading in the opposite direction. The twin British columns, turning 16 points outwards by squadrons, reversed course to form an overwhelming escort on either side of the Germans. An unnamed 'Special Correspondent' for *The Times* was aboard *Queen Elizabeth*, the British flagship, and he described the scene:

> Between the lines came the Germans, led by the *Cardiff*, and looking for all the world like a school of leviathans led by a minnow. Over them flew a British naval airship. First came the battlecruisers, headed by the *Seydlitz* . . . The *Moltke* and the *Hindenburg* followed, then the *Derfflinger* . . . and finally the *Von Der Tann*.[2]

Arrayed in a single line behind the battlecruisers came nine great, grey battleships, the most modern and powerful the *Hochseeflotte* possessed.[3] The smaller warships, seven light cruisers and forty-nine destroyers, brought up the rear. Beatty was, just a few days later, to describe the scene with a hint of triumphalism tinged perhaps with disdain:

> I have always said in the past that the High Sea Fleet would have to come out and meet the Grand Fleet. I was not a false prophet; they are out, and they are now in. They are in our pockets . . . But we never expected that the last time we should see them as a great force would be when they were being shepherded, like a flock of sheep, by the Grand Fleet.[4]

This was echoed by at least one of the more junior members of his command; an RAF officer aboard the aircraft carrier *Furious* named Jack McCleery. He penned an article that appeared in the *Belfast Telegraph* some four days later:

> I am writing this as we round up what was once the German High Seas Fleet . . . the German battle cruisers and battleships are seen to be at anchor with our battle squadrons formed into a square around them. What a sight! Tomorrow I hope to fly over them and see more plainly for myself, the ships which we in the old *Furious*, were so often sent out to try and lure to their destruction. But what a sight to remember, the pride of Germany's navy at anchor in the Forth with a wall of steel surrounding them . . . It is almost unbelievable, but – it is true.[5]

Rear Admiral Hugh Rodman, the commander of the 6th Battle Squadron, was also unequivocal, writing how 'the last scene of the great drama' came 'in the ignominious surrender of the entire German fleet without firing a gun. No more complete naval victory was ever won.'[6] Neither were Beatty's sentiments echoed in the report by the 'Special Correspondent' who was undoubtedly alive to the likely reaction of both his editor and readership:

> The sun has just gone down on the most wonderful day in all the long history of war by sea. . . . The finest vessels in the German Fleet . . . have surrendered themselves, as hostages to the Allies. . . . the captive ships lie but a few miles away in British waters, 'fast bound in misery and iron', the tragic semblance of a navy which lost its soul . . . it marked the final and ignoble abandonment of a vainglorious challenge to the naval supremacy of Britain.[7]

There could be no doubt that the Royal Navy had defeated its German counterpart, despite only coming to inconclusive blows once, in 1916. On that occasion, the latter had been faced with an enemy so superior in numbers that it had, of necessity, fled the field. Indeed, the disdain felt by the officers and men of the Grand Fleet centred around that fact; that the Germans had refused, as Beatty termed it, to 'give us what we hoped for – a good stand-up fight'.

Rather than it being a matter of materiel superiority, with the Grand Fleet simply outnumbering its enemy, he couched their reluctance to allow themselves to be destroyed in moral terms. The Royal Navy, he went on to say, had expected their enemy 'to have the same courage that we expect from men whose work lies upon great waters' and 'their humiliating end was a suitable end and a proper end for a foe so lacking in chivalry and in what we look for from an honourable foe'. The High Seas Fleet, he told his audience, was an unworthy opponent: 'From the beginning its strategy, its tactics and its behaviour have been beneath contempt . . . the enemy . . . is despicable, nothing more nor less . . . He would not be worthy of the loss of one life in the Grand Fleet; he is too far beneath us.'[8]

Stirring stuff no doubt, but they were words that would have to be, in no uncertain terms, eaten. Having said that, it is doubtful that they, or even the sentiments expressed, were remembered at all when, some 24 years later, a British fleet found itself emulating its erstwhile enemy and refusing 'a good stand-up fight'. That it did so was for much the same reason as the earlier rejection; it was confronted with a foe so superior as to make the result of any such combat a foregone conclusion. Though on this latter occasion the superiority wasn't purely numerical, but also technological and doctrinal.

That is the rationale for this work. It seeks to explore and, hopefully, explain how it came about that the world's most powerful and advanced navy in 1918 was reduced to such straits. How the largest single battlefleet that the Royal Navy mustered up until late 1944, the Eastern Fleet, was compelled in 1942 to hide from the enemy, Japan, that the British Admiralty had spent some two decades planning to fight.

It is, basically, a story of how the technology and tactics of naval warfare underwent a quantum change with the advent of aircraft, and then sending them to sea aboard carriers. These were largely British innovations; the first true aircraft carrier with a full-length flight-deck, 'designed to launch, recover, and sustain, embarked aircraft', being the *Argus* commisioned in 1918.[9] A dedicated torpedo-bomber to operate from it, the Sopwith T1 Cuckoo, was also in service.[10] The Imperial Japanese Navy (IJN), by way of contrast, had virtually no direct knowledge of such advances in 1918 but was eager to learn. In what was an astonishingly poor decision when viewed with that 20/20 vision we call hindsight, the British Government allowed an 'unofficial' Aviation Mission, amongst other initiatives, to travel to Japan and transfer both equipment and knowledge on the subject to a grateful IJN. The tale of this transference, and other efforts made by Japan to update its capabilities (both overt and covert), and their effects, are related in the first chapter.

Subsequent chapters deal with the difficulties Britain had in common with the other powers that had won the war, and the subsequent treaties limiting naval armaments agreed between them. These impacted all the states involved, but Britain had some particularly tough decisions to make, and challenges to overcome, with regards to its eastern empire and the formulation of a strategy to protect it.

Also explored is the decision made by the British Government in 1918 to create the Royal Air Force, and thus attenuate the connection between naval aviation and the Royal Navy. Though originally approving of the idea, the Navy swiftly realized this had been an error and made strenuous, and ultimately succesful, efforts to recover control over what was now dubbed the Fleet Air Arm. By then a second war with Germany, and Italy, was looming. The performance of the Fleet Air Arm during the first years of the war that ensued in 1939 is examined, and the advances, and notable successes, it made in that period described. These were significant, including a key role in the destruction of the *Bismarck* and the earlier airborne attack on Taranto on the night of 11/12 November 1940, the latter reducing the number of operational Italian capital ships by half. Somewhat more melancholic were the attacks on French ships following the Armistice of 22 June 1940.

The threat of Japan entering the war led to the forming of the first version of the Eastern Fleet based at Singapore; Admiral Tom Phillips assumed command on 3 December 1941. His flagship was the modern battleship *Prince of Wales* and his force was formed to act as a deterrent. It failed when the Japanese 'declaration of war' came by way of its invasion of Malaya on 8 December. It was still 7 December at Pearl Harbor, on the other side of the International Date Line, when the concentrated air power from six aircraft carriers heralded not only the entry of the United States into the war, but also a new era of naval warfare. Phillips' command was unfortunate to register another first in that field on 10 December. On that day both his flagship, and the battlecruiser *Repulse*, became the first capital ships to be sunk solely by aircraft whilst defending themselves and maneuvering at speed on the open sea. A new commander, Admiral James Somerville, was informed of his appointment on 15 December, though it took some little time for significant assets to be assigned to him.

The main body of this work traces then the history of this second rendition of the Eastern Fleet, and its operations in the Indian Ocean up until its dissolution on 22 November 1944 when it split between the British Pacific Fleet and the East Indies Fleet. As stated, it became the largest battlefleet that the Royal Navy mustered up until late 1944. Yet when it came face to face, or almost so, with a substantial body of the IJN it was obliged, as the High Seas Fleet had been in 1916, to avoid 'a good stand-up fight'. Rather it was, as Somerville put it on 6 April 1942, compelled to hide. Rather than a fighting force it too became a 'fleet in being', one that was forced to largely abandon the eastern portion of the Indian Ocean and operate from the shores of East Africa some thousands of miles distant. Why this was so, and subsequent events that eventually allowed a return, will be dealt with in some detail.

It is also a story that covers the period which saw the decline of the Royal Navy from joint first place to a definite second, and that only because the new holder of the top spot, the United States Navy, destroyed the other contender.

The subtitle is of course lifted from Hough's work on an earlier, Russian, naval force that crossed oceans to do battle with the Japanese Navy; *The Fleet that Had to Die*.[11] On 27 May (14 May in the Russian calendar) 1905 the Second and Third Pacific Squadrons, which had been led halfway around the world by Admiral Zinovy Rozhestvensky, encountered the Japanese fleet in the Tsushima Strait between Korea and Japan; over two days it indeed died, or was rather killed. What little remained afloat on the second day surrendered, and a few lighter ships escaped. This was not an auspicious precedent, but history did not repeat itself. However, whilst discretion may well be the better part of valour, it rarely brings victory, and though it may exercise a deterrent, neither does a 'fleet in being'.

This is not meant to be an academic work. There are no theoretical frameworks within which the tale is constructed, nor any new or startling conclusions. It merely attempts a narrative history, which is targeted at the general reader rather than the professional historian. Having said that I have been careful to correctly attribute all sources used.

Once again it gives me immense pleasure to thank a couple of stalwarts who have greatly helped in putting together this work; Charles Blackwood and Michael Perratt. Charles once again drew the excellent maps whilst Michael applied the acid test to a volume of this sort; is it intelligible and accessible to the intelligent lay reader? Happily he thought so. I am also greatly indebted to Commander Dan Clarke OBE RN (Retd.) who was generous enough to also read it and write the foreword. Any errors within though, whether of fact or style, are my sole responsibility.

Chapter 1

The Master, The Mission, and Rutland of Jutland

A close and, particularly in naval terms, important relationship between the UK and Japan existed from the very advent of the Meiji period (or era); October 1868 to July 1912. During this period Japan transitioned from being an isolated, feudal society to something recognizable as both modern and ostensibly Western-based in form. Much the same process was applied to creating an army and navy, and even before 1870, when an Imperial decree stipulated that the Royal Navy was to be the model upon which the Imperial Japanese Navy was to be based, British influence was noticeable.[1] This buying-in, as it might be termed, of British expertise and hardware was to be paralleled some 50 years later when an Aberdeenshire man, William Francis Forbes–Sempill, also known as Colonel the Master of Sempill, was called upon.

Japan, though a formal ally of Britain through the Anglo-Japanese Alliance, had participated only peripherally in the Great War against Germany and her allies.[2] Thus, and in the naval context, the IJN had no direct knowledge of the advances in technology, and battle experience, gained by the main participants. Chief amongst these was naval aviation, including the construction and use of aircraft carriers and techniques that had been developed for dropping torpedoes, and it naturally followed that advice on creating such a force was sought from Britain.

According to Sempill's own account, in 1920 Admiral Kato Tomosaburo, the then Minister of the Navy, decided to approach the British Government for assistance.[3] The initial request was formally made on 6 October that year when the Japanese Ambassador in London asked, via the Foreign Office, that Britain send an official naval aviation mission, of some twenty to thirty experienced personnel, to Japan. The purpose of the mission was to advise and teach thirty IJN officers techniques in flying, navigation, aerial fighting, torpedo launching, and flying on and off aircraft carriers, and to establish bases and instructional establishments for further development. Advice on the construction of aircraft carriers was also sought. The British personnel would be paid at one-and-a-half times their current RAF salaries and all travelling expenses would be covered.

In addition the IJN would purchase any equipment, including aircraft and ordnance, recommended by the mission from British firms. It was proposed that Captain Kobayashi Seizo, Japan's Naval Attaché, open direct negotiations with the Air Ministry.[4]

There were differences of opinion between government departments regarding the request, so a meeting was convened to iron them out on 22 October. It was a high-level affair; the First Sea Lord, Admiral of the Fleet Earl Beatty, took the chair. Rear Admiral Ernle Chatfield, Assistant Chief of the Naval Staff, also attended, as did the Chief of Air Staff, Air Marshal Sir Hugh Trenchard, General Sir William Thwaites, Director of Military Intelligence, and Sir Victor Wellesley, head of the Foreign Office's Far East Department. The outcome can be briefly stated. The Navy and Army were in agreement that any such official Mission would provide Japan with all of Britain's naval aviation knowledge; therefore it should not be sent. Wellesley played devil's advocate, outlining the commercial and political reasons which favoured the Mission. Only Trenchard argued unequivocally in favour, pointing out that if Britain did not provide the Mission then another power would, and that there were financial and political benefits to be had in the long term. Chatfield retorted that no other power was in a position to offer any worthwhile assistance. Beatty did, however, offer one concession; the Admiralty would not object if the Air Ministry were to send a civil aviation mission.[5]

The naval men were reiterating the position they had adopted around two years earlier. Indeed, almost as soon as the war in Europe was over, the potential for a future naval clash with Japan had begun to loom large in Admiralty thinking.[6] This focus was, at least to some extent, undoubtedly prompted by the fact that only by invoking such a threat could a case be reasonably made for proposing large Naval Estimates; the post-war British battlefleet certainly appeared all-powerful, but many of its major units were obsolete or worn out, or both, and needed replacement. This would of course be an expensive business, and there were many competing financial demands in the straitened financial circumstances of the time.

Somehow the results of the meeting, and the naval veto, leaked and were picked up by the Japanese, who were not best pleased. Sir Charles Eliot, the British Ambassador to Japan, sent a telegram on 13 November reporting that the IJN were 'irritated' at the unexpected refusal.[7] Since neither he nor the Japanese had been officially informed of the British decision, the Foreign Office, which had still to craft a diplomatic response, were somewhat embarrassed. The upshot was that a diplomatic reply was sent regretting that the British Government was not in a position to render the assistance required. According to Sempill at least, this was justified mainly on the grounds of extreme shortage of personnel. However, the blow, if it may be described as such, was softened, at the insistence of the Civil Aviation Department at the Air Ministry, by the offer of a civilian mission as stated by Beatty on 22 October. On 23 November 1920 the Japanese Embassy accepted this offer.[8] This decision tends to go at least some way to confirming US Naval Intelligence reports that '. . . the aviation activities in Japan, especially naval, are more than feverish; they have all the appearances of desperation'.[9]

That it was, though, taken very much as second best may be evidenced by the fact that two days later the Japanese Ambassador appealed the original decision to the Foreign Office, and on 30 November wrote personally to the Foreign Secretary Lord Curzon. Both appeals were politely, but firmly, rejected.[10]

So began the creation of the British Aviation Mission to the Imperial Japanese Navy, headed by Sempill. The Master of Sempill is an interesting character, particularly in retrospect, though quite why he was chosen to lead the mission remains obscure.[11] Though awarded several medals, including the Air Force Cross, he does not seem to have been much in action.[12] It may have been because of his work as an instructor at the Central Flying School (CFS), the primary role of which was to provide advanced flying training for qualified army and naval personnel, and his subsequent work at the Air Ministry during 1918–19. He also had the reputation of being 'one of England's [*sic*] most brilliant aeronautical engineers' and had been one of three members of the British official air mission which went to the United States in 1918.[13] It is also possible that the opinion of Captain Jack (John Peter Ralph) Marriott, the British Naval Attaché in Tokyo, was taken into account. He had opined in a message of 30 October, whilst discussions over the matter were still going on, that because the Japanese needed to be impressed by the quality of RAF officers, then any such mission should be comprised solely of 'gentlemen'.[14]

In any event in January 1921 the undoubtedly genteel, and indisputably aristocratic, Master of Sempill came to an agreement with the Japanese Naval Attaché, Captain Kobayashi Seizo, and began gathering personnel for his team on 1 February. According to his account, he was given virtual carte blanche in regard to the organization of the Mission, and recruited eighteen officers and twelve warrant officers, mainly though not exclusively from former members of the RNAS.

Clearly this was very far from being the 'civil aviation mission' that Beatty and the Admiralty had conceded. This is particularly so given the large amount of materiel that was to accompany it. According to Ferris, it took with it '113 aircraft consisting of 17 different British models, five of which were used by the contemporary British Fleet Air Arm. They also carried accessories, including bombs, torpedoes and wireless equipment.'[15] Sempill actually put the figure higher; 'In all approximately 200 machines were ordered in the first instance. These orders were supplemented at a later date from Japanese as well as British sources.'

The Mission members didn't depart all together due to the need to keep back a number of officers in order to acquire and assemble this equipment, which took a considerable amount of time to purchase, inspect and ship. In addition to the actual machines and engines required, a vast amount of material had to be arranged for in order to provide for 'the hundred and one things which go to the making of a fully equipped Air Service'.[16] These transactions would have been more than welcomed by the British aircraft industry; several aircraft manufacturers found themselves struggling to stay solvent after the Armistice as orders were cancelled.

An advance party, under Lieutenant Colonel Cecil Henry Meares as second-in-command, consisting of three flying officers and two engineer warrant officers, departed Southampton on 12 March 1921, arriving via the USA on 15 April 1921. They proceeded at once to inspect the site proposed for the new Central Training Station of the IJNAS at Kasumigaura, which lay on the shores of a lagoon of the same name about 40 miles north-east of Tokyo. However, although the site had been selected the installations had yet to be constructed.

It is testament to the resources that the IJN were putting in to the venture that the base was formally opened on 22 July 1921. Present on this occasion were upwards of 30,000 spectators, many of whom had walked great distances, and who were undoubtedly thrilled by a display of formation flying and a parachuting exhibition organized by Major Thomas Orde-Lees. Unsurprisingly, given their investment, many senior IJN officers were present.

The Mission was organized along the lines of the now-defunct RNAS. The Japanese granted acting commissions to all members with ranks equivalent to those they had already held previously in British service. Training was divided into four principal sections: Flying, Technical, Armament and Photography, and swung into action properly on 1 September.

The Flying Section instructors comprised six officers: one in charge, one for preliminary training, one for flying boats, one for seaplanes and preliminary flying boat training, one for scouts and one for deck-landing and fleet co-operation. With each of these officers were a number of Japanese officers acting as assistant instructors. The first intake of Japanese pilots that began training were in fact re-training; the instructors had decided that the existing Japanese pilots would have to be schooled in the basics, via the 'Gosport System', before any further work could begin.[17] After successfully passing this preliminary course they would move on to a more advanced syllabus. Depending on the suitability of the pupil as assessed, and the demands of the Service, this would involve training in several areas.

The most problematic technique the IJN sought to master, indeed the most difficult in naval aviation, was that of deck-landing on an aircraft carrier, in this case the *Hosho*. This vessel had been ordered in 1918 and laid down in the Asano Yard at Yokohama in December 1919 as a seaplane carrier with a flying-off deck forward and a large hangar aft. Having observed flying-off and landing operations taking place from the decks of the Royal Navy's *Furious* and *Argus*, the design was changed. The superstructure was removed and the funnels moved to one side and hinged so as to lie horizontal during flying operations, thus creating an unobstructed full-length flight deck with only a small island to starboard.[18] A small vessel displacing only some 10,000 tons, her capacity was limited; normally only fifteen aircraft were carried on board.[19]

In any event, instruction pertaining directly to *Hosho* couldn't commence until she was commissioned, which wasn't to take place until the end of December 1922. By that time the vast majority of the Mission had returned to the UK, but Major Herbert George 'Brackles' Brackley had a 'conference on deck flying' with the designated captain of the vessel on 25 July 1921, over three months before it was launched (13 November) and almost a week prior to Sempill initially arriving.[20] Until such time as the *Hosho* was available simulated operations on a 'dummy deck', so mounted that it could be turned into the wind, at Yokosuka naval base were all that was achievable.[21]

The Armament Section taught the use of weapons and ordnance, and was headed by a pair of British officers. The other instructors were Japanese who, because of their lack of participation in the war, had little current experience. The materiel they worked with was though thoroughly up to date and essentially like that used by the RN. This included locally-manufactured 500lb bombs and torpedoes.

Instruction on bombing was practiced with a device called the 'Batchelor Mirror'. This was equipment that, as the name suggests, featured a reflector. This was placed on the ground, or a vessel in Kasumigaura lagoon to simulate an attack on a ship, and used to check if the pilot had hit his target with an imaginary bomb.[22] The lagoon was also the site of exercises in air gunnery and the dropping of practice bombs and torpedoes.

Training in such matters was paralleled with more mundane parts of the Mission's remit. According to Sempill's account, the Technical Section was composed of five officers, one in charge of section, one for aircraft, one for engines, one designer and lecturer on aeronautical engineering, and one for technical and parachute training. There were also five warrant officer engineers, four riggers and one draughtsman attached to this section.

The retraining of the class of Japanese aviators to 'Gosport' standards was deemed complete in March 1922. Advanced work, including simulated landings on the 'dummy deck' at Yokosuka, then proceeded apace and it was agreed that the work of the Mission would be largely completed towards the end of the year. Not all members were to leave, however. Five officers, including Brackley, and four warrant officers were to remain behind for a further period. This number did not include Sempill, who left Japan on 25 October 1922 along with most of his team.[23] Despite his later (1924) lauding of Japanese skills, he was not so sanguine at that time; Ferris dubs his comments on the ignorance of the IJN concerning naval aviation 'brutal'.[24] Brackley was more diplomatic:

> We are having just the same troubles here as were experienced with our own Navy when aircraft first became a recognized weapon of warfare. The senior officers have first to be convinced by practical demonstration that aircraft are of real help to the Navy and not a hindrance. We have just started the flying off the gun turrets of battle cruisers. It is quite simple once the pilot knows what he is doing. (Most of the Japanese don't).[25]

Brackley left Japan for Britain on leave, and to get married, in the summer of 1922. Before he went he was asked by the commanding officer at Kasumigaura to obtain further information:

> I have herewith to express my desire that while you are on leave in England you will so mind as to make a special study on the following subjects:
>
> 1. Latest progress of decklanding; its equipment and modes of training.
> 2. Organization of RN flying stations; also that of aeroplane (seaplane) carriers.
> 3. Latest aeroplanes (seaplanes) in use by the RNAS for night flying; their performance and methods of training.
> 4. Compass adjusting procedure for airships.
> 5. Recent progress in the torpedo-machines and their torpedoes as in service either in the RAF or RNAS.
>   (a) Performance of torpedo-planes.
>   (b) Performance of air-torpedoes.
>   (c) Cares to be exercised in flying torpedo-planes.
>   (d) The final height from which the torpedo is dropped.
>   (e) Construction of torpedo-sights and other chief attachments; also their manoeuvring.
>
> Also bring home a collection of representative printed matters on naval air tactics.[26]

Over the next two days the list was expanded to include, amongst other things, 'essential particulars of the latest aeroplanes in use by the RN', 'latest progress of metallic aeroplanes', and 'recent progress of bombs in service use by the RN'.[27]

The newly-married Brackley returned to Japan on 28 November 1922, and reported on his visit to Britain on 12 December:

> During my recent visit to England I made every endeavour to gain as much knowledge as possible in all branches of Naval air work, especially studying our latest organization of Carriers, Deck work and machines used in conjunction therewith. My objects were to gather first-hand knowledge from those experienced to give it, so as to be able to advise the IJNAS as to the safest and best methods of training pilots for deck work, and the most suitable machines for this purpose.
>
> From the outset however, I feel it is my duty to tell you frankly that for the present I am unable to give you ALL our latest information on the various subjects as some of it is still of a secret nature, so naturally I cannot divulge anything divulged to me as secret until I obtain permission from our Admiralty or Air Ministry. In any case the IJNAS in its present state of development is not ready for such advanced information.
>
> Although great progress has been made in the Naval side of our Air Force during the past two years, the IJNAS has been supplied with a number of our recent types of machines for deck work; I see no reason why training for landing on the *Hosho* should not proceed, as soon as the ship is ready, on the types of machines now at Kasumigaura . . .
>
> It is obvious of course that three distinct types of pilots are required for deck work, (a) The Scout type, (b) The Reconnaissance type, (c) The Torpedo and Bombing type. The Naval side of our Air Force being a specialized branch, the majority of our Deck pilots are experienced in and adaptable to all types of machines, but naturally in its present state of development it cannot be recommended for the IJNAS to employ the same pilot for all types of machines.
>
> The types recommended for preliminary training on the *Hosho* are:
>
> *Scout*: Sparrowhawk and Mitsubishi (NOT in its present state).
>
> *Reconnaissance*: Seal (Modified as recommended by our Air Ministry). Viking (Modified) and Avro BISON (later).
>
> *Torpedo and Bombing*: Swift and Blackburn DART.

Brackley's suggestion that IJNAS pilots specialize in either seaplane, fighter, reconnaissance, or torpedo and bombing work was adopted, with the culmination of the training being taking off and landing on the deck of the *Hosho*.

His stricture that the Mitsubishi scout aeroplane should 'NOT in its present state' be used was, however, ignored. It was though only on 22 February 1923 that a former RNAS fighter ace, and latterly test pilot for Sopwith, the South African William Lancelot Jordan took off and then landed on the aircraft carrier as she steamed into the wind in Tokyo Bay at 10 knots.[28] His machine was a Mitsubishi 1MF, also known as the Navy Type 10 Carrier Fighter.[29]

Unconnected to the Sempill Mission, Jordan represented another strand of British assistance to Japan, albeit of a somewhat more generalized type. As already mentioned, the British aviation industry found itself in desperate straits at the end of the war, and one of the foremost casualties was the famous 'Sopwith Aviation & Engineering Company' which went into voluntary liquidation in 1920. So just as Sempill was able to recruit a highly skilled and talented team from amongst the ranks of recently unemployed naval and military personnel, so Japan's aviation industry did likewise with the pool of men released from aircraft manufacturers.[30] Herbert Smith, formerly a designer at Sopwith with the famous 'Camel' to his credit, plus his assistant John Bewsher, were two of a small number of ex-Sopwith designers and experts invited to initiate indigenous aircraft design in Japan. They worked under the aegis of the Mitsubishi company, as did Anthony Archibald Fletcher, late of the Central Aircraft Company. Herbert Smith started work in February of 1921 and, with his team, produced aeroplane designs over the next two years or so. As well as the fighter mentioned above the team designed the unsuccessful Type 10 triplane torpedo bomber,[31] the successful Type 13 attack aircraft,[32] and the Type 10 reconnaissance aircraft.[33] Oswald Short of Short Brothers also led a team to Japan regarding seaplanes and flying boats, which were to become a particular area of expertise for Short's.[34]

Jordan made a further couple of landings on *Hosho* on 24 and 26 February 1923, again in the Type 10 aircraft, before Brackley emulated the feat on 13 March, though in a Vickers Viking amphibian flying boat. Such feats, which were viability studies pertaining to both the aircraft and vessel as configured, were naturally enough keenly observed by the Japanese pilots who had been trained by Sempill's Mission. But though one of them, Ensign Kamei Yoshio, had made a successful take off on 23 February, none had as yet attempted a landing. This situation was rectified on 16 March when Lieutenant Kira Shunichi tried to land in a Type 10. His first attempt was abortive, though 'provided excitement and useful study', whilst on his second effort he came a complete cropper; Kira and his machine went over the side. Fortunately, the man came to no harm and with what can only be termed commendable sang-froid went up in a reserve machine to try again. This time he was successful, thus becoming the first Japanese pilot to land on a carrier. In fact, and possibly to prove a point, he did it twice that day.[35] Following some minor modifications to the carrier's deck, a third series of landing exercises was carried out beginning on 20 June. This time it was exclusively a Japanese affair and it went well. Successful graduates of the Sempill Mission training syllabus included 52 pilots, as well as 130 maintenance, 4 reconnaissance, and 12 communication personnel.[36]

In terms of building a naval aviation corps this was but a beginning, though without doubt an important one as Japan now had the ability to maintain and expand its naval aviation service. Mark R. Peattie adjudged that the Sempill Mission (and presumably the other schemes of assistance and training) 'provided the Japanese navy with a quantum jump in aviation training and technology'.[37] Geoffrey Till was a little less hyperbolic, noting that the 'hard-won experience' Britain had acquired during the Great War 'provided a sound foundation for the development of Japanese Naval Aviation'.[38]

Such judgements are undoubtedly correct, but there had been a major change in the relationship between Britain and Japan during the time the Mission was at work; they had been formal allies at the beginning via the Anglo-Japanese Alliance, but were no longer so at the end.[39] One of the practical effects of this political shift was that the details of British warship design, and associated naval and military matters, were no longer made available to Japan.[40] Or at least overtly. It followed that, if they wanted further information, their only recourse was to the dark arts of espionage.

It might be argued that the Sempill Mission, and the other forms of assistance given to Japan over roughly the same period, straddle that twilight zone between promotion of the British arms industry and providing aid to a potential enemy. As has hopefully been shown, the transfer of knowledge and technology was of a very high order and on occasion passed into what might be termed forbidden territory. That Sempill may have continued treading such ground had been discovered within three months of his return to the UK. Evidence for this, or at least that elements of Britain's intelligence services believed it to be so, may be adduced from the contents of a 'Personal and Confidential' message from Lionel Guy Stanhope Payne, a staff officer in the Operations and Intelligence Directorate of the Air Ministry, to Major W. A. Alexander of MI5. The subject matter was 'Japanese Espionage in England':

> It is known that the Japanese are very interested at the present time in the development of their Naval Air Service.
>
> A civilian mission, under Colonel the Master of Sempill (see Clause 4 of intercepted telegram dated 26 December 1922 from Tosu, Paris, to Vice-Minister of Marine, Tokyo . . .) has just returned to this country from Japan. . . .

> Several small incidents have recently shown that the Japanese may be adopting other than orthodox methods for finding out information about the Royal Air Force, notably . . . your recent report that Colonel Sempill's servant is a Japanese Naval Rating.[41]

The 'intercepted telegram' was cryptic:

> Today I caused Hara, with the object of establishing relations, to have an interview with the person in question and casually sound his views. In a few days I shall send him again to negotiate.
>
> 1. This person's engagement: no change.
> 2. In the main there is in his opinion still no objection to our policy and . . . in the manner desired.
> 3. Undecipherable.
> 4. He was warned not to have close relations with Sempill.[42]

The 'person in question' referred to was Frederick Joseph Rutland, a former RNAS and RAF flying officer and authentic aviation pioneer and war hero; he was awarded the Distinguished Flying Cross and Bar. His exploits during the 1916 Battle of Jutland, for which he received his first DFC, had earned him the sobriquet 'Rutland of Jutland'.[43] Rutland revolutionized the aircraft policy of Britain's Grand Fleet by demonstrating that aeroplanes could be successfully launched from platforms constructed on the turrets of large warships. They couldn't land on them again, so had to head for shore after completing their mission. If that distance was too great, then ditching into the sea near a friendly warship was the only option. A ship with a flat deck upon which to land an aeroplane was the only answer to that problem, and one that Rutland, who had succeeded to the command of the air squadron aboard the hybrid battlecruiser/aircraft carrier *Furious*, pushed hard for.[44] He thus became, according to an intelligence report of August 1924 authored by Major George Joseph Ball, an officer with a 'unique knowledge of aircraft carriers and deck-landings'.[45]

Two volumes of materiel were compiled on Rutland by the British Intelligence Services, but only the second survives in the UK National Archives.[46] From those documents that have survived, and are available, it is difficult to discern why Rutland should have been considered more 'treacherous' than any of the other individuals involved with Japan around that time. In a similar manner to, for example, Jordan, he went to work for Mitsubishi, starting in September 1924 according to information in his file.[47] During an interview he had with Captain Royle, the UK's Naval Attaché in Tokyo, on 20 December 1925 Rutland stated that his work with the Japanese firm up to that time had revolved around the development of pneumatic-hydraulic shock absorbers for use in aircraft landing gear.[48] Captain Guy Charles Cecil Royle, who went on to become Admiral Sir Guy Royle and hold the most senior appointment in the Royal Australian Navy, was most certainly no fool.[49]

According to Royle's letter, Rutland came to see him to ask for advice. Having designed three sets of shock-absorbing landing gear, which were tested with 'great success', his contract with Mitsubishi was ending. However, he told the attaché, a further year's work was in the offing with a higher salary if he would 'give them advice on Naval flying, particularly with references to aircraft carriers'. 'He was', Royle continued:

> ... quite open about it and said that up till now they had particularly refrained from asking him questions outside his particular job . . . I think this latter statement is true and that he has had no access to any carriers or air stations since his appointment to Mitsubishi. He wanted to know what I thought about his new proposal because as he said and I quite agreed with him that if he took it on he would feel bound to give away everything he knew . . . The question is – does he know anything that we don't want them to know or which we could otherwise prevent them finding out? If he doesn't take on the job, presumably they will get some other person to do it of whom we shall know nothing. If he does, then he will be able, to a certain extent, as he said, keep us informed of progress made.
>
> My personal advice to him was to accept the new proposal. I am not sure how long after leaving the Service a man's experience in that Service can be used for the benefit of a foreign power.
>
> ... I rather believe that the Japanese are getting 'Smith' ex-Sopwith designer who designed the Mitsubishi machines to come out again.[50]

The letter raises some interesting issues. Rutland had been on the retired list of the Royal Navy since 19 September 1923.[51] So what, at the end of December 1925, could he have known about naval flying and aircraft carriers that the Japanese didn't already know or had already been shown by the Sempill Mission, William Jordan, Herbert Brackley, and so on? It is undoubtedly the case that Rutland's background and experience had indeed put him at the very forefront of naval aviation. But the war had been over for six years or so, and Rutland retired from the navy for nearly a year, when Ball wrote about his 'unique knowledge'. Further, and given that what he told Royle was true (the latter certainly believed him), then it must have been two years or more since he'd last flown. Put simply then, and acknowledging that he would have made an excellent instructor and consultant, Rutland could not possibly have possessed first-hand knowledge of

British cutting-edge naval aviation secrets in 1924–5. This point had in fact been made to Major Ball by the Military Attaché in Tokyo, Colonel Francis Stewart Gilderoy 'Roy' Piggott, in a letter dated 8 June 1925. He had written that 'the evidence now forwarded is inconclusive and is rather to the effect that the suspicions as regards his employment are unfounded'.[52]

Another point surely arises from Royle's letter. The oft-repeated argument that Rutland was covertly engaged with the IJN in the 1920s is surely belied by the reported discussion. Being 'quite open' about what he had been asked to do in conversation with, and seeking advice on the matter from, the British Naval Attaché is hardly textbook clandestinity.

It is not proposed to labour the point, but in the absence of further evidence it is difficult to see that his actions were any more, or indeed less, 'treacherous' than that of any of the other contributors to Japanese naval aviation. Yet none of them, with one exception that I shall return to shortly, was investigated with the object of initiating disciplinary action or indeed prosecution. This wasn't through lack of zeal, but rather through a deficiency of grounds.

The August 1924 'Notes on the Case' say that 'owing to the danger of compromising the very delicate source from which our information came, it was not possible to take any disciplinary action against Rutland'.[53] Japan's diplomatic cipher telegrams were of course the 'very delicate source'; they were being cracked and read by Britain's Government Code and Cypher School (GC&CS).[54] Leaving aside the political sensitivity, it remains a mystery as to what he could have been disciplined for. A report on him some fifteen months later pointed out that he was not debarred from seeking employment with any foreign power as the rule governing such matters hadn't been in force when he retired. It also stated that the 'Foreign Enlistment Act will not help us as it only applied [*sic*] to joining a foreign power at war with us or on the verge of declaring war against us'.[55] Given this, then we are then left with something of a mystery as to why, when resources were stretched exceedingly thin, Rutland received the degree of attention that he did? [56] There was, though, one other person who attracted a good deal of attention from the various intelligence agencies, and certainly with more justification; the Master of Sempill himself.

That Sempill was on friendly terms with, and supplied information to, Toyoda Teijiro, the Japanese Naval Attaché in London, is beyond dispute. It wasn't just the Japanese, however. The Master was of course very well connected in general, and particularly so in relation to aviation matters, and seems to have set himself up as a freelance consultant in relation to the latter subject. Indeed, he was known by British Intelligence to have offered help of one kind or another to Greece, Chile, Sweden, Norway and Finland.[57] One area that seems to have particularly exercised those in the intelligence community relates to his ability to persuade aircraft manufacturers to show him their wares. Two examples may suffice. On 1 May 1924 Major Ball wrote to Air Vice-Marshal Sir Geoffrey Salmond, Air Member for Supply and Research, warning him that Sempill was known to be 'deeply interested' in the 'Dreadnought flying machine' and an accident that had occurred to it.[58] Conceived by a Tsarist Russian exile and former attaché at the London Embassy, Nicholas Woyevodsky, the Westland Dreadnought was of an advanced, indeed revolutionary, monoplane design. The prototype, constructed by the Westland Aircraft Works at Yeovil, Somerset, was not a success; the 'accident' referred to had occurred on 9 May 1924 during its maiden flight. In fact, it was more of a disaster; the aircraft 'suddenly nose-dived, and crashed to the ground', almost killing the test pilot who was thrown clear.[59]

The long-range Blackburn Iris, a flying boat that first flew on 18 June 1926, was a less innovative but ultimately much more successful design. It was also one that the Air Ministry had placed on the 'secret' list. Sempill, who was believed to have been engaged as a consultant by the Blackburn Aeroplane Company since June 1925 in connection with the Greek Naval Air Service, was also much interested in the machine,[60] as was Toyoda and, by extension, Japan's Naval Air Service. The reason why related to the Japanese acquisition of the myriad islands and atolls that collectively comprised the major portion of Micronesia; these had been captured from Germany in 1914 and then mandated to Japan under the League of Nations in 1919.[61] The area they occupied was vast but their value was strategic. In the event of a war with the United States, when the US Navy was expected (or induced) to sortie to the Western Pacific to relieve American forces in Guam and the Philippines, they would act as 'unsinkable aircraft carriers' flanking the lines of communication across the Pacific throughout a distance of 2,300 miles.[62] In order to utilize these 'carriers' to their maximum advantage, and to carry out reconnaissance over the oceanic vastness, long-range aircraft were obviously advantageous. The Japanese Navy was to develop and put into service land-based aircraft with ranges that were to astonish their enemies, becoming in the process the only first-rank navy to emphasize land-based aviation for maritime strikes.[63] Included in this category were flying boats, but it is difficult to make a case for the Blackburn Iris influencing any of them.[64] Which brings us to the crux of the matter; how far did the transfer of Royal Navy technology and expertise to the Imperial Japanese Navy, whether acquired via espionage or legitimately, go in making that Navy the formidable force it was in relation to the former in 1942?

It seems indisputable that the Sempill Mission, which was merely the largest and best known of several similar efforts, was of immense help. The conclusions of Mark R. Peattie and Geoffrey Till have already been noted in that regard and it is most certainly not proposed to dispute them. The uncoordinated nature of the British Government's response to the Japanese request for assistance seems to have allowed a far greater transfer of expertise and technology than many individual organs of that government, particularly the Admiralty, would have approved of. However, what none of that teaching, training and transference of technology did do, or indeed could do, was put Japan's naval aviation a decade ahead of Britain's some 20 years later. Yet according to no less a figure than Arthur Marder, that was where it was in 1942.[65] Given that this opinion is valid, and it is a difficult one to controvert, then the question arises as to how and why this situation came about. What, in other words, had prevented the Royal Navy from developing to the same level in the intervening period? Perhaps part of the answer is to be found in the period of austerity, and treaty limitations, which pertained in the 1920s and later, and which are examined in the next chapter.

Chapter 2

Between Scylla and Charybdis

Following the official end of the Great War between Germany and the Allied and Associated Powers, marked by the signing of the Treaty of Versailles on 28 July 1919, the British Government adopted the 'Ten Year Rule'. This stipulated that future military and naval plans and Estimates should be drafted 'on the assumption that the British Empire would not be engaged in any great war during the next ten years'.[1] Despite this there were a number of matters requiring rather urgent attention. The pre-war naval 'Two Power Standard', with a 'real margin' over and above it of 10 per cent as enunciated in 1903 and 1908, was now nothing more than a fond memory.[2] So too was the ability to achieve it through outbuilding any rival, as had been done with the Imperial German Navy. In short, the outpouring of treasure between 1914 and 1918 had left Britain in financial difficulties; the national debt had increased from £706 million in 1913–14, amounting to 26.2 per cent of GDP, to £7,481 million in 1918–19, over 127 per cent of GDP.[3]

The problems weren't just economic. Indeed Britain, having successfully seen off the challenge of Imperial Germany, now had an even more formidable naval rival; the USA. Evidence for this may be adduced by noting that on 20 August 1916 the Naval Appropriations Act 1916 had been signed in Washington. This committed $313,384,212 towards creating 156 new ships, including ten battleship, and six battlecruisers, for the US Navy, with construction commencing over the next three years and completed by 1921.[4]

Among the vessels planned and started were the six ships of the *South Dakota* class – *South Dakota, Indiana, Montana, North Carolina, Iowa* and *Massachusetts.* These vessels, which should not be confused with the class of the same name constructed in the late 1930s, were to displace some 40,000 tonnes and carry twelve 16in (410mm) guns in four triple turrets. The battlecruisers laid down were six vessels of the *Lexington* class – *Lexington, Constellation, Saratoga, Ranger, Constitution* and *United States.* Designed to be 10 knots faster than the battleships, with a design speed of slightly over 33 knots, they also displaced some 40,000 tonnes, but carried less armour and armament, with a main battery of eight 16in guns.

There were several varied factors that influenced the successful passage of this legislation, including the Battle of Jutland which, at least as far as naval wisdom had it, reaffirmed the capital ship as the final arbiter of naval power. The impetus for the programme came from President Woodrow Wilson, who had, somewhat euphemistically, dubbed it a programme of 'preparedness'. Whatever it was called, it amounted to a massive challenge to the previously supreme Royal Navy; indeed on 2 February 1916 during an address at St Louis, the President had told his audience, to 'overwhelming applause', that he desired the US Navy 'to be incomparably the greatest navy in the world'.[5]

The accession of the US to a position of naval pre-eminence was further indicated in 1918 when, on 15 October, Wilson approved a further three-year construction programme. It virtually replicated that of 1916 inasmuch as another ten battleships and a further six battlecruisers were mooted as well as some 140 smaller warships.[6]

The choices facing Britain with regard to this potential onslaught were stark. In order to achieve even a 'One Power Standard' of equality with the US, Britain would have to embark on an arms race, and one moreover from a greatly inferior position. Almost the entire capital ship strength of the Royal Navy in 1918 was coal burning, and so faced obsolescence. One decidedly unpalatable alternative was to drop to second position in world naval power, and, with Japan also constructing new tonnage, perhaps to third position in the Pacific – or even globally.

Japan became engaged in what became known as the '8:8 Programme', constructing eight battleships and eight battlecruisers, and suffering 'the greatest financial difficulties' in so doing.[7] Indeed the programme was extensive; four 30-knot battlecruisers of the *Amagi* class, *Akagi*, *Amagi*, *Atago* and *Takao*, of some 42,000 tonnes displacement, were budgeted for in 1918–19. The planned battleship construction envisaged two 40,000-tonne ships of the *Kaga/Toso* class – *Kaga* and *Toso*. Also planned were four *Kii* class ships. The first two, *Kii* and *Owari*, displacing around 42,000 tonnes, were scheduled to be laid down in 1922 and 1923 respectively. All these vessels were to have had main batteries of ten 16in guns. If nothing were done to remedy this situation, the British Empire, particularly in the Pacific, would become a hostage to the 'unlikely indulgence of others'.[8]

Keenly aware of their potential vulnerability now that Japan had displaced Germany, the Australian government had, in 1919, requested Admiral Lord Jellicoe to survey the situation.[9] Jellicoe's *Report on the Naval Mission to the Commonwealth*, which was submitted to the Governor-General in August 1919, stated it thus: 'It must be recognized that Australia is powerless against a strong naval and military power without the assistance of the British Fleet.'[10] The 'strong' power mentioned wasn't named, but there was no doubt as to exactly which country he was referring. He concluded that 'the naval interests of the Empire are likely to demand within the next five years, a Far Eastern Seagoing Fleet of considerable strength'.[11]

The cost was, in percentage terms, to be split in the ratio of 75:20:5 between Britain, Australia, and New Zealand respectively. Though Jellicoe was undoubtedly correct in purely naval terms, particularly given the proposed Japanese expansion, it was way beyond what could be conceivably afforded and so was totally unrealistic. Indeed, when asked his views on the naval situation in view of his recent study of this question at Washington, Arthur Balfour (a former Prime Minister and First Lord of the Admiralty) stated that '. . . the country . . . had to choose between Scylla and Charybdis, between a naval peril and a financial peril. The Cabinet and the House of Commons had to choose between these risks.'[12]

Indeed in an attempt to avert the first of Balfour's 'perils' the British seemed prepared to court the second; in March 1921 funds were authorized to begin four new battlecruisers.[13] The designs, provisionally entitled 'G3 Class Battlecruisers', were for huge vessels of nearly 50,000 tonnes mounting nine 16in guns in three turrets as main armament and capable of over 30 knots. A class of similarly configured battleships, mounting nine 18in (457mm) guns and capable of 23.5 knots, were also mooted.[14] Further, if Jellicoe's solution to the potential difficulty with Japan was rejected, his conclusion that there was a problem was accepted. Indeed the whole focus of British, and particularly naval, thought had shifted to the other side of the world. General Jan Christiaan Smuts, the Prime Minister of South Africa, put it thus at the 1921 London Imperial Conference:

> In shaping our course for the future we must bear in mind that the whole world position has radically altered as result of the war. . . . No; the scene has shifted on the great stage. . . . away from Europe to the Far East and to the Pacific. The problems of the Pacific are, to my mind, the world problems of the next fifty years or more. In these problems we are, as an Empire, very vitally interested. Three of the Dominions border on the Pacific. India is next door there, too, are the United States and Japan.[15]

The Admiralty subsequently compiled a War Memorandum, the main feature of which, in the absence of an unaffordable permanent naval presence, was a strategy to despatch a powerful fleet from North European and Mediterranean waters to the Far East as and when required.[16] However, because there was no base with sufficient facilities to accommodate a fleet of capital ships, both proposed and existing (once they had been fitted with anti-torpedo bulges), one would have to be constructed. At a Cabinet meeting of 16 June 1921 the decision was taken to build this at Singapore, which was entirely in line with Jellicoe's recommendation that 'Singapore as a naval base . . . is undoubtedly the naval key to the Far East'.[17]

And so the strategy of projecting naval power halfway around the world became known as the 'Singapore Strategy'. The purpose of the envisioned deployment, 'Main Fleet to Singapore' as it also became known, was to defend Imperial 'main interests', defined as trade and territorial integrity.[18] It was calculated that some 23 per cent of the total trade of the British Empire and 60 per cent of Australia's trade passed through the Indian Ocean; a figure vital to the existence of Australia.[19] That severe disturbance to this trade was likely from Japan in any future conflict, and much more troublesome than it had been from Germany in a previous one, was obvious. The whole notion was of course famously, if retrospectively, condemned by Admiral Sir Herbert Richmond as the '. . . illusion that a Two-Hemisphere empire can be defended by a One-Hemisphere Navy'.[20]

To be fair to Richmond he had, during his brief tenure as Commander-in-Chief of the East Indies Station,[21] critiqued the version of the War Memorandum that was sent to him.[22] He opined that the document concentrated on the need to get a British fleet to the Far East, but was vague about operations thereafter; 'How are we going to make war?' he asked.[23] Much the same complaint was raised the following year following receipt of the latest, July 1924, version[24] which, he argued was 'not a war plan, but a plan of naval movements' that visualized 'war between Great Britain and Japan purely as a struggle at sea'. It discounted or disregarded 'the proper co-ordination of all our elements of strength', meaning the Army and RAF. 'Success in war', he wrote, 'depends upon the proper co-ordination of all our elements of strength, not the employment of them in water-tight compartments.'[25] What he did not do however was criticize the 'Main Fleet to Singapore' strategy overall, merely how it, the fleet, was supposed to achieve its operational ends when it got there. And this, it must be remembered, was the post-Washington Treaty fleet. The same of course applied to Japan, but, and to jump forward several years, as the controversial ex-Royal Naval Commander Russell Grenfell was to put it in 1938:

> If we send the fleet to the Far East in sufficient strength to dispute the command at sea with the Japanese, what must that strength be? The Japanese capital ships now number nine. In the last war a fifty per cent superiority in capital ships was deemed barely sufficient to ensure our command at sea against the Germans. If we reduce that necessary superiority to as low as thirty per cent, for our Far Eastern force, we should need to send out at the very least twelve capital ships. Two of

our fifteen capital ships being under reconstruction, this means that at the moment the whole of our capital ship fleet but one would have to proceed eastward. . . .[26]

In June 1921, Beatty had estimated that a war with Japan would require a 'large proportion' of the navy's strength, including eight battleships and sixteen cruisers.[27] Given Grenfell's analysis was correct this proportion had clearly risen; risen indeed to near 100 per cent. To understand why, we need to go back again.

The potential for the UK to become embroiled in an unaffordable naval race after the Great War had prompted the government, under David Lloyd George, to offer something in the way of an olive branch to the United States. Walter Long, the First Lord of the Admiralty, first broached this matter in the House of Commons on 17 March 1920:

> Before the war various Governments had to consider what the strength of the possible enemies on the sea opposed to them might be, and there were various standards taken. But I think it was generally accepted that our strength ought to be equivalent to that of the two next strongest powers. . . . We are very fortunate in the fact that the only navy approximating in strength to our own is that of the United States of America . . . and we . . . hope and believe that if there is to be any emulation between the United States of America and ourselves, it is likely to be in the direction of reducing that ample margin of naval strength which we each alike possess over all other nations. That is the foundation of the naval policy of His Majesty's Government.[28]

The timing of this announcement may not have been entirely random. Wilson had been succeeded on 4 March 1921 by Warren G. Harding whose chief campaign slogan had been a 'return to normalcy', to the way of life before US entry into the Great War. His inaugural address had also mentioned relieving 'the crushing burdens of military and naval establishments' and that the war had involved the US 'in the delirium of expenditure, in expanded currency and credits, in unbalanced industry, in unspeakable waste, and disturbed relationships'.[29] In any event, the exposition of the British position, and its implicit concession, did not go unheard, at least in certain quarters in Washington. Senator Irvine Luther Lenroot raised the matter directly on the floor of the Senate on Tuesday 31 May 1921: 'If we . . . are to adopt as a policy that we are to be the first naval power in the world and Great Britain has adopted a like policy, where will the race for supremacy in armaments end?'[30]

Where indeed? It was a very good question, and one moreover that the Royal Navy, and the British Government, were quite evidently not keen to have to address. If the US Navy were to continue growing at the rate postulated by Wilson then keeping up would have necessitated a massive British financial commitment, without diminishing other commitments one iota. These had, of course, not gone away.

Unlike many of the capital ships, whether afloat or only on the drawing boards and slipways of Britain, Japan and the US, the Singapore Naval Base and its associated strategy, was to survive the Naval Conference held at Washington, DC from November 1921 to March 1922 at the instigation of the US Government. The US was probably the only one of the three naval powers that could have, in financial terms, afforded the level of fleet expansion that was in progress after the First World War, and then only with severe difficulty. Harding's Secretary of the Treasury was the banker and industrialist Andrew W. Mellon, who argued soon after taking office on 9 March 1921 that 'In the absence of drastic cuts in military and naval expenditures there is almost no prospect . . . of any substantial available surplus even in fiscal [year] 1922'.[31]

Diplomatically, there was another strand of US thinking that came into play respecting the Anglo-Japanese Alliance, the existence of which aroused deep suspicions within the US naval planning fraternity. Whilst it was no doubt accepted that the original intent of it was very different, after 1918 the Alliance was viewed as being anti-American.[32] Given that their policy was to find accommodation with the United States, the British had no political or strategic difficulty in disengaging from the Alliance. An agreement that left her superior to Japan, the third naval power, was automatically a better deal than an agreement that put her at odds, potentially at least, with the premier naval power.[33]

The Washington Conference was seen as a method whereby these various problem areas might be resolved. A set of proposals was formulated, which would be put to the Conference by the US Secretary of State, Charles Evans Hughes, a distinguished lawyer.[34] Delegates from nine nations with interests in the East Asia and Pacific regions attended, representing the United States, Britain, Japan, France, Italy, Belgium, The Netherlands, Portugal and China. On 6 February 1922, the first five states concluded an agreement on limiting the size of their navies; the Naval Armaments Treaty. This agreed a ten-year naval holiday during which no new capital ships (ships over 10,000 tons with guns larger than 8in [203mm]) were to be built. The ratio of existing capital ships between the five powers, it was agreed, would be 5–5–3–1.67–1.67. This meant that Britain and the US were each allowed 525,000 tons, Japan 315,000, and France and Italy 175,000 each. Total tonnage of aircraft carriers was restricted and a maximum size fixed for capital ships, aircraft carriers and cruisers. If Singapore (and Hawaii) survived, few other schemes to build or fortify bases in the Pacific did likewise; the signatory powers agreed not to fortify their possessions in the region.

Indeed, despite that they had obtained copies of Jellicoe's report, and so were well aware of the strategic purpose behind Britain's desire to construct a base there, the Japanese were prepared to concede the exclusion of Singapore from the non-fortification clause.[35] This followed a good deal of horse-trading in which, amongst other things, Japan succeeded in preventing the USA strengthening fortifications in the Philippines and Guam. For the Japanese, the British policy of constructing a fleet naval base in Singapore was acceptable on the condition that Britain would agree to the Japanese proposal of preventing the USA building advanced naval bases in Guam and the Philippines. This trade-off was successful; the agreed perimeter excluded Singapore.[36]

In terms of capital ships, the new allowances meant not only the cancellation of new construction, such as the four battleships of Japan's *Kaga* and *Kii* classes and battlecruisers of the *Amagi* class already laid down, and the battlecruisers of the US *Lexington* class and the British 'G3' class, but also the scrapping of significant existing tonnage. In total, the US plan consisted of proposals to scrap fifteen of its own existing battleships and another fifteen planned. The British were requested to scrap or not build twenty-three vessels, whilst Japan was asked to sacrifice seventeen existing or putative capital ships.[37] Admiral Beatty, at the conference in his position as First Sea Lord, is said to have physically staggered upon hearing the list of capital ships that it was proposed Britain should scrap.[38] Indeed, according to another account, he 'came forward in his chair with the manner of a bulldog, sleeping on a sunny porch, who has been kicked in the stomach by an itinerant soap-canvasser'.[39]

Despite this apparent shock, the British delegation managed to negotiate the construction of two brand-new battleships for the Royal Navy. This was the genesis of *Nelson* and *Rodney*, the only 16in-gun battleships to be commissioned by Britain, which were launched on 3 September and 17 December 1925 respectively.

US diplomacy at the conference was assisted in no small measure by having detailed inside information on the Japanese negotiating position and secret exchanges between Britain and Japan. This information was provided to Hughes by MI-8, more famously known as the 'Black Chamber', the cryptanalysis organization headed by the eccentric Herbert O. Yardley. The 'Black Chamber' had broken the Japanese diplomatic cipher used by the Japanese delegation, and Japan's Ambassadors, to communicate with Tokyo; Hughes thus knew the Japanese position each day before beginning negotiations.[40]

Other significant outcomes of the Washington Conference were the dissolution of the Anglo-Japanese Alliance and the return of the former German protectorate of Kiautschou, which Japan had taken in 1914, to China, a treaty being signed by both powers on 4 February 1922.[41] The conference also agreed a ten-year building holiday for major warships and set down the maximum size of battleships, aircraft carriers and cruisers as well as the size of the gun armament.[42]

So having, Odysseus-like, negotiated the passage between a naval Scylla and a financial Charybdis, what state did the Royal Navy find itself in after Washington? There were, I would argue, many positives even though it still had much the same worldwide empire to defend as it had pre-war, but now only a 'one-power' standard navy to do it with. Having said that, there was little or no chance of it coming to blows with its equal, whilst the only real potential enemy, Japan, now had a navy only 60 per cent as large. In order to deal with that potential enemy it also had a strategy and had managed to protect the cornerstone of it, the development of the Singapore fleet base, from the non-fortification clause. That this strategy was some twenty years later found to be deeply flawed is now well known. It wasn't held as such contemporaneously, though there were one or two admirals that criticized it mightlily.[43] This was certainly prescient, but having decided on the policy the British Government, or at least the Admiralty, decided there was no alternative but to stick with it.[44]

As already noted, the Royal Navy also gained the right to construct what became *Nelson* and *Rodney*.[45] In addition they added three aircraft carriers with the conversion of the three 'large light cruisers' *Glorious*, *Courageous* and *Furious*, the latter already partially converted, as permitted under the Treaty.[46]

The Washington Treaty was only the first of several such that limited the size of the Royal Navy, as it did its rivals particularly in relation to capital ships. It did nothing though to restrict or impede the development of naval aviation, apart from impose tonnage limits for aircraft carriers. There were, however, those, such as the aforementioned Grenfell, who argued that Britain had 'lost' by way of the treaties. In his analysis, which he dubbed 'a very startling conclusion to reach', there existed 'a large, well-paid, highly educated, officially encouraged, and extremely powerful sixth column in Whitehall which is, in complete safety, working away continuously to assist the country's potential enemies by trying to cut down the national defences'.[47]

That it did 'cut down the national defences' is undoubted, but that was a factor that cut both ways; it did the same to 'potential enemies' as well. It can be viewed then as a rational diplomatic solution to engaging in an unaffordable alternative. Similarly, the Singapore Strategy can also be perceived as coherent, it being ultimately a way of attempting to reconcile a strategic end with inevitably limited means. One politician who did put his finger on a forseeable problem with it was Smuts. He censured the strategy on the grounds that any trouble in the Far East was likely to coincide with difficulties in Europe. These problems, he argued, would prevent or at least inhibit the despatch of the Royal Navy to the other side of the world.[48]

He was proven correct. However, it is arguable that even if there had been no 'prevention' or 'inhibition', then the strategy would have failed. Not because it was flawed as such, nor because, as Richmond had pointed out, it gave no consideration to how the fleet was to make war once it got there, but because in 1942 any such fleet would have been summarily defeated or, as happened, forced to hide. It is perhaps ironic then that one of the main architects of this state of affairs was none other than Smuts himself.

Chapter 3

'Shattering, blasting, overpowering force'

Just before noon on Wednesday, 13 June 1917, London was attacked from the air by seventeen Gotha G.IV bombers. This operation, conducted by aircraft from *Kampfgeschwader der Obersten Heeresleitung* 3 (*Kagohl* 3, the *Englandgeschwader* or 'England Squadron') under the command of Ernst Brandenburg, formed part of a strategic offensive code-named *Türkenkreuz* ('Turk's Cross') carried out by the *Luftstreitkräfte*, the air arm of the German Army. The city had anti-aircraft defences, put in place against earlier, nocturnal Zeppelin raids, but these failed to prevent the heavier-than-air machines from unloading their ordnance. The bombers returned on 7 July, dropping seventy-six bombs along an arc encompassing Tottenham, Leytonstone, Stoke Newington, Dalston, Islington, Clerkenwell and Hoxton. Fifty-seven people were killed, including 18 children who were attending Upper North Street School in Poplar, and 193 injured.[1] As the official historian of the war in the air put it in somewhat understated fashion:

> This second daring attack on the heart of London created a tense atmosphere. . . . the enemy had flown unimpeded across England in the full light of day for the second time in a few weeks, and for that the public could find no excuse.[2]

Goaded by vitriolic attacks in the press and signs of panic amongst the population, the War Cabinet set up a committee to examine what could be done. It was, nominally, a two-man affair comprising the Prime Minister, David Lloyd George, and General Jan Christiaan Smuts, Prime Minister of South Africa and member of the War Cabinet. In fact, Smuts did all the work and presented two reports, the first, on the air defence of London, on 19 July. The second report was placed before the War Cabinet on 17 August. Smuts noted that '[An] Air Service . . . can be used as an independent means of war operations. Nobody that witnessed the attack on London on 11th July [*sic*] could have any doubt on that point.' His recommendation was that in order to reinforce this 'independent means' on the British side, the Army's Royal Flying Corps and the Navy's Royal Naval Air Service should be merged to form what would become the Royal Air Force under its own Air Ministry. He did not duck the question of whether or not the Army and Navy should retain their own special Air Services in addition to the Air Forces which will be controlled by the Air Ministry. He answered it by arguing that retention would make 'the confusion hopeless and render the solution of the Air problem impossible'. He went on:

> The maintenance of three Air Services is out of the question, nor indeed does the War Office make any claim to a separate Air Service of its own. But as regards Air work the Navy is exactly in the same position as the Army . . . the proper and indeed only possible arrangement is to establish one unified Air Service which will absorb both the existing services under arrangements which will fully safeguard the efficiency and secure the closest intimacy between the Army and the Navy and the portions of the Air Service allotted or seconded to them.[3]

There is a clear implication in the above that the Navy were against losing their own air arm. According to a US Intelligence assessment marked 'reliable', certain conditions that existed at the time of the amalgamation tended to strengthen the arguments in favour of the combined air force. These included the fact that many RNAS aircraft were fighting alongside the RFC on the Western Front and that, in general, the role played by the RFC during the war was of vastly greater importance than that played by the RNAS. Since the establishment of an air force would take over the RFC's work, it would hardly disturb the existing organization.[4] Nevertheless, the C-in-C Grand Fleet, Admiral Beatty, was one of the few supporters of an amalgamation of air services.[5] Indeed Trenchard credited him with moving the Admiralty behind the Smuts' plan, believing, as he did, that it was in the 'national interest'.[6] If so, then he swiftly changed his mind.

However, on 24 August the War Cabinet met and decided to accept, in principle, the recommendation that a separate service for the air should be formed.[7] This took place on 1 April 1918 and, as the RAF Museum website has it, the Smuts report 'laid the foundations for the creation of the RAF'.[8] Given one of the factors in Smuts' decision, the official historian's point that 'Hauptmann Brandenburg's No. 3 Bombing Squadron may lay claim to an important share in the foundation of the Royal Air Force'[9] is also valid.

The Air Ministry was formed on 2 January 1918; a direct equivalent to the War Office (Army) and Admiralty (Navy). Politically it was headed by a press baron, Lord Rothermere, who was appointed President of the Air Force Council (usually just Air Council), whilst the professional head of the Royal Air Force, and Chief of the Air Staff, was Major General Sir Hugh Trenchard. Orders to transfer personnel from the RNAS and RFC to the RAF were promulgated on 9 March and King's Regulations establishing the duties and responsibilities for various positions within the Air Staff were published on 26 March 1918.[10]

The advent of the new fighting force on 1 April 1918 raised a whole new set of problems of its own, but it did not bring immediate, revolutionary changes to the Navy.[11] By this time aircraft, mostly operated from flying-off platforms fitted to twenty-six capital ships (though all had been earmarked for modification), had become integral to Grand Fleet operations.[12] Their stated roles included strategic long-range reconnaissance, followed by tactical observation during the approach of the enemy battlefleet and the subsequent engagement by observing and correcting the fire of individual ships. Defensively, they were expected to prevent enemy aircraft fulfilling the same roles, whilst in offensive terms their task was to conduct torpedo strikes on the capital ships of the High Sea Fleet. A secondary task was the strafing of German destroyers and capital ships.[13] Immense resources were available to fulfil these and other roles; at the time of its absorbtion into the RAF, RNAS strength stood at 55,066 officers and men, and 2,929 aircraft.[14] By the time of the Armistice in November over 100 airships were employed in support of naval operations, whilst the Grand Fleet was operating 99 aircraft with a further 77 operating from shore stations in direct support of its operations.[15]

This was a massive, and massively complex, organization to potentially disrupt. That such was avoided was due to arrangements arrived at over a period of several months. Under these, admirals continued to issue operational orders directly to these air contingents, and operating routines and techniques went on as before. In other words, the Royal Navy kept operational control of its air contingent. The changes were subtle. For example, former RNAS officers retained their commands under the new regime though now came under the RAF for administrative and disciplinary purposes and were deemed to be Air Force Contingents serving with the Navy. This itself generated a degree of fairly low-level friction, for the Air Ministry leaned somewhat towards former RFC practice and so adopted the War Office model of administration. This was resented by the Admiralty.[16] They were even further aggrieved by some of the implications of RAF administrative control, such as the re-numbering of naval squadrons.

It is not proposed to delve into every twist and turn of the argument, which went on with varying degrees of intensity for some 20 years before the Royal Navy regained control of what was then called the Fleet Air Arm on 24 May 1939. But that the system of dual control led to some curious anomalies is surely beyond doubt.

This somewhat dysfunctional relationship was, at least in its early stages, further aggravated by the inevitable growing pains that the RAF suffered in trying to establish itself alongside the other two services. It was also the case of course that many senior naval figures fervently desired the demise of the

the RAF, or at the very least wanted to divest it of its naval component and assets. There was then, to put it mildly, an inbuilt bias against the Air Force. Indeed, the Admiralty deployed skullduggery of a high political order, and made common cause with the War Office on occasion, in pursuit of their aims.[17] Their Air Force counterparts were all too aware of this, which did little to promote an open or cooperative mindset within the senior personnel, or even more generally, of either organization.[18] Indeed, according to Major General Sir John Kennedy, the Assistant Chief of the Imperial General Staff, the use of air power in direct support of naval and military operations was 'regarded by the Air Staff as a "prostitution of the Air Force"'.[19] Such opinions were, no doubt, extreme and far from the norm, but the embuggeration[20] of divided control was exacerbated, greatly so, by the financial constraints within which the Royal Navy had to operate. The Air Ministry, responsible for naval aircraft, was hit just as hard and it followed that naval air power found itself low on the list of operational priorities of the Royal Air Force.

If there are few arguments about the Royal Navy being kept on a tight financial leash in the interwar period, there are difering opinions amongst those who have studied the matter as to the harm, or not, that dualism did to British naval aviation over the same timescale. It is not proposed to enter here into a review of the relevant historiography, which is vast, but it is certainly the case that at least some senior officers maintained a strong interest in aviation.

Captain Stephen Roskill, the self-ascribed 'official historian of the Royal Navy' from 1949 to 1960 and a critic of the dualist system, pointed out that in the years leading up to the Second World War 'there was one branch of naval aviation in which steady progress was made and that was in the design and construction of aircraft carriers'.[21] This progress was embodied in *Ark Royal*, laid down in September 1935 as part of what Roskill called 'the period of reluctant rearmament', and launched some twenty months later.[22] This purpose-built carrier, together with her older counterparts *Glorious* (converted 1930), *Courageous* (converted 1928), *Furious* (reclassified 1925), *Eagle* (1924), *Hermes* (1924), and the venerable *Argus* (1918), formed a substantial aviation capability.

That such vessels might profitably be used together tactically in multi-carrier operations had been foreseen in 1930, and acted upon the following year with the appointment of Rear Admiral Sir Reginald Henderson, a former commander of *Furious*, as the first 'Rear Admiral, Aircraft Carriers'. Henderson was the man to whom, in the opinion of David Lloyd George, the Allied cause in the Great War 'owed much'.[23] This was due to him finding evidence in 1917 that a convoy system was feasible. Henderson's brief as 'the recognized naval advisor to other fleets on all matters connected with the Fleet Air Arm', included studying and preparing 'a common doctrine for the tactical employment' of aircraft. Towards this end he was to be afforded the opportunity to operate the combined aircraft carriers of both the Mediterranean and Atlantic fleets.[24] This was a quantum leap from the situation in 1923 when a mere two officers, Commander Richard Bell Davies VC and an assistant, formed the Air Section of the Naval Staff, which had itself only been set up in 1920 by Chatfield in the teeth of opposition from the Air Ministry.[25]

Henderson was responsible, in May 1933, for establishing a squadron organization of twelve aircraft, which superseded the six-aircraft flight that up until then had been the largest tactical unit of the Fleet Air Arm.[26] He advocated fighter defence of the fleet, as opposed to anti-aircraft gunfire, against attacking aircraft. These aircraft, he argued, should remain concentrated so as to be able to engage the attackers as a coherent formation; 95 per cent of aircraft downed were shot down by other aircraft during the Great War. His ideas on naval aviation were not followed up. Roskill puts it thus: 'It is at this stage that one feels the lack in the Royal Navy's counsels of one or two naval aviators with plenty of gold braid on their sleeves, which had arisen because almost all of its experienced aviators had turned over to the RAF on its formation in 1918.'[27]

This lack is perhaps reflected by the fact that there are only three editions locatable in the National Archives of the 'Confidential Books' published by the Admiralty devoted to inter-war naval aviation. Curiously, and perhaps not coincidentally, two of these were produced during Henderson's tenure, the final one in the year he was promoted.[28] In any event, the Navy failed to approach the Air Ministry with a view to developing the necessary high-performance fighters, or indeed other aircraft, for its aircraft carriers. It was felt that an effective combat air patrol could not be mounted around a carrier; by the time attackers were observed and identified it would be too late.[29]

So, whilst Roskill's point about 'steady progress' being made in terms of aircraft carriers is undoubtedly true, it fails to address any questions about the weapons they carried both offensive and defensive. The Royal Navy had nevertheless a worked-out doctrine for the use of carriers, which was articulated in the 1939 version of what were known as the 'Admiralty Fighting Instructions'.[30]

Of interest in the current context is the portion that deals with the 'Protection of Aircraft Carriers' when 'subject to attack by shore-based or carrier-borne aircraft'. Protection may be afforded, the Instructions state, by 'stationing her in the line between two capital ships' and/or 'providing a close escort of two cruisers with a good AA armament'. What is perhaps noteworthy is that whilst the Instructions do pronounce that 'attacks by aircraft can be countered by gunfire, manoeuvre and fighter patrols', the latter method is hardly developed at all. In other words, it is implicit that the best defence against attack by aircraft was not defence by aircraft, but rather anti-aircraft gunfire. Fighters had other roles. They were tasked with protecting fall-of-shot spotters, and supporting torpedo attacks by machine-gunning the enemy fleet's anti-aircraft positions.[31]

That this reliance on anti-aircraft artillery was something of a triumph of hope over experience, albeit only of the kind gained in peacetime exercises, is a matter that will be explored later. But studying how the overall aviation doctrine was applied in actual combat is instructive.

On 24 September 1939 the British submarine *Spearfish*, tasked with giving advance warning of enemy ship movements, was badly damaged after being repeatedly depth-charged by German surface warships off the Horns Reef in the Heligoland Bight. Her commanding officer, Lieutenant John Eaden, somehow managed, with commendable coolness, to bring her to the surface after lying doggo on the seabed for several hours.[32] Though left unable to dive she nevertheless evaded her attackers and after effecting repairs successfully transmitted a distress signal from Danish territorial waters. The Admiralty responded by ordering a powerful task force from the Orkney-based Home Fleet to the rescue. The core of this force consisted of the battleships *Rodney* and *Nelson* (flying the flag of Admiral Sir Charles Forbes, C-in-C Home Fleet) along with the carrier *Ark Royal*. Embarked on the latter were Blackburn Skuas, Blackburn Rocs and Fairey Swordfish.[33] Also aboard was Sir Lionel 'Nutty' Wells, who held the position of Vice Admiral Commanding Aircraft Carriers (VA Aircraft Carriers); 'a seaman of the old school' according to a later assessment.[34]

The Germans too were on alert and had a number of reconnaissance aircraft in the air, which included several obsolete Dornier Do 18 flying boats. One of the latter, despite the sky being full of thick cloud, spotted Forbes' command at 11:00 hours on 26 September whilst it was approximately 250 miles west of the island of Heligoland. The British ships went to action stations and, with only Swordfish patrolling above the Fleet, launched three Skuas to intercept the enemy aircraft. This headed for safety, undoubtedly at its maximum speed of around 140–150 knots.[35] Given that the maximum speed of the Skua was only about 40–50 knots greater, then it is to the credit of the pilots that they managed to get anywhere near their prey at all. They were unable to down the German machine, however, though they may have damaged it. In any event, the Luftwaffe now knew were the British ships were and another Do 18 appeared half an hour later. This time the Skuas were faster off the mark and reached their target, the first confirmed British air-to-air kill of the war.[36] An hour later, at 12:30 hours, a further three Skuas were sent up to intercept yet more Do 18s which had appeared. No further enemy aircraft were downed, but the shadowers were at least driven off. The problem now was that more formidable enemy aircraft were likely to appear, which they duly did. But by then *Ark Royal* had recovered all her aircraft and, by 13:30 hours, struck them below.

At approximately 13:45 hours *Rodney*, which was equipped with Type 79Y radar, reported two or three groups of aircraft at about 80 miles and closing.[37] One of these groups comprised nine Heinkel He 111 aircraft of the 'Lion' *Geschwader* (No. 1 Squadron of *Kampfgeschwader* 26) under Captain Vetter, which made high-level attacks from 3,600m (12,000ft) on an accompanying cruiser squadron with no results. The other, four Ju 88A dive-bombers comprising the readiness section of the 'Eagle' *Geschwader* under the command of Lieutenant Walter Storp, went for the *Nelson*, *Rodney* and *Ark Royal*, which were steaming in close order line ahead.[38]

One of the aircraft, piloted by Corporal Carl Francke, unexpectedly got a clear view of the aircraft carrier through the eight-tenths cloud cover whilst at 3000m (10,00ft). He immediately pushed his machine into a steep dive towards the target. To his surprise the descent went untroubled by anti-aircraft fire, though had to be broken off when his view of the ship was interrupted by thick cloud. He pulled away and regained height, waiting another eight minutes for visibility to improve. Then Francke dived again, this time into the teeth of heavy though ineffective anti-aircraft fire and released his bombload before heading to safety. The aircraft's radio report as quoted went: 'Dive-bombing attack with two SC500 bombs on aircraft carrier: 1. Hit next to the ship's side. 2. Possible hit on the foredeck. Effect not observed.'[39]

Where the second bomb went remains a mystery, but the first missed by about 30m (100ft) causing a huge water fountain (*wasserfontäne*). Despite the modesty of Francke's report, German propaganda went into overdrive and claimed that *Ark Royal* had been sunk. In fact, both the ship and the aircraft involved escaped without harm.[40] As did the rest of Forbes' command, though another Ju 88 bombed the battlecruiser *Hood*, which was five miles on the port quarter of the *Nelson*, *Rodney*, and *Ark Royal*, along with *Repulse* and various escort vessels, at 14:48 hours. The weapon failed to explode, merely striking a glancing blow immediately above the bulge on the port side, and caused only superficial damage.

The Royal Navy had been lucky. As Cajus Bekker was to put it: 'There was the bulk of the British Home Fleet, at sea, far from its bases, shadowed by German reconnaissance, and the Luftwaffe "exploits" this chance of attack with only thirteen combat aircraft!'[41]

Whether the game overall had been worth the candle, the putting of the bulk of the Home Fleet at risk of attack in order to attempt to rescue a single submarine, was a matter that exercised the mind of the political head of the Navy, Winston Churchill. His memo of 29 September to Admiral Sir Dudley Pound, the Navy's professional head, and Rear Admiral Sir Thomas 'Tom' Phillips, Deputy Chief of the Naval Staff, reflected this:

> While anxious not to fetter in any way the discretion of C-in-C, Home Fleet . . . there might easily have been losses disproportionate to the tactical objects in view . . . we do not want to run unnecessary risks with our important vessels until their AA has been worked up to the required standard against aircraft flying [at] 250 miles an hour.[42]

Churchill was perhaps being circumspect. Admiral Forbes' report stated that: 'During the attacks all heavy ships opened fire with long range and close range weapons but fire was ineffective. The control personnel were obviously unprepared for such high performance dive bombing targets.'[43] One problem was that the maximum speed of the Ju 88 was in the order of 300 miles per hour.[44] It was then indeed fortunate that, to paraphrase Roskill, the bombing was as ineffective as the anti-aircraft gunfire. Both could of course become better with experience, but the Royal Navy didn't seem to understand the threat that dive-bombing by high-performance aircraft now represented, nor that their current doctrine of countering it was seriously deficient. Both battleships at sea that day were heavily armoured as were, though to a lesser extent, the two battlecruisers. The *Ark Royal*, unlike later British carriers, had an unarmoured flight deck.[45] Therefore and for example, had the 500kg bomb that struck the *Hood* exploded, and it was a general purpose rather than armour-piercing type, then it may have caused damage. Had the same ordnance hit the flight deck of *Ark Royal* then it would likely have penetrated and, at best, put the ship out of action for a long period of time.[46]

There were those that offered, or at least thought they did, a better way; the 'air enthusiasts'. They criticized, amongst other things, the tactic of striking all aircraft below during air attacks. According to Poolman:

> Whenever Forbes put to sea with the main body of the Home Fleet the *Ark Royal* went with him, her planes scouting ahead of the battleships and searching the sea for signs of U-boats. We had little enough air power to cover the northern seas, and the carrier's aircraft were priceless, although the Admiralty was cautious in probing their potentialities at this time. . . . It was infuriating for her pilots to have to stand on deck staring helplessly at the sky, waiting for enemy bombers to attack, while their own machines lay down in the hangars drained of fuel for fear of fire, and *Ark Royal* staggered along in the wake of the cumbersome *Nelson* and *Rodney*, which could only make eighteen knots. To use a potential battle winner as a floating anti-aircraft battery for the protection of the battleships seemed to them the height of big-gun stupidity.[47]

This was obviously written with the benefit of hindsight, but the question is whether, or not, it represented a realistic appraisal of possibilities in September 1939? The short answer is 'not'. There are a number of points to support this position.

Positioning the carrier in proximity to the battleships wasn't done with the aim of using it to protect them. It was rather the other way around. The anti-aircraft batteries of the battleships would, at least in theory, help defend the carrier; a tactic that, albeit weakly, foreshadowed the deployment of fast battle-ships with the fleet carriers of USN Task Force 58 (38) in 1944 and afterwards.[48] This made sense, at least in theory. Many, perhaps most, senior figures in the Royal Navy and Admiralty were of the opinion that whilst aircraft presented a comparatively small danger to armoured ships (a question that had become over-simplified as 'bombs versus battleships'), there was little doubt that they presented a very real danger to an unarmoured carrier.

Further, even if 'Nutty' Wells had wanted to defend his command, and by extension the rest of the Home Fleet, by unleashing his fighter aircraft he would have been unable to do so. None of the fighters aboard the carrier was capable of taking on a Ju 88 on anything but unfavourable terms. They were slower, had poorer rates of climb and there was no way of vectoring them onto targets (the only radar was aboard *Rodney*), particularly given the poor visibility. Arguably the most serious deficiency in this regard though was that neither Wells, nor his command, been imbued with any such doctrine.

Perhaps the most striking example of this lack of 'air-mindedness' within the Royal Navy came with the loss of one of Wells' carriers on the afternoon of 8 June 1940. The story behind the destruction of the *Glorious* has become mired in controversy of one kind or another, but this need not concern us overly as the basic facts are relatively straightforward.[49] The carrier had been taking part in the operation ('Alphabet') to evacuate British, French and Polish forces from Norway following their defeat at the hands of German invaders. During the process of covering the evacuation of Narvik, some twenty RAF land-based Gladiators and Hurricanes were successfully landed on the carrier. Having embarked these, and operating in concert with *Ark Royal*, the final phase of the operation was to perform escort duties for the transport convoys as they returned to the UK. However, at 03:00 hours (British time) *Glorious* and her destroyer escorts, *Ardent* and *Acasta*, detached themselves from the main body of the flotilla to proceed independently back to Scapa Flow. This was in accordance with a request made by the carrier's commanding officer, Captain Guy D'Oyly-Hughes, and which Wells had granted. D'Oyly-Hughes was a highly decorated former submariner with an impressive record of achievement, both during the Great War and subsequently. Unfortunately, he seems to have become mentally unbalanced at some point during his tenure as commanding officer, a position held since June 1939. That this was so is evidenced by his behaviour on that fateful day.

Though zig-zagging as a precaution against submarine attack *Glorious* was at cruising stations, steaming at 17 knots with only twelve of her eighteen boilers lit. The destroyers were stationed some two cables on either bow. The sea was calm, the wind negligible and visibility out to the horizon. Despite the latter there was no lookout aloft on the carrier nor any aircraft in the air. According to one of the Fleet Air Arm pilots who survived, this was not in error: 'The captain said there was to be no flying on the way back . . . which flew in the face of all proper practice.'[50] Compounding this was the fact that none of the ships under his command were fitted with radar, and no aircraft were ready on deck for quick take-off. Even given that *Glorious* had, similarly escorted, made the journey four times previously, this was surely top-down dereliction of a high order. It was almost as if D'Oyly-Hughes was unaware of being at war with an enemy who possessed powerful naval assets.[51] Unfortunately for him and the rest of his command two of these, the battlecruisers *Scharnhorst* and *Gneisenau* (flag), had sortied in an attempt to disrupt the UK bound Norwegian convoys.

Negligence was compounded by luck most malign when at 16:45 hours (German time) an undoubtedly eagle-eyed midshipman named Siegfried Goss, who was stationed in *Scharnhorst*'s foretop, reported smoke to the west at a distance of some 28 miles. The German ships, under the overall command of Admiral Wilhelm Marschall (another former submariner of note) increased speed to *circa* 30 knots and altered course to close what could only be the enemy. *Scharnhorst* was in the lead and opened fire on the largest target with her main armament at an incredible range; a little over 26km (16.25 miles) at 16:22 hours (German time). At 16:38 hours the third salvo of 283mm shells made at least one direct hit, bursting in the upper hangar and causing a large fire.

The two destroyers made heroic attempts to fend off the attackers, *Ardent* coming under fire from both battlecruisers at about 16:30 hours at a range of some 14.5km (9 miles). She withdrew, discharging a salvo of torpedoes at the heavy ships and making smoke in an effort to screen the carrier. The torpedoes were ineffective, but the smoke caused a twenty-minute cessation of fire as it briefly masked the target. During this period however *Scharnhorst* heavily engaged the destroyer with her 150mm secondary armament, sinking her at about 17:25 hours. Some five minutes later *Acasta* managed to place herself to the starboard of *Scharnhorst* and discharged eight torpedoes at the capital ship, one of which struck home causing severe damage. This heroism came at a heavy price; she sank at about 18:20 hours after being crippled by heavy and accurate fire. *Glorious* had gone down some ten minutes earlier after being hit repeatedly. Marschall had turned his command for home at about 18:15 hours, with *Scharnhorst* only able to make 20 knots.

Not only had an extremely valuable carrier been lost in avoidable circumstances but, and even more tragically, despite about 900 of them being still alive after the battle only forty-odd men were to ultimately survive. The rest perished in the cold sea whilst awaiting rescue; the British were unaware that the ships had been lost until the following day. The death toll of 1,519 was the largest loss of life the UK was to suffer from a single naval disaster during the course of the Second World War. Perhaps the last word should go to one of the survivors:

> The man in charge (D'Oyly Hughes) was not an aviator. He'd sacked
> his aviator . . . an aviator would have said that the security of this ship
> depends on the aeroplanes and would have had a search out.[52]

Though the Norway Campaign represented a total failure of British arms in general, the Fleet Air Arm notched up a distinct success in dive-bombing and sinking the German light cruiser *Königsberg* on 10 April 1940. The vessel had been badly damaged by Norwegian coast defence artillery, rendering her unmanoeuverable, so she was anchored at Bergen at the time of the attack. This was not carrier launched, rather two squadrons of Blackburn Skuas flew from RNAS Hatston (or HMS *Sparrowhawk*) in the Orkneys, a round trip of around 650 miles.[53]

Carrier strikes were, however, mounted during Operation Catapult, the British attempt at seizing or neutralizing French naval power following the Franco–German Armistice of 22 June 1940. This was achieved relatively peacefully where the French vessels were in British, or British-controlled, ports, but this was not to be the case at the French naval base at Mers-el-Kébir near Oran in Algeria. There were four battleships there, two of which, *Dunkerque* and *Strasbourg*, were modern, fast and powerful.[54] A superior Royal Navy force (Force H) under Vice Admiral Sir James Somerville was assembled and sent. This force, which arrived on 3 July 1940, included *Ark Royal*, aircraft from which mined the harbour mouth to (unsuccessfully) prevent any ships leaving. Negotiations took place, the British envoy being the French speaking Captain Cedric Holland of *Ark Royal*. They failed when the French refused to accept any of the choices on offer and Somerville then ordered that fire be opened at 17:55 hours. Spotting for fall-of-shot was provided by aircraft from *Ark Royal*.[55]

The two old and obsolescent capital ships, *Bretagne* and *Provence*, were quickly disabled, the former exploding. *Strasbourg* however cleared the confines of the harbour despite the mines and, with attendant destroyers, made for Toulon at maximum speed. *Dunkerque* was hit by four 15in shells and badly damaged, though this was not plainly visible to the attackers. Somerville ordered a cease fire after some twenty minutes, and pursued the fleeing *Strasbourg* aboard *Hood*, his flagship, with the battleships *Valiant* and *Resolution* following. It was too late; the French ship had an unassailable lead, unless of course it could be slowed down.

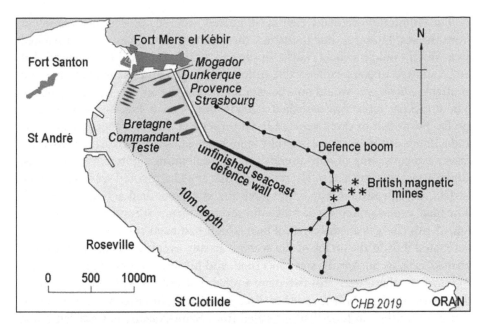

The French ships at Mers-el-Kébir. 3 July 1940. © Charles Blackwood.
The battleships *Bretagne* and *Provence* were quickly disabled by heavy gunfire, the former exploding. Of the battlecruisers, *Dunkerque* was hit and badly damaged, whilst *Strasbourg* escaped both the harbour, avoiding the magnetic mines sown to prevent such an event, and the subsequent pursuit. On 6 July Force H returned to finish off *Dunkerque* by air attack. Twelve Swordfish in three waves launched eleven torpedoes, reporting six or seven hits. In fact, though several may have struck, none had actually exploded. The huge explosion reported, which did severe damage, was caused when forty-four depth charges aboard a patrol boat, sunk by the first wave, detonated during the attack of the second.

Six Fairey Swordfish TSRs (Torpedo-Spotter-Reconnaissance), each armed with four 250lb SAP (semi armour-piercing) bombs, were launched from *Ark Royal* together with an attendant escort of Skuas. They quickly caught up and bombed *Strasbourg* to no effect for about ten minutes from 19:45 hours (British time), afterwards mistakenly reporting that one bomb had struck the target. An hour later, and after sunset, six more Swordfish armed with torpedoes attempted to cripple the battleship; to no avail though one hit was claimed. At 20:20 hours Somerville, with *Strasbourg* some 25 miles ahead of him, abandoned the chase.[56]

Two days later he was 90 miles off Mers-el-Kébir with orders to finish off *Dunkerque* for good. This second attack, codenamed Lever, was probably prompted by a radio broadcast put out by the French Governor General at Tunis, Admiral Jean-Pierre Esteva, in which he claimed that the ship was not badly damaged.[57]

The Admiralty originally envisaged, indeed ordered, another bombardment from the sea. However, due to the fact that the target was close to an inhabited area which would inevitably suffer in such an action, Somerville requested that he be allowed to compromise. The Admiralty agreed and changed the method of attack. *Dunkerque* would now be assaulted from the air by torpedo bombers. The attacking force was launched at 05:15 hours on 6 July and consisted of twelve Swordfish in three waves. Eleven torpedoes, set for a speed of 27 knots and a depth of 13ft, were successfully launched against an increasingly effective resistance consisting of anti-aircraft fire and defending fighters. Nevertheless, all the attackers returned safely, reporting that they had scored six or seven hits. In fact, though several may have struck the ship none had actually exploded. The huge explosion reported, which did severe damage, was caused when forty-four depth charges aboard a patrol boat which had been sunk by the first wave detonated during the attack of the second. In any event it was mission accomplished as far as Somerville was concerned, and his force returned to Gibraltar.[58]

However, there were still two more French battleships with the potential to disturb the British; *Richelieu* and her sister *Jean Bart*. The latter was a fairly minor threat; unfinished in June 1940 she sailed from Saint-Nazaire to Casablanca just before the Armistice. Since there were no dockyard facilities there she remained incomplete; only one of the turrets of her main battery had been fitted, she had no gunnery-control system, and her propulsion system was only half built.[59]

Richelieu was a different matter entirely. Though not fully shaken down, or complete in every sense, she had made over 32 knots on sea trials in mid-June 1940. The battleship was at Brest on 18 June 1940 when, mindful of the advancing Germans, orders were received to proceed to Dakar, Senegal, then part of French West Africa. She reached Dakar on 23 June to find the British aircraft carrier *Hermes* moored in the inner harbour.[60] Two days later the vessel's commander *Capitaine de vaisseau* Paul Marzin, fearing that the Royal Navy would trap his ship with the assistance of local officials (whom he considered overly pro-British), decided to leave for Casablanca in Morocco. Though neither knew Marzin's intentions, both the British and French Admiralties were perturbed by this manoeuvre. Amongst other actions, the former ordered Somerville to leave Gibraltar and intercept *Richelieu* at the Canary Islands. The latter commanded a return to Dakar. This directive was obeyed.[61]

The ship was still at Dakar on 7 July when Acting Rear Admiral Rodney Onslow, *Hermes*' commanding officer, presented the same offer to the French authorities there as had been sent to those at Mers-el-Kébir. This approach was ignored but an intercepted message revealed that orders were given to 'meet attacks from the English enemy with the utmost ferocity'.[62] These attacks went in overnight, the first being an intrepid, stealthy incursion by motor launch. Manned by Royal Marines, this managed to get close enough to *Richelieu* to drop four depth charges close by her stern. Unfortunately for the attackers these failed to explode, but the boat and occupants got safely away. The second phase of the attack manifested itself at 05:00 hours or so, when six Swordfish torpedo bombers from *Hermes* attacked in line ahead from the north-east, the only feasible line of approach given the position of the target and the defensive measures (the tactical mooring of merchant vessels) that had been put in place against just such a strike. Anti-aircraft fire was heavy but ineffective, all six torpedoes entered the water, and the aircraft escaped with only minor damage. They reported observing a column of smoke rising from *Richelieu*, indicating hits had been made.

In fact there had only been one, on the starboard aft quarter, which caused significant damage that may – shades of the attack on *Dunkerque* – have been exacerbated by one or more of the depth charges laid earlier detonating sympathetically.[63] In any event *Richelieu* sank by the stern, but was re-floated a few days later. It took a year to render her seaworthy, and then only in an emergency, so she remained largely immobilized at Dakar as a gun platform.[64]

Successfully delivering torpedoes into the water in shallow, confined harbours like Mers-el-Kébir and Dakar was a notable achievement by any standards, and the Fleet Air Arm in particular, and the Royal Navy more generally, learned from it. The launching of torpedoes from aircraft, though the practice dated from the Great War, had largely transitioned from an art to a science through experimentation and the application of technology during peacetime. There were several difficulties to overcome, one of the most obvious being that torpedoes are not designed to fly. Yet once released from an aircraft that is exactly what one is required to do for the brief period before it enters the water. Unless it is somehow controlled during this transition then it could be damaged when initially hitting the surface or be deflected from its intended trajectory, or both. Air-launched torpedoes had been known to bounce, somersault and snap in two upon hitting the water. The optimum dive angle necessary to avoid such undesirable outcomes had been reckoned at between 14 and 24 degrees. To achieve this, and to keep the torpedo on the right track so that it hit its target, a dual system had evolved. The first component involved fitting an 'air rudder' or 'air tail' which induced stability to the short flight and then broke off once in the water. The second comprised what was titled Drum Control Gear (DCG).

Developed during the first half of 1938, this consisted of an aircraft-mounted device featuring two pulleys fixed to a shaft that spun a weighted flywheel. Two 18ft (5.4m) wires were wound around each of the pulleys, with the end of each attached to the tail of the torpedo. Releasing the weapon caused the wires to spin the pulleys; the inertia in the flywheel ensuring they remained taut. This in turn restrained the tail of the weapon, keeping it higher than the nose, so that it maintained a suitable trajectory for entering the water until after it had

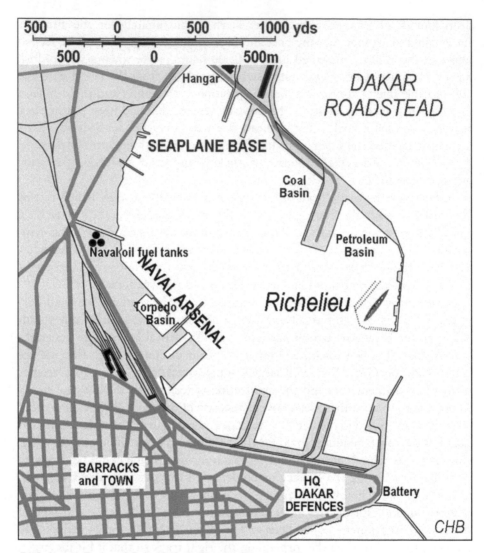

Richelieu at Dakar. 8 July 1940. © Charles Blackwood.

At 05:00 hours, six Swordfish torpedo-bombers from *Hermes* attacked *Richelieu* in line ahead from the north-east. All six torpedoes entered the water, and the aircraft escaped with only minor damage. They reported observing a column of smoke rising from *Richelieu*, indicating hits had been made. There had only been one, on the starboard aft quarter, which caused significant damage that may have been exacerbated by depth charges laid earlier detonating sympathetically. The hull was breached and three compartments flooded. Other damage included a fractured sternpost and distortion to the starboard inboard propeller shaft.

cleared the aircraft's slipstream. It also prevented the torpedo rolling from side to side until the 'air tail' took over. Whilst helping to ensure accuracy, there was a distinct disadvantage in using the device; the torpedo was still attached to the aircraft for a few seconds after release, so the pilot had to fly straight and level until it was clear. This was a perilous enterprise in the face of defensive fire or in the vicinity of enemy fighter aircraft. It thus required a considerable amount of both nerve and technical skill to deliver a torpedo accurately.[65]

Though the attack on *Richelieu* had been successful, post-battle analysis revealed that it could have been even more efficacious had the torpedoes been set to run at a lower speed and a shallower depth. The Mark XII torpedo had two speed settings, 40 knots or 27 knots, giving ranges of 1,500 yards (1,400m) and 3,500 yards (3,200m) respectively.[66] The problem wasn't that the longer range was needed, but rather that the 40-knot setting tended to make the weapon dive deeply after it had entered the water. This was a factor considerably mitigated at the lower speed. It was further adjudged that a shallower running setting of 33ft (10m) would have resulted in a greater number of hits, as would the fitting of duplex pistols to all the torpedoes.[67] All these lessons were put into practice for the famous attack at Taranto, Italy, on the night of 11/12 November 1940 where the water depth was similar to that at Dakar.[68]

According to some scholars the concept of a carrier-launched air strike on Taranto dated back to 1935–6 and the time of the 'Abyssinian tension'. Though as Smithers has remarked, 'no firm evidence seems to exist now', Marder identified Henderson's successor as Rear Admiral Aircraft Carriers, Alexander Ramsay, as the proponent of this 'first offensive action'.[69] In any event, the Commander-in-Chief, Mediterranean, Andrew Cunningham, related how the arrival of the new armoured aircraft carrier *Illustrious*, complete with Rear Admiral, Aircraft Carriers, Lumley Lyster in the summer of 1940, led directly to the attack:[70]

> At our first interview he brought up the matter of an attack on the Italian fleet in Taranto harbour, and I gave him every encouragement to develop the idea. . . . To Admiral Lyster and myself the project seemed to involve no unusual danger.[71]

Taranto lay in the gulf of the same name, and its harbour was divided. To seaward was the large harbour (*Mar Grande*) which communicated with the smaller, almost landlocked, inner harbour (*Mar Piccolo*) by way of a narrow channel. Since nothing larger than a cruiser could pass this channel, Italian capital ships were obliged to anchor in the outer harbour. In 1940 the *Regia Marina* had six such vessels in commission, and all of them were tied up in the *Mar Grande* on the night of the attack.[72] Also in port were seven cruisers and twenty-eight destroyers, all but three of the former in the *Mar Piccolo*.

Lyster had intended to attack using both his aircraft carriers, *Eagle* and *Illustrious*, but was forced to proceed with only the latter after *Eagle* had to be withdrawn. Five of her Swordfish were transferred to *Illustrious*, which gave twenty-four aircraft for the strike, though this number was reduced by way of technical problems to twenty-one. The crews, reduced to two per aircraft through the need to accommodate extra fuel, had been well trained through a series of exercises, and would be going in during the hours of darkness. A nocturnal attack was necessary because it would prevent any interference from fighters, and also make life more difficult for the anti-aircraft batteries, of which there were plenty both afloat and on land. Passive defence was catered for by lines of tethered barrage balloons, though several of these had been damaged or otherwise removed by a gale a week earlier, and anti-torpedo nets around the capital ships. As with the balloons, however, there were deficiencies in the amount of netting deployed and it was set shallow, so did not reach the harbour bottom.[73] Crucially the Italians had no operational radar to provide any element of early warning.[74] Instead they were reliant on sound locators (*aerofoni*) manned by blind volunteers (*aerofonisti*) encadred as MDICAT (*Milizia per la Difesa Interna Antiaerea Territoriale*/Militia for Internal Territorial Air Defence, normally shortened to DICAT). These hardy souls, it was hoped, would be able to accurately locate incoming aircraft from their engine sound as amplified through a system of paraboloidal trumpets (usually four). Thirteen separate *aerofono*, two of which were slaved to searchlights, with a purported maximum detection range of some 40km, were arrayed around the harbour.[75] Some Italian sources, including the official history, state that the attacking aircraft cut their engines and glided into the attack to avoid being detected acoustically, but there is no mention of this in any of the British accounts.[76] In any event the attackers, in two waves, met with heavy though largely ineffective anti-aircraft fire from the start. The first wave of twelve aircraft had half the complement torpedo-armed, whilst the rest carried either six 250lb bombs or four bombs and sixteen flares. As the official report put it:

> The squadron of 12 aircraft to pass up the centre of the Gulf of Taranto and approach the harbour from the southwest. The primary attack to be by six torpedo aircraft against the battleships in the *Mar Grande*. This attack to be immediately preceded by two aircraft dropping flares (and bombs) along the eastern side of the *Mar Grande* in order to illuminate the targets and distract attention from the torpedo aircraft, and by four aircraft making a dive bomb attack on the attractive target presented by the line of cruisers and destroyers in the *Mar Piccolo*. It was expected that this attack would also distract attention from the torpedo attack.[77]

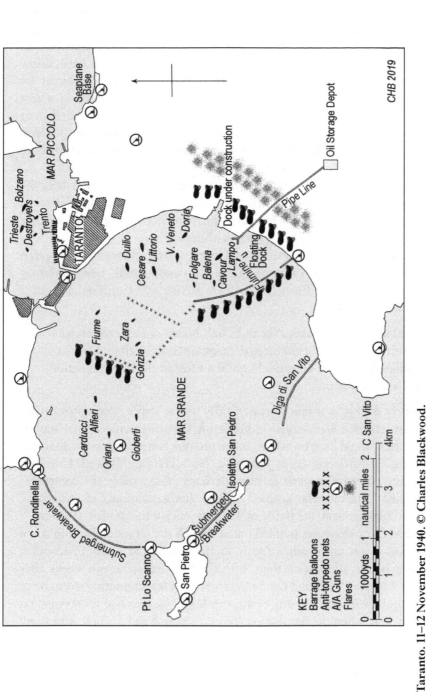

Taranto. 11–12 November 1940. © Charles Blackwood.

The first wave of twelve Swordfish had half the complement torpedo-armed, whilst the rest carried either six 250lb bombs or four bombs and sixteen flares. The second wave of eight aircraft, two of which carried bombs and two flares and bombs, followed some 90 minutes. later In all, the attackers successfully launched eleven torpedoes, though only five struck, or exploded under, the targets; the Italian battleships. *Conte di Cavour* and *Caio Duilio*, old though modernized ships, were each struck by single torpedoes, whilst three hit the modern *Littorio. Cavour* was never to return to service, whilst repairs to the others took until the following year. Half the Italian battlefleet had been put out of action in one fell swoop: 'Twenty aircraft had inflicted more damage upon the Italian fleet than was inflicted upon the German High Sea Fleet in the daylight action at the Battle of Jutland.'

The second wave of eight aircraft, two of which carried bombs and two flares and bombs, followed some 90 minutes later at 21:34 hours (British time), though one had to turn back. A late launch of a final bomb-armed aircraft returned the total number back to eight. In all, the attackers successfully launched all eleven torpedoes, though only five struck, or exploded under, the battleships. Curiously, out of the three pairs of sister-ships present one of each was hit whilst the other survived intact. *Conte di Cavour* was hit by a single torpedo whilst *Giulio Cesare* was undamaged. The same applied to *Caio Duilio* and *Andrea Doria* respectively, whereas *Littorio* was struck by three torpedoes but *Vittorio Veneto* remained unscathed. There was also some bomb damage to onshore infrastructure, but nothing of a serious nature.[78]

With the exception of two aircraft shot down, one of the crew being killed, the other taken prisoner, the attackers all successfully made it back to the *Illustrious*. It had been intended to repeat the operation the following night but bad weather intervened and the carrier and her escorts withdrew.[79]

A 'black day' for Italy according to Count Ciano, Mussolini's Foreign Minister and son-in-law, the Taranto strike was an undoubtedly famous victory for the Royal Navy and the Fleet Air Arm in particular.[80] Cunningham put it thus in his memoirs:

> In a total flying time of about six and a half hours – carrier to carrier –
> twenty aircraft had inflicted more damage upon the Italian fleet than
> was inflicted upon the German High Sea Fleet in the daylight action
> at the Battle of Jutland.[81]

Proportionately the loss was much greater; fully half of Italy's operational battle-fleet had been rendered *hors de combat*. Following Cunningham's comparison for the moment, this would have translated into a pro rata loss of thirteen or fourteen battleships and/or battlecruisers at Jutland; a 'New Trafalgar' indeed. However, and despite the polemics of some authors, perhaps most notably the controversialist Antonino Trizzino who accused various Italian admirals of cowardice, espionage and high treason, the Battle of Taranto was not the 'Italian Trafalgar'.[82] Indeed, and as Caravaggio has pointed out, although the attack at Taranto was a tactical success it was essentially a failure in the operational sense.[83] Sadkovich makes similar points, illustrating them with the fact that some two weeks after the battle the *Vittorio Veneto* and *Giulio Cesare* were at sea attempting to intercept a convoy bound for Malta.[84] In any event, the *Regia Marina* had its revenge on 19 December 1941 when the battleships *Queen Elizabeth* and *Valiant* were sunk at Alexandria by Italian frogmen.[85] Given that the battleship *Barham* and the *Ark Royal* had both been lost the previous month to U-boat attacks, it is clear that the struggle for mastery in the Mediterranean had not been settled at Taranto.[86]

What the raid had done, however, was prove that the Fleet Air Arm had, in the relatively short time it had been at war, honed its strike techniques to the point where they constituted a deadly opponent to capital ships. Aircraft were now demonstrably as capable as the big gun in delivering that 'shattering, blasting, overpowering force' which Churchill had characterized as being the *raison d'etre* of the Admiralty as long ago as 1912. The 'air enthusiasts' had of course been arguing that point for many years. However, they had very little in the way of empirical evidence to support their case, and what hadn't yet been demonstrated was whether or not air attack could cause a similar level of damage to a modern capital ship that was capable of defending itself whilst also manoeuvring at speed in open waters.

The first opportunity to put such matters to the test came in late May 1941 during the Royal Navy's pursuit of the German battleship *Bismarck*. An attack by nine Swordfish launched from *Victorious* on the night of 24 May resulted in one torpedo strike which caused no significant damage. However, and ominously for the Germans, none of the aircraft were downed by the heavy anti-aircraft fire and all returned safely to the carrier. How much truth there is in the story that the Swordfish flew too slowly for the anti-aircraft gunnery directors to target them is unknown, but several authorities claim it was so. Even more portentously for those on the receiving end though was the fact that one of the attacking aircraft was equipped with ASV II radar, which allowed them to find the target whatever the weather or visibility.[87]

In any event, the early hours of the following morning saw *Bismarck* temporarily shake off her multiple pursuers and leave them searching too far north. What this meant in effect was that, even after *Bismarck*'s course became known again, the heavy ships necessary to take her on could no longer intercept her before she reached safety. There was though one force heading westward from Gibraltar which might make contact; Force H under Somerville. However, consisting as it did of the aircraft carrier *Ark Royal*, the battlecruiser *Renown* and the light cruiser *Sheffield*, this was in no way adequate to take on such a powerful opponent in a gunnery duel. An air strike was a different matter and Somerville launched one in the afternoon of 26 May despite the atrocious weather conditions. It failed, which was fortuitous since the Swordfish attacked the wrong ship; nobody had warned them that *Sheffield* had advanced to shadow *Bismarck*. This 'blue on blue' encounter did, however, give notice that the duplex-triggered torpedoes were failing to explode. Rearmed, this time with torpedoes fitted with contact pistols and set to run at 22ft, the fifteen aircraft tried again some four hours later. The attack, in which the aircraft struck from a number of points of the compass as and when they could, lasted some thirty minutes (from about 20:55 hours to 21:25 hours) and seemed at first to have been a failure.

In fact three torpedoes had struck *Bismarck*. Two, abreast of the after super-structure to both port and starboard, caused fairly minor damage leading to controllable flooding. The third, hitting close to the stern on the port side, just aft of the 70mm armoured bulkhead of the steering gear room whilst the ship was in the midst of executing a sharp turn to port, was catastrophic. It jammed her rudders, whilst leaving her propellers undamaged. Able to steam but only in a circle, *Bismarck* could no longer avoid interception by her vastly superior fleet of pursuers.[88]

Battered unmercifully by the combined heavy metal of *Rodney* and *King George V*, later augmented by fire from the heavy cruisers *Norfolk* and *Dorsetshire* who also launched several torpedoes, *Bismarck* finally sank at 10:39 hours on the morning of Tuesday, 27 May 1941. There is still some dispute as to whether or not her end was hastened by scuttling, but there can be no doubt that she had been defeated.[89] Nor can it be contested that the Royal Navy's Fleet Air Arm had been instrumental in causing that defeat. It had in the twenty or so months since regaining independence from the RAF, whilst also being at war, demonstrated a formidable ability to attack and damage or sink capital ships.[90] Moreover, the ability to do this at night was unique.

Whether or not the *Bismarck* could have been sunk by aerial attack alone is a moot point. Logic dictates that she must have eventually foundered given enough hits, and the 175kg warhead of the British Mark XII torpedo did not compare unfavourably with that of the 'relatively humble', but remarkably effective in action, Japanese Type 91.[91] That, if necessary, a sufficient number could have been delivered on target is unknowable, but it would certainly have been well within the bounds of possibility. So had it been shown that, as the 'air enthusiasts' had long predicted was the case, the aircraft carrier had superseded the battleship as *the* capital ship?

The short answer is, of course, no. For example, and though also giving fulsome praise to all involved, Churchill commented in his memoirs that, vis-à-vis the pursuit and destruction of *Bismarck*, 'the battleship and the gun were dominant both at the beginning and at the end'. He sent a telegraph to the US President Roosevelt contemporaneously (28 May) in much the same vein:

> I will send you later the inside story of the fighting with the *Bismarck*. She was a terrific ship, and a masterpiece of naval construction. Her removal eases our battleship situation . . . The effect on the Japanese will be highly beneficial. I expect they are doing all their sums again.[92]

It is probably safe to say that the Japanese Navy (and Army) were indeed 'doing their sums' in May 1941, but if so they were not arriving at the answers Churchill seems to have expected.

Chapter 4

The Grandsons of The Master

Basil Liddell Hart's witticism that 'no battle in history has spilt so much – ink' was made in reference to Jutland in 1916.[1] He was probably right, at least in terms of works in the English language, but what was termed the 'Naval Battle of Malaya' by the Japanese, though remains unnamed in the English-speaking world, surely cannot be very far behind.[2] The destruction of *Prince of Wales* and *Repulse* on 10 December 1941, whilst a disaster in itself, was only a part of a much larger military and strategic catastrophe. More immediately, naval control of the South China Sea was gained by Japan, and the Indian Ocean, a vital British strategic interest, was laid wide open. Churchill later related his feelings, after hearing the news whilst abed, in his memoirs:

> I was thankful to be alone. In all the war, I never received a more direct shock . . . There were no British or American ships in the Indian Ocean or the Pacific . . . Over all this vast expanse of waters Japan was supreme, and we everywhere were weak and naked.[3]

The grand strategic situation proved to be recoverable following the expenditure of much blood, toil, tears and sweat, but what could never be retrieved was the position of the battleship (or battlecruiser) as the yardstick for gauging naval power. This one action was indeed, as many writers have remarked, the final judgement on the 'Bombers versus Battleships' question and a decisive one at that. As stated, the tale of the destruction of the two ships and the background to the decision to send them has been investigated at huge length, and it is certainly not proposed to go over it again here.

What is perhaps worth going into a little is the fact that whilst, with hindsight, the question was on the very cusp of settlement, such matters were not so apparent at the time. Acting Admiral Sir Tom Phillips has been generally, and almost (but not quite) universally, excoriated for the loss of Force Z. But it is only fair to judge him and his actions based on what he knew, or could have been expected to know, at the time.

What he didn't know, or at least for certain, was that a rapidly manoeuvring, heavily-armoured, modern battleship equipped with fully-functioning anti-aircraft defences, as *Prince of Wales* was, could be sunk purely by aircraft-launched ordnance. This was so because it had never been done before. The Royal Navy had been operating in the Mediterranean for two years and had at times undergone intensive aerial attack from both the *Luftwaffe* and *Regia Aeronautica Italiana*. Many ships had been lost to air attack, but no capital ships had been sunk, and several convoys had been fought through to Malta against heavy aerial opposition. These experiences demonstrated that it was not impossible to operate in waters covered by enemy aircraft. The only precedent for a successful attack on a battleship was that launched on the *Bismarck*. This, as has already been related, caused enough damage and delay to allow her to be destroyed by gunfire and torpedo attack later, but it did not sink her.[4] Given though that Phillips was a highly intelligent individual, and few have disputed this, then he must surely have realized that it was a matter of quantity; a sufficient volume of ordnance delivered on target must eventually tell.

Even so, he didn't know that the Japanese had the ability to deliver an attack of that nature. Both he in particular and British Intelligence more generally were distressingly ill informed about the capabilities of Japanese aircraft. Students of the subject have generally agreed with the conclusions arrived at in the 1953 Admiralty Historical Section's study:

> Little was known about the capabilities of either their Naval or Air Forces . . . War experience up to this time indicated that attacks by torpedo carrying aircraft had not been carried out at long range, and attacks by dive bombers had been confined to within 200 miles of airfields.[5]

As Boyd has demonstrated, reasonably accurate intelligence on Japanese naval air power was available, but was not disseminated to the correct recipients, most notably of course to Phillips.[6] Having said that, he could not have been unaware that his command was within range of Japanese aircraft; Singapore was bombed in the small hours of 8 December 1941 whilst *Prince of Wales* and *Repulse* were berthed there. Arthur Percival, General Officer Commanding (GOC) Malaya, reckoned it came as '. . . rather a surprise, for the nearest Japanese aerodromes were 700 miles from Singapore . . . and we hardly expected the Japanese to have any very long-range aircraft'.[7] In fact the Imperial Japanese Navy possessed the long-legged Mitsubishi G4M and G3M2, and there were more than eighty of these aircraft (the 22nd Air Flotilla comprising the *Genzan*, *Mikoro* and *Kanaya* air groups) based at Saigon.

Phillips was probably surprised by the raid too, but there can be no doubt that he now knew that his command was within range of bomber, but not necessarily torpedo-bomber, aircraft. Only seventeen bombers raided Singapore that morning according to most accounts, but their full capabilities were not realized. In fact, these air groups specialized in bombing and torpedo attacks against ships, deployed very experienced and competent pilots, and had undertaken 'special torpedo attack training' with live torpedoes, including at night.[8] These techniques had evolved as part of the IJN's 'interception-attrition' strategy for dealing with an American fleet approaching Japanese waters. Long-range land-based aircraft (*rikujo kogeki ki*, often shortened to *Rikko*) stationed in the Micronesian islands had a large part to play, and the skills of their crews were honed through constant peacetime exercises.[9]

Of these matters Phillips was oblivious, but that he was aware, to some degree at least, of the danger is evidenced by the recollection of Lieutenant Commander Francis Cartwright. Cartwright was commanding officer of the destroyer *Express*, one of the four escorts assigned to *Prince of Wales* and *Repulse*. Force G, as it was known until being renamed Force Z on 8 December,[10] had of course been despatched as a deterrent to Japanese aggression. That this had comprehensively failed became obvious when an amphibious landing at Kota Bharu on Malaya's north-east coast commenced in the early hours of 8 December 1941, followed of course by the air raid already mentioned. Further landings were also undertaken further north at various points along the Kra Peninsula, which was Thai (Siamese) territory, including Pattani and Songkhla (Singora).

Phillips called a council of war with the senior officers of his command, including the destroyer captains, at 12:30 hours that day. According to Cartwright he emphasised that the mission, to destroy enemy shipping off Kota Bharu (about which he had already informed the Admiralty), was 'extremely hazardous' and likened it to 'taking the Home Fleet into the Skagerrak without air cover'. He then added, 'Gentlemen, we sail at five o'clock'.[11] His mention of the Skagerrak was probably hyperbole, and in any event shortly afterwards he requested 'fighter protection off Singora during daylight' on 10 December.[12] The mention of Singora is interesting inasmuch as it indicates an intention to venture some 110 nautical miles closer to known Japanese air bases than Kota Bharu.

Force Z began leaving Singapore at 17:20 hours and, after forming up, headed north-easterly at 17.5 knots to pass to the south of the Anambas Islands. After that Phillips intended turning roughly north-north-west towards the Gulf of Thailand (Gulf of Siam), but even before reaching the first waypoint he received a setback in the form of a two-part message from Rear Admiral Arthur Palliser, his Chief of Staff, whom he'd left behind in Singapore. The first portion stated that the fighter protection requested would not ('repeat not') be possible on 10 December, whilst the second informed the Admiral that the 'Japanese have large bomber forces based Southern Indo-China and possibly also in Thailand'.[13] He did not add that the northern airfields from which the fighters would have operated were already in Japanese hands or were 'either untenable or else had been badly damaged by bombing'.[14]

It is doubtful if the level of air cover that might have been provided would have been of much use anyway. Malaya, and the Far East in general, was accorded a low priority in terms of equipment including modern aircraft with the consequence that their numbers were woefully inadequate. For example, of the estimated 582 aircraft that were required for the defence of Malaya only 164 were available with 88 in reserve.[15] Britain simply couldn't spare up-to-date fighters because of her immense commitments in Europe and the Middle East. If quantity was a problem, the situation as regards quality was just as bad. The most important front-line fighter was the Brewster Buffalo. This had been designed for the US Navy, but that organization had declared them obsolete and unreliable, and was rapidly replacing them with something better. They were though supposed to have been 'good enough for Malaya'.[16] There were four operational Buffalo squadrons: 243 Squadron (RAF), 21 and 453 Squadrons (RAAF), and 488 Squadron (RNZAF), a total of sixty aircraft.[17]

Despite these rather discouraging messages Phillips decided to press on. His plan, reconstructed later from the testimonies of officers who survived, revolved around detaching the escorts, then making a high-speed surprise descent on the Japanese shipping believed to be at Singora with the capital ships alone. Having wreaked havoc with their big guns these would then quickly retire. He calculated that any aircraft which might pursue would not be armed with armour-piercing bombs nor torpedoes, and that such an attack would have had to be hastily organized and thus uncoordinated.[18] The element of surprise was deemed necessary for success, however, and when this was lost, via an enemy reconnaissance aircraft spotting the force, Phillips decided to turn back. He was, as is well known, distracted by a false report of a further Japanese landing on the Malayan coast some 200 nautical miles north of Singapore and investigating this caused delay. The Japanese knew Force Z was at large and were searching hard. At around 10:15 hours on the morning of 10 December it was spotted by a Japanese aircraft, and an hour later Japanese bombers and torpedo-bombers were converging on it.

Phillips' apparent lack of concern about air attack may well have been conditioned by, as already noted, the fact that no capital ship had thus far been sunk by aircraft. The legend that he treated it over-lightly, one that persists 'as legends will' according to Marder, has been pretty much debunked.[19] There is, though, evidence that Japanese air power was greatly underestimated; it was widely accepted within Phillips' command, that 'the Japanese Air Force [*sic*] was about on a par with the Italian'.[20] According to Lieutenant Timothy Cain, the Gunnery Officer of the destroyer *Electra*, it was believed that Japanese torpedo bombers would equate to being 'a somewhat inferior edition of the early Swordfish'.[21]

It might also have been the case that Phillips had faith in the anti-aircraft weaponry of, in particular, *Prince of Wales*. As Friedman has pointed out, the ship had the best available anti-aircraft battery, with the best available radar and fire-control technology that could have been provided. It also seems likely that Captain John Leach, who had tactical control of the ship, chose to use this firepower over trying to evade the torpedoes.[22] And of course, anti-aircraft fire control worked best if a ship followed a more-or-less straight course.[23] The story of the development and effectiveness, or not, of the anti-aircraft control system used by the Royal Navy in the Second World War, the High Angle Control System (HACS) is convoluted and, in some quarters, controversial. It had, and has, many critics.

For example, there are several versions of the tale of the 'Queen Bee' radio-controlled drone, which was used for target practice, and the inability of the pre-war Home Fleet to shoot it down. One version, written by Geoffrey Shakespeare MP, a member of the Board of Admiralty from 1937–40, will suffice. In 1937 Shakespeare visited the Home Fleet off the north of Scotland during some anti-aircraft trials using HACS. As he later described the occasion:

> The target was an aircraft nicknamed the Queen Bee. It was con-trolled by wireless and sailed majestically and slowly overhead. The high-angle ack-ack guns of the battleships and cruisers fired contin-uously at it, but to my surprise the Queen Bee continued her steady course unmolested.[24]

This incident is probably the Ur-source of Corelli Barnett's tale (essentially sim-ilar to that of several others) about a 'Queen Bee' drone circling the Home Fleet for two and a half hours, constantly under fire from HACS-equipped ships, but with not a single hit being scored. He also quotes the Admiralty's Director of Research describing HACS as a 'menace to the service'.[25]

Of actual combat conditions in the Mediterranean some five years later, Admiral Cunningham was to remark that in the 'early months' of the war (Italy declared war on France and the United Kingdom on 10 June 1940) 'the Italians [*sic*] high-level bombing was the best I have ever seen, far better than the German'.[26] The torpedo-bombers of the *Regia Aeronautica* were also a problem. Cunningham says that they were 'little danger in broad daylight' when they could be seen coming in low, but developed more dangerous tactics 'by attacking in the grey half-light just after sunset'.[27] The Mediterranean Fleet had found that bar-rage fire could force Italian torpedo bombers to launch their weapons at ranges of 3,000–5,000 yards, which lessened the accuracy of the attack.[28] As Friedman suggests, accounts of wartime anti-aircraft action in the Mediterranean suggest that barrage fire was much preferred to aimed HACS fire.[29]

That was so because placing a high-explosive shell so that it occupied much the same place and time as a fast-moving aircraft, and then detonating it there, was not a problem easily solved. It could not be done visually, and mechanical analogue computing, combined with powder-burning or clockwork fuses, proved only partially adequate. The latter part of the problem was solved by the development and deployment of the proximity, or VT, fuse.[30] That was for the future, and it is difficult to argue with Friedman's conclusion that HACS was badly outclassed by 1939.[31]

To return to the morning of 10 December 1941; what happened to Force Z has been analysed and reanalysed over the years, but the latest research from close examination of the wrecks is informative. Contemporary British accounts stated that five torpedoes struck *Repulse*, four on the port and one on the starboard side. The attackers claimed no fewer than thirteen hits; nine on the port side and four to starboard. An analysis of the wreck carried out in May 2007 confirmed one hit on the starboard side, but could only find evidence of a single torpedo strike on the port.

Similar discrepancies exist with respect to *Prince of Wales*. The attackers claimed seven hits with torpedoes, five to starboard and two to port, whilst the defenders claim six hits, four to starboard and two to port. The 2007 survey found only four confirmed strikes; three on the starboard side with one to port.[32] A later 'Marine Forensic Analysis' of the photographs taken, and data gathered, in 2007 concluded the single torpedo hit on the port side sealed the fate of the ship.[33] Only one of the three starboard strikes was deemed 'serious', with the remaining two being 'somewhat superfluous in the cause of her demise'.[34]

These conclusions are stark; a single aerial torpedo with a 150kg warhead had fatally wounded one of the Royal Navy's newest battleships.[35] Yet *Prince of Wales* was fitted with the very latest in anti-torpedo protection that was supposedly proof against a 500kg warhead.[36] *Repulse* was fitted with less sophisticated 'bulges' against torpedo attack but was fatally wounded after being struck aft and, echoing the fate of *Bismarck*, having her rudder jammed.[37]

If the shade of David Beatty had been present he might have reprised his Jutland comment about there being 'something wrong with our bloody ships to-day'. Perhaps Phillips thought along the same lines. We shall never know; he joins the list of admirals whose largely unexplained decisions led to their own demise.[38] Phillips undoubtedly made several tactical errors on the day, but he had been placed in an operationally impossible situation by his superiors. The Admiralty had advised Churchill as long ago as 2 August 1940 that there was no point in sending a fleet to Singapore unless it was strong enough to fight the Japanese.[39] Yet out one had been sent; the British Government had, it appeared, willed the end without providing the means.[40] Indeed, Boyd has convincingly disposed of the 'long standing belief' that the aircraft carrier *Indomitable* had been allocated to Phillips, but ran aground in Jamaica and so was prevented from joining his command.[41]

Or perhaps not? One recent study contests that Phillips, who was a highly experienced Staff officer but had not seen any actual combat since the Great War, was given command of Force Z not for his fighting skills (or lack thereof) but because of his abilities at diplomacy.[42] His mission as originally conceived was to deter Japanese aggression: 'an eleventh-hour attempt to prevent the Japanese attacking the British rear'.[43] In fact deterrence, though the British Government could not have known it, was a dead duck; Japan had decided to advance south-wards in 1940.[44] After the fall of France Malaya was there for the taking. The diplomatic part of his mission involved co-ordinating with the US Asiatic Fleet, under Admiral Thomas C. Hart, based in the Philippines. Phillips met with him, and MacArthur, on 5 December at Manila and though Hart agreed to transfer some destroyers to Singapore, but not as many as Phillips would have liked, events transpired to frustrate this.[45] He returned to Singapore having received information that large-scale Japanese shipping movements, invasion convoys, had been observed heading for Thailand or Northern Malaya, arriving in the early hours of 7 December. Shortly afterwards there was no doubt that war with Japan had broken out.

In the absence of orders to the contrary, and with the enemy having initiated hostilities, Phillips' mission perforce changed. Few would argue that, given the information available to him, he had little option but to attempt to interdict enemy support and supply lines. Even if the invasion forces had already sub-stantially accomplished their mission, the 'routes between Indo-China and the Siam-Malaysia coastline would be thick with transports'.[46] If not that, then the only real choices open to him were to remain at Singapore doing nothing (not a particularly inviting prospect after Taranto and, especially, Pearl Harbor) or withdraw to safety. In the latter case he could have gone eastwards to Australia, though there was no fleet base there, or west to Ceylon or beyond; the Prince Edward Graving Dock at Durban was the only place closer than Gibraltar that could accommodate a capital ship.[47] Phillips could not have known it, but orders to do something very like that were being mulled over in London. According to Churchill's account, a meeting, 'mostly Admiralty' (which included the First Sea Lord, Dudley Pound) in the Cabinet War Room held at ten o'clock on the night of 9 November had talked over the question.

> The *Prince of Wales* and the *Repulse* had arrived at Singapore. They had been sent to these waters to exercise that kind of vague men-ace which capital ships of the highest quality whose whereabouts is

unknown can impose upon all hostile naval calculations. How should
we use them now? Obviously they must go to sea and vanish among
the innumerable islands. There was general agreement on that.[48]

This was nonsense, and it is hard to see that the professional head of the
Royal Navy, Admiral Pound, would have signified his general agreement to
it. Capital ships were not like the buccaneering, and coal-burning, *Emden* of
1914 fame, and could hardly 'vanish' no matter how innumerable the islands
might have been. They needed a fully-equipped dockyard, or at least a functioning logistical support network, if they were to operate successfully for
any length of time, which is of course precisely what His Majesty's Naval
Base, Singapore, was for.[49] Churchill also stated that in his opinion 'they
should go across the Pacific to join what was left of the American Fleet'
which was at least realistic. In any event, the meeting resolved only to 'sleep
on it, and settle the next morning what to do with the *Prince of Wales* and
the *Repulse*'. These remote decision-makers were however too slow and too
late: 'Within a couple of hours they were at the bottom of the sea.'[50] Even the
Japanese Navy was surprised at the completeness of the victory.[51] According
to Middlebrook and Mahoney none other than Genda Minoru, one of Japan's
most prominent and innovative naval aviators and a planner behind the Pearl
Harbor strike, remarked that 'it was the grandsons of the Master of Sempill
who sank the *Prince of Wales* and *Repulse*'.[52] There is also Marder's (probably
apocryphal) story that, on receiving the news of the sinkings, Lord Sempill
declared, 'Well done!'[53] Whatever the apocryphalness of these statements,
there can be little doubt that the one attributed to Genda contains at least a
modicum of truth.

It had been made plain to Sir Robert Brooke-Popham, upon his assuming
the positon of Commander-in-Chief in October 1940, the strategic priority his
command enjoyed (if that is the correct term):

> It was pointed out to me that the requirements of Home Defence, the
> Battle of the Atlantic, and the Middle East, must take precedence
> over those of the Far East; at a later date Russia also took precedence,
> and, at one time, Iraq and Iran.[54]

The Middle East was vital for several reasons, including the fact that a defeat there
would allow Italy and Germany, and most particularly the latter, to gain access
to the oil of the Caucasus and Persian Gulf. As Churchill put it; 'The Persian oil
fields were a prime war factor.'[55] Indeed they were. The Abadan refinery in Iran,
constructed by the Anglo-Persian Oil Company in 1912, was one of the world's
largest oil refineries. It, or more properly its product, was deemed 'essential' to

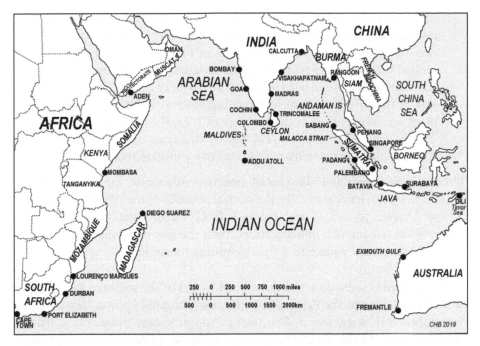

The Indian Ocean. © Charles Blackwood.
The Middle East theatre in particular, and Britain's war effort more generally, were crucially dependent on the vital sea routes through the Indian Ocean. But with the loss of Force Z, and the imminent fall of Singapore, there was little to prevent the nightmare scenario of a Japanese fleet operating there. As *Großadmiral* Erich Raeder put it: 'When Germany and Japan touch hands in the Indian Ocean, the final victory is not far away.' Somerville and the Eastern Fleet had the task of preventing this, and keeping open the crucial sea lines of communication.

continuing the British and larger Allied war effort.[56] So important was it that Operation Countenance, the military invasion of Iran by Britain and the Soviet Union, was undertaken between 25 August and 17 September 1941 largely in order to secure it.[57] As the official history of BP (British Petroleum) puts it, following the loss of Burma and the Netherlands East Indies, the refinery was 'the sole remaining large source of oil for the eastern theatre of war operations. Activity at Abadan was raised to cope with the growth in the demands made upon it, which were further increased by the preparations being made for the North African campaign.'[58] There was more:

> Though oil went out in increasing quantity – 648 tankers in 1942 as against 462 the previous year – there now rose an extra-special need. As the Allies steadily built up . . . the greatest air armada in history,

there came a desperate call for aviation spirit. This is the most highly refined form of all the products obtained from oil . . . The air forces of pre-war years had not run on this form of fuel . . . thus at the beginning of the war they were turning out at Abadan a mere 600 gallons a day – or enough to run one Hurricane for about twenty hours. . . . The first of the three . . . superfractionating towers of the aviation spirit plant was in operation in the summer of 1943, the second in January 1944 and the third in May 1945 and by this time there was flowing from Abadan not two tons a day but nearly a million tons a year.[59]

Thus was demonstrated the crucial interdependence of both the Far and Middle East and, more generally, the crucial reliance of the Allies on the products of Abadan. Indeed, if one accepts J. F. C. Fuller's analogy that logistics is the 'blood stream' of a military effort, then the loss of Abadan's production to the Allies would equate to a tightly-wound tourniquet being applied to a vital artery.

This is doubly so because also threatened would be the southern supply route to the Soviet Union; the Persian Corridor, as it became known. Beginning in September 1941, some five million tons of supplies were eventually delivered via this route.[60] So the Middle East in particular, and Britain's war effort more generally – between April 1940 and December 1941 the Indian Army swelled to almost 900,000 troops[61] – were crucially dependent on the vital sea routes through the Indian Ocean.

But with the loss of Force Z, and the imminent fall of Singapore, there was little to prevent the nightmare scenario that the Deputy Chief of Naval Staff, Vice Admiral Sir Tom Phillips, had outlined in the autumn of 1941; a Japanese fleet in the Indian Ocean. This would effectively sever the 12,000-mile trip around Africa to the Middle East as securely as any German and Italian victory in the Mediterranean would do.[62]

Indeed, the realisation of such a scenario could have knocked the British Empire out of the war, or at least several German and Japanese officers so thought. Perhaps chief amongst them was *Großadmiral* Erich Raeder, Commander-in-Chief of the German Navy, whose so called 'Great Plan' was presented to Hitler on 13 February 1942. This visualized a series of combined and coordinated operations involving all three Axis powers, Germany and Italy in the Middle East, and Japan in the Indian Ocean and subcontinent, that were intended to knock Britain out of the war. As Raeder put it: 'When Germany and Japan touch hands in the Indian Ocean, the final victory is not far away.'[63]

Chapter 5

The Ratcatcher, the Common, and 'Old Ming'

If the Royal Navy was stunned by the loss of Force Z then it recovered with remarkable speed. Vice Admiral Sir Geoffrey Layton, the former C-in-C of the China Station, whose command had been dissolved at the same time as he was superseded by Phillips, was almost literally dragged back to duty. He thus became the second flag officer to command the Eastern Fleet, albeit in a temporary capacity. Not that there was much of a fleet to command.

The only capital ships available were the *Revenge* and *Royal Sovereign*, and the sole carrier *Hermes*. All were of strictly limited value. Of more utility, albeit scattered across the Indian Ocean and Pacific, were six modern 6in cruisers. The former ocean also contained nine older cruisers of doubtful worth. Destroyers were in desperately short supply, and what was available included many old and inefficient vessels. In terms of land-based air support there was virtually nothing.[1]

In any event Layton informed the Admiralty some three days after assuming command that Singapore was untenable as a naval base and that such naval assets as existed should concentrate at Colombo, Ceylon. He recommended two days later that the focus of his efforts should be on maintaining communications in the Indian Ocean.[2]

His points were largely unarguable, and the Admiralty had been thinking along somewhat similar lines anyway. The Vice-Chief of the Naval Staff, Sir Henry Moore, had drawn up a Memorandum for the Chiefs of Staff on 14 December 1941 entitled 'Future British Naval Strategy'.[3] Global in scope, it made the point that next in importance to communications across the Atlantic were those in the Indian Ocean. It pointed out that since the US Fleet, or at least what remained of it after Pearl Harbor, had to concentrate in the Pacific to protect Hawaii and the west coast of the continental USA there was no possibility of a combined effort; the Royal Navy would have to take care of the Indian Ocean unaided.

The memorandum went on to argue that the best way of achieving this aim was to send to Singapore 'a fleet capable of disputing command of the sea with the Japanese'. This depended of course on:

> . . . the provision of a balanced fleet of modern capital ships, carriers, cruisers, and destroyers capable of matching any forces which it is considered likely that the Japanese might employ in the South China Sea.

In addition, there would have to be an upgrade of anti-aircraft defences at Singapore. This would include shore-based long and short-range fighters and radar. Moore went on to admit that it was apparent that 'we cannot in the immediate future provide a balanced fleet'. Particularly one which might have to take on the five or six capital ships, and perhaps five carriers, that the Japanese could probably deploy against it. Instead then, and whilst Singapore relied on the army, the RAF and minor vessels such as submarines to defend itself, he proposed building up a fleet in the Indian Ocean. Only once this was of sufficient strength and capability to contest the matter with the IJN would it proceed to the 'relief' of Singapore.

The composition of this future fleet, which would amount to 'three quarters of our naval strength', was also laid down. The battleships *Valiant* and *Queen Elizabeth* would be withdrawn from the Eastern Mediterranean, and would be joined by *Warspite*, *Nelson* and *Rodney* once they became available. Four carriers were also mooted: *Indomitable*, *Formidable*, *Illustrious* and *Hermes*. Also detailed, and to be 'employed possibly as close convoy escorts', were the four remaining battleships of the 'R' class: *Ramillies*, *Resolution*, *Revenge* and *Royal Sovereign*.[4]

The potential naval campaign was considered as encompassing two phases, the first being the 'period of the land battle in Malaya and the assembly of our fleet in the Indian Ocean'. The second phase would commence following the concentration of the fleet. Moore considered it 'improbable' that the Japanese would sortie into the Indian Ocean with an 'organized fleet' during the first phase; whilst the fighting continued in Malaya in other words. In this scenario the only enemy forces likely to be encountered would be of the fairly light variety; 'cruisers accompanied by carriers, armed merchant raiders', and submarines, though the possibility of a raiding capital ship could not be excluded.

The premise that the Japanese wouldn't send a fleet into the Indian Ocean led the author to argue that the naval forces he enumerated, less the 'R' class, would best be employed as 'striking forces'. Though it was not possible at the time of writing to forecast how the striking forces should be deployed, Moore considered five possible bases from which they could deploy: Trincomalee in

Ceylon; Addu Atoll in the Maldives; Melbourne, Australia; and Durban, South Africa. He also added that Diego Suarez could 'possibly' be used, but this was a typographical error; he meant Diego Garcia.[5]

Layton was informed of these points, which had been adopted by the wider British Government, in the answer to his signals dated 17 December. He was also told that the reconstituted Eastern Fleet's main base would, at least initially, be Trincomalee. The importance of Abadan, and the continuing need to maintain communications with it, was re-emphasized.[6]

In terms of the operational deployment of naval assets, the ideas embodied in Moore's paper might appear to indicate an abrupt about-turn in Admiralty and Government policy. This is particularly so if one considers the wrangling over whether or not to despatch the distinctly unbalanced force of *Prince of Wales* and *Repulse* to Singapore at all. However, and as has already been noted, Force Z was despatched prior to an outbreak of hostilities as a deterrent and was not intended to take on any substantial Japanese naval forces.

Contrarywise, and in the event of an outbreak of hostilities between Japan and both the US and Britain, a Royal Naval force capable of doing just that had been mooted earlier; in May 1941. The capital ship composition of this hypothetical fleet had been anticipated as *Nelson* and *Rodney*, three 'R' class battleships, plus Force H from Gibraltar; *Renown* and the carrier *Ark Royal*. These would be supported by ten cruisers, thirty-two destroyers and ten submarines.[7] Moore's memorandum can then be viewed as building on this earlier design, and indeed expanding on it.

However, and as the elder Moltke is credited with aphorising, no plan survives contact with the enemy. Britain of course now had no fewer than three main enemies, and each contributed to the undoing of her plans. *Ark Royal* was sunk on 14 November and *Barham* on 25 November 1941 by U-boats deployed in the Mediterranean. Things got worse thereafter when, as has already been mentioned, the *Regia Marina* removed two capital ships from the equation by 'Tarantoing' *Queen Elizabeth* and *Valiant* at Alexandria on 19 December. Indeed, the disabling of these ships, whether permanently or not, meant the British Mediterranean Fleet had almost ceased to exist for the moment.[8] Finally, Moore's consideration of improbability in relation to a large-scale Japanese sortie into the Indian Ocean whilst the fighting continued in Malaya was rendered null when the garrison defending Singapore surrendered to General Yamashita Tomoyuki, the 'Tiger of Malaya', on 15 February 1942.

Even at the time, some realized that the fall of Singapore foreshadowed nothing less than the 'end of the British Empire'.[9] More immediately though it left the British Admiralty and Government with the strategic conundrum of actually defending the rest of its 'Two-Hemisphere Empire' with a 'One-Hemisphere

Navy'. Conversely, this was made easier because the defence of Australasia, minus New Zealand,[10] which had long been predicated on the 'Singapore Strategy', was removed from its purview with the creation of the Southwest Pacific Area (SWPA) on 18 April 1942. US General Douglas MacArthur was appointed as Supreme Commander Southwest Pacific Area on the date of the command's creation.[11] American entry into the war of course followed the attack on Pearl Harbor, which was a strategic mistake of the highest order. Though it did succeed in destroying or disabling the American line-of-battle, it barely bought the IJN the 'six months' which Yamamoto Isoroku, the architect of the plan, is credited with claiming it would.[12] Indeed, by attacking the US at the same time as striking south against the European colonial territories, Japan now had to be prepared to fight a 'two-ocean' war of its own.

From the British point of view, what this boiled down to in effect, and no matter how weighty the blows rained upon it and the strain thus implied, was that the Royal Navy's primary operational mission in the region became the defence of the vital Indian Ocean sea routes, which were well defined. As the illustrious, and oft quoted, Alfred Thayer Mahan had put it in one of his most famous works:

> The first and most obvious light in which the sea presents itself from the political and social point of view is that of a great highway; or better, perhaps, of a wide common, over which men may pass in all directions . . . These lines of travel are called trade routes; and the reasons which have determined them are to be sought in the history of the world.[13]

Defending those trade routes was, for all the reasons already enumerated, an inescapable British obligation and one it rose to meet by deploying the majority of its assets. What the Eastern Fleet as reconstituted could not do, however, was form any kind of 'striking force' as had been envisioned by Moore. Some twenty-four years after supervising the internment of the *Hochseeflotte*, the Royal Navy had to discover what it meant to carry out the function of a 'fleet in being'. The consequences of the various policies, decisions and actions (or lack thereof) taken in the intervening period had now to be faced. Put most basically, the Royal Navy had to develop techniques and tactics to enable it to take on the Imperial Japanese Navy on something approaching even terms or avoid action altogether. There was of course a precedent of sorts for the despatching of a fleet from Europe to do battle with the Imperial Japanese Navy, though not an auspicious one from the British perspective; the voyage to, and destruction of, the Russian Fleet at the Battle of Tsushima on 27–28 May 1905. *The Fleet that Had to Die*.[14]

It is not known if Vice Admiral Sir James Somerville, the new Commander-in-Chief, who was told of his appointment on 15 December, was aware of the parallel; his biographer states that he 'did not read very much'.[15] His staff, however, were said to have been the butt of 'wry jokes' on the matter.[16] In any event, Somerville was undoubtedly the right man for what was an extraordinarily difficult job. Some of his exploits as commander of Force H have already been discussed, and his biographer's choice of title was undoubtedly well merited. Though he was probably the oldest of the Royal Navy's fighting admirals, he was certainly one of the most technically aware, having specialized as a torpedo officer; that branch being responsible for the development and maintenance of electrical equipment.[17] Indeed, he was noted as having a gift for scientific and technical matters, and all his appointments between 1909 and 1920 were as a wireless telegraphy specialist. His service during the Gallipoli campaign, maintaining communications between the fleet and the forces onshore, was recognized as 'outstanding'.[18]

His appointment to flag rank, as Rear Admiral (Destroyers) with the Mediterranean Fleet based at Malta, came in April 1936. His flagship, the *Arethusa* class light cruiser *Galatea*, was equipped with a catapult-launched Hawker Osprey floatplane and 'unlike the majority of senior officers of those days, he took every opportunity to get into the air to watch his flotillas exercising'. He also 'took a delight in functioning as the wireless operator, a role which probably no other Flag Officer could have played'.[19]

Somerville was heavily involved in the development of radar for the Royal Navy, and was largely responsible for the rapid equipment of ships with it during 1940 and 1941.[20] Indeed he was dubbed the 'foster father of naval radar' by no less an authority than Sir Robert Watson-Watt, the acknowledged real 'father' of the technology.[21]

Throughout his career Somerville had demonstrated an irreverent sense of humour that was not always appreciated by his superiors. Further, and whilst in command of Force H, he had also shown he was not afraid of criticizing Admiralty decisions and orders in no uncertain terms where he thought it appropriate. His disputatious signals concerning the attack at Mers-el-Kébir, and the British Governments attitude to Vichy France more generally, are examples.[22]

Despite the occasional displeasure visited upon him by his superiors, and whatever else may be said of him, there can be little argument that Somerville possessed what Andrew Gordon categorized as that 'ratcatcher's instinct for war'.[23] This he had developed, or honed, during his tenure of Force H whilst deprecating the lack of any such in his predecessor, Tom Phillips.[24] He would certainly need all the cunning he could muster for carrying out the task he was allotted, and this was particularly so given some of the tools with which he was provided to carry it out.

The main battleship strength of the Eastern Fleet, certainly in the numerical sense, devolved onto the four vessels that constituted the 3rd Battle Squadron. As Sir Henry Moore had postulated this was formed from the remaining 'R' class vessels, which dated back to the 1913 battleship programme. Originally conceived as forming a class of eight, they were designed for slotting into the line of battle and so were rather slower (21 knots) than their predecessors, the five fast (24-knot), oil-fuelled battleships of the *Queen Elizabeth* class. The initial design called for them to be coal-powered, with oil as a secondary feature, but this changed to all-oil before launch. Sometimes, and interchangeably, called the *Revenge* or *Royal Sovereign* class, they were smaller (33,500 tons as against 36,500 tons at full load) than *Queen Elizabeth* and her sisters, but with similar main batteries of eight 15in guns. Unlike them however, the 'R' class were not heavily reconstructed in the 1930s, so remained largely unchanged during the years Roskill dubbed the 'Period of Reluctant Rearmament'.[25] This meant that they were effectively obsolete when the Second World War broke out in 1939. This might not have mattered if their intended replacements, the *Lion* class, had actually been built.[26] Unfortunately they weren't.

Compounding their inherent problems though was the poor shape, in terms of maintenance and serviceability, that the vessels were in. Commander William Crawford, a gunnery officer on the staff of Vice Admiral Sir Algernon Willis, commanding the 3rd Battle Squadron and Second-in-Command of the Eastern Fleet, was highly critical of them in general, and considered that the state of their engines was 'appalling'.[27]

Not all the ships earmarked for Somerville's command were quite so broken-down. One of them, the *Illustrious* class fleet carrier *Formidable* with the C-in-C embarked, sailed from the River Clyde on 17 February in company with *Malaya*, *Eagle* and *Hermione*.[28] The latter three were headed for Mediterranean duty, whilst the former was destined for the Indian Ocean. The *Illustrious* class, *Illustrious*, *Formidable*, *Victorious* and their close sister *Indomitable*, were all laid down in 1937 and commissioned between May 1940 and October 1941. Displacing 23,000 tons and able to steam at 30.5 knots, the class were of a unique design; aircraft carriers with armoured hangars.[29]

They were the brainchild of the man who had been the first Rear Admiral, Aircraft Carriers, Sir Reginald Henderson.[30] In 1934 Henderson had succeeded Sir Charles Forbes as Third Sea Lord and Controller of the Navy and was thus responsible for responsible for procurement and matériel. His knowledge of carriers, and his deductions about the probable nature of a future European conflict, led him to consider ways and means of reducing the inherent vulnerabilities of such vessels. These stemmed largely from the nature of the weapon they carried; aeroplanes. These required ordnance, bombs and torpedoes, as well as significant quantities of high-octane aviation fuel. Any ship carrying large stocks of such materiel was in grave danger of coming to grief should it be successfully attacked with penetrating explosive ordnance of whatever description. They were then, to steal and adapt the witticism first used by Churchill in relation to battleships, eggshells armed with hammers.[31]

Henderson foresaw that the future conflict for which the United Kingdom was reluctantly rearming was likely to be with Germany. This would mean operating in narrow waters within the range of land-based bomber aircraft. Having regard to all the factors, including the relatively poor performance of Fleet Air Arm aircraft in general, and fighters and the control of them in particular, he determined the solution to the problem was hardening the 'eggshell'. Given the limits imposed by Article 5 of Part II of the 1936 London Treaty this had to be done on a hull with a standard displacement of no more than 23,000 tons. This was a difficult task; all warships are compromises and William A. D. Forbes of the Royal Corps of Naval Constructors, the naval architect responsible for *Ark Royal*, juggled the options and came up with a solution in less than three months. The ships would feature a single hangar, hardened with 4.5in armoured sides and a 3in armoured deckhead forming the flight deck; the latter was shorter than that on *Ark Royal* by some 60ft. Defensive armament comprised eight twin turrets each containing a pair of 4.5in anti-aircraft guns. A Type 79Z RDF (radar) set, able to detect aircraft at an altitude of 10,000ft from a distance of 60 miles, was fitted. If the eggshell was strengthened however it inevitably came at the cost of weakening the hammer; the hangar could contain only thirty-six aircraft.[32]

Nor were the complement that accompanied Somerville on his voyage worked up to the standard to which he was accustomed. One Albacore aircraft was lost on 21 February after it failed to return from reconnaissance. Two more were damaged the following day whilst landing, one being a complete write-off with the second repairable, and a third machine crashed on 23 February whilst landing. These events led to him commenting in a letter to his wife that he was 'beginning to be seriously disturbed by the lack of skill and pep in this party here'. The next day he insisted, despite the disapproval of Arthur Bisset, the carrier's captain, that the air crews practice deck landing.[33] He also stated that he thought that Bisset and his Flight Commander 'view with great dislike the fact that I know too much about operating aircraft and refuse to accept blindly any stuff they like to hand out'. Training of the 'green as grass' squadrons wasn't confined to landing practice. Somerville instituted a complete flying programme. His account for 28 February indicated a 'full day's flying. ALT [Air Launched Torpedo], Martlets, long range RDF (Radar) tests . . .'.[34]

Formidable had two squadrons aboard, both equipped with Albacores. Designed to a 1936 Air Ministry specification, the Fairey Albacore was a three-seater, single-engine, fixed undercarriage biplane. A replacement for the TSR Swordfish, it could operate as a bomber (level, dive and torpedo) and conduct reconnaissance and spotting missions. One of the last biplanes to see operational service, and with a top speed of 140 knots (161mph), opinions tend to differ on its effectiveness.[35] Also aboard was as squadron of Grumman Martlet fighters. The Martlet was a slightly modified Grumman F4F Wildcat; the US Navy's mainstay. British-designed and constructed carrier fighters, the 'slow and stately Skuas and Fulmars',[36] were outmatched by just about anything they might have been required to enter combat with, hence the requirement to purchase these American alternatives.[37]

Allied fortunes, particularly in the naval context, declined even further as Somerville was on his way. The Battle of the Java Sea took place on 27 February 1942. That defeat was followed by several smaller battles, with entirely similar results, over the following days; the Second Battle of the Java Sea, fought on 1 March 1942, being the last naval action of the Netherlands East Indies campaign.[38] With these victories Japan had achieved the virtual elimination of Allied naval opposition.[39]

This then was a time of both myth-busting and myth-making. The myth that was comprehensively shattered was that of white European (in general) and British (in particular) racial superiority over the Japanese. In naval terms this had been exemplified by the now-infamous 1935 report from Captain John Guy Protheroe Vivian, the Naval Attaché at Tokyo. He stated: 'I have to strain my imagination to the utmost to believe that these people are capable of springing a technical surprise of any importance on us in a war.'[40] There was much more in this vein, which was rather poetically summed up by Marder:

> There was, too, the supreme confidence engendered by the British naval tradition. How could officers brought up on Drake, Blake, Hawke, Howe, St. Vincent and Nelson believe that little chaps in the Far East who ate rice could ever hope to be a match at sea for honest, beef-eating Englishmen who had had salt water running through their veins for the past 400 years?[41]

It is, however, uncertain how seriously such twaddle was taken.[42] There were certainly cautionary voices; one belonged to Admiral Sir Reginald Henderson who pointed out that 'one must be careful not to belittle the general efficiency of a possible enemy'.[43]

It is tempting to invoke Hubris. However, and if anything, that now applied even more so to the Japanese. By March 1942 their war machine appeared unstoppable, which bred the notion, and fed the myth, of 'Japanese Invincibility' in the minds of those that had been trampled underfoot by it.[44] It also, or at least according to the later account of Commander Fuchida Mitsuo, inculcated what turned out to be a fatal case of 'Victory Disease', an overconfident mental attitude, in the vanquishers.[45]

That Somerville was at least aware of some of the nonsense about Japanese capabilities is evidenced by a letter he wrote to his wife whilst at Freetown, Sierra Leone: 'I'm told the Japs are afraid of the dark so I must try and specialise in night attacks.'[46] He was clearly thinking out tactical matters. Operationally, and as has already been mentioned, his task was to maintain the Eastern Fleet as a 'fleet in being'. He was to write to his wife on the matter two days later, telling her that he hears 'a lot of blah about how everything now depends on our maintaining control of the Indian Ocean. That's poor bloody me and I wonder how the devil it's to be accomplished. My old battle boats are in various states of disrepair and there's not a ship at present that approaches what I would call a proper standard of fighting efficiency.'[47]

Somerville arrived in Ceylon on 24 March 1942, flying the last 90 miles in one of *Formidable*'s aircraft, and took over formally as Commander-in-Chief, Eastern Fleet, at 08:00 hours on 26 March;[48] 'and now', as he confided to his diary, 'my troubles begin'.[49] His account dated Sunday, 29 March has the Eastern Fleet disposed at three different points as follows:

At Colombo were *Formidable* plus the heavy cruisers *Dorsetshire* (refitting) and *Cornwall*. Also there were the light cruisers *Enterprise*, *Dragon* and *Caledon*, along with the destroyers *Paladin*, *Panther*, *Nestor* and *Express*.

At Trincomalee: the battleship *Warspite*, the aircraft carrier *Hermes*, the light cruisers *Emerald* and *Jacob van Heemskerck* (Dutch), and the destroyer *Vampire* (Australian).

Stationed at Addu Atoll were the four "R" class battleships, with *Resolution* flying the flag of Vice Admiral Sir Algernon Willis, and the aircraft carrier *Indomitable*; the latter being the flagship of Sir Denis Boyd, Rear Admiral Aircraft Carriers. Also present were eight destroyers; the Australian *Napier*, *Norman* and *Nizam* and the Dutch *Isaac Sweers*, plus the British *Fortune*, *Foxhound*, *Griffin* and *Decoy*.

Addu Atoll was one of Somerville's 'secret weapons'; secret because the Japanese were not aware of its existence. Generally referred to only by its codename of Port T in an effort to keep it that way, a fleet anchorage had been constructed there by the Mobile Naval Base Defence Organisation (MNBDO), a Royal Marine formation tasked with setting up defences at such anchorages at short notice. Port T had first been surveyed as an operational fleet base only in autumn 1941. By early 1942, it provided a sheltered anchorage offering fuel and water and had coastal defence batteries installed. There were rudimentary underwater defences but as yet no airfield.[50] Despite an appearance that suggested otherwise, it was not a place that was much liked by those that served there.[51] Commander Leslie Newton Brownfield, serving on board *Ramillies*, later recalled the place and the status of the vessels gathered there:

> We assembled at Addu Atoll, which is a ring of coral islands surrounding a considerable deep-water anchorage, and situated roughly in the centre of the Indian Ocean and just south of the equator. Though our force looked quite imposing on paper, we were, in fact, a pretty good collection of 'Old Ming'.[52]

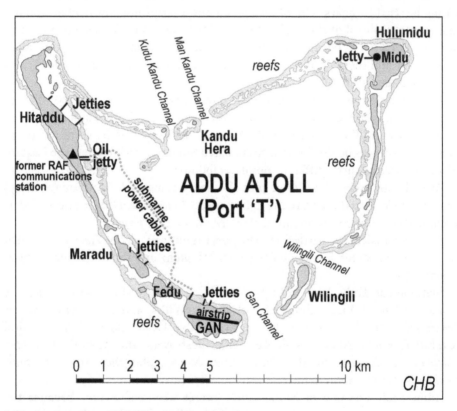

Addu Atoll or 'Port T.' © Charles Blackwood.

The base at Addu Atoll was one of Somerville's 'secret weapons'; secret because the Japanese were not aware of its existence. Generally referred to only by its codename of Port T in an effort to keep it that way, a fleet anchorage had been constructed there by the Mobile Naval Base Defence Organisation (MNBDO), a Royal Marine formation tasked with setting up defences at such anchorages at short notice. Advance parties had arrived in August 1941 to begin the work. By early 1942, it provided a sheltered anchorage offering fuel and water, had coastal defence batteries, plus rudimentary underwater defences. The airstrip on Gan, built subsequently, later became an RAF base.

'Old Ming' was British naval slang for an out-of-date and obsolete ship, and whilst this certainly applied to the battleships the same could not be said of *Indomitable*. Originally conceived as the fourth vessel of the *Illustrious* class, she was redesigned so as to incorporate a second hangar above the original in a double-decker arrangement. This raised the flight deck 14ft (4.3m), with a concomitant reduction in the side armour to 1.5in (39mm) to compensate, but increased aircraft capacity to forty-eight; a trade-off between 'eggshell' and 'hammer'. When completed in October 1941 she was, according to Hobbs, 'without doubt, the best equipped and most capable British aircraft carrier'.[53] She carried four squadrons of aircraft: one of Sea Hurricane Ibs (nine aircraft) and one operating the Fulmar II (twelve aircraft), plus two operating twenty-four Albacores between them.

The adaption of ex-RAF Hurricane fighters, Sea Hurricanes, to carrier operations had been forced upon the Admiralty by the lack of Martlets. The Hurricane had of course proved itself as a superb fighter.[54] It was, however, found to be unsuitable for operating from carriers for several reasons. The lack of folding wings being one; they could not be used in the small aircraft lifts of *Victorious*, *Illustrious* and *Formidable*. Their short endurance was another issue:

> Their small endurance requires a Carrier to be turned into the wind
> so often in order to relieve fighter patrols that the consequent reduc-
> tion of speed of advance of the ships from which it may be operating
> is quite unacceptable under certain circumstances.[55]

Sea Hurricanes also had a characteristic that hardly endeared them to their pilots:

> . . . to ditch a Hurricane safely was impossible because of the huge
> cooling radiator located like a scoop under the fuselage. The radiator,
> as soon as it touched the sea, would inevitably cause the aircraft to
> bunt upside down and hard into the sea without possibility of survival
> for the pilot.[56]

One of Somerville's first actions on assuming command was to nominate *Warspite* as his flagship despite, as he wrote to his wife a few days later, the ship having been 'gutted of all the things she ought to have as a flagship'.[57] Heavily reconstructed during the 1930s, she was a powerfully-armed and well-armoured ship though fairly slow, her maximum speed being 23.5 knots.[58] She would thus be unable to keep up with, and so slow down, the two 30.5-knot carriers. The venerable *Hermes* was a different story. Her air wing consisted of twelve Swordfish, but given her maximum design speed was 25 knots she had difficulty getting these airborne unless steaming into a 'good breeze'.[59]

Somerville knew, and informed his superiors in no uncertain terms, that he could do nothing offensively with this 'fleet' before it had been trained and worked up. Until then, as his Staff Officer Plans, Commander William Kaye Edden, later put it, it was a mere collection of warships and little more than a 'rabble'.[60] That was of course a process that required time, but within days of taking over Somerville discovered that time was on thing that he didn't have. The Japanese were moving to destroy the Eastern Fleet.

Chapter 6

Unknown Unknowns

Less than two days after hoisting his flag in the *Warspite*, on 28 March 1942, Somerville, in the words of the Royal Navy's Battle History, 'received a report of a Japanese force indicating an intention to attack Ceylon by air about 1 April'.[1] In fact the 'report' came from the Far East Combined Bureau (FECB), which, from 1936, was an outstation of the Government Code and Cypher School (GC&CS).[2]

The codebreakers at Colombo had begun to suspect that Japan was planning an incursion into the Indian Ocean about the middle of that month. 'The probable force was given as two or more carriers, two large 6-in. cruisers, possibly several 8-in. cruisers and a large number of destroyers. Battleships of the Kongo class might be in support.'[3] This striking force had been concentrated at a forward base, Staring Bay (*Staring-baai*) on the coast of Celebes (now Sulawesi), in the newly conquered Netherlands East Indies. Now, according to the available intelligence, it was foraying into the Indian Ocean with the intention of attacking a place identified only as 'DG'. This was thought to be Ceylon.

Somerville called a conference on 29 March between his staff and the Head of the FECB, Paymaster Lieutenant Commander Arthur 'Harry' Shaw, in order to assess the dependability of the intelligence.[4] When asked how reliable the information about 'DG' being Colombo was, Shaw replied that there was no doubt at all.[5] There was also some American input into the equation.[6] Having accepted the intelligence presented as accurate, both Somerville and Vice Admiral Sir Geoffrey Layton, who had been appointed Commander-in-Chief, Ceylon, after the former had taken over the Eastern Fleet, acted decisively. Colombo and Trincomalee were cleared of shipping as far as was possible and the defences, such as they were, put on alert. The fighter aircraft component of these comprised sixty-seven Hurricanes and forty-four Fulmars.

Somerville deployed his 'ratcatcher' instincts; what a later generation would call 'strategic empathy'.[7] He conjectured that both Colombo and Trincomalee were likely to be attacked simultaneously, and calculated that a carrier-launched attack would be made from a point around 100 miles south-east of Ceylon and thus approximately 180–200 miles from both Colombo, on the south-west coast, and Trincomalee, on the north-east coast. He also deployed Catalinas on reconnaissance missions, flying out over 400 miles from Colombo, to search along the south-east line of approach which he expected the Japanese would take. Seemingly there were only six of these aircraft available and operational. Given that these long-range patrols could last up to 32 hours, then only three aircraft could be available for patrol on any one day. Each searched an arced sector of about 15 degrees.[8]

When the Japanese arrived at the expected point, then Somerville planned what might be termed a nocturnal ambuscade whilst avoiding the risk of engagement with what could well be a superior IJN force. He ordered the whole Eastern Fleet, minus its submarine component, to concentrate by 16:00 hours on 31 March at a position where his carriers could launch torpedo-carrying aircraft during the hours of darkness. The chosen concentration area lay on a bearing of 198° (between south-by-west and south-south-west) some 80 nautical miles from the southernmost tip of Ceylon, marked by the Dondra Head Lighthouse. In accordance, and having furthest to travel, the 'Old Ming' under Vice Admiral Willis left Addu Atoll at 23:30 hours on 29 March. The warships at Colombo, which had meanwhile been joined by *Warspite*, steamed south to the rendezvous on the morning of 30 March whilst the vessels at Trincomalee did likewise.

The decision to attempt a night interception, albeit when the moon was full so not in total darkness, may have been prompted by Somerville's belief, already mentioned, that the Japanese were 'afraid of the dark'. If so, then he was falling prey to dangerous nonsense. Not only was the Imperial Navy distinctly unafraid of the dark, but it had been intensively trained in, and had practised for, night-fighting over many years.[9]

It seems unlikely that Somerville was aware of this expertise, which can only be marked down to a gap in the intelligence available to him. In any event, he was planning a nocturnal carrier-on-carrier battle where he thought he had the technological edge; his force was equipped with radar. Or at least mostly. In terms of airborne sets, the Albacore strike aircraft aboard *Formidable* were equipped with ASV II, whilst their counterparts aboard *Indomitable* had yet to be so fitted. A single ASV-fitted Swordfish had been retained aboard the latter vessel to provide radar coverage, but this had been lost on 28 January 1942 off the coast of Java.[10]

Though this discrepancy would likely have complicated matters somewhat, his plan overall was relatively simple; he would remain well out of the path of any likely Japanese force during daylight hours to avoid being detected by enemy reconnaissance aircraft. Following nightfall however, he would steam the fleet towards the anticipated Japanese launch point, at 15 knots, whilst carrying out a continuous ASV search ahead and to the southward. His intention was to catch the Japanese unawares and perhaps in the midst of launching their own strike. To this end, and aware that the greater part of his command in the numerical sense had little role in such operational methodology, he split the fleet in two.

Under his direct command was Force A: *Warspite*, the two large carriers, the cruisers *Cornwall*, *Emerald* and *Enterprise*, together with the destroyers *Napier*, *Nestor*, *Paladin*, *Panther*, *Hotspur* and *Foxhound*. Force B comprised the four 'R' class battleships, *Hermes*, the cruisers *Caledon*, *Dragon* and *Jacob van Heemskerck* together with the destroyers *Griffin*, *Decoy*, *Norman*, *Fortune*, *Arrow*, *Scout*, *Vampire* and *Isaac Sweers*. This formation under Willis, flying his flag in *Resolution*, was assigned a back-up role; 'a supporting force to Force A, keeping 20 miles to the westward and conforming to Force A's movements throughout the night'.

The feasibility, or otherwise, of Somerville's plan and subsequent actions can only be judged in the light of what he knew, or thought he knew, at the time. To steal the phraseology made famous by Donald Rumsfeld, there were things he knew (and knew he knew), things he knew he didn't know (known unknowns), and things he didn't know he didn't know (unknown unknowns).[11]

In the context of the operational situation pertaining, the list of things he knew, or thought he knew, was rather short. Probably top was the capabilities of the force under his direct command. He knew, from the attacks on *Bismarck* and Taranto amongst others, that his strike aircraft were capable of delivering torpedoes which could disable and sink capital ships including, by extension, the 'two or more carriers' that were his target. On the other hand, he also knew that his ships had had no time to train together, and no time at all to practise multi-carrier operations.

He also knew that his prime objective was to keep the Eastern Fleet, the single largest concentration of capital ships and aircraft carriers that the Royal Navy would deploy against an active enemy fleet throughout the Second World War, in being. This included the 'Old Ming' in Force B, which he employed for their defensive value against enemy capital ships; 'I considered it a cardinal point in any operation that Force A should not proceed outside supporting distance from Force B unless it could be presumed that enemy capital ships would not be encountered.' Since the intelligence he'd received stated that there were probably *Kongo* class battleships in support, then having Force B available as a back-stop made sense.[12]

What he didn't know, and knew he didn't know, was the composition and definite strength of the Japanese force that was on its way to attempt a re-enactment of the Pearl Harbor strike at Colombo; the information available to him suggested that whilst it was powerful it was also opposable. Nor did he know the area from where it would launch its attack, or that it actually would attack Trincomalee at the same time. He had to rely on what information the FECB could gather in respect of the former matter.[13] For the latter, and in the absence of any intelligence, he could only utilize his, and his staff's, judgment on what was most probable. This was a course of action that carried inherent risks, but given he was indeed an officer 'brought up on Drake, Blake, Hawke, Howe, St. Vincent and Nelson' then he was no doubt mindful of the injunction issued by the last named prior to fighting the Battle of Trafalgar: '. . . something must be left to chance. Nothing is sure in a sea fight beyond all others. . . .'[14]

Nelson, however, knew more or less what he was dealing with; there were probably no unknown unknowns as far as he was concerned. This did not apply to Somerville; there were several crucial matters about which he knew nothing and, moreover, didn't know that he didn't know. In order to consider them it is useful to go back a little and, to steal a different Napoleonic War metaphor, to look at 'the other side of the hill'.

Japan, like the United States, did not create a separate, unified air force. This meant that the aviation arm of the Imperial Navy was able to develop operational doctrines and tactics, as well as specify equipment designs, that focused purely upon naval requirements. It also had full control of the recruitment and training of its aviators. Before the Sempill Mission had completed its work, the proportion of naval academy graduates who applied to become aviators had been small. Following the Mission's departure, this greatly intensified, as did naval aviation generally.[15] At first, Japanese doctrine around aircraft and their carriers pretty much equated with that of Britain and the US; they were generally considered as having a support role vis-à-vis the line of battle, with missions centred around reconnaissance and patrol. Something of the future was perhaps glimpsed in 1928 when a Carrier Division (containing two or more carriers, together with screening forces) was formed. The same year 'The Third Revision of Principles in Naval Operations' was published, which defined the aim of naval air operations as carrying out attacks on a hostile fleet in support of a friendly fleet.[16] This marked the acceptance that aircraft had an important part to play, but still very much in an auxiliary role.[17]

Some ten years later, on 15 November 1939, Rear Admiral Ozawa Jisaburo became commander of the First Carrier Division. Ozawa quickly became convinced that current carrier doctrine and organization, whereby each carrier division was attached to a corresponding battleship division, was ineffective. He proposed grouping them into one independent command, into an air fleet, where they could both train and fight together.[18] Admiral Yamamoto Isoroku, the Commander-in-Chief of Japan's Combined Fleet since 30 August 1939, was also a proponent of air power and had been for many years.[19] He actively promoted the aircraft carrier and foresaw the critical role of aviation in the future. However, many in the upper echelons of the IJN were just as conservative as their RN and USN counterparts, if not more so. To them the future lay with vessels such as the *Yamato* class super-battleships to which Yamamoto was vehemently opposed.[20] Further impetus was lent to Ozawa's ideas by Lieutenant Commander Genda Minoru, a 1924 graduate of the Japanese Naval Academy and one of the most brilliant 'Young Turks' of Japanese naval aviation.[21] The idea of tactically grouping carriers is said to have come to Genda from a newsreel of several such American vessels parading for the camera in a box formation.[22] In any event, and though too junior to be able to exert serious influence, he began to pester his superiors on the matter.[23] He was, as the saying has it, pushing at an open door with regards to Ozawa, and much the same applied with Rear Admiral Onishi Takijiro, who was rated as one of Japan's few 'genuine air admirals' who had 'consistently advocated expansion and improvement' of the naval air arm.[24] He was also a good friend of Yamamoto's.[25] Another major proponent of air power, and denigrator of super-battleships, was Vice Admiral Inoue Shigeyoshi, the head of the Naval Aviation Department from October 1940 to January 1941.[26] Yamamoto, who was already considering how best to successfully attack, and hopefully destroy, the American Pacific Fleet at Pearl Harbor saw the potential of what was being proposed. On 10 April 1941 the First Air Fleet, also designated as the Mobile Force (or in transliteration *Kido Butai*) within which were gathered Japan's six largest fleet carriers as one unit, was created. This marked a revolutionary leap in naval warfare; the revolution lay in moving from utilizing carriers as tactical weapons, very much auxiliary to the line of battle, to deploying them as a stand-alone force that could use its combined air power to operational and strategic effect at long distances. The person appointed as Air Officer of First Air Fleet was Commander Genda Minoru.[27]

Overall command of the force, however, was given to Vice Admiral Nagumo Chuichi, who had no background, nor familiarity, nor experience, in naval aviation and was appointed simply by virtue of his seniority via a Japanese rendition of the Buggins' turn principle.[28] He seemingly had the sense though to allow Genda a free hand in developing doctrine.

By the time of its first operational usage, the 7 December 1941 strike on Pearl Harbor, the Mobile Force had honed its doctrine and technique to the extent that aircraft from all six carriers concerned could be launched, formed up as appropriate, and headed off in pursuit of their target within 15 minutes. In this scenario, each carrier contributed what was termed a 'deckload strike': a squadron of either dive or torpedo bombers, plus escort fighters, to a total of between twenty-one and thirty-six aircraft, dependent on the size of the carrier flight deck. The 'deckload strike' could be launched uninterruptedly without the need to reorganize or bring up aircraft from the hangar. Once airborne, each aircraft type, whether fighter or bomber of whatever description, would be commanded by a single officer regardless of which carrier they came from. Thus, the attack would be made by coordinated groups which, afterwards, would then reform for return to the carriers. The 7 December attack saw two attack waves, of 183 and 171 aircraft respectively, strike targets which went beyond the warships berthed at Pearl Harbor; simultaneous air raids were made on every major airfield across the breadth of Oahu. Equipped with strike aircraft of long range, and fighters that could outrange and outfight any likely opponents, the Mobile Force could project force over several hundred miles and was virtually unopposable.

The carriers dispersed after Pearl Harbor to fulfil more traditional roles; two, *Soryu* and *Hiryu*, supported the amphibious landings at Wake Island on 23–24 December 1941, and another pair, *Kaga* and *Akagi* assisted at Rabaul during January and February 1942. All four carriers, plus the light carrier *Ryujo*, took part at various times, and at various points, in the Dutch East Indies Campaign that lasted from December 1941 until early March 1942.[29]

It was during the course of this operation that the four fleet carriers reunited to unleash the full force of their innovatory mode of warfare at Darwin in Australia's Northern Territory. In order to interdict supplies and reinforcements being sent to the Dutch East Indies in general, and in support of amphibious landings on the island of Timor which lay some 400 miles to the north-west across the Timor in particular, 188 aircraft were launched in a single wave from the carriers on the morning of 19 February 1942.[30] The ships and port facilities of Darwin Harbour comprised the targets of the eighty-one Nakajima B5N torpedo bombers (designated 'carrier attack aircraft') and seventy-one Aichi D3A dive-bombers (designated 'carrier bomber aircraft') that comprised the strike force.[31]

Though purpose-built for its task, the B5N, which had a maximum range of over 1,200 miles (1,992km) and a maximum speed of 235mph (378km/h), could carry an alternative bomb load of 1,800lb (800kg) and did so on this occasion.[32] The D3A had a similar top speed, 242mph (389km/h), though slightly less range, 915 miles (1,473km), and a much smaller bomb load. It could though deliver its one 551lb (250kg) bomb, or alternative load of two 132lb (60kg) bombs, with near-pinpoint accuracy.[33] These strike aircraft were escorted by thirty-six Mitsubishi A6M Zero fighters. Fast, 346 mph (534km/h) at 15,000ft (4,550m), long ranged (circa 2,000 miles (3,104km)), and well-armed with two 7.7mm machine guns and two 20mm cannon, the Zero '. . . ruled the air in the Far East from 1939 until mid-1943. It had the impressive combat kill ratio of 12:1 . . .'[34]

The raid, popularly remembered as 'Australia's Pearl Harbor', achieved surprise and, combined with a later attack by land-based naval bombers, killed around 250 people, wounded a further 300–400, and destroyed 30 aircraft.[35] It also sank eleven vessels whilst damaging another twenty-eight to a greater or lesser extent; '. . . most of the available cargo shipping was wiped out, and Java was sealed off from further surface shipments from Australia'.[36]

In attempting to repeat such destruction in Ceylon, Nagumo sortied from Staring Bay on 26 March. He had five carriers under his direct command: *Akagi* (Carrier Division 1), *Hiryu* and *Soryu* (Carrier Division 2), plus *Zuikaku* and *Shokaku* (Carrier Division 5).[37] In support were the 3rd Battleship Squadron, containing all four members of the *Kongo* class, and the 8th Cruiser Squadron comprising the heavy cruisers *Tone* and *Chikuma*. Escort duties were undertaken by Rear Admiral Omori Sentaro, who commanded two divisions of destroyers (nine in total) from his flagship, the light cruiser *Abukuma*. Sources differ somewhat, but the total aircraft complement of the fleet, divided more or less equally between torpedo bombers, dive-bombers and fighters, was somewhere between 270–280.[38]

Somerville of course knew none of this critical information. The intelligence available to him had indicated that the force he was attempting to intercept and surprise was broadly comparable, at least in size and composition, to his own. He was also expecting it to be somewhere close to Ceylon on 1–2 April. This had been calculated from the supposed departure date of the Japanese from Staring Bay; 21 March according to the information provided by the FECB.

The Japanese were thus five days behind the schedule which the British had assigned them. They were also, in plain numbers, about twice as strong in ships, and three-and-a-half times in aircraft, compared to what had been expected. This doesn't tell the whole tale though, because in terms of striking power, of delivering 'shattering, blasting, overpowering force', they were superior many times over. Indeed, several authors have described the concept embodied in, and the methodology adopted by, the *Kido Butai* as being the naval equivalent of the 'blitzkrieg' tactics used by the German Army.[39] This is surely a comprehensible, if arguable, analogy. Perhaps Vice Admiral Sir Arthur Hezlet put the essence of it most succinctly in his 1970 book. He argued that the Japanese had organized their air power, which was capable of competing with shore-based opponents, to deliver powerful, coordinated strikes at great range. The British, on the other hand, had a naval aviation arm comprised of inferior aircraft, which had been basically designed to give air support to a battlefleet.[40] And therein lay the vast difference; the unknown that Somerville didn't know he didn't know as his fleet assembled on the afternoon of 31 March 1942 some 80 miles south of Dondra Head.

The sun dipped below the horizon at 18:15 hours, which was followed by about an hour of twilight. Only when the light had faded, albeit the moon was bright, did Somerville take his fleet to the north before turning east-by-north towards the anticipated Japanese launch area. Proceeding at 15 knots in order to allow Force B to keep up, he had the radar-equipped Albacores fly continuous search patterns ahead and to the south.[41] Wallace makes an interesting point in respect of this: 'If sufficient Albacores were despatched to cover a wide search area they then would not be available for any subsequent air strike.'[42] Having no choice in the matter, Somerville was forced to juggle his available assets in order to maintain a balance between the requirements of reconnaissance and the potential for launching a strike if and when the search found something worth striking. Until then, or at least until he knew rather more, he sensibly adopted a policy of what Scots call ca'canny; going carefully. There was after all, and to paraphrase Sir Francis Walsingham in 1568, less danger in fearing too much than too little.[43] Indeed, given what seemed to be at stake and the fact that from the British point of view Japan's strategy seemed to be unfolding with some precision, the sobriquet retrospectively bestowed on Jellicoe vis à vis the 1916 Battle of Jutland, 'the only man on either side who could lose the war in an afternoon', seems (the necessary changes having been made) rather appropriate for Somerville in 1942.[44]

By 02:30 hours on 1 April the area where he expected to find the enemy had been reached with of course no sign of them at all. The Fleet then withdrew to the south-west to a point where it would be beyond the estimated outer range of any daylight air-searches that the enemy might instigate should they appear. Both the Eastern Fleet and the RAF in Ceylon carried out wide diverging searches to the east and south-east during daylight hours, but again there was no sign of any enemy. Somerville penned a letter to be later sent to his wife, relating that the sea was 'flat calm' and that the sun 'scorches the skin off you' which had left his face and arms like 'raw beetroot'. He went on:

> The trouble is that the Fleet I now have is much bigger than anything anyone has had to handle before during this war. On top of that, most of my staff are pretty green so I have to supervise almost everything myself. It will improve as time goes on. But it certainly is the devil of a job at present.[45]

Reinforcement for Force A, in the form of the heavy cruiser *Dorsetshire* which cut short her refit at Colombo, arrived in the afternoon. That evening the operation of the previous night was repeated with a sweep to the north-east, though keeping clear of areas already traversed. Gordon Wallace aboard *Indomitable* at the time later wrote:

> The Albacores on *Indomitable* and *Formidable* were capable, if inadequately practiced, in the execution of a night torpedo attack . . . There was a full moon on 1 April so there seemed a reasonable chance of success if we were given the chance. The Swordfish on *Hermes* were . . . not fitted with ASV; being part of Force B we saw little of her. However, when the sun rose on the 2nd we were back again in the same position steaming slowly west. 'Where were all these Japanese?' was all we could say to each other.[46]

Somerville was asking the same question. As he put it to his wife:

> Still no news of the enemy. I fear they have taken fright which is a
> pity because if I could have given them a good crack now it would
> have been very timely. Unfortunately I can't hang about indefinitely
> waiting for them.[47]

The reason why he couldn't linger revolved around the battleships in Force B;
they 'confessed with salt tears running down their sides that they must return
to harbour quickly as they were running out of water'.[48] Indeed, Willis had
informed him at the beginning of the operation that three days was their endurance limit, which was in part due to the failure of a water tanker to arrive at
Addu Atoll before Force B left. He did not immediately abandon the operation
however, but during the hours of daylight manoeuvred the Fleet in an arc about
50 miles to the westward of its position on the previous two days. He was of
course worried about the presence of enemy submarines, particularly as 'several unconfirmed echoes were reported by destroyers in the screen'.[49] Aircraft
reconnaissance continued, with at least some of the Albacores being substituted
for Fulmars which 'had about the same range, but, with . . . higher speed[50] . . .
could cover the area in a shorter time and, if intercepted . . . had a better chance
of defending [themselves]'.[51]

Somerville also pondered his options that day. He had several factors
to consider, including of course the requirements of the battleships in
Force B. Also of concern was the likelihood that, after operating for three
days and two nights in the same general area, the chance of his force being
located by enemy submarines was increasing. No sign of the enemy fleet had
been forthcoming, nor had any further information arrived, which led him
to think that perhaps the air raid on Ceylon was unlikely to develop in the
immediate future. He calculated that the most probable reason for this was
that his activities had been discovered, and that the attack had been merely
delayed until the need to refuel drove him back to Colombo or Trincomalee.
Then his command would be 'Pearl Harbored'. His decision was to undertake
a smaller sweep to the east that night. As nothing was seen by 21:00 hours,
he abandoned the operation and headed south-west to Addu Atoll some
600 miles distant. Four ships were though detached and sent north to Ceylon;
Dorsetshire and *Cornwall* to Colombo whilst *Hermes* and *Vampire* went to
Trincomalee.[52]

Force A, with Albacores from *Indomitable* scouting up to 150 miles ahead
on anti-submarine patrol, arrived at Addu Atoll at 12:00 hours on 4 April.[53]
Force B followed some three hours later. It was of course Somerville's first sight
of the place. He was horrified: 'This beats the band for an abomination of heat

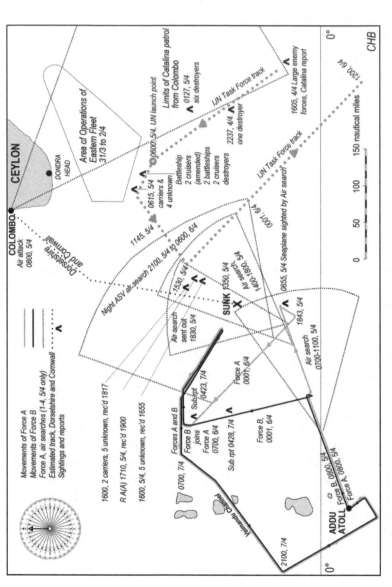

Fleet Movements: the Eastern Fleet and the *Kido Butai*. 31 March–5 April 1942. © Charles Blackwood.

Less than two days after hoisting his flag in *Warspite*, on 28 March, Somerville received a report of a Japanese force intending to attack Ceylon about 1 April so put to sea immediately. He conjectured that both Colombo and Trincomalee were likely to be attacked simultaneously, and that a carrier launched attack would be made from a point around 100 miles south-east of Ceylon. Long-range reconnaissance patrols were launched from Ceylon to try and locate the Japanese. Nothing was found so he returned to Addu Atoll. No sooner had he arrived than, on 4 April, the *Kido Butai*, based around five carriers under Nagumo Chuichi, put in a belated appearance. Somerville took his fleet back to sea as soon as possible in an attempt to engage. Soon realising that he was up against a much superior force, he avoided contact and preserved the greater part of his command. Nagumo meanwhile, who had neglected to carry out adequate reconnaissance, and had also failed to 'Pearl Harbor' the Eastern Fleet at Colombo, moved around southern Ceylon to have another try at Trincomalee. Somerville, perforce, retreated.

and desolation . . . I just don't know where to begin to put things in some sort of order.'[54]

The defences at Ceylon also were also stood-down somewhat, but the Catalina flying boats continued long-range reconnaissance patrols from their base at Koggala Lagoon on the coast, about 68 miles south of Colombo. One of these, of 413 (RCAF) Squadron captained by Squadron Leader Leonard Birchall, had taken off before dawn on 4 April for a long patrol. Having arrived at its designated, southernmost, patrol area at about 06:15 hours it began flying a search grid: 150-mile east-west lines spaced 50 miles apart.[55] Some ten hours later, at about 16:00 hours, one of the crew, Sergeant L. A. Colarossi, spotted a speck on the distant horizon and Birchall moved to investigate, losing altitude as he did so. As they got closer it became obvious that it was a ship, then came the realisation that it was only one of many proceeding in a line-ahead formation some 360 miles from Dondra Head on a bearing of 155 degrees (between south-east-by-south and south-south-east) heading towards Ceylon.[56] According to their later testimony the crew, who had only arrived in Ceylon two days earlier, had not been briefed about the potential for a Japanese force to be in the area. They therefore thought they were viewing Somerville's Eastern Fleet.[57] They were soon disabused of this notion when Zero fighters swarmed to the attack. According to Birchall's account:

> As we got close enough to identify the lead ships we knew at once what we were into but the closer we got the more ships appeared and so it was necessary to keep going until we could count and identify them all. By the time we did this there was very little chance left. . . . All we could do was to put the nose down and go full out, about 150 knots. We immediately coded a message and started transmission.[58] We were halfway through our required third transmission when a shell destroyed our wireless equipment and seriously injured the operator; we were now under constant attack. Shells set fire to our internal tanks. We managed to get the fire out and then another started, and the aircraft began to break up. Due to our low altitude it was impossible to bail out, but I got the aircraft down on the water before the tail fell off.[59]

Despite the Catalina crew basically sacrificing themselves, their signals were garbled on arrival in Ceylon and requests for further information obviously went unanswered.[60] Enough information was, however, gleaned to indicate that the air attack would take place the next day. What didn't get through though was the likely scale of the attack, given that the Japanese had sent a substantial fleet rather than a raiding force headed by two carriers which the original intelligence had indicated; this, it seemed, had been wrong only on timing.[61] Somerville was seriously annoyed when he received the news:

> Damn and *blast* it looks like I've been had because a Catalina has just reported a large enemy force 350 miles SE of Ceylon – evidently the party I've been waiting for and here I am miles away and unable to strike . . . its maddening to think they've slipped me this time. . . . Expect the India people not to mention those in Whitehall will want to know what the E[astern] F[leet] was doing. Crocks can't play centre court tennis and that's the answer. . . .[62]

A second Catalina, from 205 Squadron RAF piloted by Flight Lieutenant 'Jock' Graham, was despatched at 17:45 hours to continue surveillance of the enemy force. At 22:37 hours Graham reported seeing a single destroyer and, at 00:45 hours (5 April), a further six some 200 miles south-east of Ceylon. A third report at 06:48 hours stated that a battleship and two cruisers, subsequently amended to two battleships, two cruisers and several destroyers, were 120 miles south of Dondra Head steering 290 degrees (between west-north-west and west-by-north) towards Ceylon. That was the last heard from Graham and his eight-man crew, who were all lost when their aircraft was detected and shot down.[63]

The Eastern Fleet could do nothing in respect of the forthcoming attack on Ceylon; in the matter-of-fact words of the Admiralty's later account, it 'was 600 miles distant, short of water and fuel, and could by no possibility intervene'.[64] Somerville calculated that he might be able to cause the attackers some damage following the raid, particularly if the land-based air defences had managed to 'wing' some of the enemy ships during the course of the action.[65] He had first to get his command ready to sortie, so throughout the evening of the 4 April, in 'a burning, torturing heat from which there is no escape', tankers and water-boats went from ship to ship.[66] By dint of these efforts, Force A was able to exit Addu Atoll at midnight, leaving Force B to follow at 07:00 hours the following morning (5 April). The cruisers at Colombo, *Dorsetshire* and *Cornwall*, were ordered to leave Colombo and rendezvous with the rest of Force A on the afternoon of the 5 April.

Once again Somerville attempted to get inside the mind of his opponent, and divined that an attack on Colombo, and possibly Trincomalee, would take place 'either before dawn or shortly afterwards' on 5 April and be launched from a position about 150 miles south-east of Ceylon. Upon the aircraft recovering to the carriers the whole force would then retire to the east, and so be vulnerable to a night attack as it did so. In other words, Somerville would attempt to put his original strike-plan into action, though this time after, rather than before, the event. Meanwhile all he could do was steer straight for where he expected to find the Japanese.

The 'event' began at 07:30 hours over Colombo and, amazingly, caught the defences unprepared. Why this was so is outside the scope of this work, but the attack lasted about 80 minutes and did surprisingly little major damage particularly to shipping because Layton had ordered the harbour cleared. Perhaps the greatest effect was to cause an enormous exodus of people from Colombo, whereby 'work in the harbour, workshops, etc., suffered seriously in consequence'.[67]

What of course the attack singularly failed to achieve was the main object of the exercise; the destruction of the Eastern Fleet. This, or at least the fast portion of it, was steering east-north-east at 18 knots with the intention of being some 250 miles south of Ceylon at dawn on 6 April. Force B had cleared Addu Atoll at 07:00 hours and was following in its wake some 130 miles astern.

Steaming hard in more or less the opposite direction were the two cruisers that had left Colombo harbour at 22:00 hours the previous night in anticipation of the raid; *Dorsetshire* and *Cornwall*. At 07:00 hours they had changed course to head almost due south, the intention being to intercept and of course join Force A. At about 08:00 hours a report of strong enemy forces to their east was received and the senior officer, *Dorsetshire*'s Captain Augustus Agar, ordered speed be increased to 27 knots, the maximum that *Cornwall* could manage.

The Japanese Navy, with its emphasis on the offensive at almost all costs, had 'solved' the conundrum noted by Wallace earlier; strike aircraft used for reconnaissance had to be subtracted from the strength of any subsequent attack. This had been achieved by, as Parshall and Tully put it, 'off-loading scouting duties from the carriers' by developing heavy cruisers like *Tone* and *Chikuma*.[68] Both these rather extraordinary vessels had all their main armament, eight 8in guns in four turrets, concentrated forward. This left the aft section devoted to aircraft operations, and as designed the vessels would carry eight floatplanes each, launched by gunpowder-propellant catapults and recovered from the surface of the water by crane. This complement was not reached in practice and five each was the norm.[69] It was one of these floatplanes from *Tone* that spotted the two cruisers, and was in turn seen by them.[70] In Agar's later account:

> At 11:30 am we sighted a dot bobbing up and down the horizon every minute or so. It was an aircraft. . . . There was no doubt it was a Jap 'shadower' and must, by our calculation of the plotted positions, have placed the enemy Carrier Force 100 miles nearer the ship than we reckoned; or alternatively, it gave the Jap 'recco' plane a performance of 100 miles more than we thought they had.[71]

Agar's last point, the actual performance of enemy aircraft as against what was expected, was to become something of a recurring theme over the next few days.

In any event, and after observing what was thought to be a second aircraft at about 13:00 hours, he decided to break radio silence, which was strictly enforced ordinarily, and report that the cruisers had definitely been spotted. They were by now only some 90 miles from the point of rendezvous with Force A and the danger, as Agar saw it, was 'exposing the Fleet to the "Shadower"'.[72] What this would have meant was soon to become apparent.

'It was', as the Admiralty account noted, 'a calm day, with little or no cloud, and a slight haze over the sun; visibility was extreme'.[73] The strike Nagumo ordered against what were initially thought to be a pair of destroyers took some time to arrange. At first the attempt was to be made by B5N torpedo bombers, but because these had been loaded with bombs for a second strike on Colombo if one was required, a change of ordnance was required. This took time, so Aichi D3A dive-bombers were deployed instead; fifty-three of them from *Akagi* (Carrier Division 1) and *Hiryu* and *Soryu* (Carrier Division 2), under the command of Egusa Takashige, 'the Navy's best dive-bomber pilot'.[74]

Whilst this strike was airborne a second report came through from the reconnaissance floatplane to the effect that the destroyers were both cruisers. At 13:38 hours Egusa spotted their wakes below, and signalled this back to *Akagi*, at the same time ordering his command to divide their attention; the Carrier Division 1 aircraft to attack the leading ship (*Dorsetshire*), whilst those from Carrier Division 2 concentrated on the second (*Cornwall*).[75] Despite *Dorsetshire* being equipped with radar, the attack materialized without warning. Anti-aircraft fire was ineffective and by 13:51 hours the last bombs had been dropped. By then *Dorsetshire* had sunk, and the final order to abandon *Cornwall* was given at 13:55 hours.[76] It was estimated that the dive-bombers, using tactics devised by Egusa, achieved a hit rate of 88 per cent; 'an incredible achievement' in the words of his biographer.[77]

Force A was 84 miles away to the south-west and heading east when the strike took place, close enough indeed for the attackers to be detected on *Warspite*'s radar and then to fade from the screen after five minutes.[78] Somerville recognized what had been seen and is reported to have exclaimed 'that's a Jap air strike'.[79] That the Eastern Fleet seemed to be powerless to do anything was a matter that exercised the minds of those that made up its fighting component. Or at least according to the recollection of one of them. Sub-Lieutenant Hugh Popham, a fighter pilot aboard *Indomitable*, recalled the frustration felt by him and his colleagues:

> . . . the fighters on deck were put at instant readiness, pilots strapped in. We sat there, sweltering, fingers on the starter button, muscles aching with the effort of waiting. There were enemy aircraft on the radar screen. A W/T message had just been received from *Dorsetshire* and *Cornwall* . . . 'we are being attacked by enemy dive-bombers'.

> Then why weren't we airborne and on our way? For Christ's sake, why?. . . The thought of an enemy fleet just over the horizon, simply waiting to be torpedoed, was too tantalising to be borne.[80]

That Somerville refused action during the hours of daylight was of course because he was still pursuing his plan for launching a nocturnal ambush. Having said that, it is apparent that he was beginning to realize that the enemy were far more powerful, and in far greater strength, than anticipated. He had continued probing eastwards after hearing of the attack on Colombo, whilst waiting anxiously for further information on the enemy force and its where-abouts. At 10:20 hours a report was received indicating Japanese battleships about 320 miles to the north-west (some 120 miles from Dondra Head); 'they seemed to be marking time and I appreciated that probably they were waiting for the carriers – which had not been located – to recover their aircraft'.[81] No further news came in until a 'mutilated signal' was received about a 'shadower' at 13:30 hours, which was only identified as having come from *Dorsetshire* some 30 minutes later. Nothing more was heard from either of the cruisers, though four Albacores had been despatched to investigate and to look for any sign of the enemy.[82] At 15:52 hours one of these reported sighting wreckage and survivors in the water and a destroyer was detached to investigate.

This was, however, recalled when reports came in of enemy battleships and carriers about 100 miles to the north, steering south-west.[83] That was a heading that led towards Addu Atoll. Somerville didn't know, and knew he didn't know, if the Japanese were aware of his 'secret weapon'. If they were, and were on the way to attack it, then he had lost his only secure base. It was then necessary for him to keep clear to the southward, and for Force B, then estimated 135 miles astern, to do likewise.[84]

At 18:00 hours on 5 April Somerville received a report that his reconnaissance aircraft had, some 50 minutes earlier, spotted an enemy force, of two aircraft carriers and three unknown vessels, around 120 miles to the north-north-east of Force A. This correlated with the information already received. However, 17 minutes later, this was followed up with another report stating that the force was in fact steering north-west, and not south-west as reported earlier. Of the quartet of search aircraft involved in the search, the two that covered the most northerly sectors were attacked by Zero fighters, one escaping and one being shot down. The former had managed to send in the report before attempting a return to its carrier. The second disappeared without trace.

Still seemingly determined on a night attack, Somerville altered course to north-west in order to keep within striking distance of the enemy. He ordered Force B to conform, and arranged for the two forces to rendezvous at dawn. At 19:30 hours he deployed radar-equipped Albacores to cover a sector from north-by-west to north-east-by-north out to a range of 180 miles. This was modified at 21:00 hours to cover the sector north-north-east to east-by-north out to 200 miles and the search continued until 06:00 hours on 6 April. No contact was made with Japanese vessels throughout the night, but at 04:00 hours Force B was reported as being 25 miles to the south-west. Junction of the two forces was effected 3 hours later. By 07:20 hours the fleet was formed up and their course altered to due east.[85] The reason for the course selected was twofold. Somerville's Chief of Staff, Commodore Ralph Edwards, enumerated them in his diary entry for 6 April:

> During the previous 24 hours and at this time there were continual tracks of reconnaissance aircraft being abroad and it was astonishing that the enemy never found us. We appreciated that the enemy would expect us to move W[est] away from his main force. We had furthermore some 1500 men in the water 100 miles to the E[ast] of us. We reckoned that probably the best way of dodging the enemy – which had by this time become the C-in-C's chief object – would be to move to the Eastward which would be the last direction in which the Japanese would expect us to proceed. This would not only (we hoped) fox them but also enable us to pick up our 1500 survivors.[86]

The section of Somerville's letter to his wife of the same date revealed why 'dodging the enemy' had become his chief object: 'By this time [the evening of 5 April] it was clear that I was greatly outnumbered by the enemy forces in the vicinity.' It had been, he went on, 'A black day – Colombo had been bombed and I had lost two 8" cruisers and nothing to show for it except 25 enemy aircraft shot down at Colombo . . .'[87] In fact he had even less to show for it than that, inasmuch as the Japanese had lost far fewer aircraft than was then thought. Inflated claims in that regard are of course common, but Boyd makes an interesting point respecting numbers. He points out that the amount of Japanese aircraft involved in the Colombo raid, reported at the time as seventy-five, suggested a launch from more than two carriers. Moreover, Somerville and his staff were aware of this figure on the morning of the attack.[88] The later loss of *Dorsetshire* and *Cornwall* that day may have reinforced this point, yet he had still determined to launch a night attack if at all possible. His letter of 6 April however makes clear that he was forsaking an offensive posture: '. . . I've come to the conclusion that *until* I get a proper fleet out here I will simply have to hide, more or less.'[89]

Indeed his woes had multiplied. In addition to the situation he was in, he was aware of further Japanese depredations. His letter continued: 'Today the Japs have been roaring up the Bay of Bengal and sinking right and left but I can do nothing. I haven't even a secure base to go to . . .'[90] The 'roaring up' he referred to was the secondary incursion into the Indian Ocean by Vice Admiral Ozawa

Jisaburo which began on 4 April. With his flag in the light carrier *Ryujo*, and accompanied by five heavy cruisers, Ozawa sank twenty-three merchant ships. Five more were disposed of by submarines off India's west coast. Air attacks launched from *Ryujo* against various towns along the eastern Indian coastline, including Visakhapatnam and Cocanada, resulted in considerable panic amongst the civilian population. The balance of power had been totally upended; the Bay of Bengal had been a 'British Lake' for over a century.[91] As the Commander-in-Chief, India, was to put it:

> In the Bay of Bengal Japanese light forces and aircraft sank just on 100,000 tons of merchant shipping . . . This was India's most dangerous hour; our Eastern fleet was powerless to protect Ceylon or Eastern India; our air strength was negligible.[92]

The Eastern Fleet, whilst seeking to avoid the enemy – 'we were no longer the hunters, we were the hunted' Somerville had declared the previous day[93] – was also engaged in a rescue mission. At 13:00 hours the cruiser *Enterprise*, together with the destroyers *Paladin* and *Panther*, were sent ahead to pick up survivors from *Dorsetshire* and *Cornwall* who had been in the water for 30 hours. Air search and fighter cover was flown off to assist the operation, which was successful: out of total complements numbering 1,546 from both ships, 1,122 were picked up alive.[94]

At about 14:00 hours a signal was intercepted in *Warspite* from Layton in Ceylon to the Admiralty in London, estimating that a strong Japanese force, estimated to be at least four carriers and three battleships,[95] was somewhere between Addu Atoll and Colombo and that 'the Eastern Fleet now faces immediate annihilation'.[96] This was mainly hyperbole, and probably meant as a warning to Somerville who was bound to read it, but it still contained a great truth. Indeed, despite utilizing his 'ratcatcher' instincts in heading in the last direction the enemy might expect, Somerville's Eastern Fleet was still in peril. Indeed, in the event of an enemy attack his fighter strength was deeply inadequate; two days later he reported it as six Martlets, eight Fulmars, and eleven Hurricanes (only one of which was the Mark II version).[97]

At 18:15 hours, and with the cruiser survivors rescued, he threw out all-round air searches to a distance of 200 miles and reversed course onto a north-west heading. His intention now was to return to Addu Atoll. As he explained it: 'Now I'm in the unpleasant situation that I have to get oil and water and there is no guarantee that I shan't get roared up when I'm doing it as the place I have to use is quite unprotected.'[98] At 02:00 hours on 7 April the Fleet altered course to the west, but at 04:30 hours one of the radar-equipped patrol aircraft reported two submarines to the south, potentially interdicting the eastern approach to Addu.[99]

In order to avoid these, Somerville decided to pass through the Maldivian archipelago via the Veimandu Channel between Haddummati and Kolumadulu Atolls. Though the channel was 'deep and free from dangers' a later edition of the Admiralty Pilot stated 'it is not advisable to proceed through it at night'.[100] Navigating it at night was though precisely what Somerville proposed, which would then allow him to approach Addu Atoll from the west during daylight the following morning. The passage was successfully navigated, and at 07:00 hours on 8 April an all-round air search to a depth of 175 miles was flown off. Nothing being found, the Eastern Fleet arrived at Addu at 11:00 hours.[101]

It was not to stay long, only until refuelling and re-watering could be completed. During the afternoon Somerville conferred with his deputy, Vice Admiral Willis, Rear Admiral Denis Boyd, Admiral Commanding Aircraft Carriers (who flew his flag in *Indomitable*), and Captain Arthur Bisset, the commander of *Formidable*. The latter were, in Somerville's words, 'a little difficult. They both resent the fact that when it comes to carriers I know what I'm talking about.'[102] What Somerville didn't mention to his wife was the admonition delivered by Willis, who accused him of taking 'grave risks with the fleet, the preservation of which ought to have been the main object'. Somerville now agreed, but said 'he felt we ought to have a crack at the enemy'.[103]

It was now agreed by all three flag officers that discretion was definitely the better part of valour. Somerville's subsequent signal to the Admiralty laid out the situation as they saw it and how this 'discretion' was to be achieved:

> Enemy has complete command of Bay of Bengal and can, at his selected moment, obtain local command of the water S[outh] and S[outh] W[est] of Ceylon.
>
> Our present naval forces and land-based air forces are quite inadequate to dispute this command. The Battlefleet is slow, out-gunned and of short endurance. Its available carrier-borne protection would be of little use against repeated air attack on the scale used against the 8" cruisers. There is little security against air or surface attack at our naval bases in Ceylon and none at Addu.[104]

Somerville's proposed solution to the problem was to send the Battlefleet, and Force B as a whole, well out of harm's way. As Churchill was later to phrase it in respect of the 'R' class:

> . . . when . . . the possibility of bringing them into action against the Japanese fleet which entered the Indian Ocean in April 1942 presented itself the only thought of the admiral on the spot, of Admiral Pound, and the Minister of Defence, was to put as many thousands of miles as possible between them and the enemy in the shortest possible time.[105]

This was a curious way of wording it. One is tempted to view it as a rhetorical device by which the author sought to distance himself from the matter. To succumb to that temptation would however be to venture into the realm of cod psychology; an area of distinct unprofitability. Suffice then to note that the Minister of Defence was of course one Winston S. Churchill, and that his statement of physical distance was correct. In the words of the Admiralty account: 'Vice Admiral Willis with Force "B" accordingly sailed from Addu Atoll for Kilindini at 0200, 9th April.'[106] Kilindini Harbour comprised the 'portuary facilities of Mombasa', then part of the British Colony and Protectorate of Kenya, and was some 2,000 nautical miles from Addu.[107]

Somerville's proposed that Force A continue to operate in the Indian Ocean, 'using Colombo, Addu, Bombay, Seychelles, Mauritius and occasionally E[ast] African ports as fuelling bases'. This reduced fleet's maintenance bases would be Bombay and Durban, and the object of the exercise revolved around deterring the enemy from attacking our communications using light forces and making it 'necessary for him to employ substantial forces for this purpose'.[108]

The Admiralty vetoed his Colombo proposal, ordering him instead to Bombay.[109] It wasn't as far as Kilindini, being some 1,200 nautical miles distant from Addu Atoll, but it was a substantial strategic withdrawal that left Ceylon undefended. As Macintyre put it: '. . . the resurgent American naval power in the Pacific must be relied upon to force the Japanese to call home their heavy ships and carriers.' He went on: 'First, however, the penalty for failure to deploy adequate air power in Ceylon had to be paid in full.'[110]

As Force A left Addu Atoll at 06:00 hours on 9 April for Bombay, the enemy it was seeking to escape from was around 200 miles east of Trincomalee, Ceylon, and being searched for by one of the invaluable Catalina flying boats. An aircraft carrier and three battleships had been sighted by a different Catalina in the afternoon of the previous day some 400 miles distant to the south east heading north-west-by-north. After shadowing these vessels for about an hour the aircraft was attacked by Zero fighters. The Catalina survived but the contact was lost.[111]

The likelihood of an air strike on Trincomalee was, however, apparent so the tactic of emptying the harbour, as had been employed with success at Colombo, was put in train. Four warships, *Hermes* escorted by *Vampire*, plus the anti-submarine corvette *Hollyhock* and auxiliary minelayer *Teviot Bank*, as well as a number of naval auxiliary vessels, were ordered to steam south along the coast with the object of being at least 40 miles from Trincomalee by dawn 9 April. There were only two warships of note remaining, one being the First World War Dutch light cruiser *Sumatra*.[112] The other, of similar vintage, was the monitor *Erebus*. This ship had been fitted with six 3in anti-aircraft guns and Type 285 radar for

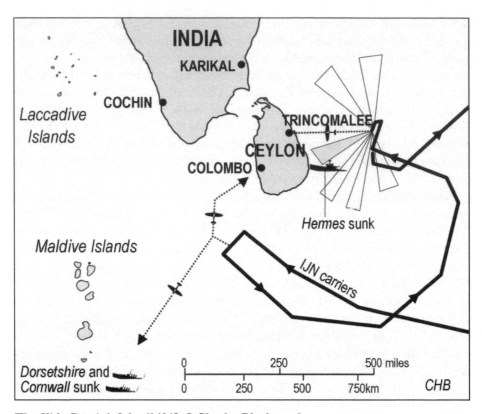

The *Kido Butai*. 4–9 April 1942. © Charles Blackwood.

The strike on Trincomalee took place on the morning of 9 April. The harbour had been largely cleared of shipping, with *Hermes*, escorted by the Australian destroyer *Vampire*, plus the anti-submarine corvette *Hollyhock* and the auxiliary minelayer *Teviot Bank*, sent to steam south along the coast with the object of being at least 40 miles (64km) away when the raid arrived. Whilst the raid itself caused little damage, Nagumo had despatched floatplanes to carry out reconnaissance. These aircraft, seven in total, searched an arc roughly 180 degrees from north to south between the Japanese fleet and Ceylon (indicated by the cones on the map), and out to a distance of 150 miles (240km). One of them, the greyed search cone on the map, spotted *Hermes*. Nagumo had eighty-five dive-bombers in reserve and quickly started launching them. It was to be a repeat of the attacks on *Dorsetshire* and *Cornwall* with aircraft diving at an angle of about 65 degrees out of the sun. *Vampire* and *Hollyhock* were also sunk, as were several merchant vessels. The discovery and destruction of these ships transformed the otherwise rather underwhelming results of the Trincomalee raid into something approaching a respectable result. Nagumo then withdrew and headed for home.

anti-aircraft fire control and sent specifically to Trincomalee in March 1942 to provide air defence.[113] Nine merchantmen of 3,000 tons or more, and up to eight minor warships and naval auxiliaries were also left in the harbour.[114]

Further indications that a raid was in the offing manifested themselves around dawn on 9 April, when land-based radar at Elizabeth Point, a promontory just north of Trincomalee, plotted aircraft between 15 and 30 miles distant in a sector between north-east-by-east and east-by-south of the harbour. These were undoubtedly battleship and cruiser-launched floatplanes sent between about 05:00 and 06:00 hours to reconnoitre the target and adjacent coastline. A search in the opposite direction was also underway via a single Catalina that had taken off from Koggala at 02:56 hours piloted by Flight-Lieutenant Rae Thomas. At 07:08 hours this aircraft spotted large enemy force some 205 miles almost due east of Trincomalee and heading north-west-by-north. Unfortunately, Thomas' aircraft was spotted, attacked by Zeros from *Hiryu* at 07:15 hours, and destroyed before it could send a detailed message; 'as the signal faded without giving a position or time of origin'.[115]

This was the third Catalina downed by the enemy since 4 April, and even if it had managed to send a full message then it wouldn't have helped greatly. Nagumo had begun launching the strike group, again led by Fuchida, at about 06:00 hours. Curiously, no dive-bombers were included in the complement which comprised ninety-one B5N 'carrier bomber aircraft', each loaded with a single 800kg high explosive bomb, escorted by forty-one Zero fighters. Approaching in three waves on a bearing of east-by-north, these were detected on radar at 07:06 hours whilst still 91 miles distant. A red alert was sounded at the RAF airfield at China Bay, located approximately 4.5 miles south-west of Trincomalee, at 07:15 hours and at Trincomalee itself five minutes later.

There were eighteen British Hurricane fighters (mainly the Mark II version) in the air (out of an available total of thirty-six fighter aircraft in total) to meet the attackers. They drew first blood, shooting down three Zero escorts for the loss of one of their own after intercepting the raiders some 30 miles off the coast. The bombers, however, got through. Eighteen of them struck the harbour, mistaking *Erebus* for a cruiser. Flying at 9,000–10,000ft (2,750–3,000m) in formations of six, which dropped together, the monitor was damaged by one of these salvoes which near-missed, killing nine men and wounding a further twenty-two. *Sumatra* was probably hit by one bomb which failed to explode and escaped serious damage; she was able to depart under her own steam for Bombay on 16 April. In fact the only vessel sunk was the *circa* 8,000-ton merchant ship *Sagaing*. Twelve bombers went for China Bay, destroying thirteen aircraft under repair there (seven Swordfish, four Fulmars and two Albacores), causing some damage to infrastructure and facilities, and killing three airmen and wounding six. The airfield was a long way from being put out of action, however. The other bombs fell on the dockyard and other targets, such as what the Japanese thought was the governor's residence, barracks and coast defence artillery positions. Also destroyed were twenty-seven aircraft, or twenty-eight if the reconnoitring Catalina piloted by Rae Thomas is included, for the loss of three Zero fighters and two B5N bombers.[116] As Stuart put it, the attack on Trincomalee produced meagre results and the damage inflicted was of no lasting significance.

What was of much more moment was the sighting of several ships that had vacated the harbour prior to the attack. Amongst these were *Hermes*, under the command of Captain Rodney Onslow of Dakar fame, and *Vampire*. Both had cleared the defensive boom at 01:00 hours on 9 April then steered east before turning onto a south-south-east heading in order to reach the specified 40 miles distance from Trincomalee by dawn. This was achieved, and more so, so that at about 08:00 hours the two ships were effectively loitering about five miles offshore some 15 miles south-east of Batticaloa; a city some 70 miles south of Trincomalee. Arbuthnot had stated that they, along with all the other dispersed ships, were to return to harbour without further orders before 16:00 hours.

As had been detected by the radar station at Elizabeth Point, Nagumo had despatched floatplanes to carry out reconnaissance before launching the Trincomalee strike. These aircraft, seven in total, searched an arc roughly 180 degrees from north to south between the Japanese fleet and Ceylon, and out to a distance of 150 miles. One of them, a Nakajima E8N launched from the battleship *Haruna*, had been assigned to cover a sector on a heading of south-west-by-west. This involved flying out to the required distance, turning 90 degrees to starboard onto a heading of north-west-by-north, then following this course for 50 miles before executing a second starboard turn onto a return course to the ship. It so happened that this final turn would take place about 30 miles offshore from Batticaloa. The inevitable report, sent uncyphered, was intercepted by the signals intelligence unit at Colombo at 08:58 hours and interpreted some thirty minutes later. A warning was sent immediately to *Hermes* and orders sent to scramble RAF fighters for her protection.

It was already too late. Nagumo had eighty-five dive-bombers in reserve on his carriers and started launching them at 08:43 hours under the command of Lieutenant-Commander Takahashi Kakuichi from *Shokaku*. Nine Zero fighters provided the escort. *Hermes* meanwhile had increased speed to her 24-knot maximum on a heading for Trincomalee. Ten minutes later the floatplane from *Haruna* sent a message, reporting that the carrier was around 20 miles south-south-east of Batticaloa. This was to be its final message before heading home; the E8N had an endurance of less than five hours at normal cruising speed and had by then been airborne for almost three of them.

One consequence of using low-endurance floatplanes for recconnaisance was realized when Takahashi's force arrived at *Hermes'* anticipated position to the south-east of Batticaloa at 09:50 hours. There was no sign of the ship. He searched south to a distance of about 40 miles before reversing course, then sighting the fugitive vessel at around 10:30 hours; the diversion occasioning a delay of about 40 minutes. It was to be a repeat of the attacks on *Dorsetshire* and *Cornwall* with aircraft diving at an angle of about 65 degrees out of the sun. The words of the impressively succinct official report say it all:

> At 1035 the first bombs struck the ship, hits being registered aft and on the forward aircraft lift. From this time on HERMES was repeatedly hit. Both boiler rooms were put out of action and the forward aircraft lift was wrecked. At 1050 the ship was immobilized, on fire, and had a heavy list to port. At 1055 HERMES capsized to port and sank.[117]

Twelve dive-bombers turned their attention to *Vampire* even before *Hermes* slipped beneath the water, the first attack going in at the same time as the latter ship sank. The destroyer broke in two about seven minutes later and had disappeared by 11:05 hours. The oil tanker *British Sergeant*, was spotted about 12 miles north-west of *Hermes* and was bombed from about 11:00 hours by six aircraft. Four direct hits and two near misses resulted in the crew abandoning ship; she sank at 13:00 hours. A second tanker, the *Athelstane*, was together with *Hollyhock* some 30 miles south of *Hermes'* final position. Both vessels were attacked at about noon by nine dive-bombers that had split off from the main body which, having expended its ordnance, had begun the return flight to the carriers. Five bombed *Athelstane* which foundered almost immediately. The remainder attacked *Hollyhock* in pairs. The first two, at 12:09 hours, missed; one by a wide margin the other rather closer, putting a boiler out of action. The second pair scored direct hits at 12:17 hours which sank the corvette in less than a minute.[118]

The fate of two other ships involved in Takahashi's strike may be considered of interest, the first being the Norwegian-owned freighter *Norviken*. This vessel committed the cardinal sin of being in the wrong place at the wrong time. Already in the Far East when Norway fell to the German invaders, there she remained tramping around and about the Indian Ocean. On 6 April, manned by six Norwegian officers and forty-two Chinese crewmen, she departed Madras for Bombay. Three days later, at about 10:00 hours, she found herself heading south just off the Ceylonese coast within sight of Batticaloa Lighthouse. Alert crew members might well have noticed an aircraft carrier and a destroyer heading in the opposite direction some way out to sea. At about 11:20 hours the ship was attacked and directly hit by three bombs, which disabled her and killed her captain and three crew. She was promptly abandoned but did not sink and drifted ashore to be looted and, eventually, burned two days later.[119]

By way of contrast, the hospital ship *Vita* was a vessel that was most definitely in the right place at exactly the right time.[120] On passage from Trincomalee to Colombo, she had passed *Hermes* and *Vampire* heading in the opposite direction at about 09:30 hours. An hour or so later she was off Batticaloa when the attacks commenced, whereupon she turned immediately about and went to offer assistance. Clearly marked as a hospital ship, being painted white overall with prominent red crosses, she picked up a total of 595 survivors between 13:00 and 19:00 hours, whilst being left entirely untroubled by the enemy. As the author of the Official Naval Medical History of the War put it: 'Enemy aircraft were still attacking with cannon fire, but it is recorded that on *Vita*'s arrival all hostile activity ceased and all due respect was accorded to the Red Cross.'[121]

The discovery and destruction of the various ships off the east coast of Ceylon transformed the otherwise rather underwhelming results of the Trincomalee raid into something approaching a respectable result. The cost to the Japanese of this latter episode was six aircraft lost, five shot down and one damaged beyond repair, plus five more damaged to one degree or another. The human cost was nine airmen killed. The damage inflicted, however, totalled one aircraft carrier, a destroyer, a corvette, two tankers, and a freighter, all destroyed, plus 374 dead and about 164 wounded. Counted amongst these casualties were six airmen killed in attempts to both attack the Japanese fleet and defend the British vessels. The former was attempted by nine Blenheim light bombers of the RAF's No. 11 (Bomber) Squadron under the command of Squadron Leader Kenneth Ault which had taken off at 08:20 hours. They arrived above their target unobserved and bombed *Akagi* and *Tone* from 11,000ft, scoring near misses but no hits and, of course, thereby alerting the Combat Air Patrol to their presence. Four aircraft were quickly shot down by the Zeros, though one of the attackers fell as well. The remaining five got away but ran into the aircraft returning from the attack on *Hermes*, three of which were fighters. Ault's Blenheim was downed, as was one Zero, but the remainder managed a second escape, albeit all were badly shot up and rendered unserviceable by their ordeal.[122]

Due to problems with disrupted communications, caused by both the Trincomalee raid and the 5 April attack on Colombo, there were delays in getting fighters airborne above the attacked ships. Eight Fulmars, from 803 and 806 Naval Air Squadrons based at Ratmalana airfield near Colombo, arrived just after 12:00 hours as *Athelstane* was going down. This was, in one sense, fortunate inasmuch as the Zero fighter escort had by then departed. It seems likely that if that hadn't been the case then the Fulmars would have been massacred. According to Wing Commander Wilfrid Russell (who was in a position to know): 'the Fulmar was far too slow for these little bastards, who could turn on a sixpence, pull up into a stall, do a roll off the top, and cock ten thousand devils of a snook at you'.[123] As it was they, together with six further Fulmars from 273 Squadron RAF Kokkilai, a satellite airfield of Ratmalana located some 35 miles north-west of China Bay, engaged with the D3A dive-bombers.[124] The two aircraft were comparable in terms of speed but, once their bombs were gone, the Japanese aircraft were much more manoeuvrable than their British opponents though less heavily gunned. In any event, three D3As and two Fulmars were downed. Small wonder that Somerville, who thought they would 'have approximately the performance of our Albacores', dubbed them 'fighter-bombers'.[125]

These engagements however were the last involving the *Kido Butai* in the Indian Ocean. Nagumo, who had been at sea with the core of his fleet since deploying to strike Pearl Harbor, then withdrew and headed for home, reaching the Strait of Malacca on 12–13 April.[126] Somerville had also opined that whilst the British could lose the war in the Indian Ocean, it could not win it there. However, by withdrawing to avoid certain defeat ('I will simply have to hide, more or less') the Eastern Fleet appeared to have finally answered the question ('How are we going to make war?') posed by Admiral Sir Herbert Richmond in 1923.

Chapter 7

'. . . Aircraft fit for sailors to fly in'

Despite both sides withdrawing relatively unscathed after the events described in the previous chapter, the question as to which came out best is not difficult to answer. Indeed the Royal Navy, at least as represented by the views of the senior commanders, considered they had suffered a 'considerable' defeat. Sir Geoffrey Layton certainly thought so:

> As a Naval operation, the Japanese raid must be held to have secured a considerable strategical success. . . . Although the Japanese did not follow this up by further attacks on Ceylon, it enabled them to disregard the Eastern Fleet for the time being.[1]

A year after the events described, when the above was published, the British still didn't know the full strength of the force they had skirmished with.[2] It had, in truth, been a lucky escape for Somerville and his command, who had no idea initially of the comparative superiority their enemy enjoyed. Only after the short order destruction of *Dorsetshire* and *Cornwall* by Nagumo's 'fighter-bombers' did he seem to begin to realize the extent of what he was facing. Even then, if what he wrote to his wife can be taken at face value, he merely thought that he was 'greatly outnumbered'.[3] That there was a qualitative difference, based around both materiel and tactics, was a matter that took much longer to be accepted. For example, Captain Stephen Roskill, who had fought against the Imperial Japanese Navy, offered his opinion of the matter in 1956:[4]

> Given two or three more fleet carriers in substitution for the old and cumbersome R-class battleships, a dozen more long-range reconnaissance aircraft and a few squadrons of shore-based torpedo-bombers, he [Somerville] could have challenged Nagumo with confidence.[5]

There is little or nothing to be gained in indulging in an exercise of 'what if' in this regard, but it is nevertheless difficult to accept Roskill's contention. To reiterate Hezlet's point, the navies of Britain and Japan had evolved differing philosophies and doctrines in respect to the use of carrier-based naval aircraft; the former as battlefleet support, the latter as a striking force in its own right.[6]

Even if the Eastern Fleet had contained all the Royal Navy's most modern carriers, the four vessels of the *Illustrious* class, plus the available battleships of the *King George V* class, it would still have been unable to match the First Air Fleet in delivering 'a few minutes of shattering, blasting, overpowering force' where it mattered most. In short, and to put it plainly, in a head-to-head battle against an adversary able to command the degree of aerial firepower that was deployable by the *Kido Butai*, the Royal Navy's inadequacies would have been mercilessly exposed. Regardless of the scale of their deployment, the British simply did not have the requisite capabilities to withstand Japanese air-naval superiority; extra resources could not have offset the gap between the Royal and the Imperial Japanese Navies.

It wasn't just better aircraft, though they certainly had those, that tipped the balance, it was how this materiel was used. The Japanese had evolved a superior technique of carrying out naval warfare. This was, at least somewhat, analogous to the line-breaking tactics evolved by Nelson, the culminative application of which appeared at Trafalgar to devastating effect.[7]

Having said that, Nagumo was no Nelson and history has not been kind to him. It is self-evidently true that he failed to achieve his main operational objective; the Eastern Fleet was not brought to battle and destroyed. That this was so was down to Somerville being both cunning and lucky which, in combination with several Japanese mistakes and shortcomings, allowed him to escape otherwise certain destruction. One of the main deficiencies that the IJN in general, and the *Kido Butai* in particular, suffered from was its reconnaissance doctrine; the use of floatplanes launched from battleships and cruisers to perform scouting work. Despite that there were downsides to such methodology, mainly that the mother-ship had to stop to recover the aircraft, there was nothing inherently wrong with the floatplanes themselves, or at least the modern, long-range types.[8] The weak point, as has been noted by several authorities, including Zimm and Peattie for example, is that the aviators who operated them were not of the same quality as their carrier-based counterparts. Indeed, the latter describes the doctrine and training of the crews as hindering reconnaissance capabilities, and the men themselves as being 'often ill trained, inexperienced, and careless'.[9]

This may be so, but it is certainly the case that they located *Dorsetshire*, *Cornwall*, *Hermes* and the other ships that were sunk in short order. They would perhaps have found the main body of the Eastern Fleet as well; if they had been sent to look for it! As Somerville had said, 'it was astonishing that the enemy never found us'. That they didn't was less to do with the aircraft or crews of the reconnaissance aircraft, and much more to do with what can only be described as the curiously disinterested attitude of their commander Vice Admiral Nagumo. In Murfett's judgement, he was 'wary and conservative' in

Japan's 1942 Perimeter. © Charles Blackwood.

The area of Japan's initial conquests, encompassing some 200,000 square miles within a massive amoebic-shaped perimeter that was largely oceanic, had to be somehow defended. The only really defensible portion, whereby offensive naval action could be severely inter-dicted by submarines and land-based aircraft, was that formed by the so called Malay, or East Indies, Barrier. This comprised a hypothetical line running southward from Malaya, through Singapore, then south-easterly to encompass the westernmost and southerly islands of the Netherlands East Indies, then on to New Guinea. The policy, however, was not for defence in the passive sense, but rather defence according to an ancient principle: 'Attack is the secret of defence; defence is the planning of an attack.' In pursuit of this the Japanese decided to take Port Moresby in New Guinea and Tulagi in the south-eastern Solomon Islands. The result-ant Battle of the Coral Sea, 4–8 May 1942, was the first carrier-carrier battle, leading to an operational-level victory for the United States; the first time that a Japanese invasion force was turned back.

general, and the same author is downright accusatory about his conduct south of Ceylon:

> On this latter occasion, he might have discovered Somerville's Eastern Fleet had he devoted a little effort, rather than none at all, to even the most rudimentary of reconnaissance duties. He didn't and most of Somerville's force lived to fight another day.[10]

This conclusion might be thought somewhat over-harsh and, like many similar opinions, probably influenced by the disaster he suffered at Midway in June 1942. On the other hand, it is unarguably the case that Nagumo singularly failed to initiate comprehensive measures to search out the opponent he had been sent specifically to destroy. The possession of a superlative, and basically irresistible, striking force able to deliver a 'shattering, blasting, overpowering' attack was no use at all if the intended victim couldn't be located.

The reasons quite why Nagumo was so undeniably lackadaisical in terms of carrying out effective reconnaissance, and thus failing to locate the Eastern Fleet, are elusive. But these failings were not apparent to his opponents at the time. From their perspective at least, the Japanese appeared to be uncontainable and working to a well thought-out plan. On the other hand, Somerville made great efforts in attempting to locate his opponent in order to deliver an attack on him, and very nearly got into a position to do so. Had his reconnaissance assets managed to confirm that the enemy were indeed within striking distance on the evening of 5 April then it is possible he would have launched his favoured option of a nocturnal strike. On the other hand, the evening of 5 April was just about the time when he realized he was up against a much more powerful enemy than he had first thought. How successful a hypothetical strike might have been is impossible to judge, particularly given that it would have involved relatively few aircraft, and numbers grant an important tactical advantage in helping to saturate enemy defences. Even taking the most optimistic view of any such strike, it is difficult to visualize all the enemy carriers being rendered unfit for action. It follows that retaliation would have followed at some point, lending validity to Willis' accusation about Somerville having taken 'grave risks' in order to 'have a crack' at them.

In judging the relative performances of both commanders and their fleets over the period in question, particularly with the inestimable benefit of hindsight, it is probably right to conclude that Nagumo played the part of the 'regulator' to Somerville's 'ratcatcher'. Nagumo's strategic objective was to find and destroy the Eastern Fleet, which was thought to be at Colombo or Trincomalee. When it was not found at the former he resolved that it must be located at the latter. Having discovered that it wasn't there either he then seemed to conclude that his mission was accomplished and retired eastwards.[11] So whilst the British thought they'd come off worse and had no choice but to withdraw and hide, 'Nagumo returned triumphantly to Japan'.[12]

The retirement of the Eastern Fleet from the eastern half of the Indian Ocean generally, and the Bay of Bengal in particular, repurcussed in several areas including that of the grand politico-strategic. If the fall of Singapore had established in no uncertain terms that Britain, the 'mother country' and traditional protector, no longer had the power to defend the Australasian portions of her Empire, then the mutually-agreed subsumption of Australia and New Zealand into the American-dominated Southwest Pacific Area (under MacArthur) and South Pacific Area (under Nimitz), demonstrated unequivocally who now had that power.[13] Somerville's withdrawal to the east-coast of Africa then accentuated the already fractured relationship. That this, or something like it, would indeed be the case had long been postulated. As Admiral George Ballard, a naval historian of some note, put it in 1927:

> . . . the Empire may be roughly divided into an occidental half – including the British Isles – and an oriental; which are held together commercially and strategically by the Imperial lines of communication across the Indian Ocean . . . If those connections are cut, the two halves of the Empire will fall apart as surely as night follows day.[14]

If the results of the *Kido Butai*'s foray fostered division with respect to the British Empire's self-governing Dominions, then it massively exacerbated the discord between India and its rulers, which was already remarkably close to being a crisis of existential proportions. The Viceroy, Lord Linlithgow (Victor Hope, 2nd Marquess of Linlithgow), had announced that India was at war with Germany in September 1939 in line with the British declaration. This had been done without regard to, or consultation with, any of the elected representatives.[15]

The resulting situation, which led to the 'Quit India' movement, is far too complex to relate concisely, but Japan's entry into the war and subsequent string of victories had certainly exacerbated the matter; in Raghavan's words, it 'cracked the edifice of the Raj and left large parts of India cowering at the prospect of war'.[16] According to the Viceroy, the programme of airfield construction was held up for between four and six weeks whilst sabotage on the railways caused a three-week delay regarding the movement of troops and supplies to the Army. Some 10 per cent of steel and textiles production was lost, with a knock-on effect on the output of weapons, military equipment and clothing. Also, no fewer than fifty-seven infantry battalions, equating to five divisions more or less, had to be taken away from training for six to eight weeks at a time and redeployed on internal security duties.[17] Christopher Bayly well makes the point that 'the colonial system in India was on the point of almost complete dissolution as late as July 1942'.[18]

More immediately, the incursion into the Bay of Bengal by Ozawa, and the bombing of the cities on the east coast particularly, caused panic, both public and official. The civil authorities in Madras, under Governor Sir Arthur Hope, were informed by the local military command that a Japanese 'invasion in force' was expected south of Masulipatnam on the Coromandel Coast. South of Masulipatnam meant just to the north of Madras, and Sir Arthur's government issued a communiqué asking people whose presence was not essential to leave that city. They also gave orders that government offices and their staff were to evacuate Madras and move inland. 'The effect of the Government's decision to move offices', Sir Arthur reported on 18 April 1842, 'did far more than the advice in their communiqué.' Between 8 and 14 April, about 200,000 people fled the city.[19] This was though merely a precursor to chaos. Following the Japanese occupation of Burma, essentially complete by the end of April 1942, and with the Eastern Fleet unable to dispute control, the Bay of Bengal was closed to shipping.[20] All the seaborne traffic from ports on the east coast – such as Calcutta, Chittagong, Vizag, and Madras – was diverted to Bombay, Karachi, Cochin, and other ports on the west. As Raghavan notes, the 'magnitude of the dislocation can be gauged from the fact that Calcutta alone had handled an annual traffic of 8.25 million tons' and that in 'May 1942, Bombay handled over 220 ships a day, up from the pre-war daily average of 25.71'.[21]

That the Royal Navy in general, and the Eastern Fleet in particular, with its relatively poorly-equipped naval air arm and unsuitable tactical doctrine, was no longer capable of exercising command of the sea and so rectifying the situation was also now acknowledged. A memorandum by A. V. Alexander, the First Sea Lord, recognized this in part some two weeks after the events around Ceylon. Outlining details of new construction proposed for 1942, it had very little to say about battleships beyond noting that they would not figure 'in this year's programme'.[22] He had a great deal more to say about aircraft carriers however:

... as a short-term policy, complimentary to the building of additional Fleet carriers, I propose to order four carriers of a new 'Intermediate' type, designed to be comparatively easy and rapid in construction, yet of sufficient speed to operate with the Fleet.[23]

The Eastern Fleet's encounters with the Japanese were not the trigger for the emphasis on the 'intermediate' aircraft carriers. In fact the need for such a type had been identified earlier and a final design approved by the Board of Admiralty in February 1942. Of 14,000 tons, capable of 25 knots, and with a complement of forty-one aircraft, two of these were ordered in March; *Colossus* and *Glory*.

Unarmoured and designated 'Light Fleet Carriers', the ships could be con-structed by civilian shipyards, but still had build-times of about two years.[24] More immediately, the experiences that the Eastern Fleet had undergone laid bare the inadequacy of the aircraft that equipped the Fleet Air Arm. Both Somerville and Layton let fly in uncompromising terms, the latter on 9 April:

1. It is now quite clear that the Eastern Fleet will not be able to afford any appreciable protection to Ceylon or the East Coast of India for some considerable time. It follows therefore that Ceylon requires a much more powerful Air Force than now exists.
2. The FAA [Fleet Air Arm] aircraft are proving more of an embar-rassment than a help in comparison with land [-based aircraft] as they cannot operate by day in the presence of Japanese fighters and only tend to congest airfields.[25]

Somerville's broadside on the matter was delivered some 22 days later, the context being a series of messages between himself, the Admiralty and Wavell in India, over the role, strength and future capabilities of the Eastern Fleet. He had informed them that 'until such time as my carrier-borne aircraft are adequate in numbers and of first class performance I shall not be able to operate my fleet against a concentration of enemy aircraft carriers or in waters which are within operating range of land based aircraft attack'.[26] Only at night would his Albacores or Swordfish have any chance of making an attack, but he had also suggested ways of improving his striking power, taking his cue from the 'fighter-bombers'[27] that he perceived the Japanese as possessing: 'In order to provide Eastern Fleet with an effective day striking force, however limited, request 880 Squadron[28] may be lent or equipped with 14 Hurricane II with bomb racks.' These aircraft he envisioned as being able to attack enemy ships at long range, as well as handle any defending fighters. That they might actually compete with the Zero on equal terms was, as the editor of his papers put it, 'highly debatable'.[29] In any event, the inability, as reported by Somerville, of his fleet to engage enemy carriers in daylight, and thus to cede the 'initiative to [the] Japanese', was characterized by Pound as being 'unattractive' and 'defen-sive'. He requested 'you will signal more fully reasons supporting your policy'.[30] Somerville, who had never been backward in speaking truth to power, let fly with both barrels:

> The unattractive policy you refer to is forced on me by the very unat-tractive aircraft with which my carriers are equipped.
>
> The situation is comparable to that at home, where low performance bombers are no longer used for daylight operations in clear weather.

It is no use disguising the fact that for day striking we are outclassed by the Japanese, whose dual purpose fighter-dive bombers
can be switched from attack to defence whilst in the air.

. . .

. . . I thought by now that it would be appreciated that our FAA,
suffering as it does from arrested development for many years, would
not be able to compete on all round terms with an FAA which has
devoted itself to producing aircraft fit for sailors to fly in.[31]

This was strong stuff, but difficult to controvert. It followed that without 'aircraft fit for sailors to fly in', the development of offensive tactics whereby they
might deliver 'shattering, blasting, overpowering force' was also arrested. In this
regard Rear Admiral Alva D. Bernhard, a former commanding officer of the
carrier *Lexington*, Commander, Air Force and Naval Air Force Atlantic Fleet
from 1 January 1943–8 March 1943, and then aviation adviser to Vice Admiral
Raymond Spruance, was censorious. He argued, in December 1943, that the
Royal Navy knew 'less of the proper use of carrier air power than we did when
Langley was our only carrier'.[32] Given that *Langley* had ceased to be the USN's
only carrier with the commissioning of *Lexington* and *Saratoga* in 1928, this was
a clear indictment.

Given that new aircraft carriers, different and better aircraft, and the evolution of tactics suitable for employing them effectively, could not be extemporised
overnight, it followed that Somerville and the Eastern Fleet had to make do
with what was available. That they might have at least some prospect of success
was indicated by the withdrawal of Nagumo's force from the theatre, which
Somerville did not hear about until 11 April.[33] Indeed a week or so after his blast
about the deficiencies in the aircraft available to him, came the first sign that
the hitherto 'invincible' Imperial Japanese Navy was in fact distinctly vincible.

The Battle of the Coral Sea, 4–8 May 1942, was the first carrier-carrier
battle in naval history, in which neither side's ships even sighted, never mind
fired upon, each other.[34] Whilst in retrospect it is viewed as an operational-level
victory for the United States, being the first time that a Japanese invasion force
turned back without achieving its objective,[35] it was nevertheless costly to the
Americans. One matter unequivocally demonstrated was that whilst the carriers,
on both sides, wielded mighty hammers, they were indeed eggshell-like in their
fragility. In terms of fleet carriers the Americans lost *Lexington* whilst *Yorktown*
was badly damaged; on the other side *Shokaku* too was damaged, taking her out
of action for three months, whilst *Zuikaku* was unhurt but suffered grave losses
amongst her aircrew. The Japanese also lost the light carrier *Shoho*. Nimitz
signalled his superiors afterwards, stating that the USN could not sustain equal

losses with the IJN as they had more aircraft carriers. He called for an urgent increase of American air strength in the Pacific, especially carrier-based.[36] On 17 May 1942 he was forbidden to engage in any 'decisive action' with the IJN as the USN simply not afford to meet the Japanese in a head-on battle.[37]

The IJN focus on the Pacific, and with destroying what remained of the US Navy, did however grant the Eastern Fleet, and the Royal Navy more generally, a certain freedom to carry out operations in the Indian Ocean, or at least its western portion. The fear that Japan would 'persuade' Vichy France to grant them the use of Diego Suarez or other ports and bases in Madagascar, as had happened in Indo-China previously, weighed heavily.[38] In the words of the Admiralty Historical Section: 'Here, if anywhere, was the spot for the Germans and Japanese to join hands; here it was imperative to avoid any repetition of the events in French Indo-China, and preparations were begun accordingly.'[39]

Chapter 8

Ironclad

The preparations for the invasion of Madagascar, dubbed Operation Ironclad, involved Somerville detaching *Hermes* from his command on 4 April 1942 and sending her, along with *Vampire*, to Trincomalee. The operation as a whole was not an Eastern Fleet responsibility but was to be undertaken by Somerville's old command, Force H, now designated as Force F for the occasion. Normally based on Gibraltar and commanded by Rear Admiral Sir Edward Syfret, it is a measure of how seriously the Indian Ocean danger was taken that it was considered feasible to redeploy Force H from the western Mediterranean, and indeed augment it.

Only with the inestimable benefit of hindsight does the danger of Japan, possibly in conjunction with Germany, establishing a naval base on the island seem fanciful. In early 1942 it seemed all too realisable. Between December 1941 and January 1942, the Axis Powers had agreed that the 70th degree of longitude would constitute the demarcation line between German/Italian and Japanese spheres of operations in the Indian Ocean.[1] Madagascar was in the German/Italian portion, and Allied intelligence indicated several high-level conversations on the subject were taking place, especially between Germany and Japan.[2] The Vichy French government, whilst not legally at war with Britain and not formally allied to any of her enemies either, was not exactly friendly towards Britain either. This was unsurprising following Mers-el-Kébir, the attempt to sink *Richelieu* and then the full-scale, if abortive, attack on Dakar itself.[3] There was also a precedent in respect of Japan reaching an 'accommodation' with Vichy; the latter had allowed the former to establish bases in Indo-China from whence the air power to aid in the invasion of Malaya, and the destruction of Force Z, had emanated. Jan Smuts, Prime Minister of South Africa, was exercised by the matter, writing to Churchill on 12 February 1942:

> I look upon Madagascar as the key to the safety of the Indian Ocean, and it may play the same important part in endangering our security there that Indo-China has played in Vichy and Japanese hands. All our communications with our various war fronts and the Empire in the East may be involved.[4]

Churchill and the British Government more generally needed little if any persuasion, and Syfret left Gibraltar accordingly on 1 April aboard his flagship *Malaya*. As well as the battleship, the naval forces assigned to support Ironclad comprised the carriers *Illustrious* and *Hermes*, the heavy cruiser *Devonshire* and the light cruiser *Hermione*. Allocated as support were nine destroyers, six corvettes and six minesweepers.[5]

The object of the exercise, at least in the first instance, was limited: 'to capture and hold the naval and air base at Diego Suarez'.[6] This was to be accomplished by making use of military forces already in transit. As Churchill was to later put it: 'The stream of reinforcements which was flowing round the Cape to India could, it seemed, be made to do this job on their way without any great loss of time.' He went on to relate another important facet of the venture: 'With memories of Dakar in our mind we could not complicate the operation by admitting the Free French. The decision was taken for a purely British expedition.'[7] The attitude of the Vichy French colonial regime and, more pertinently, the military forces under its command could not be accurately predicted. The rules of engagement imposed on the British forces precluded them from opening fire, except against submarines and aircraft, until they had been engaged first.

The composition of the naval force changed before the invasion went in. *Hermes* was of course no longer available and so Somerville ceded *Indomitable* in her place. *Malaya* reached Cape Town in South Africa but was subsequently ordered to return to Freetown. Syfret then shifted his flag, first to *Illustrious* and then to *Ramillies* which was drafted as a replacement. Apart from forming a 'pool' upon which Force F was permitted to draw resources as and when, the Eastern Fleet, consisting of the battleships *Warspite* and *Resolution*, the carrier *Formidable*, the heavy cruiser *Newcastle*, and the light cruisers *Emerald*, *Enterprise*, *Caledon* and *Dragon*, together with seven destroyers was tasked with covering the operation, and remained between 130 and 220 miles to the eastward of Diego Suarez playing 'long stop' as Somerville put it.[8]

The assault landing, which was 'thoroughly prepared, well executed and built upon a close liaison between Rear Admiral Syfret and Major General Sturges leading the assault force (Force 121)', went in on 5 May 1942.[9] Air support was provided by nine squadrons of Albacores, Fulmars, Martlets, Sea Hurricanes and Swordfish, flying off from *Indomitable* and *Illustrious*.[10] The attack achieved complete tactical surprise and was a great success. This news was rather slow to filter through to Somerville, who was positioned 150 miles off the north-east coast of the island at the time. He intercepted a French signal stating that the defenders would refuse to surrender and 'fight to the last', though he received a later report from Syfret that the operation was proceeding according to plan and without 'much opposition'.[11] His instructions were to engage any force the

Japanese might send in an attempt to interfere with the attack, provided that it was inferior to the strength of Force F and his fleet combined. On the other hand, if the enemy appeared to be superior then he was authorized to cancel Operation Ironclad and withdraw the entire force.[12] Reconnaissance was provided by long-range Catalina patrols into the Indian Ocean which observed no enemy activity at all.[13]

The more immediate threat to the seaborne components of the invasion force came from submarines. British intelligence estimated that the defenders had five such vessels available.[14] Grehan lists only four, however, and three of these were located and destroyed in fairly short order: *Bévéziers* was sunk by aircraft on 5 May, *Le Héros* likewise on 7 May and *Monge* following a destroyer attack on 8 May. The fourth, *Glorieux*, escaped and eventually made its way back to France.[15] None of them succeeded in causing any harm.

Of much greater concern were Japanese submarine activities. *Großadmiral* Karl Dönitz was to later write that:

> The political and the military leadership of Germany – reared in continental concepts, and caught in them – did not recognize the decisive importance of the naval war to grand strategy. This lack of understanding was one of the fundamental reasons for the political and strategic errors committed by the German state and war commands.[16]

Be that as it may, Vice Admiral Kurt Fricke, Chief of Staff to *Großadmiral* Erich Raeder, tried hard to persuade the Imperial Japanese Navy via discussions with Vice Admiral Nomura Naokuni, Japan's naval attaché in Berlin, of the crucial position the Indian Ocean held in Axis fortunes because of the strategic importance of the Allied maritime trade routes there.[17] During a meeting between the two admirals on 8 April 1942, Nomura imparted the information that four or five long-range submarines, supported by two supply ships doubling up as auxiliary cruisers, would be deployed off the east coast of Africa from May until July.[18] In accordance with this, the 1st Division of the 8th Submarine Flotilla was redeployed from Kwajalein Atoll in the Marshall Islands to Penang in north-west Malaya. Commanded by Rear Admiral Ishizaki Noboru flying his flag in *I-10*, the division was made up of five large fleet submarines: *I-10*, *I-16*, *I-18*, *I-20* and *I-30*. The flagship was a 'Type-A1' boat equipped with a Yokosuka E14Y (Type 0 Small Reconnaissance) seaplane. The *I-30* was similarly equipped but was of the newer 'Type B1' class, whilst the others were 'Type-C' vessels, each equipped with a detachable 'Type-A' two-man midget submarine. Surface support was provided by the *Aikoku Maru* and *Hokoku Maru*, both 18-knot ex-liners.[19] The division sortied westward on 30 April and crossed the ocean undetected.

The harbour at Diego Suarez was reconnoitred by the seaplane from *I-10* at about 22:30 hours on the night of 29 May, the darkness alleviated by a bright moon, and *Ramillies* was observed to be at anchor there. According to the Official History:

> . . . an aircraft arrived over the harbour and seemed to be about to alight on the water near the *Ramillies*, when it switched on its engine, banked steeply, and flew away making a wrong reply to the challenge. Witnesses agreed that it was a monoplane with two floats, but its identity could not be established.[20]

Suspecting that it had been an enemy spotter plane, the battleship raised steam and was under way early the following morning. Moving around the bay was thought to be an effective protection against a surprise dawn attack by submarine or aircraft, whether French or Japanese. As none materialized at or just after sunrise, then she anchored in a new location a short while later. Extensive airborne reconnaissance was undertaken out to sea, but no enemy activity was detected.

Unbeknown to the British, *I-16* and *I-20* had been ordered to make an attack with their midget submarines the following night; the unit attached to *I-18* had been damaged on the voyage and had to be ditched.[21] Launched some ten miles offshore, only the submarine from *I-20* crewed by Lieutenant Saburo Akeida and Petty Officer Masami Takemoto managed to get inside the harbour, the other being presumed lost.[22] At 20:55 hours they discharged one of their two torpedoes at *Ramillies*. It struck on the port side abreast of 'A' turret, blowing a hole some 20ft (6.1m) in diameter in the hull, the highest part being 22ft (6.7m) below the forecastle deck. It also dislodged a plate on the anti-torpedo bulge, leaving a 20ft (6.1m) section sticking out on the forward side of the hole. The vessel began listing some 4.5 degrees to port, whilst her forward draught increased considerably, being calculated an hour later (after damage control measures had been instigated) as 43ft (13m) forward and 29ft (9m) aft. The 'Flower' class corvettes *Thyme* and *Genista*, the only anti-submarine resources available at that time, immediately began searching for the culprit and depth-charging any suspected contacts. They failed to destroy the boat, however, and at 21:02 hours its second torpedo struck the tanker *British Loyalty* in the engine room, causing her to sink rapidly by the stern, though her bows remained above the water.[23] *Ramillies* did not sink and was able to steam to Durban for temporary repairs before returning to Britain, although she was out of action for almost a year. *British Loyalty* was also salvaged. Somerville immediately ordered two destroyers to Diego Suarez, but it was too late.[24]

Ishizaki had moved away and deployed his command to interdict shipping in and south of the Mozambique Channel, which comprised a maritime choke point between Madagascar and Mozambique some 260 miles across at its narrowest point. *Aikoku Maru* and *Hokoku Maru* remained well to the south-east of Madagascar. From 5 June to 8 July 1942 the submarines sank twenty-one Allied merchant ships, while one, the *Elysia*, was intercepted and sunk by gunfire from both support vessels.[25] Reconnaissance missions were also flown over the Natal coast and city of Durban by seaplanes, prompting concern over Japanese intentions; the possibility of invasion was seriously countenanced.[26] Despite numerous sorties by both the South African Air Force and the British RAF, the Japanese vessels, both surface and submarine, were never found.[27] This despite the British being aware of their presence, though not their location: 'Signal from C-in-C SA [South Africa] shows that here are two Jap raiders off Durban to eastward. 20-knot ships well armed. [Danckwerts] has taken all necessary steps. Told him to use *Indomitable* if necessary.'[28] The aircraft carrier was indeed used, but to no effect, and by the time it retired from the area in July, Ishizaki's division had, in addition to crippling *Ramillies*, sunk some 120,000 tons of merchant shipping.[29]

That the Japanese were unlikely, indeed unable, to venture in anything approaching fleet strength into the Indian Ocean again was one result of the Battle of Midway. On 4–5 June 1942 the *Kido Butai* was effectively eliminated with the loss of four of its carriers; *Soryu*, *Kaga*, *Akagi* and *Hiryu* respectively. The loss of veteran aviators and their highly-skilled support was equally devastating, and it is far from hyperbole to state, as have many historians, that the result changed the course of the entire war.[30] Churchill was quick to appreciate the transformation, writing to Sir Dudley Pound less than a week after the battle:

> The loss of these four aircraft carriers sensibly improves our position in the Indian Ocean and Bay of Bengal. For instance, Addu Atoll which can only be attacked by seaborne aircraft becomes pretty secure and is worthy of more attention. There still remain shore-based aircraft at the Andamans, but these are not very numerous and the distance is great from there to Colombo or Trincomalee. It seems to me that severe restraint is imposed upon the Japanese by their need to husband their large naval units. Perhaps you will consider what further instructions should be given to Admiral Somerville . . .[31]

It is fair to say that Churchill harboured certain reservations about Somerville's offensive spirit, and indeed his abilities as a whole. For example, on 1 June he had composed a memorandum to the Chiefs of Staff Committee, mentioning in less than glowing terms his evaluation of the admiral: 'There is a good deal in Admiral Somerville's telegrams which favours the idea of his playing a passive role, avoiding "frittering away" his strength in the Bay of Bengal etc. . . . when our shore-based air is established on the east coast of India in adequate strength he may have to escort an amphibious expedition of our own.'[32] The Prime Minister had also written to Pound, stating 'No satisfactory explanation has been given by this officer of the imprudent disposition of his forces in the early days of April, resulting in the loss of *Cornwall*, *Dorsetshire* and *Hermes*'.[33] Both Pound and Alexander were quick to point out the facts of the case in respect of the latter point, and Pound wasted no time in responding to the former:

1. Our position in the Indian Ocean is improved inasmuch as the Japanese are less likely to stick their head into it.
2. Note. It is true that the Japanese Carriers attacked both Colombo and Trincomalee without suffering damage because we had no striking force of any value.
3. I am of the opinion that the correct thing for Admiral Somerville to do is get his Carrier force properly trained so that if the Japanese stick their heads out into the Indian Ocean we shall give them a knock. *Formidable* and *Illustrious* should be efficient by now but . . . the *Indomitable* will not be efficient for some little time.
5. Whilst working up his carriers he should endeavour to destroy the Japanese surface raiders which are becoming active in the Indian Ocean.
7. I would propose to instruct Admiral Somerville in the sense of Paras. 4 & 5, adding that it is not desired that he should expose his carriers to attack by shore based aircraft.[34]

A lengthy message from Somerville to Pound of 29 June showed that he was thinking and planning very much along the lines expounded by the latter, but was also mindful of the need to be taking the offensive: 'The outstanding need at the moment is action of some sort.' He went on to explain that he had considered launching a carrier attack on Port Blair, in the Andaman Islands, and Sabang, an island off the northern tip of Sumatra. However, he reckoned that the results likely to be achieved would not justify sending in the carriers, though 'it would certainly be a good tonic to the fleet'. The rationale behind this decision lay with the limitation imposed by the aircraft with which his fleet was equipped.

> The Martlets, except for certain technical defects, are undoubtedly very good and very robust. Fulmars are now relegated to fighter reconnaissance as they are no match for Jap Zero fighters. Both Albacores and Swordfish are too slow for day strikes in clear weather and except for relatively short distance strikes cannot be escorted by Martlets or Hurricanes owing to the wide discrepancy in cruising speed and endurance. If our fighters can have additional detachable fuel tanks, this would make all the difference.[35]

Intelligence showed that there were Japanese flying boats based at Port Blair, which were susceptible to attack from fighters. The problem, as he explained it, was that in order to mount such a strike he would have to take the carriers to within 70 miles or so of the target. This would of course leave them open to attack from land-based Japanese aircraft. There was also an additional problem with Sabang. According to information received from *Luitenant-Admiraal* Conrad Helfrich, the former commander of the Royal Netherlands Navy in the East Indies, the harbour at Sabang was so dispersed in nature as to make the location of targets difficult to establish. Somerville doubted therefore if an attack using Swordfish and Albacores would produce sufficiently good results. As he had so often pointed out, the only feasible way of using these aircraft was for night-striking to which end he and his staff 'continually reviewed' their methodology. However, as he stated it to Pound, he had not yet had an opportunity to determine the extent to which three carriers could operate at night and still receive sufficient support and protection from the main body of the fleet. Nevertheless, 'night strikes are being continually practised and should prove most effective'.[36]

The action that Somerville hankered after for morale-boosting purposes was of a different scale to the 'amphibious expedition' Churchill mooted him as escorting. Be that as it may, neither was really feasible until such time as the Eastern Fleet could compete with its opponents in the air in daylight. This meant reequipment with new and better aircraft, which was no easy task. It is surely unarguable that despite the UK aircraft industry produced many excellent land-based aircraft, it failed miserably with respect to their naval counterparts. As one former Fleet Air Arm pilot put it in his post-war writings: 'Between the first day of the war and the last, the Fleet Air Arm received not one single British aircraft which wasn't either inherently unsuited to carrier-work or was obsolete before it came into service.'[37]

Commodore Matthew Slattery, the Chief Naval Representative at the Ministry of Aircraft Production (MAP), was a former naval aviator. He noted contemporaneously that the responsibility for this state of affairs in the latter part of 1941 and the summer of 1942 lay with the Admiralty rather than elsewhere:

> The outlook of the Board of Admiralty to aircraft has been one of scepticism. They have never been convinced until six to nine months ago that they were really important. They realised it was a new factor but did not really understand the possibilities because they did not know anything about the technical side and were unable to state their case to the Cabinet or Chiefs of Staff meetings.[38]

There is some justification for this accusation, but it is also the case that towards the end of 1941 the Admiralty had recognized the requirement for improved single-seat fighters along the lines of those operated by the Japanese and American navies. Having said that, they still clung to the somewhat outmoded concept of a two-seater strike escort, as embodied by the Fulmar. Also required were new torpedo-bomber reconnaissance aircraft:

> . . . the main reason which led to the adoption of a three-type policy was the paramount necessity of providing a really high performance fighter for Fleet defence. The only way that this could be attained was to confine this type to the bare requirements of Fleet defence, which entailed abandonment of navigational facilities and a considerable reduction in endurance, these latter being previously required for a fighter which might be called upon for striking force escort duties.[39]

The ordering of almost 200 American Grumman F4F Wildcats (Martlets) in 1940 is evidence that deficiencies in home-grown naval fighter aircraft, particularly of the 'high performance' variety, had been recognized.[40] Problems with the Albacore's proposed replacement, the Fairey Barracuda, the following year led to the acknowledgment that American models would have to be sourced for strike and reconnaissance as well. Two types of American aircraft, Vought SB2U Vindicator dive-bombers (dubbed the Chesapeake for British service) and Grumman Avenger torpedo-bombers, were earmarked for the roles.[41] The advent of Lend-Lease in March 1941 had greatly facilitated the likelihood of such aircraft arriving in significant numbers.[42] However, the Japanese attack in December of that year inevitably meant that the United States Navy would claim first priority.

As well as producing 'aircraft fit for sailors to fly in' the United States also helped to make those sailors fit to fly. The 'Towers Scheme', named for the Chief of the Navy's Bureau of Aeronautics Rear Admiral John H. Towers who originated it, was a training programme initiated in 1941.[43] Under the auspices of the scheme, Fleet Air Arm recruits were sent to the United States and given access to the latest aircraft. The results were impressive: 'By November 1944 it was providing 44 per cent of the pilots required by the Royal Navy. In particular, the Fleet Air Arm had come to rely on the scheme to turn out the pilots needed to fly the American aircraft on which it increasingly depended.'[44]

Commander Richard Smeeton, the assistant Naval Attaché at Washington DC responsible for ordering all US-built aircraft for the Fleet Air Arm, was of the opinion that the F4U Corsair would make a 'useful' single-seat fighter. He 'strongly' recommended that it be accepted despite that, with its wings folded, it was too tall to fit in the hangar of a British armoured carrier. He pointed out that 'delivery prospects in late 1942 are fairly promising'.[45] It turned out to be an inspired recommendation. The US Navy was at first dubious about the aircraft due to reported difficulties recovering it aboard carriers, and so assigned it largely to Marine Corps units operating from land bases. The Fleet Air Arm evolved techniques to overcome these problems, which were in any event eased by slightly shortening the wings so that Corsairs could be accommodated in carrier hangars.[46] It has been claimed that, once assimilated, the Corsair 'made the single biggest impact on Royal Navy aviation in the Second World War'.[47] This was undoubtedly so, particularly given that over 2,000 of the type were delivered to the Fleet Air Arm between 1943 and 1945, with the first arriving in November of the former year.[48]

This was of course unhelpful in respect of the Eastern Fleet, or the Royal Navy more generally, in 1942 when Martlets and Sea Hurricanes formed the only possible answer. The former, being the only effective fighter available to the United States Navy and Marine Corps at the time, was inevitably in short supply; only 300 were available in January 1942.[49] Sea Hurricanes were very much a second-best option as tests carried out the previous year had demonstrated:

> Several opportunities have occurred during the past month of comparing the performance of the Martlet with Hurricanes flown by the Royal Air Force. Dog-fights have been arranged in which the Martlets have had not the slightest difficulty in shooting down the Hurricanes at heights up to 15,000 feet.[50]

They were nevertheless, better than nothing though, as Alexander made clear to Churchill in a communication of 15 May 1942, availability was limited as production of the type had ended. Their place, at least until the arrival of American aircraft, was to be taken by another adaption of a British land-based fighter:

> . . . adapted Spitfires which will be called Seafires I and II. The estimated production of Seafire II's is 6 this month, 20 next and 24 in July with completion of the whole order for 250 by the end of this year.[51]

Alexander also expressed grave concern at the Eastern Fleet's lack of up-to-date aircraft for strike purposes, attaching the 'utmost importance to getting Barracudas at the earliest possible moment'. In the meantime, he wrote, 'the best we can do is to supply *Indomitable* with Hurricane II's fitted to carry bombs'. He went on to tell the Prime Minister that 'unfortunately *Indomitable* is the only modern carrier whose lifts will take this type'.[52] The Spitfire was of course a superlative fighter which first gained its outstanding reputation during the Battle of Britain. It did not, however, readily convert to a naval fighter, a type that required somewhat different characteristics.[53] Nevertheless, towards the close of 1942 it had become imperative to get as many improved aircraft into service as rapidly as possible. Indeed, despite it being essentially extemporised, the Seafire was by far the best performer out of the trio of types the Royal Navy was trying to get into service:

> . . . it has been decided to adopt the short term policy of developing the Seafire, Barracuda and Firefly to provide improved Fighter, Reconnaissance and Torpedo–Dive–Bomber aircraft.[54]

As far as the Eastern Fleet was concerned the matter of carrier aircraft became, perforce, somewhat academic. This was because, as the editor of his papers put it, 'Somerville found that his fleet became virtually a floating reserve for operations elsewhere, especially in the Mediterranean'.[55] Thus the means to conduct an offensive fleet action, whether in support of large-scale amphibious operations or small-scale raids, was removed. A very different kind of warfare began to be conducted in the Indian Ocean, however.

Chapter 9

'In the belly of Death'

The ships destroy us above
And ensnare us beneath.
We arise, we lie down, and we move
In the belly of Death.[1]

Imperial Japanese Navy doctrine regarding the use of submarines differed greatly from that of their main Axis partner. Whilst German U-boats concentrated on interdicting sea lines of communication, the prime targets for Japanese attacks were warships, most especially capital ships: 'There was no consideration given to using submarines to interrupt enemy [Sea Lines of Communication].'[2] Notwithstanding that, the withdrawal of Ishizaki's submarine division was shortly followed by Dönitz' decision to begin U-boat operations in much the same area that the Japanese had vacated. Rather than heralding a departure from his undoubtedly correct conviction that the 'war decisive'[3] campaign was the one being fought in the Atlantic, the decision was made on strategic grounds. Though he was in no doubt that the 'focal point' of the submarine campaign was the east coast of the United States, his entry in the U-boat Command War Diary of 15 April 1942 is revealing. It demonstrates his global conception of the campaign he was waging; the attempt to interdict supplies of food, raw materials and manufactured goods, especially weapons, without which Britain would have to surrender:

> The enemy's shipping constitutes one single, great entity. It is there-
> fore immaterial where a ship is sunk. Once it has been destroyed, it
> has to be replaced by a new ship; and that's that. In the long run the
> result of war will depend on the result of the race between sinkings
> and new construction. . . . I am therefore of the opinion that tonnage
> must be sought in those localities where, from the point of view of
> U-boat operations, it can most readily be found, and where, from
> the point of view of keeping down our own losses, it can most easily
> be destroyed. It is infinitely more important to sink ships when and
> where we can than to sacrifice aggregate sinkings in order to concen-
> trate on sinkings in any particular locality.[4]

By ordering his U-boats into the South Atlantic and Indian Ocean Dönitz hoped thereby to create a diversionary effect. The Allies would be compelled to redeploy anti-submarine forces to cover the extensive African coast as well as the North Atlantic and the Eastern American seaboard. Indeed, even though 1942 was the very height of the Battle of the Atlantic with huge losses inflicted on Allied shipping (in November 117 ships, totalling over 700,000 tons, were sunk by U-boats in all areas), it was also the year when Allied anti-submarine warfare techniques began to produce decisive results.[5]

German surface raiders, both warships and merchantmen converted to auxiliary cruisers (*Hilfskreuzer*), had operated in the Indian Ocean, and even further east, since the early days of the war. Perhaps the best-known of the former type was the *Admiral Graf Spee*, which sortied across the dividing line between the Atlantic and Indian Oceans on 3 November 1939 to raid the shipping routes. Pickings were slim with only one victim claimed, the small British tanker *Africa Star* on 15 November. On 20 November the *Panzerschiff* returned to the Atlantic, an event swiftly followed by her demise following the Battle of the River Plate on 13 December 1939.[6]

A little over a year later *Admiral Graf Spee*'s sister, *Admiral Scheer*, made a rather more successful foray. She entered the Indian Ocean on 3 February 1941 and rendezvoused with a supply ship and the auxiliary cruiser *Atlantis* eleven days later at a position some 1,000 nautical miles east of Madagascar. Having taken on supplies and shared intelligence on shipping movements, *Kapitän zur See* Theodor Krancke took his command north to the Seychelles where two Allied ships were encountered. One, the tanker *British Advocate*, he took as a prize whilst the second, the Greek vessel *Grigorios*, was sunk. A third ship, *Canadian Cruiser*, was also sunk on 21 February but managed to transmit a distress signal prior to going down as did a Dutch vessel, *Rantaupandjang*, which was sunk the following day. These messages got through and despite then being hunted by a flotilla of Allied warships, including the aircraft carrier *Hermes*, Krancke avoided interception and was back in the Atlantic by 3 March. He managed to get his ship home in one piece.[7] The actual damage caused, in terms of ships sunk or captured, by these vessels was less important than the resources necessary to catch and kill them. For example, the hunt for *Admiral Graf Spee* involved the British and French deploying four aircraft carriers (*Ark Royal*, *Béarn*, *Eagle* and *Hermes*), three battlecruisers (*Dunkerque*, *Renown* and *Strasbourg*) plus sixteen cruisers, both light and heavy, as well as the requisite support in terms of destroyers etc.[8]

Much the same applied in terms of auxiliary cruisers, though they lacked fighting strength and speed, and were completely unarmoured, so could not (usually) take on warships. Five of them, *Atlantis*, *Orion*, *Komet*, *Pinguin* and *Kormoran*, were despatched to the South Atlantic, South Pacific and Indian Ocean in 1940, to wage a trade war (*Handelskrieg*). Their operational strategy, as it applied to *Kormoran* in particular, was explained by one of her officers as follows:

> The main guideline was to disturb the sea traffic of our adversaries with the aim of keeping enemy warships busy protecting their trade routes. The mission of KORMORAN was to remain at sea for a very long period and disturb trade routes, rather than just sinking enemy merchant ships.[9]

These vessels had some successes, the case of *Atlantis* capturing the *Automedon* being one of the more notable.[10] The *Kormoran* also managed a rare feat when, having become unavoidably 'engaged with an enemy warship' she managed to defeat her adversary, albeit at the cost of her own loss: 'The action lasted 30 minutes with both ships being crippled and set ablaze. Both sank and the entire complement of HMAS *Sydney* was lost.'[11] The destruction of the *Sydney*, a modified *Leander* class light cruiser, off the coast of Western Australia on 19 November 1941 is probably unique, though it seems that the commander of the warship made several mistakes.[12]

One feature of both the types of surface ships mentioned was their extensive range, a factor augmented by the deployment of supply and support vessels. What would have improved their capabilities immensely were bases in the region, and attempts at acquiring such facilities had been made by the Kriegsmarine in December 1939. The recipients of this request, the Imperial Japanese Navy, had demurred.[13]

The third member of the Axis, Italy, did of course have ports that might have proven useful at that time, particularly Massawa (Massaua) situated on the Red Sea in Italian Eritrea. Then a part of Italian East Africa (*Africa Orientale Italiana*), it had been developed as the base of the Red Sea Flotilla (*Flottiglia del mar rosso*), and was home to eight submarines, amongst other vessels. However, with Britain controlling the Suez Canal these ships were effectively a wasting asset cut off from home. The submarines, despite being mostly modern, made little impact; the last successful attack occurring on 6 September 1940 when *Guglielmotti* sank the Greek-registered tanker *Atlas* south of the Saudi Arabian Farasan Islands.[14] When the fall of Italian Eastern Africa to Allied forces became imminent at the end of 1940, the submarines were ordered to escape. By then four of the complement, *Evangelista, Galileo Galilei, Luigi Galvani* and *Macallé*, had already been captured, sunk or scuttled. The remainder, *Archimede, Galileo Ferraris, Guglielmotti* and *Perla*, made it back to Bordeaux in France,[15] after voyaging some 12,500 nautical miles.[16]

Such distances made submarine sorties from Europe problematical. The advent of the Type IXC U-boat in 1941, the third generation of the Type IX long-range attack boats with extra fuel capacity and a range of 13,450 nautical miles at 10 knots, mitigated this somewhat.[17] In October 1941 Dönitz despatched two of these boats, *U-129* and *U-68*, along with the Type IXB boat *U-124* and *U-A*, a modified Type IX U-Boat originally built for the Turkish Navy, from the 2nd U-boat Flotilla (*2. Unterseebootsflottille*) based at Lorient, France, to the area around Cape Town. There were many agents in South Africa willing to assist Germany.[18] Intelligence from them indicated that hundreds of Allied ships had passed through the area in recent months, and that there were as many as fifty moored within the harbour and its approaches at any given time.[19] Here then were, potentially at least, rich pickings indeed, but it was not to be. The U-boats were to be succoured en-route by the auxiliary cruiser *Atlantis*, currently making her way back to Germany, and the supply ship *Python*, which had steamed from a French port. *Atlantis*, on her way home after 622 days at sea during which time she'd travelled around 100,000 nautical miles, was ordered by radio to rendezvous with *U-68* some 450 nautical miles south of St. Helena and refuel the submarine, then to do the same in respect of *U-126* north of Ascension Island. But the message had been intercepted, and subsequently decrypted by Britain's codebreakers at Bletchley Park.[20]

Atlantis rendezvoused with *U-68* on 13 November 1941, but it wasn't until the next day that the weather abated enough to allow the resupply to take place. It was completed successfully, and on 22 November *U-126* met the auxiliary cruiser as planned. Unbeknown to the Germans, three Royal Navy cruisers were also seeking to attend that rendezvous: *Devonshire*, *Dorsetshire* and *Dunedin*, all acting independently. The submarine escaped but *Devonshire*, which arrived on the scene first and unexpectedly, bombarded and sank the German ship from long range whilst *U-126* crash-dived to avoid destruction.

There were many survivors, most of whom were saved when the U-boat resurfaced to take them onboard. The submarine's captain, Ernst Bauer, reported what had occurred to U-boat Command by radio, a signal which was intercepted by *Python* who hurried to the scene. Arriving on 24 November she took aboard 305 survivors and replenished *U-126*, which then turned for home because of engine problems. *Python* meanwhile steamed to a new rendezvous some 1,500 nautical miles to the south in order to resupply the other boats. Unfortunately for the Germans, the British again learned what was afoot via intercepted and decrypted radio transmissions and acted accordingly. Unfortunately for the British, *U-124* had sighted *Dunedin* on 24 November and fired three torpedoes at her from extreme range. Two struck home whereupon she blew up and sank instantly, with heavy loss of life.[21]

Python rendezvoused with *U-68* and *U-A* on 30 November as planned, but their designs were rudely interrupted the next day when *Dorsetshire* appeared without prior notice. The two submarines crash-dived whilst *Python* attempted to make off at top speed before, realizing that escape was impossible, scuttling herself.[22] Fearing being torpedoed *Dorsetshire* vacated the area, leaving hundreds of survivors in the water as well as in, and on, the two now-resurfaced U-boats. Dönitz ordered *U-124* and *U-129* to assist, and aborted plans for the operations around Cape Town. He also requested the Italians to send four of their boats from Bordeaux to the rescue, which they did: *Luigi Torelli, Enrico Tazzoli, Giuseppe Finzi* and *Pietro Calvi*. Being bigger than their German counterparts, they had more internal space for accommodating survivors.[23] All eight submarines made it back to safety, with no loss of life on the voyage home, an exploit straight out of a *Boy's Own* adventure tale.

There were two main repercussions. Firstly, and as Dönitz wrote: 'After the sinking of *Python*, it is now impossible to refuel in the Atlantic. It will be impossible to resume refuelling on the surface – the time for such operations is now passed.'[24] In other words, missions such as the one to Cape Town had to be abandoned until such time as U-boat tankers (*Milchkühe*), which were then under construction, became operational.[25] The second was, potentially at least, of far more import; it provoked an inquiry into whether or not the enemy were reading German signals. As Heinz Bonatz, the head of B-Dienst (which was, very broadly, the German navy's equivalent of Bletchley Park; there was no central German cryptography agency comparable to the British set-up), put it on 2 December 1941: 'It is the third time a supply ship has been caught by the enemy at a meeting point . . . the fact that there have been three interceptions is remarkable.'[26] Fortunately for the Allies, the subsequent investigation concluded that the naval Enigma cypher was secure and that it was 'unimaginable' that the enemy could read it.[27] Indeed, it was the case that the 'enemy' couldn't read naval Enigma during 1942; see below.

Thus, when Dönitz again sent his units to hunt around Cape Town they were succoured by a U-boat tanker rather than surface vessels, and his command still used the Enigma machine to communicate. Four Type IXC boats were sent, *U-68, U-156, U-172* and *U-504*, together with the Type XIV U-tanker *U-459* in support. Though the decision to send the complement south had been made in July, it wasn't until the following month that *Gruppe Eisbär* (Polar Bear Group), as they were dubbed, set off, the name, according to Paterson, being chosen as a 'vague attempt at disguising the group's destination'.[28] The first three *Eisbär* boats, *U-156, U-172* and *U-459*, began their voyage south on 19 August 1942. The tanker was directed ultimately to grid reference GG, some 500–1,000 nautical miles off the west coast of South-west

Africa (the former German colony of *Südwestafrika*, now Namibia) and to the south of the British island of St. Helena.[29] There she would hold position ready to replenish the other boats. The operational areas of the attack boats were divided as follows; *U-68* was to operate in an arc from south-west to south-east of Cape Town and Cape Agulhas, whilst *U-504* would cover the area north and north-west of Cape Town. The other two were to operate closer inshore, on the approaches to Cape Town itself; these were not the *Rudeltaktik* (wolfpack tactics) used in the North Atlantic. Dönitz wanted the group to remain in their operational areas until the end of October, when other boats would arrive to relieve them. He considered that they would require this length of time to achieve results commensurate with the resources devoted to this long-range operation.[30]

There was of course a *circa* 6,000-nautical mile voyage to the southern tip of Africa to complete first, and this was to prove problematical. In accordance with his global vision, that enemy shipping was one single, great entity, Dönitz wanted the group to attack any targets they came across whilst in transit. His superiors in the SKL (*Seekriegsleitung* or Naval Warfare Command), however, wanted the boats to keep their powder dry, as it were, and achieve maximum surprise on arrival. A compromise was reached. The group could attack any shipping found between the equator and the 5th Parallel south, lines of latitude roughly encompassing the extent of the French Equatorial Africa (*Afrique équatoriale française*) littoral to the east (now Gabon). This decision was to have far-reaching consequences when, on 12 September 1942, *U-156* spotted the Royal Mail Steamer *Laconia*. The ship was on her way from Cape Town to Freetown, Sierra Leone, and was some 550 nautical miles to the north-east of Ascension Island and about 1,200 nautical miles west of Pointe-Noire, then in the Belgian Congo, and so fractionally outside the specified zone of attack.[31] Aboard were 1,800 Italian prisoners of war, 80 civilians and 428 British and Polish soldiers.[32]

The commander of *U-156*, Werner Hartenstein, put two torpedoes into *Laconia* which immediately began to founder, then surfaced in order to try and capture the ship's senior officers. When he observed the scale of the disaster he had instigated, however, Hartenstein immediately adopted a humanitarian role and went to assist those in the water.[33] To this end he also radioed his command in France, who then directed, at the personal order of Dönitz, three other submarines, *U-506*, *U-507* and the Italian *Comandante Cappelini* (which had been patrolling off Freetown, Sierra Leone) to help. As part of this effort, they took the ship's lifeboats in tow and packed their own hulls and decks with survivors; such medical aid as was possible was given. A rendezvous was arranged with two Vichy French warships, the light cruiser *Gloire* and the minesweeping sloop (*aviso dragueur*) *Annamite*, despatched from Dakar for the purpose of taking onboard the survivors. A third, the sloop (*aviso*) *Dumont-d'Urville*, was also despatched.

Despite displaying prominent Red Cross banners, and having broadcast the object of its mission on the international frequency, *U-156* and its attendant string of lifeboats were attacked on 16 September by a US Army B-24 Liberator bomber based at Wideawake Airfield on Ascension Island. Damaged by bombs, and forced to dive to avoid destruction, the U-boat nevertheless survived the attack. Less fortunate were the *Laconia* survivors, dozens of whom were killed or subsequently drowned. The next day, a similar aircraft attacked *U-506* which had 142 survivors on deck. The submarine crash-dived and survived unharmed, whilst the fate of those that had been sheltering on deck need hardly be described. Indeed, it is reckoned that about 1,500 of those that had been aboard *Laconia* perished in one way or another; a toll entirely comparable numerically with that pertaining to the rather better known *Titanic* disaster. These events led Dönitz to issue the '*Laconia* Order' to his U-boat commanders stating, in effect, that any attempts at rescuing the crews of sunken ships must cease forthwith.[34]

The damage caused to *U-156* was sufficient to prevent it continuing with its mission, its place being taken by *U-159*, which had been voyaging to the mouth of the Congo River. Between 22 and 24 September the *Eisbär* boats rendezvoused with *U-459* and took on supplies and fuel, which enabled them to continue for a further 30 days; they arrived off the coast of Cape Town during the first week of October 1942.[35]

The deployment of *Gruppe Eisbär* took place during a period when the ability of the British codebreakers at Bletchley Park to read the Kriegsmarine's communications had been compromised. This was due to the introduction of the M4 four-wheel Enigma machine, on 1 February 1942. From then on the Atlantic U-boats used it for their Triton cipher (codenamed 'Shark' by the British). This, in conjunction with the introduction of a new edition of the Short Weather Cipher (*Wetterkurzschlüsse* or WKS) book, which provided 'cribs', proved devastating. Without these cribs, and lacking four-wheel bombes, the codebreakers 'became blind against Shark'. It wasn't until a version of the WKS book was captured on 30 October 1942, and the realisation that 'M4 emulated M3 [the three-rotor Enigma machine] when enciphering weather short signals', that progress was made.[36] 'On 13 December, Hut 8 solved 'Shark' keys for 5 to 7 December.'[37] Thus the arrival of the *Gruppe* a month earlier came as a surprise. On the night of 6/7 October 1942, *U-172* managed to penetrate the Cape Town roadstead undetected, but found it empty of shipping. *U-68*, on the other hand, was shadowing several ships on the approach to the same location. Both boats radioed their findings back to their command HQ in France, apparently without attracting any attention, and were ordered to commence attacking at midnight on 8 October. Over the next three days thirteen or fourteen – the sources differ – merchant ships were sunk.[38]

The Eastern Fleet, as such, was not responsible for the defence of the sea routes around Cape Town and the southern coast of South Africa. That was the responsibility of the South Atlantic Station whose remit extended into the Indian Ocean as far as the 35th Meridian east, a line that bisects the town of Inharrime in Portuguese East Africa. Therefore the entire east coast of South Africa fell under the command of the C-in-C South Atlantic, Vice Admiral Sir Campbell Tait.[39] Nevertheless, it was Somerville's command that had to find the resources to deal with the incursion, and, as he reported on 7 November 1942, he only had sixteen destroyers available at the time of the first U-boat attacks. Four, *Arrow*, *Active*, *Foxhound* and *Nizam*, were at Simonstown, South Africa. The first two were scheduled to sail for Freetown as escorts, whilst the second pair were about to commence refits; 'Both ships well overdue to boiler clean, and *Nizam* limited to 22 knots by shaft defects.'

Three more were at Durban; the recently-refitted *Hotspur*; *Norman*, under repair for boiler defects until 14 October; and *Derwent*, in the Prince Edward Graving Dock along with the carrier *Illustrious*, both due to undock on 14 October. Two of the three were then earmarked to escort *Illustrious* to Kilindini the following day. There were a further three at Madagascar: *Napier*, *Inconstant* and *Blackmore*. These, however, had been assigned to escort troopships containing the 29th Independent Infantry Brigade Group, which had recently completed Operation Stream Line Jane (the three-stage occupation of the whole of Madagascar), from Madagascar to South Africa before they were shipped to India.[40] On their arrival all three destroyers were scheduled for a 'well overdue' boiler clean.

Somerville also had six destroyers, which included two Dutch vessels, at Kilindini. Two of them, *Fortune* and *Nepal*, were scheduled to escort the battleship *Warspite* to Durban on 11 October for dry-docking, where they would have their boilers serviced at the same time. The two Dutch destroyers, *Van Galen* and *Tjerk Hiddes*, had already been nominated for service in the American Southwest Pacific Force under Vice Admiral Arthur S. Carpender and were scheduled to leave for Fremantle imminently.[41] That left him with two destroyers, *Catterick* and *Express*, which could be employed on fleet escort duties. On 10 October, Somerville informed the Admiralty that the refits of *Foxhound* and *Nizam* could be deferred and that *Hotspur* could be spared to proceed to the Cape at once.[42]

The next day he confided his evident frustrations to both his pocket diary and his wife:

> [The] Admiralty have asked if I can send destroyers to Cape [Town]. Have replied that this can only be done if Force A is completely immobilized and continuation of this state of affairs is most undesirable . . . looks as if at least 11 ships have been torpedoed off the Cape so situation is serious but hard to see what we can do.[43]

> The blasted U-boats have appeared *en masse* off the Cape and [the Admiralty] are shouting for me to send little boats down there. They seem to have forgotten how to count or else they would have known that I have practically none in the bag.[44]

He had also informed the Admiralty on 10 October that a further five destroyers, *Express*, *Catterick* and *Nepal*, plus *Fortune* and *Inconstant* after their boilers were attended to, could be deployed to the Cape. This would though, as per his diary entry, have resulted in Force A, for which read the Eastern Fleet, being effectively immobilized. He asked if the Admiralty would accept this and, on 13 October, a reply came to the effect that no less a body than the Cabinet approved of such a course of action; *Express* and *Catterick* sailed accordingly.[45]

Most things in war, as in life itself, are a matter of priorities and it is clear that the British Government considered that in October 1942 protection of the sea lines of communication in the Indian Ocean was of greater significance than anything else. This was a distinct change, brought about of course by force of circumstances. To understand why we need to go back in time a little.

The amphibious operations mooted by Churchill for the Eastern Fleet in June revolved around a proposed operation dubbed Anakim. This was a scheme drawn up by General Archibald Wavell, the Commander-in-Chief in India, for the re-invasion of Burma by amphibious assault along the Arakan coast and in the vicinity of Rangoon (Yangon) and Moulmein (now Mawlamyine or Mawlamyaing).[46] For various reasons, mainly a severe lack of resources, Anakim was, however, postponed and could not take place in 1942.[47] Churchill had continued to chafe at what he saw as the inactivity of the Eastern Fleet, and particularly wanted it to instigate operations that would draw off Japanese forces; the Guadalcanal Campaign in the Solomon Islands was in preparation and would commence on 7 August.[48] Churchill had written to Pound on 12 July, stating that he had 'promised we would assist the [the Americans] by making diversions in any way possible'. He went on:

> We must now show a helpful attitude. I understand you have sent a telegram to Admiral Somerville asking him what he can do . . . He has

two first-class carriers and the *Warspite*. He has been doing nothing for
several months and we really cannot keep his fleet idle indefinitely.[49]

As has already been argued, whilst the *Formidable* and *Illustrious* were undoubtedly first-class ships, the aircraft they carried, and the strike aircraft in particular, were mostly second class.[50] As Somerville noted in a letter of 11 August:
'until I get more Martlets and until I get Barracudas instead of Swordfish and
Albacores, my [two] carriers are equal to about half a Jap carrier.'[51]

Churchill's 'promise' had been made following requests from Admiral Ernest
J. King, Commander in Chief United States Fleet (COMINCH) and Chief of
Naval Operations (CNO). With the US Navy stretched to the limit and about
to embark on the campaign to capture the Solomon Islands, King wanted
diversionary attacks on the Malay Barrier to force the Japanese to disperse their
resources. Anakim, despite King's offer to provide landing craft in support, was
not feasible. Strikes on two major oil refineries, both about six miles east of the
town of Palembang in south-eastern Sumatra, were King's second choice.

There were, however, difficulties. Palembang could only be reached by
an air strike. However, being situated on the eastern side of Sumatra, then a
short-range attack from the sea would involve breaching the Malay Barrier; the
carriers involved would have to pass through the Sunda Strait separating Java
and Sumatra, before steering north to launch. This would be a perilous exercise, exposing the fleet to Japanese land-based air attack. The alternative was to
launch from off the western coast. This too involved problems. Palembang is
around 180 miles distant from the west coast of Sumatra, so any flight from one
to the other not only involved a long round trip, but also necessitated crossing
the 11,000ft Barisan Mountains twice.[52]

As Somerville's biographer noted: 'It is sad to record that, when asked for his
views, Somerville was forced to give his opinion that the most his fleet could
be asked to undertake was a diversionary cruise towards the Andamans.'[53] The
'diversionary cruise' referred to was code-named Operation Stab, the general
outline of which was communicated to the Admiralty on 27 July. Somerville
summarised its object as being to 'contain Japanese air and surface forces' by
carrying out a feint, a diversion, in the Bay of Bengal suggestive of a seaborne
attack on the Andaman Islands. To that end, three small dummy convoys
made up of available merchant and Royal Fleet Auxiliary ships would sail in
daylight from Vizagapatam, Madras and Trincomalee with local escorts;
these were dubbed respectively, if perhaps a little unimaginatively, Force V,
Force M and Force T. The first would comprise *Blackheath*, *Trader Cranfield*
and *Mahout*, escorted by the Royal Indian Navy[54] sloop *Jumna* and the old 'S'
class destroyer *Scout*. The Madras contingent comprised *Tasmania*, *Hoperange*,

Clan Mciver, *Yuensang* and *Custodian* with the *Abdiel* class minelayer *Manxman* and the Indian anti-submarine patrol vessel *Sonavati*. Force T was made up of three Royal Fleet Auxiliary vessels, the tankers *Appleleaf* and *Broomdale* plus the supply ship *Shengking*, and the merchant vessel *Marit Maersk*, escorted by the Indian sloop *Hindustan* and the 'Flower' class corvette *Marguerite*.[55]

These three 'convoys' were to set out on 1 August and proceed eastwards at their best speed until nightfall. Then they would reverse course and return to their ports, arriving before dusk the next day. Due to 'unserviceability of aerodromes' around Vizagapatam no air support was available for Force V, but the other two would be escorted by fighter aircraft on both legs of their voyage out to a distance of 50 miles of port. Whilst out, they would also be screened by anti-submarine air patrols where possible.

Force A meanwhile would have left Colombo so as to be east of Trincomalee by the time Force T was due to sail. Thereafter it would stay to the eastward so as to cover that force during 1–2 August. Catalina patrols would also be established to provide reconnaissance over the Bay of Bengal whilst the operation was ongoing. Subsequent movements of Force A would depend on the situation as it developed, but the initial plan was for it to return to Colombo on 4 August or thereabouts. So as to attract the attention of the enemy, Force A would carry out a spurious radio conversation, dubbed Operation Spark, on the night of 1/2 August. This would report, in plain language, that there had been a collision between two of the merchant ships and that one of them could no longer proceed. One of the escort vessels would then supposedly order her to maintain radio silence, and then report to the Commander-in-Chief that Force M was unable to proceed. The latter would then postpone the operation and order all forces to return to their ports.

Force A, *Warspite*, *Illustrious* and *Formidable*, plus the cruisers *Birmingham*, *Mauritius* and *Jacob van Heemskerck*, and the destroyers *Napier*, *Norman*, *Nizam*, *Inconstant* and *Van Galen*, sailed from Colombo rather earlier than planned, on the afternoon of 30 July, following receipt of a message from the Dutch submarine *O 23*. This vessel was on patrol in the far northern portion of the Malacca Strait just west of Perak Island, and it reported on 29 July that it had been in action with a group of Japanese warships, consisting of two cruisers, of either the *Takao* or *Mogami* class and four destroyers of the *Fubuki* class. Torpedoes and depth-charges had been discharged by both sides as appropriate, but no damage had been caused to either. The surface vessels were on a heading of north-north-west when spotted.[56] Somerville related the import of the message in an account to his wife:

> We left harbour in a hurry . . . because I got news that two Jap 8"
> cruisers and 4 destroyers had been sighted at the N[orth] end of the

Malacca Straits apparently heading for the Bay of Bengal. . . . We may be lucky and meet them or else they may get wind I'm on the war-path and sugar off back inside the Andamans where I can't get at them.[57]

His later analysis was that it was unlikely that the enemy cruiser force was a reaction to the 'planted' rumours in India that an attack on the Andaman Islands was in progress. Rather they were either engaged in a raid on shipping in the northern part of the Bay of Bengal, or on a visit to Rangoon to coincide with the establishment of what he termed 'the new Burmese puppet government'.[58] In any event, it was an enemy force that Force A could defeat if it could only come to grips with it; Somerville went looking.

After leaving Colombo he shaped course to keep out of sight of land, and to be in a position 35 miles to eastward of Trincomalee by 10:00 hours on 1 August, whilst despatching air searches ahead to a distance of some 150 miles. They found nothing, and since no further information concerning the cruiser force was forthcoming he ordered Force M from Madras to postpone its departure from 10:00 hours until 14:00 hours. He also decreed that, once it had departed, a Catalina be deployed to patrol to the north-eastward of it to warn of any enemy approach. Force T left Trincomalee on schedule at 09:00 hours and Force A, which was steaming some 40 miles to the east, paralleled it on a north-easterly course for the rest of the day. Again, an air search revealed nothing, but radar contact was obtained at 10:40 hours on an aircraft some 73 miles distant on an east-by-south bearing. It proved impossible to identify as hostile, or not, due to the inability to detect an IFF (Identification Friend or Foe) signal, which was 'the rule rather than the exception' according to Somerville.[59] The unidentified aircraft circled Force A at a distance of around 24 miles before, some 75 minutes later, heading off to the north-east-by-east. Officers on *Formidable* obtained visual contact and reported the aircraft as a Catalina. Accordingly, and despite the fact that no Catalina was scheduled to be in the vicinity or to behave as such, no fighters were launched to intercept; it was accepted that the behaviour of the aircraft could well have due to the lack of training of many of the newly-arrived Catalina crews.

However, and according to Somerville, subsequent investigation and a warning of the presence of British forces broadcast from Tokyo established this was an enemy aircraft; probably a Kawanishi H6K from Port Blair in the Andaman Islands, which bore a resemblance to a Catalina at a distance.[60] Given that *Illustrious* had launched a Combat Air Patrol of two Martlets at 12:00 hours, the C-in-C was convinced that the flying boat could have been intercepted were it not for its misidentification. The small size of the fighter umbrella was dictated by the need to conserve the Martlets, one of which crashed on landing in any event.

An air search was launched at 15:00 hours covering a sector from north to east-south-east to a depth of 150 miles. This found nothing, but one of the returning aircraft, a Fulmar from *Illustrious*, crashed on landing and was badly damaged. That wasn't the end of the aviation problems; two Fulmars from *Formidable* were unable to find their carrier and radioed asking for Direction Finding (D/F) bearings to be transmitted. Somerville immediately complied, ordering radio silence to be broken and, at 18:40 hours, the fleet to turn towards one of the aircraft when its position had been established by radar. He also ordered searchlights to be turned on to assist the pilot, who closed in but ran out of fuel before being able to attempt a landing. The crew were picked up by the destroyer *Norman*. Nothing further was heard from the second Fulmar, however. At 23:00 hours Operation Spark was carried out and Force A reversed course, heading back to the area where the survivors of the lost Fulmar might be expected to be found. Air searches were launched at 06:30 hours on 2 August and the fleet manoeuvred to try and locate the survivors. They were not found, but Catalinas traversing the area were requested to continue to search for them; they were never found unfortunately.

At 11:00 hours *Formidable* flew off two Martlets as Combat Air Patrol, and twelve minutes later both carriers reported radar contact with an aircraft some 55 miles distant on a bearing of north-east-by-east and flying at 10,000ft. The Martlets were directed to intercept. Their initial sighting indicated a Catalina. A closer look, however, revealed a Kawanishi H6K, which was promptly despatched. There were no survivors. Four more Martlets had been launched at 11:15 hours, two from each carrier, but one of them, from *Formidable*, crashed into the sea on take-off; the pilot was rescued by *Jacob van Heemskerck*. Also at 11:00 hours, Somerville received information from Layton in Ceylon indicating that RAF signals intelligence in Bengal (Air Headquarters Bengal) predicted a naval attack on Madras at dawn on 3 August. This was predicted from unspecified naval activity that had been detected south of the Andaman Islands on 31 July. The C-in-C replied requesting amplification, as he considered that any such attack was unlikely given that, from sightings and radio broadcasts, whether spurious or otherwise, the Japanese were aware that Force A was at sea. Nevertheless, he determined on heading immediately to Trincomalee to refuel his destroyers so as to be ready in case any attack materialized; course was altered and speed adjusted at 12:15 hours accordingly. Whilst the fleet was so proceeding another Martlet, from *Illustrious*, was lost. It crashed at 15:30 hours whilst attempting to land and the pilot perished.

Trincomalee was reached at 19:15 hours on 2 August, where a message from Air Headquarters India was received; the warning of an attack on Madras was probably a false alarm. After discussing the matter with his senior officers

Somerville agreed and decided to return most of Force A to Colombo whilst *Formidable* and *Birmingham*, being required for the Madagascan Operation Stream Line Jane, would proceed to Kilindini. Whilst en route the next day there was a further aviation-related failure when, at 18:50 hours, *Illustrious* reported that an aircraft had been sighted just above the horizon and bearing south-by-west. The two Fulmar fighters providing the Combat Air Patrol were directed to investigate what looked to be a Catalina, but could not be definitely identified as such. As noted earlier, the Kawanishi H6K and the Catalina were visually similar, despite the former being larger and four-engined, and were thus not readily distinguishable at a distance. It seems that the Fighter Directing Officer mistakenly designated the target as a 'Bandit' (an aircraft positively identified as being an enemy) rather than a 'Bogey' (an aircraft whose identity is unknown) with the result that one of the Fulmars opened fire on it as soon as it was within range. Only then did it become apparent that the aircraft was indeed a Catalina, and the fighters withdrew. One Catalina crew member was killed and two injured, whilst the aircraft suffered damage to its rudder but was able to return to its base at Koggala, Ceylon.

It was a miserable ending to what has been characterized as 'a sortie of debatable success'.[61] Nevertheless, and despite losing or damaging several aircraft, including the Catalina, Somerville considered that Operation Stab had been worthwhile. He based this observation on information received from a photographic reconnaissance of the Andaman Islands on 7 and 8 August. This revealed that there was a Japanese aircraft carrier of about 10,000 tons, and a small cruiser or destroyer, at Port Cornwallis on the northern east coast of North Andaman Island. Subsequent analysis of the photographs however showed that the 'carrier' was a seaplane tender carrying fighter floatplanes.[62] Somerville took the presence of these aircraft as clearly indicative of a defensive, as opposed to offensive, posture which, in conjunction with information that an additional bomber squadron had been sent to Sabang, off the northern tip of Sumatra, suggested to him that 'Operation STAB more than achieved its object in containing Japanese forces in the western Malayan barrier'.[63] He also noted on 5 August that there had been a 'Report from Tokyo of [the] presence of *Warspite* and 2 carriers etc. in [the] Bay of Bengal. Diversion seems to have been quite good.'[64] The 'official history' by Roskill is less upbeat:

> . . . there were indications that the Japanese moved bomber rein-
> forcements to northern Sumatra at about that time; but it is doubtful
> whether the diversion deceived the enemy, or caused him to move any
> substantial force in the direction of the Indian Ocean.[65]

Indeed, for the Japanese the main focus of the war had shifted; they had no reason to venture west.[66] Indeed, towards the end of 1942 it became plain that the Indian Ocean was no longer as vitally important to Allied fortunes as pre-viously: 'After the cataclysmic Japanese defeat at Midway in June 1942 it was obvious that a joining of forces in the Middle East would not become possible.'[67] Making it even less possible was the result of the Second Battle of El Alamein, 23 October–11 November 1942. This began the retreat of the German and Italian forces in North Africa westwards, whilst the success of the Anglo-American invasion of French Morocco and Algeria (Operation Torch: 8–16 November 1942) threatened them from the opposite direction. We, however, must return to the depredations of *Gruppe Eisbär*.

As noted, the U-boats had opened their attack on 7 October and within 24 hours six ships, aggregating 33,000 tons, had been sunk within a radius of 100 miles of Cape Town by *U-68*, *U-172* and *U-179*, the last, a Type IXD with greater speed but somewhat reduced range in comparison to the IXC, being a reinforcement for the group that had sped south to join. Because the attack was unexpected, most South African lighthouses were still functioning and merchantmen routed independently around the South African coast. As per Somerville's report of 7 November, the destroyers *Nizam* and *Foxhound* were at Simonstown for refitting, but the Admiralty ordered Tait to cancel this work for the moment and also reassigned *Arrow* and *Active* to him.

Early on the morning of 8 October the four destroyers deployed to the south-south-west of Cape Town to search for both survivors and submarines. They found several of the former; those who had taken to the boats of the Greek-registered *Koumoundouros*, which had fallen victim to *U-68* at 02:30 hours that morning. These were all picked up by 13:00 hours and the ships began patrolling, in line abreast two miles apart, to hunt for U-boats and further lifeboats. This time they found both. At around 22:00 hours the survivors from *City of Athens* were picked up and taken aboard *Active*, which some 40 min-utes later registered a radar contact at a distance of some 2,500 yards. *Active* moved to investigate at speed, making visual contact with a surfaced submarine that appeared to be stationary. The destroyer continued to close and at around 800 yards illuminated the target and began an attack with her 4.7in guns. The submarine was the recently-arrived *U-179* on her first mission and one feature of these large cruiser U-boats was their relative sluggishness when surfaced and inability to crash-dive rapidly. Thus, by the time the boat had managed to get out of harm's way of 4.7in shells, the destroyer was upon her and able to drop ten depth charges directly over her last observed position. Set to explode at between 50–100ft (15–30m), these drove *U-179* up to the surface before she plunged back under; this time for good and with all hands.[68]

The sinking of *U-179* was to be the only kill made by the defenders and her loss was more than made up for by the arrival of *U-177* and *U-181*, both Type IXD boats. In conjunction with *U-178* they moved up the east coast of

South Africa to operate off Natal and Mozambique, an operation attended with great success if judged by tonnage sunk, but one also by great tragedy in the destruction of the RMS ship *Nova Scotia* at 06:12 hours on 28 November. *U-177* sighted the vessel east of Cape St Lucia, on the northern Natal coast zigzagging at 14 knots. Incorrectly identified as an Auxiliary Cruiser, the ship was attacked from periscope depth with a spread of three torpedoes, of which two were on target whereupon she burst into flames and settled quickly. Some lifeboats and rafts were lowered, around which sharks of the aggressive Oceanic Whitetip variety quickly began to mill. Many more were no doubt attracted by the greater number of survivors who went directly into the water.[69]

Upon surfacing to interrogate the lifeboat occupants, which was a standard procedure when safe to do so, *Korvettenkapitän* Robert Gysae, the U-boat commander, discovered he had initiated another *Laconia*-type situation. There were over 1,000 souls aboard, at least 750 of which were Italian prisoners of war or former colonists from Italian East Africa, including several women and children. Forbidden by the '*Laconia* Order' from attempting any rescue, he radioed his superiors and informed them of the situation before taking two Italians aboard and departing. His message – 'over a thousand Italian civil internees ex Massawa'[70] – even if somewhat inaccurate – prompted the despatch of assistance: 'Within 7 hours of the attack the Portuguese East African Government was requested by the German government to search for survivors.'[71] The sloop (*Aviso de 1ª classe*) *Afonso de Albuquerque*, under Captain Jose Augusto Guereiro De Brito, was accordingly despatched from Lourenço Marques and reached the scene of the sinking about 30 hours later. By that time there were just 192 souls left alive, only one of whom was female. The tally of those who perished came to 858, a figure including 650 Italians and, most gruesomely, according to the log of *Afonso de Albuquerque* at least a quarter of them had been killed by sharks.[72] One survivor recalled that 'the sea was alive with sharks, and dozens of men were taken'.[73] All in all, the torpedoing of *Nova Scotia* recorded the largest single loss of life ever to have occurred in South African waters.[74] The scale of death was thankfully unusual, but there were another forty merchant vessels that fell victim to the boats of *Gruppe Eisbär* between 8 October and 2 December 1942. This was a toll amounting to no less than 223,131 tons (202,421 tonnes) lost in the South African sea lanes.[75]

Such a scale of loss, disproportionate because it was at the cost of only a single enemy submarine, led to the belief that espionage was involved; spies had been informing the Germans of shipping movements. This belief persisted for some time, and no doubt persists still, and seems to have been held in high places. For example, Janie Malherbe, the wife of Ernst Gideon Malherbe, the Director of South African Military Intelligence from 1942 to 1948, wrote in a work published in 1965 that '[T]he Germans torpedoed . . . *Nova Scotia*, off the coast of Zululand as the result of information from a South African German spy . . .'[76] It is undoubtedly the case that white South African society (the only kind that counted at the time in every context) was divided on 'the war issue'.[77] It is also the case that there were pro-German agents and saboteurs amongst the Afrikaner population: Visser notes that documents were captured in 1942 pertaining to a plot to 'blow up the graving dock in Durban harbour'.[78] There is no question that the Germans and Italians maintained intelligence networks in South Africa and Mozambique and that the British and South Africans indulged in counterintelligence work to neutralize them.[79] Later scholarship has, however, tended to discount the effectiveness of Axis efforts in regard to shipping. Bizley for example argues that '. . . no U-boat log, as researched from those vessels operating off our coast, appears to record a predetermined ambush as by instruction'.[80]

It is though probably the case that these losses were more due to cock-up than conspiracy for several interrelated reasons; perhaps most notably the fact that the arrival of *Gruppe Eisbär* came as a surprise. This was the result of intelligence failures including, and most importantly, a hiatus in the ability to read the Triton cipher as already mentioned. Because the attacks were unexpected no convoy system had been instituted, so it followed that most of the victims were voyaging independently over a vast operational area; protection from submarine attack was therefore a task that was difficult in the extreme. Compounding everything was the lack of ability to respond. There were simply not enough anti-submarine assets available, whether airborne or naval, to initiate countermeasures, despite the Eastern Fleet being immobilized through lack of destroyers in an effort to do so.[81] A system of convoy was also instituted, firstly between Cape Town and Durban. Then shipping travelling eastwards towards Cape Town was formed into convoys upon reaching Walvis Bay in South-west Africa, whilst that travelling to South Africa via the Mozambican Channel was formed into convoys at Lourenço Marques.[82]

In order to provide protection for these convoys Somerville records that, on 23 October, Admiral Tait formed the South Atlantic Escort Force consisting of eight Eastern Fleet destroyers, plus three corvettes, including the Free French vessel *Commandant Detroyat*.[83] Marder, Jacobsen and Horsefield explained the 'dilemma' facing him thus:

> [He] could send his heavy units to sea to prepare for the eventual counter offensive, or he could protect commerce in the vast reaches of the Indian Ocean. He could not do both, and with the passage of time, it became more questionable whether he could do either.[84]

One anti-submarine scheme that Somerville could, and did, contribute to though was concocted in Cairo during December 1942. Dubbed 'Workhouse' it aimed to protect Allied shipping in the Persian Gulf by discouraging possible submarine attacks through deception; Japan and Germany were to be persuaded that the Straits of Hormuz had been sown with naval mines. In league with Somerville in respect of this *ruse de guerre* was Colonel Dudley Wrangel Clarke 'the greatest British deceiver of WW2'.[85] Clarke headed 'A Force', an unorthodox organization with the remit of manufacturing 'strength out of weakness' through skulduggery.[86] The initial idea involved sowing the strait with dummy mines, and then blowing up several dispensable ships so as to add 'verisimilitude' to the subterfuge. However, investigation revealed that the scanty coastal population would be unlikely to notice, never mind pay heed, to such dramatics, and would accordingly ignore any such 'minefields' when fishing. Consequently, and with the submarine threat in the area declining, 'nothing much ever came of "Workhouse"'.[87]

Chapter 10

The 'Unwritten Chapter' and
a Wilderness of Mirrors

The Eastern Fleet almost ceased to exist following Operation Stab. Just over a week after returning from the mission Somerville recorded that he was down to one carrier.[1] His second, and only other, carrier *Illustrious* didn't last much longer; she steamed away to the UK on 12 January 1943 where she was due for a refit and trialling new aircraft. That month also saw the losses of shipping in the Indian Ocean to enemy action fall dramatically. During November 1942 twenty-three ships, equating to 131,071 tons, had been lost, with six vessels, a total of 28,508 tons, sunk the following month. There were no losses at all in January.[2]

This hiatus was purely temporary; further submarines had been despatched south to carry on the work of *Gruppe Eisbär*. This follow-up, *Gruppe Seehund*, comprised four Type IXC boats, *U-506*, *U-516*, *U-509* and *U-160*. These had voyaged independently from their bases during December 1942 and January 1943, rendezvousing south of St. Helena with the tanker *U-459*.[3]

One unusual aspect of this mission was the participation of the Italian *Marconi* class submarine, *Leonardo da Vinci*, the *Regia Marina*'s highest scoring boat of the war with seventeen ships totalling 120,243 tons to her credit.[4] Perhaps unfortunately, from the Italian perspective, some 21,000 tons of this total came from a single vessel. This was the British Royal Mail Ship *Empress of Canada* which was sighted by the submarine on the night of 13/14 March whilst around 400 miles south of Las Palmas, Liberia, and on her way from Durban to Britain. The ship had nearly 2,000 souls aboard, including around 300–500 Italian prisoners of war and a number of women, several of whom were members of the British WRNS (Women's Royal Naval Service known colloquially as WRENS). About 440 people, including many Italians, were lost and, in a distinct and disturbing echo of the *Laconia* and *Nova Scotia* incidents, many survivors' accounts relate the presence of sharks and their depredations.[5]

The U-boats had meanwhile arrived off Cape Town, the first on 10 February, only to find slim pickings. Things had changed. As well as forming the South Atlantic Escort Force and equipping it with destroyers and corvettes seconded from the Eastern Fleet, the Allies had redeployed other anti-submarine forces to the area. These included twelve anti-submarine trawlers from UK waters and another eighteen from the American seaboard.[6] The South African Air Force (SAAF), in terms of both quantity and quality, had also been greatly reinforced.[7] The SAAF had also been reinforced by the RAF, and Catalina flying boats were based at Langebaan, Saldanha Bay (some 76 miles north of Cape Town) and Lake St. Lucia (about 168 miles north of Durban) in order to conduct long-range patrols. Thus, a system of escorted convoys had been instituted on 23 January 1943, and some 300 ships had voyaged unmolested.[8]

These measures account for the fact that only three boats, *U-506, U-509* and *U-516,* managed a successful attack and between them sent six vessels (36,650 tons) to the bottom. Such dismaying results meant the boats were ordered to proceed eastwards, in the hope that there would be better hunting off the coast of Natal.[9] There was, or at least for one boat which had been patrolling one of those Mahanian 'well-worn paths' off the Natal coast, between Durban and Port Shepstone, over the period 1–3 March.

On the afternoon of the latter date *U-160,* commanded by *Kapitänleutnant* Georg Lassen, spotted a convoy some 31 miles (50km) due east of Port Shepstone making 8 knots. It was identified as consisting of eight freighters and two tankers in two lines, with an escort of one 'U-boat hunter' with 'sound gear [ASDIC/SONAR] installed' on each side and a corvette forward. There were also three aircraft in attendance overhead. Unable to get in even a long shot, Lassen 'remained unnoticed and pursued'.[10]

He had in fact intercepted Convoy DN 21, which was being led by the 'Flower' class corvette *Nigella* with three anti-submarine trawlers, *Norwich City, Sondra* and *Viviana,* in attendance.[11] Displaying commendable coolness, and despite hearing the 'long steady tones' of the escorts' detection equipment, he surfaced after dark and ran *U-160* into the space between the lines of ships. At 21:22 hours, and at a position almost due east of the mouth of the Umngazi River, he began firing, discharging three torpedoes at the ships of the starboard line. The British steamship *Nirpura* was the first to go down, swiftly followed by the American *Harvey W Scott.* The Dutch tanker *Tibia* was hit but only damaged.

The escort immediately reacted, using searchlights and star shell to try and locate the attacker but with no success. *U-160* dropped back astern of the convoy, her War Diary noting the 'continuous tone' of the sound detection equipment and 'a strong depth charge shock' but she was neither found nor harmed. After letting 'things settle down', Lassen initiated a second attack. At 23:11 hours a pair of torpedoes hit the British *Empire Mahseer,* sending her to the bottom in two minutes. Once again Lassen allowed the remaining ships to draw ahead, though he noted at 23:20 hours that the convoy had split and there was no sign of the escorts.[12] He then stalked a group of three freighters that had headed off on an easterly course, catching up with them at 01:13 hours on 4 March and discharging a pair of torpedoes. Both missed, the inaccuracy being attributed to overestimating the targets' speed. A second attack was made at 01:46 hours, and this time it struck home, with two British vessels suffering hits; the *Sheaf Crown* and *Marietta E.* Both stopped dead in the water and were abandoned by their crews, whilst the third vessel escaped at maximum speed. Lassen let it go, his tubes needed reloading and he could 'no longer get in position for a night attack', and so turned to 'shoot a coup de grâce on the first steamer'. This either missed or failed to explode so a second shot was prepared. Before this could be delivered, however, a 'destroyer' was observed approaching; *U-160* withdrew and escaped unscathed.[13] The *Marietta E* later sank but *Sheaf Crown* remained afloat and was towed into East London on 7 March by the tug *Prudent*.[14]

It was a heavy blow. Churchill wrote on 5 March that he was 'shocked' at the 'very serious disaster' and questioned the Admiralty on the whereabouts of 'the destroyers which belong to the Eastern Fleet;' 'Are they all sharing the idleness of that fleet?'[15] The fact that the Eastern Fleet, such as it was, had become 'idle' because it had sent away its destroyers for convoy-escort duties had apparently passed the Prime Minister by. Nor, as Marder, Jacobsen and Horsefield noted, did he publish the reply from A. V. Alexander, the First Lord: 'Nowhere . . . are we sufficiently strong to be able to guarantee the safety of convoys . . . it is not possible to divert escort craft from other areas to the Cape.'[16] Churchill's response to this was that he was 'sure the Admiralty, as ever, are doing their best'.[17]

There is no indication in *U-160*'s War Diary (*Kriegstagebuch*), or indeed anywhere else, that the encounter with Convoy DN 21 occurred due to intelligence received, rather than the result of being in a known shipping lane at the right time. This was not necessarily the view of the naval and military authorities at the time. Espionage was suspected. Indeed, as noted by Bizley, on 4 March, and coincidental to the attack, Tait had issued a communique on that very subject:

> Never by word or deed give the enemy the slightest information about
> the movement of ships at sea. To win the war at sea he must have that
> information and he spends a fortune in an attempt to get it.[18]

One suspected source of intelligence on Allied ship movements originated, however, some 3,800 nautical miles distant from Durban; from Mormugao (Marmagoa) Harbour at Goa. Goa was a colonial enclave on India's west coast forming the main, and only sizeable, element of Portuguese India (*Índia Portuguesa* or *Estado da India*).[19] The particular source was later believed to be the German merchant vessel *Ehrenfels* which, along with three others (*Braunfels*, *Drachenfels* and the Italian *Anfora*), had become effectively marooned there at the outbreak of war in 1939 (or 1940 in the case of the Italian vessel). Three were basically tramp steamers, but *Ehrenfels* was a modern, fast vessel eminently suitable for conversion into an auxiliary cruiser like two of her close sisters.[20] A 'Most Secret Cipher Telegram' dated 24 December 1941 from General Wavell, the Commander-in-Chief, India, to the newly-appointed Chief of the Imperial General Staff, Sir Alan Brooke, outlined the situation as being 'intolerable:'

> . . . a number of German ships are lying in the harbour and their crews are at large. Wireless station is utilized continuously and there is a grave danger of leakage of information. There have been reports, though not confirmed, that port has recently been used by an enemy submarine.[21]

Portugal had declared, and maintained, neutrality throughout the war thus far, and the British Government was loath to do anything that compromised or breached it.[22] The Chiefs of Staff met on the same date as Wavell's message was received, and the subject of that message was the second item on their agenda. The minutes record that: 'The attention of the Committee was drawn to a telegram [21627/G cipher 23/12] . . . pointing out the unsatisfactory position in Goa.' The outcome being that the Admiralty were invited to 'examine and report on the Naval aspects of the problem'.[23] The conclusion was recorded in a letter written on Christmas Day 1941:

> Chiefs of Staff consider, and Foreign Office concur, that we should not (repeat not) attempt anything in Goa at present owing to delicate situation with Portuguese Government over Timor.[24]

So far as was publicly known or admitted, the situation of the Axis ships in Mormugao Harbour remained unchanged until March 1943. The weekly summary for the British War Cabinet in London, dated 11 March 1943, then neatly encapsulated what had occurred:

> Three German ships which have been at Mormugao since the autumn of 1939 were reported on the 8th March [*sic*] to be on fire. . . . All four ships are reported to have been scuttled as well as burnt and the crews are stated to have been taken under police supervision to Novagaya [Nova Goa, the Goan capital].[25]

Nothing further was generally known, or published, about how the ships had gone from their former state to being scuttled and burned; that is until the British author James Leasor published a book entitled *Boarding Party* in 1978.[26] This work was subsequently republished in paperback in 1980 as *The Sea Wolves*.[27] The cover also featured the wording 'Previously published as Boarding Party with a Foreword by Admiral of the Fleet Lord Mountbatten of Burma', and,

'Soon to be Major Film from Euan Lloyd, producer of *The Wild Geese*'. Indeed the film, starring Gregory Peck, Roger Moore, David Niven, Trevor Howard and Barbara Kellerman, premiered in London on 3 July that year.[28]

Leasor's book, of whatever edition, can be succinctly summarized. It reads like a novel, is unreferenced, and contains accounts of many conversations and scenes that can only have been imagined. The source of the raw material for these reconstructions is stated in the 'Acknowledgments': 'I am especially in the debt of Mr W. E. Catto, Mr Dan G. Haigh, and Major General Lewis Pugh, CB, CBE. DSO, for their kindness in supplying me with recollections, anecdotes and incidents concerning the Calcutta Light Horse and Operation Creek.'

It tells the tale of how, under the auspices of the British Special Operations Executive (SOE), a clandestine military mission was organized to stop the broadcasting of important information on Allied shipping movements from a secret transmitter aboard *Ehrenfels*.[29] Because of the location of the vessel, regular forces could not be utilized. Therefore the mission involved the recruitment of over-age members of the Calcutta Light Horse and Calcutta Scottish, both formations of the part-time Auxiliary Force (India).[30] Of the Auxiliary Force in general, a retired regular Indian Army officer (formerly of the 9th Gurkha Rifles) described it as follows:

> No race in the world, but the British could have evolved such an untidy military set up . . . Units which were clubs, in so far that no one could enlist unless he was accepted by the remainder of the unit, and who elected their Officers . . . Units which never paraded at above platoon strength and other anomalies . . .[31]

The detailed plan for the operation was drawn up by Lieutenant Colonel Lewis Henry Owain Pugh of the Royal Artillery.[32] Pugh was, at that time, seconded to SOE.[33] Two less drastic expedients were attempted before the resort to large-scale violence, the first being an attempt to bribe *Kapitän* Johann Röfer, commanding officer of *Ehrenfels*, to move the ship out of the harbour to where it could be captured. This failed: '. . . Röfer was totally unwilling to accept any bribe and would not even discuss the matter.'[34]

The second involved taking out the man perceived to be at the centre of affairs, a German codenamed Trompeta who lived in the Goan capital, Panjim (Panaji, Nova Goa). According to Leasor, Trompeta was 'in fact, one of Germany's two most important and successful spy-masters in the East. The other was Richard Sorge, in Tokyo . . .'[35] He was receiving information from a 24-year-old man named Ram das Gupta. Gupta worked as a clerk for a shipping firm in Bombay and had been persuaded by a 'middle-aged Indian woman' to 'supply details he learned in his work about ships, their ports of arrival and departure, their crews and speeds and cargoes'. This woman was, however, arrested by the police, and so Gupta stepped into her role, his task being to collect information from unknown others in the network, take it to Goa, and pass it on to Trompeta, a journey he made eleven times.[36]

Pugh and a second SOE operative, Major Gavin Burton Stewart, journeyed to Panjim in the guise of businessmen with the objective of kidnapping Trompeta.[37] The next day they lunched with the British Consul to Goa and, from him, obtained the German agent's address. Leasor then describes how Trompeta and his wife, the presence of whom had not been suspected, were kidnapped the next morning at gunpoint, forcibly bundled into a car, and sedated with pentothal before being driven away for interrogation at Bombay. There Trompeta provided 'a description of an Indian courier', Ram das Gupta, who was picked up 'as he came off the bus from Goa'. A further lead, or leads, were obtained and 'someone else' was 'also telling what he knows'. The spy ring had not, however, been dismantled; further messages were being sent and ships lost.[38] Leasor did not know what happened subsequently to Trompeta and his wife, 'whether they returned to Germany after the war, or stayed in India'.[39]

With the failure of all efforts to stop the radio messages and, according to Duckett, under 'pressure from London' the head of SOE India, Colin Hercules Mackenzie, approved an attack on *Ehrenfels*.[40] Pugh's plan was therefore sanctioned.

In the subsequent tale as related by Leasor, and often repeated and embellished, the plan was relatively simple. It involved the chosen team, consisting of fourteen men from the Calcutta Light Horse, four from the Calcutta Scottish and six regular soldiers attached to SOE, journeying to Cochin, a city bordering the Laccadive Sea on India's south-west coast. There they were to rendezvous with a vessel to take them the rest of the way by sea. This turned out to be a hopper-barge ('a bloody great floating iron bath with an engine'[41]) named *Phoebe*, normally employed in keeping the Hooghly River navigable, which had been redeployed from West Bengal. Now it was to steam northwards from Cochin along India's west coast towards Goa, a three-day voyage of around 334 nautical miles at 5 knots, a journey which had been so timed that arrival would take place on the night of 9/10 March 1943.

In the interim much skulduggery had taken place at Mormugao, the object being to lure ashore as many officers and men from the four vessels as possible. To that end, houses of ill repute had received largesse to the extent that sailors ashore that night had free use of their amenities. For those with slightly more sophisticated tastes, a local notable had been induced to host a soiree for officers and officials, whilst the services of the local taxis had been engaged to ensure passage back to the harbour was rendered problematical.[42] The British Consul at Goa and his wife were ordered to Bombay to forestall any accusations of complicity.[43]

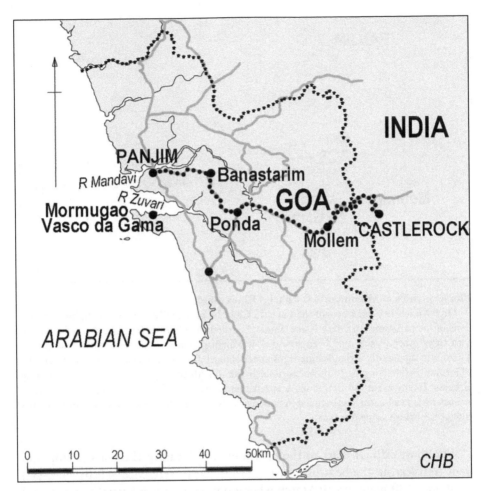

Panjim and the Road to Castle Rock. © Charles Blackwood.

On the morning of 19 December 1942, Robert and Grethe Koch, two German residents of Panjim, the capital of the Portuguese colony of Goa, were kidnapped by SOE agents and spirited away to British India. Or at least that's the tale told by James Leasor in his 1978 book entitled *Boarding Party* (subsequently reissued and filmed as *The Sea Wolves*). Robert Koch, codenamed Trompeta, had arrived in Goa aboard the German freighter *Ehrenfels* in 1939 and, along with the ship, had then been unable to leave. According to Leasor's account, he was at the centre of a spy-ring broadcasting Allied shipping information to U-boats, and thus responsible for extensive shipping losses in the Indian Ocean. Later research suggests that there was no abduction, and in any event the 'broadcasts' continued, leading to more vigorous measures being undertaken.

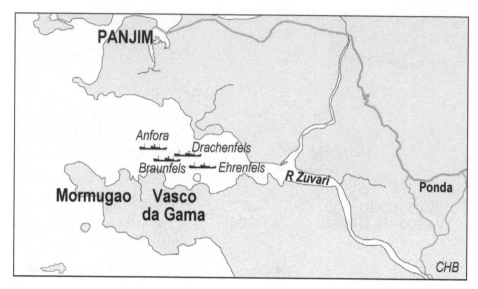

The Axis ships at Murmagao. © Charles Blackwood.

On 9 March 1943 members of the Calcutta Light Horse and Calcutta Scottish, both formations of the part-time Auxiliary Force (India), boarded the German freighter *Ehrenfels* which, with three other vessels, had been stranded at Murmagao in Goa since the outbreak of war. There was supposedly a clandestine transmitter aboard *Ehrenfels*, which had been utilized by a German-Indian spy ring to broadcast information on Allied shipping movements to waiting U-boats. In any event, all four ships scuttled themselves upon the attack. The account later written by James Leasor was branded 'A fictional story . . . Very fictional' by Anne Bremner, the wife of the British Consul at Goa.

The most difficult part of the operation was locating the correct ship and then transferring the boarding party onto it. Both were successfully managed by about 02:30 hours on 10 March whereupon there was a firefight and several Germans, though no raiders, were killed.[44] Five members of the *Ehrenfels'* crew were later found dead and three declared missing. Two bodies remained unidentified, including one assumed to be of the commanding officer of the ship, *Kapitän* Johann Röfer.[45] Dependent on which version of the tale is believed, the raiders either destroyed[46] or removed[47] the transmitter before being forced to evacuate the vessel when she began listing; the remaining crew had scuttled her. Hearing the commotion, the crews of the other three Axis ships followed suit; all the ships had made preparations for doing so in the event of an attack. Amazingly all the attackers escaped back onto *Phoebe* largely unscathed and, along with three prisoners, made it to Bombay.

Operation Creek/Longshanks,[48] as the attack was dubbed, can be categorized as falling very much amongst those 'Deeds That Thrill the Empire'. This is so even though the Empire could never know about it, and had long become 'one with Nineveh and Tyre' by the time the story came out in 1978.[49]

Indeed, a history of the Calcutta Light Horse, written by 'a Committee of Light Horsemen' and published in 1957 contains a section heading 'The Unwritten Chapter' in 'Chapter VI: The War, 1939–1945'. 'This portion of the history', the reader is informed, 'is suppressed for reasons of security.'[50]

There is no doubt that the events of 9/10 March 1943 as described by Leasor took place. Nor can it be stated that his portrayal of them is wildly inaccurate, despite that they were related to him some thirty years after the event. But there are definitely some anomalies in the account more generally. This is unsurprising, particularly when attempting to make sense of matters related to intelligence and espionage. Indeed the significance behind the phrase 'a wilderness of mirrors', as adopted by James Angleton, starts to become comprehensible.[51] The treatment of Trompeta is an example, and though it ill behoves an author to draw attention to 'clangers' in the work of another (karma always lurks patiently in the background) the comparison of Trompeta with Richard Sorge certainly comprises one. Sorge was far from being a German 'spy-master'; he was a communist agent spying for the Soviet Union.[52]

There is also evidence that the kidnapping of Trompeta and his wife was a story fabricated by Pugh.[53] Trompeta's real name was Robert Koch, and he lived in Panjim with his wife Grethe, having arrived there aboard the *Ehrenfels* in 1939.[54] He had been identified by Dutch intelligence as an *Abwehr* (German military intelligence) agent and his presence aboard *Ehrenfels* had been made known to Pugh when the ship had called at Calcutta in August of that same year. Indeed, Pugh had laid plans to 'detain' him should he have left the ship. He didn't, and of course travelled on to Goa when the ship departed suddenly without a pilot and without authorization.[55] The British Consul at Goa, Lieutenant Colonel Claude Edward Urquhart Bremner, who had been appointed in November 1940, was suspicious of Koch as well. According to Miller he 'repeatedly informed New Delhi of the threat posed by his presence'. A signal of 19 November 1942 is used as an example:

> . . . Robert Koch, the directing brain of the Nazi refugees here is allowed full liberty of movement and from his residence in Nova Goa can (and does) proceed anywhere and everywhere at all times of the day and night. From the contact he is known to have, it is unlikely that his activities are other than subversive.[56]

There are some questions about Bremner's reliability in such matters, however. Sir Olaf Caroe, British India's Foreign Secretary from 1939 to 1945 who 'served under three Viceroys',[57] opined in 1942:

> He is inclined to dramatize himself and his work, and his reports and advice are not always distinguished for a wise perspective. These aspects are a part of his nature, and are, I fear, incurable.[58]

If this were the only criticism of that nature then it might be easily discounted. However, it was not. Bremner had previously, in 1932, served in Muscat (Oman) as a Political Agent reporting to Trenchard Craven William Fowle, the Political Resident in the Persian Gulf who was responsible for Britain's relations with the entire region.[59] Fowle thought him a poor judge of character, impulsive, unable to size up situations and given to exaggeration. His final judgment, made whilst Bremner was absent, was damning: 'For as long as I am Resident, I would prefer he did not return.'[60] Similar judgements were passed on his abilities after he returned to India from the Middle East in 1936. Then his superiors noted 'a tendency to express immoderate views on insufficient data or even no data at all' and, the following year, he was judged to be 'too easily prejudiced against individuals by gossip related to him'.[61] None of these criticisms necessarily mean that Bremner was wrong in his judgment about Koch, and it is the case that activities that were definitely 'subversive' from the British perspective had been considered by Germany in relation to Goa.[62]

The evidence that the Kochs were not kidnapped and left Goa willingly is fragmentary and comes from three sources. The first, and most authoritative, is the report from Pugh to McKenzie of 15 March 1943:

> After a brief discussion they were persuaded to proceed to British India by car. They were driven openly through the streets of Panjim and across the . . . frontier at about 10:30 hours on 19 December without let or hindrance from the Customs posts, where normal formalities were observed.[63]

At least partial contemporaneous corroboration of this account was unearthed by the Goan author Dr P. P. Shirodkar, whose work is based mostly on Portuguese archival documentation available at the Goa Archives.[64] According to his research, following the disappearance the local police (*Corpo de Polícia e Fiscalização da Índia*) investigated the matter and recorded witness statements to the effect that the Kochs had left Goa with two other Europeans. The party had been seen at three places, Banastarim, Ponda and Mollem, on the road to Castle Rock (which marked the British side of the frontier and was over a three-hour drive away from Panaji at that period), but no uneasiness had been observed on the faces of the Germans, nor had they made any requests for help.[65] Shirodkar does go on to say that on arrival at Castle Rock the couple were killed.[66]

The third piece of evidence comes from the widow of the British Consul at Panaji, Anne Bremner. Mrs Bremner wrote a short, retrospective though of unknown date, manuscript account of life in India entitled 'India during the British Raj: Recollections of Kathiawar, Quetta, Goa'. The portion dealing with Goa, just over six typewritten pages entitled 'Goa. Portuguese India. November 1940. October 1943' was published in Portuguese as 'A Segunda Guerra Mundial em Goa: o manuscrito de Anne Bremner' in 2015.[67] In this she states:

> Koch's wife was unwell and he had written to the Red Cross asking if he could take her to British India. One day two men came and lunched with us at the British Consulate. They said they were staying at a hotel in town. Next day the Kochs had gone, so had the two Englishmen. At the frontier the book was signed by Mr and Mrs Cook, Journalists. The police charged into the Consulate [the Kochs's house] and turned everything upside down.[68]

Taken together, the available evidence suggests that Robert and Grethe Koch went willingly with Pugh and Stewart, rather than being forcibly abducted. We can probably discount Shirodkar's account of them being murdered upon arrival in British territory; as Miller points out, it is hardly likely that would happen before an extensive interrogation had taken place.[69] His contention that the kidnaping tale was counterfeited to cover up their defection seems the best explanation, though why this deceit was necessary some thirty years after the event remains a mystery, as does what happened to the couple afterwards.[70]

But perhaps the most important point is that even after the removal of Trompeta, Gupta, and 'someone else', from the equation, the radio broadcasts continued.[71] According to one account the mole in the Ministry of Shipping and Transport at Bombay, now delivered information on Allied shipping movements to 'the German Consulate at Panaji'.[72] This cannot have been the case; Germany had no such representative in Goa. German diplomatic services for Portuguese-India (*Portugiesich-Indien*) had fallen under the remit of *Generalkonsul* Count Bogislav von Dönhoff based in Bombay. He, of course, had been compelled to leave at the outbreak of war in 1939.[73] Confusingly, Anne Bremner says that Koch (whom she always refers to as 'Herman') was the German consul.[74] Whatever the methodology employed however, the unintended destruction of *Ehrenfels* seemingly put a stop to it.

Indeed, according to conventional wisdom, the effect of the raid was rapid and 'produced a dramatic and almost immediate decline in shipping losses from German U-boats'. Leasor relates how, amongst losses amounting to twelve ships during the first eleven days of March, '*U-160* alone sank 10'.[75] In fact the *U-160*, whilst it had *torpedoed* ten ships, had sunk only eight. Four of these ten, plus the pair that were hit but survived, had been in Convoy DN 21 which had originated at Durban.[76] In any event, and whatever the numbers, he made the point so as to demonstrate a sharp contrast between the period before, and that following, the events of 9/10 March; that there was, in other words, a question of cause and effect. In this he is explicit, going on to say:

> . . . without the radio messages to give precise details of speed, destination, cargo and other material factors, U-boat commanders now had to rely only on luck or chance for their kill. During the rest of March, the 13 German U-boats operating in the Indian Ocean only sank one ship.[77]

In fact U-boat Command had not been satisfied by *Seehund*'s overall performance and the *Gruppe* was recalled on 14 March; all had reached their pens at Lorient by 11 May. The only real success achieved was that by Lassen and *U-160*; as Bizley put it: 'It had been an almost one-man affair.'[78] Moreover, the contention that messages from Goa had been instrumental in the depredations Lassen inflicted on Convoy DN 21 is unsupported by evidence. It appears even more doubtful that detailed information pertaining to the convoy would have been obtainable in Bombay and, even if it was, easily accessible to a clerk. However, even if such precise data relating to 'speed, destination and cargo', were available and had been acquired, it would then have had to be conveyed to Goa, handed over to someone, encoded and then broadcast to the waiting U-boats. Leasor, via what can only be a reconstructed conversation involving Pugh, records that the British were able to read these messages.[79] This at least makes sense. If the *Ehrenfels* had an Enigma machine then it would have been the M2 version, introduced in 1938 and not superseded until 1940 by the M3.[80] In other words, the British would have been able to take pre-emptive action. That they did not suggests the messages were never sent. Interestingly, Anne Bremner's short account of her time in Goa gives a slightly different twist to the story in general:

> The Germans had radio equipment to radio out messages and receive them. They were able to transmit the names of allied shipping arriving in Bombay or departing. Their receiving equipment was on the *Ehrenfels*. To transmit to a submarine they had a vehicle that they were able to drive about in. The Portuguese were unable to do anything about it except to protest, which they did regularly.[81]

Be that as it may, according to Miller, who has studied the matter carefully, nowhere in the available records is there 'the slightest suggestion that the U-boats were receiving information from clandestine transmitters anywhere on the Indian sub-continent, let alone Goa'.[82] If this be accepted, as I think it must be, then it raises a further matter. For if there were no secret radio transmitter aboard the German vessel, then the whole downstream espionage organization disappears. What would have been the point of it? A rhetorical question of course, but in answering it the conclusion that Trompeta wasn't in receipt of any classified shipping information brought to him by Ram das Gupta via the Bombay-Goa bus, or the 'middle-aged Indian woman' in Bombay, is inescapable. We are indeed in a 'wilderness of mirrors' made even more unnavigable by noting that, unless the couple were indeed shot out of hand once they were across the Goa-India border, Koch would have surely told his interrogators this and, accordingly, dispelled any *idée fixe* pertaining. If this is so, then why was Creek/Longshanks carried out at all?[83]

The simplest explanation is probably that which Leasor relates Pugh giving to Colonel William Henry Grice, the Commanding Officer of the Calcutta Light Horse, which Grice then passed on to the team whilst aboard *Phoebe*: that *Ehrenfels* might make a break for Singapore and there be fitted with weaponry to become 'a most dangerous merchant cruiser'.[84]

Perhaps this was felt to be a little too mundane for popular consumption. The espionage story at least imbues the episode with some glamour, which the mere sinking of four merchant vessels at anchor probably lacks. Perhaps the last word, from a handwritten appendix to her manuscript, should go to Anne Bremner:

> With regard to the sinking of the ships, I swore to keep a secret. I have never told anyone, although questioned by American and British journalists. So I was surprised when, in 1978, I saw a Sunday Express poster about the sinking of the ships in Goa. A fictional story by James Leasor. Very fictional.[85]

Chapter 11

The Penang Submarines

President Roosevelt and Prime Minister Churchill, together with their foremost military and naval advisors, met in conference at Casablanca in French Morocco from 14–24 January 1943. The leader of the third mainstay of the Grand Alliance, Stalin, was unable to attend; 'Front business absolutely prevents it', he had informed Roosevelt on 17 December 1942.[1] The 'Front business' in question was the titanic, and decisive, Battle of Stalingrad. Indeed, Stalin himself wrote out the 31 January newsflash proclaiming the eventual result: 'Today our armies trapped the commander of the Sixth Army near Stalingrad with all his staff . . .'[2] The most well-known outcome of the Casablanca Conference, codenamed Symbol, is probably the surprise announcement by Roosevelt that the Allies would accept nothing less than the 'unconditional surrender' of the Axis powers.[3]

Such decisions were of course a matter of high politics. At a slightly less elevated level, and with the job of working out how to actually achieve the goals set by their political chiefs, of reconciling means with ends, sat the Combined Chiefs of Staff (CCS) comprising the British Chiefs of Staff (COS) and the American Joint Chiefs of Staff (JCS). Set up in January 1942, the CCS were tasked with formulating the military and logistical strategies 'that seemed best suited to bring about Allied victory in World War II as quickly as possible'.[4] Given that the CCS was based in Washington DC, the actual Chiefs themselves met only intermittently, though liaison between them was maintained via the British Joint Staff Mission to the United States.

Unsurprisingly, the US Navy, as represented on the CCS by Admiral Ernest J King, who was both Commander-in-Chief (COMINCH) of the US Fleet and Chief of Naval Operations (CNO), had its main focus on the campaigns in the Pacific.[5] The minutes of the CCS meeting of 14 January 1943 reflect this.[6] They record the opinion of the US Army, as embodied by Chief of Staff General George C. Marshall, concerning the allocation of resources between the two major theatres of war; the Atlantic 'which included for this purpose the Mediterranean', and the Pacific. He suggested that the 'broad allocation should consist of 70 percent in the Atlantic theater and 30 percent in the Pacific theater'. King reckoned that, at the time, only 15 per cent of Allied total resources were being deployed against the Japanese in the Pacific, an area within which he included the Indian Ocean and Burma. 'This', he argued, 'was not sufficient to prevent Japan consolidating herself.' Marshall agreed and made the point that the United States Chiefs of Staff were 'anxious to find some method whereby they can strike in the rear and against the flank of the Japanese defenses'. Operations in Burma would 'serve to weaken the Japs' defensive front' therefore the Americans were 'most anxious' that they were undertaken. Northern Burma formed the only available 'land-bridge between India and China' so operations there would also have the object of 'reopening the supply routes to China'.[7]

Reinforcing China was a vital American strategic interest. The Chinese were tying down a huge amount of Japanese manpower and resources, the best part of a million troops, but needed logistical support via the only possible land route; through Burma. Keeping these Japanese resources out of the Pacific and away from American forces was the aim of Admiral King and of the US in general.[8]

The actual land route in question, the Burma Road, had been built in 1938. It ran from Lashio, a town in northern Burma about 120 miles north-east of Mandalay, for a distance of some 717 miles to Kunming, the capital and largest city of Yunnan province in south-west China. It has been described as 'a dirt-track, only some 9 ft. wide' which wound 'in and out of heavily wooded hills, plumbing the depths of fantastic gorges, rising precipitously to giddy heights, wriggling back and forth, up and down'. Nevertheless, it was 'the artery through which was pumped the life-blood of China at war'.[9] Supplies for China were landed at Rangoon then shipped via metre gauge (3ft 3⅜in) rail over a distance of some 580 miles to Lashio. The last section of this line, the 180 miles from Mandalay, had been constructed in the early 1900s 'in the face of considerable engineering difficulties'.[10] In short, and to maintain the arterial metaphor, the Burma Road was somewhat atherosclerotic and could only trickle life-blood into China. Nevertheless, it had been, perforce, all that was available until the Japanese Army conquered northern Burma in 1942 and shut it down permanently.

The substitute for the Burma Road, for furthering the American strategy of keeping China in the war, was the trans-Himalayan airlift over 'The Hump', the eastern end of the Himalayan Range. This, according to Plating, 'is recognized . . . as the first sustained and most ambitious combat airlift operation in modern history'.[11] Maintaining this 'aerial umbilical' was an incredible effort.[12] Small wonder then that the United States Joint Chiefs wanted the Burma Road reopened as quickly as possible. The problems associated with conducting military operations against northern Burma from bases in India were, however, manifold and severe. The communication difficulties, and concomitant supply problems, have already been mentioned. Even limited, narrow-front operations that could be supported, such as the Arakan Offensive that began

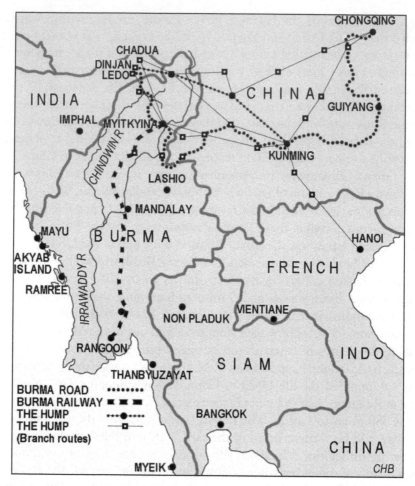

The China-Burma-India Theatre and the Burma Road. © Charles Blackwood.

Sustaining and reinforcing China was a vital American strategic interest; the Chinese were tying down the best part of a million Japanese troops, which might otherwise be redeployed to the Pacific. The only possible land route for providing logistical support to Chiang's regime was though via the Burma Road, which had been constructed in 1938. It ran from Lashio, a town in northern Burma about 120 miles north-east of Mandalay, for a distance of some 717 miles to Kunming, the capital and largest city of Yunnan province in south-west China. The Japanese conquest of northern Burma in 1942 shut it down permanently, leaving the trans-Himalayan airlift over 'The Hump', the eastern end of the Himalayan Range, as the only substitute. The Japanese occupying forces were however dependent upon sea lines of communication, which passed through the Malacca Strait and the Andaman Sea, to Rangoon. The Eastern Fleet was too weak to take advantage, but in an effort to at least partially overcome this potential vulnerability, the Japanese Army began the construction of the infamous 258-mile Burma Railway, connecting Non Pladuk in Thailand with Thanbyuzayat in Burma, in June 1942.

The British Aviation Mission to Japan. The ranks stated are those that were used in Japan. Warrant Officer Earwaker is missing from the photograph. Rear Row L–R: 1. Warrant Officer Bond. 2. Warrant Officer Crisp. 3. Warrant Officer Ford. 4. Warrant Officer Sherras. 5. Warrant Officer Satchell. 6. Warrant Officer Hunter. 7. Warrant Officer Williams. 8. Warrant Officer Adams. Middle Row L–R: 1. Warrant Officer Ellis. 2. Warrant Officer John Redmond. 3. Lieutenant Robert Malcolm Brutnell. 4. Lieutenant George Rudolph Volkert. 5. Lieutenant Arthur George Loton. 6. Unknown Japanese Officer; possibly Rear Admiral Tajiri Tadatsugu. 7. Lieutenant William Pollard. 8. Lieutenant Arthur Wellesley Hatfield. 9. Lieutenant Alfred Stanley Sheret. 10. Lieutenant Edward Charles Landamore. 11. Warrant Officer Manton. Front Row L–R: 1. Lieutenant Walter Edward George Bryant. 2. Lieutenant Hugh Raymond Vaughan. Fowler. 3. Major Charles Henry Chichester Smith. 4. Major Felton Clayson Atkinson. 5. Major Fowler. 6. Captain the Honourable William Francis Forbes-Sempill. 7. Lieutenant-Colonel Cecil Henry Meares. 8. Major William Hugh Jackson Eldridge. 9. Major Herbert George Brackley. 10. Major Thomas Orde-Lees. 11. Surgeon Lieutenant W. F. Jones.
(Source: Frida H Brackley (ed.), *Brackles: Memoirs of a Pioneer of Civil Aviation* (Chatham; W & J Mackay, 1952))

An Italian Sound Locator.
(Source: *L'Illustrazione Italiana*, 27 Agosto 1939 XVII)

The German ships at Mormugao (Marmagoa) Harbour, Goa. (Source: http://www.ddghansa-shipsphotos.de/ehrenfels500.htm)

The Officers of the Calcutta Light Horse in 1944. Colonel William Henry 'Bill' Grice, commanding officer from 1939 to 1944, is seated in the centre of the front row. (Source: A Committee of Light Horsemen, *Calcutta Light Horse AF(I), 1759-1881-1947* (Aldershot; Gale & Polden, 1957))

HMS *Cornwall*. (Source: Author's collection)

HMS *Dorsetshire*. (Source: Author's collection)

HMS *Erebus*. (Source: Author's collection)

HMS *Glorious*. (Source: Author's collection)

HMS *Hermes*. (Source: Author's collection)

Hosho. (Source: Kure Maritime Museum)

HMS *Indomitable*. (Source: http://www.militarystory.org/hms-indomitable-torpedo-damage-16th-july-1943/)

Penang: Japanese and German sailors at a reception for the crew of *U-511* which berthed there on 17 July 1943 whilst voyaging to Japan. (Source: Public domain)

HMS *Ramillies*. (Source: Author's collection)

HMS *Renown*. (Source: Author's collection)

HMS *Repulse*. (Source: Author's collection)

Richelieu. (Source: Public domain)

Shokaku. (Source: Yamato Museum)

HMS *Warspite*. (Source: Author's collection)

Admiral Sir James Somerville. (Source: Donald Macintyre, *Fighting Admiral: The Life of Admiral of the Fleet Sir James Somerville* (London; Evans Brothers, 1961) frontispiece)

The Combined Chiefs of Staff with Roosevelt and Churchill at Quebec 1944.

Rear Row L–R: Major General Leslie Hollis (Secretary to the Chiefs of Staff), General Hastings Ismay, Admiral Ernest J. King, Air Chief Marshal Charles Portal, General Henry H. Arnold, Admiral Andrew Cunningham.

Front Row L–R: General George C Marshall, Admiral William D Leahy, President Roosevelt, Prime Minister Churchill, Field Marshal Alan Brooke, Field Marshal John Dill.

(Source: Public domain)

on 17 December 1942 along the Mayu Peninsula, ran into trouble because of
the terrain:

> The Arakan is the swampy jungle covered mountainous tract in west
> Burma bordering on East Bengal . . . [It] comprises jungle-covered
> swamps which run down to a narrow coastal strip of paddy fields
> and mangrove swamps. The hills and the coastal are intersected by
> hundreds of *chaungs* [watercourses] and tidal creeks often many miles
> long. Most of them were unfordable and offered few landing points.
> The whole region is highly malarial.[13]

The main goal of the Arakan advance, dubbed Operation Cannibal, was Akyab
Island, which had a port and all-weather airfield. These facilities were prominent in Allied notions of recovering Burma, or at least useful in harassing
the Japanese occupiers; Akyab was some 310 miles distant from Rangoon, the
Burmese capital and premier port, by air. Aircraft based at Akyab would also be
able to support any future Allied advances into central Burma. The attack on
Akyab struggled and eventually failed for various reasons, not the least of which
were the difficult conditions and the Japanese Army's ability to exploit them for
defensive purposes.[14] In Churchill's mellifluous, and oft-quoted, phraseology:
'going into swampy jungles to fight the Japanese is like going into the water
to fight a shark'.[15] Nor, at that time, was an advance deep into Burmese territory anything more than an aspiration. What was planned was 'a very modest
advance to the banks of the Chindwin River'.[16]

Code-named Operation Ravenous, this circa 60-mile advance was to be
based on Imphal in the Kingdom of Manipur, one of British India's princely
states. This movement was to be supported by Chinese forces driving south
from Yunnan. There was though a complication; Chinese participation, as iter-
ated by Generalissimo Chiang Kai-shek, the head of the National Government
of the Republic of China (Nationalist China), was conditional upon the Japanese
being prevented from reinforcing their forces in northern Burma.[17] This was a
constant refrain from Chiang, who was still pushing the point later the same
year.[18] That he had a point was unquestionable; the occupiers were dependent upon seaborne transport for their logistical support until such time as the
infamous 258-mile Burma Railway, connecting Non Pladuk in Thailand with
Thanbyuzayat in Burma which had been started in June 1942, was completed.[19]

Preventing the Japanese reinforcing therefore meant interdicting the sea lanes
from the south. These stretched along a 2,000-mile sea lane through the Malacca
Strait and the Andaman Sea, to Rangoon. There was though, '. . . no question of
the Eastern Fleet pursuing serious naval operations in early 1943, for its strength
had shrunk further to three battleships (the *Warspite*, *Revenge*, and *Resolution*),

three cruisers and some half a dozen destroyers.'[20] Indeed, Somerville had opposed lending any naval support to amphibious operations, including those that might have assisted with the operations along the Mayu Peninsula, without substantial carrier-based air support.[21] The lessons attendant on the destruction of *Prince of Wales* and *Repulse* were only just over a year in the past. His was not a lone view. Layton, the C-in-C at Ceylon, had noted as far back as 21 January 1942 that:

> . . . retaining control of the coastal waters of Burma was quite beyond our powers in the absence of either air superiority or fast patrol craft with good anti-aircraft armament so numerous that we could afford substantial losses.[22]

Nevertheless, at the Casablanca Conference, General Marshall explained that the United States Joint Chiefs of Staff were anxious that Operation Ravenous should go ahead. Offensive operations in Burma, he argued, 'will serve to weaken the Japs' defensive front'. He went on:

> A successful Operation Ravenous would result in an eventual economy of tonnage by relieving the Japanese pressure in the Southwest Pacific.[23]

Admiral Pound responded that though the creation of a significant Eastern Fleet had been intended, the requirements of higher-priority operations in the Mediterranean and North Africa had stymied this. The fleet had lost its only carrier *Illustrious* on 12 January 1943 when she had returned to the UK. He went on: 'Without the protection of carrier aircraft, the Eastern Fleet is unable to operate in the eastern part of the Indian Ocean against Japanese naval forces accompanied by aircraft carriers.' He might have added that the same applied to land-based bombers as well.

Neither could the Eastern Fleet emulate their opponents, or indeed their American allies, in conducting an effective submarine campaign; Japanese shipping in the sea lanes off Burma and Malaya's west coast remained largely undisturbed due to a paucity of resources. In January 1943 there were only two submarines, based at Colombo, available for operations; the modern British 'T' class boat *Trusty*, launched in 1941, and the Dutch *O 21* class boat *O 24* of similar vintage. A second boat, *O 23*, had been rendered non-operational by engine problems in December 1942; the Dutch pair had been placed under British operational control in December 1941.[24] Even when all three boats were available it was not possible to keep one out on patrol continually. Such patrols, mainly operating in and around the Malacca Strait, had three primary objects; to give warning of Japanese naval forces debouching into the Bay of Bengal; to interdict the sea-lanes to Burma; and to intercept Japanese submarines toing and froing from Penang.[25]

The Japanese Navy had first started to create a submarine base at George Town, capital of Penang Island, in the first week of February 1942.[26] Separated from the mainland by a narrow strait and located in a strategically important spot at the northern end of the Malacca Strait, the island had never featured a naval base and so had neither a skilled workforce nor infrastructure. The extemporized base was located on George Town's Swettenham Pier, an iron T-shaped structure completed in 1904 and extended over the next seven years to provide 1,200ft of wharfage.[27] Three or four boats could tie up at any one time and at high tide their decks were about level with the pier. It wasn't an easy task to come alongside due to the powerful tidal race, and approaches had to be from the north due to the south channel being mined.[28]

Though routine maintenance and minor repairs could be undertaken at Penang, major overhauls necessitated a voyage to Singapore, 415 nautical miles distant, or mainland Japan, a journey of some 3,500 nautical miles.[29] As already noted, the 1st Division of Japan's 8th Submarine Flotilla had been redeployed to Penang, but of greater significance for the Allies in the Indian Ocean was the arrival at Swettenham Pier, on 28 August 1943, of the German submarine *U-178*.[30] Her captain, *Korvettenkapitän* Wilhelm Dommes, became the commander of the base there, where both he and his command managed to live in some style. The crew members were housed in George Town's Elysee Hotel where 'electric chamber fans are constantly spinning on the ceilings, and the ice cabinets are always well filled'.[31]

This rare joint venture by the Axis was actually a tripartite enterprise. On 26 August the Italian *Marconi* class boat *Aquila VI*, formerly *Luigi Torelli*, had arrived at Sabang; an island off the north-west tip of Sumatra and about 300 nautical miles east of Penang.[32] Two more Italian boats, the *Liuzzi* class *Reginaldo Giuliani* and the *Marcello* class *Commandante Cappellini* (re-designated as *Aquila II* and *Aquila III* respectively), had already made similar voyages to Singapore and Sabang.[33]

The Penang base lacked most of the facilities required for a proper dockyard, but it was out of range of Allied land-based bombers. The strengthening of the logistical chain, attendant on the deployment of supply submarines, meant that it could at least potentially support a U-boat campaign in the Indian Ocean, and its use would remove the requirement for the boats to make long voyages to and from France.[34]

Given Dönitz's strategic philosophy that enemy shipping constituted a single entity, and it was therefore immaterial where a ship was sunk, then the Indian Ocean became attractive as a theatre in mid-1943. It did so because it was where that 'race between sinkings and new construction' might be tilted in favour of Germany. They had had started inclining very much in the other direction

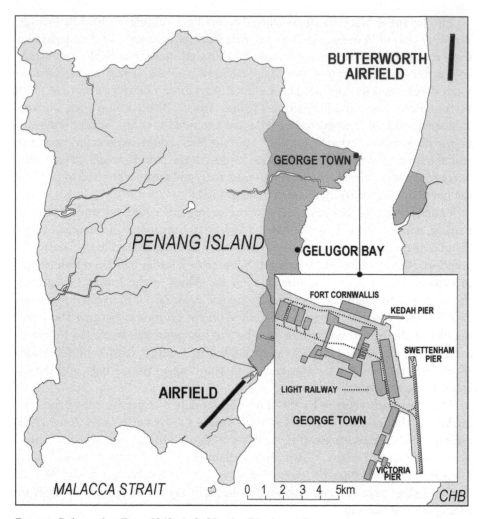

Penang Submarine Base 1943–4. © Charles Blackwood.

The Japanese Navy had established a submarine base at George Town, capital of Penang Island, in the first week of February 1942. Separated from the mainland by a narrow strait, and located in a strategically important spot at the northern end of the Malacca Strait, the extemporized base was located at Swettenham Pier, an iron T- shaped structure with 1,200ft of wharfage. The first U-boat, *U-178*, arrived at Swettenham Pier on 28 August 1943 and her commanding officer, *Korvettenkapitän* Wilhelm Dommes, became the commander of the base. Whilst routine maintenance and minor repairs could be undertaken at Penang, major overhauls necessitated a voyage to Singapore.

in April when the man fighting the Battle of the Atlantic on the Allied side, Admiral Sir Max Horton, went on the offensive. Thanks to Ultra intelligence he knew that more than a hundred U-boats were working in wolf-packs in mid-Atlantic where they were out of range of Allied land-based aircraft. A fierce proponent of air-sea cooperation, Horton had established a school of anti-submarine warfare at Larne, Northern Ireland, where fast naval support groups, increasingly including small escort carriers, learned their trade. When Horton unleashed these resources in conjunction with an additional air offensive to destroy U-boats as they crossed the Bay of Biscay the results were devastating.[35] The combined depredations inflicted on the German forces was such that at the end of May, Dönitz withdrew his U-boats stating, 'we have lost the battle of the Atlantic'. Though far from final, it was nevertheless a famous victory.[36]

The move in search of easier pickings began in June 1943 with the staggered despatch of eleven U-boats from French, Norwegian and German ports. Legend has it that their voyages were timed so that arrival in the theatre coincided with the end of the monsoon season, and this gave rise to their designation as *Gruppe Monsun*.[37] The Indian Ocean might have been considered safer to operate in than the Atlantic, but the boats still had to run the gauntlet of increasingly effective Allied anti-submarine measures on the voyage. Indeed, only six, *U-168*, *U-183*, *U-188*, *U-516*, *U-532* and *U-533*, reached southern Africa successfully where *U-516* refuelled the rest before turning around for home.[38] Replenishment was also undertaken by the five remaining boats when they rendezvoused with the supply ship *Brake* some 450 nautical miles south of Madagascar on 8 September.[39] This was of course the date upon which it was announced that Italy had surrendered to the Allies following the signing of the Armistice of Cassibile in Sicily five days earlier.[40]

The chaos that followed the announcement 'traumatized Italy' according to O'Hara and Cernuschi. They note however that whilst the army and air force disintegrated, the *Regia Marina* maintained its discipline and most of its forces, and stomached the terms that had been agreed.[41] Indeed, most of the navy then changed sides, forming the *Regia Marina Cobelligerante* to fight alongside their former foes. It thus became a 'useful ally' and 'the only one of Italy's armed forces to effectively fight the Germans'.[42]

The detaching of Italy from the Axis had effects on the Indian Ocean theatre. It had become possible for Allied convoys to be routed through the Mediterranean since victory in North Africa had been achieved in May 1943.[43] Now the Italian fleet had not only been removed from the enemy part of the equation, but a large proportion of it had moved to the other side. This gain was, all things considered, probably exceeded by the increase in Allied merchant capacity which came about when the necessity of routeing convoys around

South Africa disappeared. This extra capacity was, in effect, 'new construction', thus allowing the Allies to draw further ahead in the race with the 'sinkings' that Donitz was attempting to compete in. It also meant of course that there were fewer opportunities for Axis submarines on the Indian Ocean trade routes, the protection of which east of the demarcation line with the South Atlantic Command was the responsibility of the Eastern Fleet.[44]

There were also repercussions on the micro scale. *Aquila VI* (*Luigi Torelli*) had voyaged to Singapore on 31 August to discharge her cargo and enter drydock. As soon as news of the surrender reached Japan, the order went out to local commanders to detain the Italians in Japanese ports. Accordingly, the boat's crew were rounded up, without resistance, and imprisoned. They joined their compatriots from *Aquila II* (*Reginaldo Giuliani*) and *Aquila III* (*Commandante Cappellini*). The crew of the latter had decided to continue the war and, believing that their wishes were being respected, had voyaged from Sabang to Singapore under Japanese escort. Upon arrival, however, they were taken captive and imprisoned, most of the crews eventually ending up in the notorious Changi prisoner of war camp.[45]

Somerville had only returned to Kilindini in July, having been called 'home' to the UK for 'consultation' on the 'vexed question of the proposed Burma offensive' on 10 April 1943.[46] His two fellow commanders, Wavell and Air Marshal Richard Peirse, also returned at the same time. The three C-in-Cs had also travelled across the Atlantic as part of the British delegation to the Trident, or Third Washington Conference, which took place between 12 and 25 May. They had been, as Churchill later put it, summoned:

> . . . because I was sure that our American friends would be very anxious that we should do everything possible – and impossible – in the way of immediate operations from India. The conference must hear at first hand the views of the men who would have to do whatever task was chosen.[47]

Somerville later summarized the proceedings for Admiral Guy Royle, the First Naval Member of the Australian Commonwealth Naval Board (the operational head of the Royal Australian Navy):

> The situation on our arrival [at Washington] was that, so far as the Americans were aware, ANAKIM [an amphibious assault upon Burma to recapture Rangoon and eventually reopen the Burma Road] was being actively planned and would be executed. They were naturally upset when they found out the plan was no longer acceptable . . . After considerable discussions, the Americans agreed

that the original plan was no longer workable, and accepted in lieu a modified ANAKIM, now called BULLFROG, which envisages an advance in Upper Burma, coupled with a seaborne assault on Akyab and Ramree[48] by what approximates roughly to two divisions.[49]

Once again, disagreement with the Americans had loomed. The Joint Chiefs still considered the expulsion of the Japanese from Burma a matter of urgency so that the Burma Road, and thus logistic support of China, could be resumed in full. The divergence between British and American perspectives on China, and more particularly Chiang's regime, was large. Maurice Matloff, chief historian of the US Army, put it diplomatically: 'The two staffs seemed to be in general agreement as to the need to reopen the Burma Road, but the US Chiefs dwelt more on the urgency of doing it.'[50] The operative word in the above sentence is 'seemed'. This is so because the British were reluctant to engage in a protracted and difficult military campaign in northern Burma. Churchill authored an alternative based on naval operations which was accepted by his colleagues and put to the Americans at Trident. It involved seizing 'some strategic point or points which will force the Japanese to counter-attack under conditions detrimental to them and favourable to us'. It should, he argued, 'be possible to carry up to 30,000 or 40,000 men across the Bay of Bengal' to occupy one or more of several key points. A prerequisite for any such operation was of course that 'the naval command of the Bay of Bengal must be secured' and that the landings, if opposed, 'can only be achieved by the provision of a large seaborne air force in carriers of all classes'.[51] As Churchill explained it to the Americans, the advantages lay in the fact that these proposed operations would draw Japanese resources away from the Pacific. Carriers aside, this was classic British maritime strategy and in general terms would have been recognized by Nelson. It was though unachievable until such time as the Eastern Fleet had been greatly reinforced. The Americans, particularly Admiral King, were not impressed, and they largely had their way. The conclusions of the Joint Chiefs deliberations were unambiguous:

> . . . offensive operations in the Pacific and Far East in 1943–44 have the following objectives:
>
> a. Conduct of air operations in and from China.
> b. Operations in Burma to augment supplies to China.
> c. Ejection of the Japanese from the Aleutians.
> d. Seizure of the Marshalls and Caroline Islands.
> e. Seizure of the Solomons–Bismarck Archipelago and Japanese held New Guinea.[52]

Thus was set out the three-pronged (four if one counts the Aleutians) strategic advance the Allies would employ to defeat Japan. Northwards from the Southwest Pacific Area under General Douglas MacArthur; westwards under the auspices of the Pacific Ocean Areas command, more particularly the Central Pacific Area, under Admiral Chester Nimitz; and the Burma-India area under the 'co-equal trinity' of Peirse, Somerville and Wavell (the latter soon to be elevated to the position of Viceroy of India, his place being taken by General Claude Auchinleck on 20 June 1943).[53] Since there was little or nothing that could be accomplished in terms of offensive action in the latter area, then a 'placatory gesture' was made to the Chinese. This took the form of a statement that 'all possible measures to secure the Naval Command of the Bay of Bengal by an adequate force' would take place to prevent the Japanese from readily reinforcing their forces in Burma.[54] Such reinforcements could not though be spared from European waters for the foreseeable future. The existence of the German battleship *Tirpitz* alone (*Scharnhorst* was also in Norwegian waters) had a disproportionate effect in this regard; the Admiralty policy of maintaining three *King George V* class battleships in UK waters to deal with her had been set out in 1941.[55]

Another idea first mooted at the time of the Washington Conference was appointing a Supreme Commander for the Burma-India theatre. The initial idea originated with the Secretary of State for India, Leopold Amery, who wrote to Churchill stating that he doubted if 'the system of a co-equal trinity is really the best for working purposes in the terrestrial sphere'.[56] The Chiefs of Staff formally endorsed the idea in June, and several names were considered.[57] One candidate was Somerville, though Churchill demurred at appointing an admiral.[58] The matter wasn't settled until, despite Churchill's apparent concern about sailors, acting Vice Admiral Louis Mountbatten was appointed in August 1943.

Notwithstanding the higher direction of the war, Somerville had to deal with the threat posed by the arrival of the *Monsun* U-boats. He was aided in this because their presence within the Indian Ocean was being closely followed by Allied codebreakers, who were decrypting the radio traffic between them and U-boat command and thus allowing convoys to be rerouted out of harm's way whenever possible.[59] Somerville also reorganized his anti-submarine resources into three escort groups: the Aden Escort Force,[60] the Kilindini Escort Force[61] and the Aden-Bombay-Colombo Escort Force.[62] He also instituted convoy, though this inevitably slowed up shipping movements and so came in for criticism from the Admiralty.[63]

There were naturally enough substantial problems in finding sufficient resources to escort shipping in a sea area as vast as the Indian Ocean. Marder, Jacobsen and Horsefield argue that Somerville was in error in only accepting convoys when they could be escorted, and that he failed to 'grasp the benefits . . .

merely of convoys by themselves – escorted or unescorted'.[64] This was perhaps unsurprising. That the larger the convoy the lesser chance that it would suffer submarine attack, and if it did then the damage percentage-wise would be less, was a counter-intuitive proposition. That it was though indeed the case had been demonstrated by the new discipline of Operational Research.[65]

Somerville either didn't know of this research, or he disregarded its conclusions. The latter is not impossible; as Marder, Jacobsen, and Horsefield show, he had 'no use for this kind of analysis', citing as evidence his comment that he 'felt better situated to judge the efficiency of my aircraft and ships than a scientist making guesses'.[66] That had been written at the end of January 1944; eight days later he noted in his diary that the 'only solution' to a lack of convoy escorts in the Gulf of Aden was to form a 'hunting group', though there were not enough vessels to do so immediately.[67] The concept of searching for enemy submarines via the use of hunting groups, as distinct from the support groups established by Horton mentioned above, had long (September 1939) been discredited.[68] Roskill was highly critical, writing:

> It seems incredible that the hardly learned lessons of the Atlantic battle were thus regarded as inapplicable to the Indian Ocean: and that the old heresy of the hunting group should have been revived at this late date and in defiance of so much previous experience.[69]

There is, though, a significant caveat. Roskill was writing at a time when the Allies successes in cryptanalysis, the Ultra secret, had yet to be revealed, so he can perhaps be forgiven for underestimating the amount of intelligence-led information these groups would be utilizing. Yet using Ultra tactically to effect the sudden appearance of naval and air forces in remote areas of the Indian Ocean was, as has been discussed, an inherently risky business in terms of keeping the secret. Indeed *Gruppe Monsun* had been whittled down to four following the loss of *U-533* on 16 October to a surprise air attack whilst in the Persian Gulf, though this appears to have been nothing more than luck, rather than being an intelligence-directed interception.[70] These boats sank six ships totalling 25,833 tons during the rest of October before heading to Penang to refit.

As a U-boat base Penang left a lot to be desired. A US appreciation from 1945 summed it up as follows:

> Innumerable difficulties were placed in the way of the Germans. Services and supplies were of poor quality; bases were never well equipped with personnel or supplies . . . U-boat and blockade runner crews had to load, unload and repair their own vessels . . . U-boats had to go to Japan proper to change worn out batteries.[71]

Indeed, the Indian Ocean as a whole was not a theatre conducive to German submarine operations. The humidity and heat caused premature deterioration of the boats' battery-banks which had been designed with cooler climes in mind.[72] Much the same applied to the boats' primary weapon; the G7e/T3 electric torpedo.[73] This was a complex device powered by a 52-cell lead-acid battery that weighed some 635kg and was 2.5m long. In order to achieve maximum performance (30 knots for 5,000m) the battery had to be heated to 60° Celsius before use, being stored ideally at half that temperature with continuous ventilation mitigating the risk of a build-up of explosive gas. The downside to this was that it led to water loss from the cells, with the result that they had an optimum life of only 120 days.[74] The long voyage to the theatre, plus the climate, caused several problems with the torpedoes; of the four discharged by *U-188* three failed, whilst *U-183* suffered no fewer than eight faulty torpedoes.[75] Nor did the personnel manning the boats escape. Paterson states that 'tropical rashes and skin infections were rampant' amongst the crews when they finally arrived at Penang.[76] The quality of the supplies they found there were also a problem. Even such a basic commodity as diesel fuel was found to be inferior.[77] The interrogation of the sole survivor from *U-533* revealed that Japanese fuel, 'could only be used when they were well away from enemy shipping as it gave a very dirty exhaust'.[78]

The five Indian Ocean U-boats, *U-168*, *U-183*, *U-188*, *U-516* and *U-532*, became eight when the Germans, after lengthy negotiations by *Konteradmiral* Paul Wenneker, the German naval attaché in Tokyo, persuaded the Japanese to give them the three Italian boats. These were put back into service as transport boats (*Untersee/Unterwasser Italien Transport*) with mainly German crews (some Italian sailors volunteered in order to escape Japanese captivity) and renamed. The *Aquila II* (*Reginaldo Giuliani*) became *UIT-23*, *Aquila III* (*Commandante Cappellini*) *UIT-24* and *Aquila VI* (*Luigi Torelli*) *UIT-25*.[79]

Whilst the U-boats refitted and recuperated at Penang, seven Japanese vessels, *I-162*, *I-165*, *I-166*, *I-10*, *I-27*, *I-29* and *I-37* managed to cause some severe damage. Between September and the end of December 1943, twenty-one ships were sunk in the Indian Ocean, mostly by these submarines.[80]

Somerville had returned his HQ to Colombo on 4 September 1943, the threat of a Japanese invasion or major incursion being held to have passed, but no amount of juggling could increase the size of his fleet. Indeed, during 1943 he had lost most of what he had to more active theatres; forty-eight ships were redeployed to the Mediterranean for the invasion of Sicily in July. As the authors of the official British history put it; 'for a time the Eastern Fleet had been reduced below the strength even of a trade protection force'.[81] As already mentioned, it was the case that the theatre he was responsible for suffered from a great lack of shipping in general. This had come about due to the British Government's fear of an 'import crisis' following the crippling shipping losses in the Atlantic in late 1942 and the diversion of shipping necessary to support Operation Torch, the invasion of North Africa.

There were then, in total, only roughly half as many potential targets for enemy submarines as had been the case previously, but organizing what was available into convoys meant delays in ship turnaround, which had the knock-on effect of exacerbating the shortage. It became, perforce, a case of fire-fighting. On 27 November Somerville instituted convoy on the Calcutta-Colombo route when Japanese submarine activity in the vicinity of Aden increased, but de-convoyed the faster ships on other routes; Persian Gulf-Bombay, Colombo-Bombay, and Durban-Kilindini. Still the Admiralty demanded more action, arguing that some 1,800 ship-days were being lost per month in relation to 'relatively modest and local threats'.[82] Accordingly on 13 December, and excepting the Bombay-Colombo-Calcutta route and movements involving troopships and landing craft, he discontinued convoys overall. 'The Germans', to use Marder, Jacobsen, and Horsefield's wording, 'took advantage of this generosity.'[83]

The degree to which theatre shipping shortages, and the inability to protect what there was from enemy action, contributed to the devastating Bengal Famine of 1943 is impossible to compute. Churchill, in his message of 5 January, had argued for logistical cuts to military forces. However, as Leighton points out, the ships that carried military cargo along the route to India also carried food and other basic economic necessities for the civilian populations, and:

> . . . in their cross voyages they contributed to the complex inter-regional trade on which these countries also depended. The removal of so much tonnage endangered the delicate balance between subsistence and famine in the whole Indian Ocean area, particularly in India itself and in fact contributed to the outbreak of famine in Bengal later in the year.[84]

The famine, and more particularly the attempts at relieving it (or the lack thereof), remains a controversial topic much given to partisan interpretation and analysis. Brennan, Heathcote and Lucas argue that the British Government could have attempted to ship wheat to Bengal in 1943 but, given the paralysis that would have entailed in other theatres and the 'import crisis', they instead chose to focus on winning the war.[85] In other words; 'there were reasons for the British reluctance to meet their imperial obligations'.[86]

Mukerjee acknowledges that there were indeed reasons, but categorizes them as malign and selfish. Shipping that could have been used to transport food relief to Bengal was instead involved in creating massive stockpiles of food in the

United Kingdom.[87] Contemporary opinion, at least as exemplified by Wavell, the recently-appointed (18 September 1943) Viceroy and Governor General, was scathing of the Imperial Government's policy. He let his masters know this in no uncertain terms in February 1944, opining that the famine was 'one of the greatest disasters that has befallen any people under British rule and damage to our reputation here both among Indians and foreigners in India is incalculable'. He went on to warn the government 'with all seriousness' that they were risking a 'catastrophe of far greater dimensions' than the famine.[88] It was already too late. The most critical period of deaths from starvation lasted from March 1943 to November 1943, though ongoing epidemics 'stalking a famine-ravaged land' meant that the death rate for most of 1944 was higher than it had been in 1943.[89]

Churchill did eventually ask the US for help with shipping food to Bengal, but not until, by his own estimation, at least 700,000 people had perished and the effect was being felt with respect to military operations.[90] Cordell Hull, the US Secretary of State, sent a memorandum to Roosevelt after consulting the Joint Chiefs of Staff on the matter dated 29 May:

> . . . the Joint Chiefs of Staff . . . are unable on military grounds to consent to the diversion of shipping necessary to meet the Prime Minister's request, because of the adverse effect such diversion would have upon military operations already undertaken or in prospect.[91]

The 'catastrophe of far greater dimensions' as alluded to by Wavell began to develop when the famine, as might have been expected, became a focal point of nationalist criticism of British imperial policy. As Sen wrote, 'The refusal of the British Government to permit more food imports into India through realloca-tion of shipping as an emergency measure . . . was severely criticized.'[92] Smith opined that the British Government's actions, or rather inactions, were symp-tomatic of a 'waning power [that] could no longer suffice to maintain protection for its Imperial subjects'.[93]

In the end of course it was a matter of priorities, of choices; choices that were, ultimately and in the grand scheme of things, made for India in London. For that, by definition, was the nature of colonialism; of British rule. What this meant in practice was exemplified in the official view from the British capital, as interpreted by Leopold Amery in 1944: 'it was better to take the risk of a second famine than risk the failure of the Second Front.'[94]

Chapter 12

Tweaking the Tail of a 'Fireless Dragon'

If 1943 had been a lean year for the Eastern Fleet, then the start of 1944 boded well for its return to full-blown battlefleet status. By the end of January, the battlecruiser *Renown*, the battleships *Queen Elizabeth* and *Valiant*, and the carrier *Illustrious* had been assigned to duty.[1] Also despatched was the carrier *Unicorn*, an interesting vessel designed in the late 1930s as a maintenance carrier. Towards this end she carried numbers of replacement aircraft and was equipped with double hangars containing extensive workshop facilities. Thanks to the farsightedness of Reginald Henderson, she was also equipped with a full-length armoured flight deck and could operate effectively as a light fleet carrier.[2]

These capital units, designated the 1st Battle Squadron, were under the command of Vice Admiral Sir Arthur Power. He had led the squadron in the Mediterranean with distinction and was characterized by the C-in-C there, Andrew Cunningham, as 'an officer of fierce energy and outstanding character and ability'.[3] As well as commanding the squadron, he was also tasked with filling the role of Second-in-Command (Vice Admiral, Eastern Fleet) under Somerville; Algernon Willis had departed in March the previous year to command Force H in the Mediterranean.

Though the battleships and battlecruiser had undergone extensive modernization programmes they were, excepting the latter, still relatively slow compared to the 30-knot *Illustrious*. The same applied to the *Unicorn*, which could only make 24 knots. The point being that this was not a fleet that could manoeuvre together as a unit, such as the US Navy task groups were now accomplishing in the Pacific. In order for that to occur then fast battleships, and more fleet carriers, would be needed and whilst there were plans for the latter, the former could not be accomplished until the remaining *King George V* class battleships became available. This would only be when the *Tirpitz*, laid alongside in her heavily protected berth in Norway but still greatly exercising the minds of the Admiralty in London, was finally put out of action. But whilst the Eastern Fleet's heavy ships were perhaps only a step or two away from 'Old Ming' the carriers were immeasurably more capable than had been the case in 1942. The intervening period had seen them equipped with 'aircraft fit for sailors to fly in'; American Corsairs and Avengers plus, arguably less fit, British Barracudas and Seafires.

A collection of ships does not, however, equal a fleet. The transition from one to the other requires training, practice and general working up, but the opportunities for that were curtailed somewhat by a distinct lack of destroyers. As per the previous chapter, the depredations of the Axis submarines based at Penang continued to absorb the energies of all available escorts, leaving the big ships immobilized and unable to put to sea.[4]

The base at Penang had very limited capacity in every context and the decision to withdraw *U-532*, *U-188* and *U-183* was taken. They were to load cargoes of strategically important materiel and carry out attacks en route to Europe. Supporting this enterprise were two *Z-Schiff* (*Zufuhrschiff* – supply ships); *Charlotte Schliemann* and the previously-mentioned *Brake*, merchant tankers based on Japanese ports, carrying fuel, torpedoes, water and so on.[5] Unbeknown to the Germans, Somerville had put in place plans to locate and destroy both vessels using 'special intelligence'. Under an overall codename of Thwart, Operation Canned was the hunt for *Charlotte Schliemann*, whilst that to destroy *Brake* was dubbed Operation Covered.[6] The former was found first, initially by Catalina air search, while in the process of refuelling *U-532* on the night of 9 February 1944. The modern 'R' class destroyer *Relentless* rushed to intercept and upon arrival discharged eight torpedoes at 2,000 yards range, obtaining two or three hits. Gunfire was also opened, and *Charlotte Schliemann* sank, or was scuttled, a few minutes later. Forty-one out of the crew of eighty-eight were picked up by *Relentless*. *U-532* submerged and escaped.[7] The *Brake* suffered a similar fate some four weeks later on 12 March. The veteran U-boat commander *Fregattenkapitän* Günter (sometimes spelt Günther) Hessler, who was also Dönitz' son-in-law, later (but before the existence of Ultra had been revealed) wrote:

> The sinking of this second tanker, in an area far removed from all air and naval bases and at the exact time that replenishment was in progress was indeed remarkable.[8]

It was thought so at the time too. The commander of *U-532*, *Fregattenkapitän* Ottoheinrich Junker, who had been present when both ships were sunk, sent a message which was itself intercepted stating that these 'provisionings have been systematically compromised'.[9] The Allies were then taking a risk in using Ultra intelligence tactically. This has to be viewed, however, in the context of what was happening in terms of the Axis submarine campaign at that time. For example, and despite the difficulties occasioned to them by the paucity of bases, Axis submarines caused some serious damage.

Particularly noteworthy as an example was the sinking of the liner *Khedive Ismail* on 12 February 1944 whilst she was traversing the Suvadiva, or 'One and a Half Degree', Channel between Haddhunmathi and Huvadhu Atolls in the

Maldives. Despite being in an escorted convoy of five troopships en route from Kilindini to Colombo, the Japanese submarine *I-27* managed to close in undetected and launch four torpedoes, two of which struck the liner. Aboard were 178 crew plus 1,333 passengers, the largest single grouping being Kenyan gunners of the 301st Field Regiment, East African Artillery. There were also a significant number of females aboard; fifty-four nurses, nineteen WRENS and nine members of the ATS (Auxiliary Territorial Service). Also present was a naval officer's wife travelling with her husband and infant son.

The *Khedive Ismail* broke in two and foundered in minutes. Many of those aboard went down with her, leaving those that escaped in the water. Two escorts, the 'P' class destroyers *Paladin* and *Petard*, sped to pick up survivors and in doing so gained ASDIC contact with the attacker.[10] They counter-attacked, and *I-27* was eventually sunk by a torpedo after depth charges, gunfire and even an attempt at ramming by *Paladin* had damaged both it and the destroyer; *Paladin* weighed some 2,286 tonnes at full load whilst the Type B1 submarine displaced some 2,631 tonnes on the surface. It was, Somerville remarked, 'a singularly tough submarine'.[11] There was one survivor from *I-27* and only 208, including 6 women, from *Khedive Ismail*. Many more had made it off the stricken liner, only to perish from the detonation of depth charges. In the grim league table of Allied merchant shipping disasters over the course of the war, the incident comes third in terms of fatalities. It holds the record, though, for being the British Empire's largest loss of servicewomen ever.[12]

Destroying the two tankers deprived the U-boats of their support network and was undoubtedly a major coup. Indeed, *U-188* was the only boat to receive sufficient replenishment to enable her to journey to Europe; she arrived at Bordeaux on 19 June 1944. The other boats were ordered back to Penang.[13] The Ultra secret was kept because the Kriegsmarine in general, and the U-boat arm in particular, concluded after investigation that messages enciphered via Naval Enigma could not be broken.[14] Alternative explanations for the extraordinary success rate of Allied air and naval forces were adopted. These included traitorous Germans, espionage and the possession of advanced radar systems.[15]

The Axis submarine campaign tapered off somewhat following the destruction of *Brake*, and there were no Allied shipping losses at all in the Indian Ocean during April and May.[16] The menace had not gone away, however, and attacks began again in June and continued in line with Dönitz's global strategic conception of it being immaterial where a ship was sunk. In the face of ever-growing Allied air and naval power in the theatre this dispersed strategy, which also attempted to tie down the greatest number of enemy forces, was however doomed to fail. It was though definitely the case that the submarine menace continued to plague the Indian Ocean until the end of the war.

If Axis submarines constituted a chronic problem, then a more acute version began to impinge on the theatre in early 1944. In late February the Japanese Navy began moving major fleet units to Singapore; seven battleships, plus three aircraft carriers including the new armoured 29,000-ton *Taiho*, supported by a large number of cruisers and destroyers were eventually reported as being in the area by March.[17]

What Admiral Koga Mineichi, who had succeeded Yamamoto as Commander-in-Chief of the Combined Fleet on 18 April 1943, intended to do with this concentration of naval power was unknown. Somerville feared that it would carry out a repeat of Nagumo's 1942 incursion and his response to any such attack would be the same as it had on that occasion:

> The present E[astern] F[leet] was not only numerically inferior but was not yet fully trained and it would be necessary for the Fleet to withdraw if the threat of a Japanese attack in force should appear likely to materialise. Until the Fleet is reinforced we have to rely on the air for defence.[18]

The potential for any such an event caused disquiet in Australia, with Prime Minister John Curtin sending Churchill a message on 4 March asking for his advice:

> . . . could you inform me of the opinion of your naval advisers about the probability of Japanese incursions into the Indian Ocean and whether they are likely to attempt a diversion to relieve the pressure in the Pacific.[19]

Perhaps anticipating such an inquiry, Churchill had addressed these matters in a message which crossed Curtin's. It was also sent to Peter Fraser, the Prime Minister of New Zealand. Reassurances were given to both premiers:

> We have studied this new development which has interesting features. The Japanese must have appreciated that Truk, where normally they stationed half their fleet, was becoming too exposed, and evidently withdrew before the recent American attack . . . It is possible that the Japanese intend to raid our communications between Calcutta and Ceylon, or in other parts of the Indian Ocean. Nevertheless, it is not thought that any serious danger, either to India or to Western Australia, is likely . . .[20]

Churchill was correct, inasmuch as the withdrawal of the Japanese fleet from its base at Truk in the Caroline Islands had been occasioned by the imminence of a massive US Navy attack; Operation Hailstone. This took place on

17–18 February and was carried out primarily by three of the four carrier task groups that constituted Task Force 58 (the Fast Carrier Task Force) under Vice Admiral Marc Mitscher. This demonstration of offensive air power showed, according to Samuel Eliot Morison, that 'Carrier warfare had now come of age'.[21] In other words, it was the Japanese fleet that was now having to hide to avoid certain destruction at the hands of American carrier-borne aircraft. On the Japanese side, the retreat was characterized as a husbanding of resources for the decisive battle within the Inner Defence Ring, which the Imperial Navy hoped to fight and in which US naval power would be crushed. This of course was a fantasy, but one that was pursued until destruction intervened.

That was for the future, and Somerville was to write on 24 February that whilst his intelligence department were of the view that the 'chief factor' in the Japanese deployment was to 'keep their fleet clear of the Americans', the possibility of an attack in the Bay of Bengal could by no means be excluded.[22] The possibility of again having to hide the Eastern Fleet, this time from an enemy that was itself hiding, was in the air. 'Nerves were,' as Hezlet put it, 'to a certain extent, steadied' by the offer of Admiral King to lend the Eastern Fleet the carrier *Saratoga* and three destroyers.[23] The request came from the Admiralty according to Somerville, and was accompanied by a commitment to reinforce the battleship strength of the fleet.[24] There were no modern British battleships to spare, but there was a newly modernized vessel that fitted the bill perfectly: the French *Richelieu*.

Following the invasion of French North Africa (Operation Torch) in November 1942, and the subsequent invasion of unoccupied France by Germany, the French Navy, under the command of Admiral (*Amiral de la Flotte*) François Darlan, had, put simply, agreed to join the Allies.[25] Subsequently *Richelieu* had left Dakar under her own steam and arrived at the Brooklyn Navy Yard, New York, in February 1943. Work to bring her up to standard took until October, whereupon she steamed back across the Atlantic to join the Royal Navy's Home Fleet. Somerville was informed on 10 March that *Richelieu* would be joining his command, allowing him to quip that 'we shall have to erect a Tower of Babel as a PWSS Station'.[26] It might have been worse if Admiral (*Ammiraglio di Squadra*) Raffaele de Courten's proposal, that Italy's best battleships should partake in the war against Japan, had been acted upon. Perhaps fortunately it wasn't.[27]

On 4 March 1944 the *Saratoga*, complete with its veteran Carrier Air Group 12 (CVG-12) plus three destroyer escorts, *Dunlap*, *Fanning* and *Cummings*, departed the newly acquired Fleet Base at Majuro Atoll in the Marshall Islands which had been captured in February. Designated Task Group 58.5, the four ships steamed south to Espiritu Santo in the New Hebrides, then on to Fremantle, Australia, via Hobart in Tasmania. TG 58.5 was met at sea on 27 March by the

Eastern Fleet under Vice Admiral Power, with personal contact being established when Rear Admiral Clement Moody, the Eastern Fleet's carrier commander (Rear Admiral Aircraft Carriers), flew over from *Illustrious* (as a passenger) aboard a Barracuda to meet Captain John A. Cassady, *Saratoga*'s captain; 'The admiral was received with full honors, and Saratoga's pilots thoroughly inspected the Barracuda.'[28] They were unimpressed; Ian Cameron quotes an unnamed American lieutenant as exclaiming 'Jesus Christ! The Limeys'll be building *air-planes* next'.[29]

Moody too had his doubts about the aircraft. Somerville recorded these on 15 March, writing how the Rear Admiral had referred to the 'disappointing performance' of the Barracudas which 'will not have a radius of action in this climate exceeding 160 miles'. He also pointed out that their cruising speed of 120mph 'makes it very difficult to match them up with Corsairs and Hellcats'. Somerville's final verdict: 'these aircraft, in fact, appear to be a thorough misfit'.[30]

The reinforced Eastern Fleet arrived at Trincomalee on 31 March 1944, to be joined on 12 April by *Richelieu*.[31] Training for joint operations commenced, though Reynolds notes that during the initial 'making friends' celebrations, 80 American pilots from *Saratoga* on their first social call to the 'wet' British carrier consumed '700 bottles of beer and three-dozen bottles each of whisky and gin'.[32] More seriously, joint training exercises in early April revealed deficiencies in British techniques; it took 90 minutes for a deckload of aircraft from *Illustrious* to launch and rendezvous.[33] The experienced commander of *Saratoga*'s Fighter Squadron 12 (VF-12), Commander Joseph C. 'Jumpin Joe' Clifton, took command of the situation with, of course, the consent of the British. By the middle of the month the launching and rendezvous time was down to 25 minutes and both groups were working as a team.[34]

The question now was how to deploy this new-found offensive power, particularly given the limited period during which *Saratoga* was to be deployed with the Eastern Fleet, basically April and May. Somerville had pondered his options even before the arrival of the Americans, and had concluded that 'a review of possible targets for carrier operations is not very encouraging':

> Palembang is a very attractive target but the distance that has to be flown over land, and the high intervening mountains suggest that the prospects of success are not good . . . Batavia is a little better in this respect, but the only readily approached target is Sabang.[35]

Sabang was located on the north-eastern tip of Weh Island, situated about 12 miles off the northern tip of Sumatra, where it commanded the northern entrance to the Straits of Malacca. There was an airfield outside the town and a radar station on the coast, though its importance lay in its oil storage tanks and dockyard. This importance was, however, relative. The target was essentially peripheral and only a hit-and-run raid was contemplated. The attack was though not launched in isolation, but in compliance with a request from Admiral Ernest King. He wanted a diversionary attack on the Andamans or on Sumatra to distract the enemy; MacArthur's Southwest Pacific Area command was preparing an assault on Hollandia, New Guinea, on 22 April.[36] In the smaller scheme of things, the Sabang attack, dubbed Operation Cockpit, would also be important in giving the Eastern Fleet valuable operational experience, and have 'an extremely good effect on morale' after '18 months in the doldrums'.[37]

Though there is little or no trace of it in his writings, at least overtly, Somerville was undoubtedly still wary of Japanese capabilities; hence of course the choice of Sabang as a target. He took it for granted that Japanese shore-based aircraft would be superior to his carrier-borne aircraft, and memories of what had happened to *Dorsetshire, Cornwall, Hermes, Vampire*, etc. lingered.[38] This was neither idiosyncratic nor unreasonable. Rather it was an intelligence-led

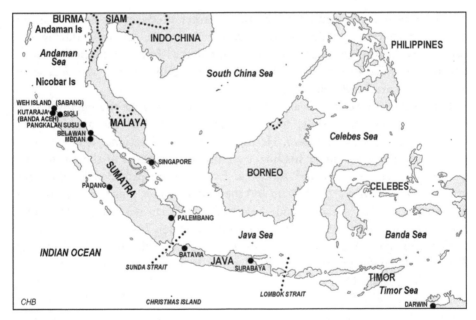

Operations of the Eastern Fleet 1944. © Charles Blackwood.
Despite not knowing how it would ultimately be used in the campaign against Japan, Somerville utilized his Fleet for a series of operations against occupied areas throughout 1944. Several of these were diversionary and in support of American operations elsewhere. All though were necessary in terms of training the Fleet for modern carrier-based warfare.

position and, as Ford argues, 'the absence of British victories over the IJN dictated caution'.[39] Also dictating caution was the fact that the fleet was formed from 'disparate units staffed by inexperienced crews and unseasoned officers'.[40] As Somerville put it on 12 March:

> I inspected the divisions on board *Queen Elizabeth* . . . and was much struck by the extreme youth of the men . . . it was quite clear to me that they have some way to go before a proper standard is reached.[41]

He made similar observations following a visit to *Valiant* on 17 March, writing of the 'extreme youth and inexperience' of the ratings and the 'heavy dilution of officers'.[42] His second-in-command, Vice Admiral Power, was even more forthright:

> . . . the RN is over expanded and dilution has already passed the sensible limit. Ships have but a sprinkling of leaders, a tremendous number of youngsters who require skilled leadership and a percentage (perhaps five per cent or even more) who are not worth their rations let alone their pay . . .[43]

These problems were caused by the much larger predicament around severe manpower shortages; a dearth which afflicted Britain generally during the Second World War.[44] Similar issues were not noted with respect to the *Richelieu*, which Somerville inspected on 11 April. There he found that 'the men were clean, well shaved and well turned out . . .'.[45]

Eschewing any reconnaissance flights for fear of giving the enemy notice of his intentions, Somerville took personal command of the attack, flying his flag in the *Queen Elizabeth*. He divided his multi-national fleet into two task forces. Force 69, under his direct command, consisted of the battleships *Queen Elizabeth*, *Valiant* and *Richelieu*. Escorts were provided by the light cruisers *Ceylon*, *Newcastle*, *Nigeria* and the Dutch *Tromp*, plus three Australian destroyers, *Napier, Nizam,* and *Nepal*, five British destroyers, *Quiberon, Rotherham, Racehorse, Petard* and *Penn*, and the Dutch *Van Galen*.

Force 70, under Vice Admiral Arthur Power with his flag in the battlecruiser *Renown*, contained the two carriers plus the light cruisers *London* and New Zealand's *Gambia*. Destroyer escorts consisted of the three USN vessels that had sojourned with *Saratoga* and the three British ships *Quilliam, Queenborough* and *Quadrant*. Also involved, though sent ahead separately, was the British submarine *Tactician*. Her role, an innovation lifted from USN current practice, was to act as a rescue vessel for any crew that might end up ditching in the sea.[46] This facility was important: 'the choice between falling into the hands of the Japanese or into the mouths of sharks had little to choose between them'.[47]

The Eastern Fleet departed Ceylon on 16 April, Somerville noting that the 'Fleet work was not bad though [the] ships were obviously out of practice'.[48] The next day, at 09:30 hours, the fleet slowed down to carry out refuelling of the destroyers from the cruisers and *Renown*. The C-in-C found cause to complain in the length of time this took; speed was only increased back to 16 knots at 14:00 hours.[49] He also took the opportunity to exercise his command in taking up cruising positions against air attack and the firing of blind barrages. This, he recorded, 'did not go too well since some ships were firing much too high and other far too low'.[50] Perhaps as a result of these exercises, a redeployment of assets took place the following day; *Ceylon* and *Nigeria* were sent to Force 70 in order to provide it with enhanced anti-aircraft capability. No flying from the carriers was permitted in order to avoid the fleet disclosing its presence.[51]

The fleet separated, Force 69 keeping some 20 miles to the west of Force 70, on the morning of 19 April. The latter, positioned around 180 miles south-west of Sabang, commenced flying off at 05:30 hours with the strikes led by 'Jumpin Joe' Clifton. The carriers had to manoeuvre at high speed due to there being practically no wind in order to get their aircraft launched. The total force comprising seventeen Barracudas, each carrying two 500lb and two 250lb bombs,[52] escorted by thirteen Corsairs, from *Illustrious*; and eleven Avengers, four with a single 2,000lb bomb and the rest carrying four 500lb bombs, and eighteen Dauntless dive-bombers each carrying a single 1,000lb bomb, from *Saratoga*. The latter also launched sixteen F6F Hellcats as escorts for the strike aircraft, plus eight more to carry out attacks on the airfields at Sabang and Lho Nga (Lhonga). A Combat Air Patrol of four Corsairs from *Illustrious* and eight Hellcats from *Saratoga*, was also sent aloft in case of retaliatory attacks.

Compete tactical surprise was achieved; the American strike arrived on target at 06:57 hours with the British, who came from a different direction, about a minute behind. There was no anti-aircraft fire until after the raid had commenced. Sources differ as to how many aircraft the Hellcats from *Saratoga* caught on the ground at the airfields, but claims of twenty-one destroyed at Sabang and a further four at Lho Nga were made. Three, which got into the air, were shot down.

It was all over in about ten minutes. Three (out of four) oil tanks were ablaze and three, albeit minor, ships were hit; the convoy escort and former mine-layer *Hatsutaka* was slightly damaged, whilst the transports *Kunitsu Maru* and *Haruno Maru* (formerly the Dutch cargo vessel *Kidoel*) were sunk. The port facilities also suffered heavy damage: 'The power-station, barracks, and wireless station were badly damaged, and large fires in the dockyard were seen by the *Tactician* to be burning fiercely hours after the fleet had left on its return to Trincomalee.'[53]

The only Allied loss was a Hellcat which was hit by anti-aircraft fire and forced to ditch. The pilot, Lieutenant Dale 'Klondike' Klahn, was rescued by *Tactician*. As soon as all aircraft had returned and been landed-on, Force 70 withdrew westwards in conjunction with Force 69. The expected retaliation failed to materialize, though three Nakajima B5N torpedo bombers were spotted on radar approaching from the east at approximately 10:00 hours. These were promptly dealt with by the Hellcats of *Saratoga*'s Combat Air Patrol, and the Eastern Fleet remained unmolested during its voyage back to Trincomalee.

Strategically Operation Cockpit was irrelevant. MacArthur's operations against Hollandia were successful and achieved against minimal opposition; the Japanese simply weren't expecting them. It was though a tactical success and, much more importantly, a great confidence booster. Churchill noted this in a message some ten days later, terming it a 'brilliant attack . . . whilst the Japanese fleet was at Singapore'.[54] Somerville remarked a few days earlier, after visiting *Illustrious*, that the 'operation had had a most stimulating effect on all the air crews'.[55] His biographer argued that it 'signified the long-delayed resurgence of the Eastern Fleet and gave the Fleet Air Arm Squadrons some badly-needed practical experience'.[56] It also highlighted several areas where there were problems.

The Royal Navy was made aware of several key deficiencies, one of which was the performance of the Barracuda: 'the gentle breezes of the Indian Ocean were to prove too much' for them.[57] In order to get them into the air *Illustrious* had steamed away from Force 70 at 30 knots in an effort to generate enough over-deck wind. Attended only by destroyers she would have been thoroughly exposed in the event of a counter-attack. In future, and in line with current American practice, the carrier force would manoeuvre as a unit with Rear Admiral Moody in tactical command during flying operations. To facilitate this, and for the next operation, the Barracudas would be replaced with Avengers redeployed from escort carriers that had been sent to the theatre.[58]

The operation in question, designated Operation Transom, was to be an attack on the Japanese installations at the former Dutch naval base of Sourabaya (Soerabaja, Surabaya) on the north shore of Java.[59] Following the Japanese occupation, it had become a centre for anti-submarine forces in the Java Sea. The Commander in Chief of the US Seventh Fleet ('MacArthur's Navy'), Vice Admiral Thomas C. Kinkaid, had been asked by Rear Admiral Ralph W. Christie, the commander of Task Force 71, the Seventh Fleet's submarines, to arrange an air attack on Sourabaya by *Saratoga*. The carrier would be in a position to effect this strike when she voyaged back to the United States from her service with the Eastern Fleet. Kinkaid referred the idea to Admiral Ernest King in Washington, who in turn raised it with the Combined Chiefs of Staff and the British Admiralty Delegation. The latter proposed that the Eastern Fleet should accompany the American carrier, which would both increase the power of the strike force and give the British further operational experience. Somerville was all for the project, though he asked for American submarines to be deployed in the Sunda and Lombok Straits in case the enemy sortied from Singapore to intercept. This was agreed and Christie deployed eight of his submarines at the two straits, through which any Japanese response would have to pass.[60]

This would be a far more complex mission than the attack on Sabang, involving a round trip of around 8,000 nautical miles from Trincomalee for the Eastern Fleet, though not of course for *Saratoga* and her escorts. Somerville wrote that '*Saratoga*', probably meaning her captain, John H. Cassady, 'suggested that *Renown* and *Richelieu* with some cruisers and destroyers would afford enough cover for the operation'.[61] This suggestion was likely made because the ships mentioned were the only ones with sufficient speed (a theoretical 31 and 32 knots respectively) to keep up with the carriers. This followed the USN's latest practice; the 32-knot *Iowa* and *New Jersey* had joined Task Force 58 in January 1944.[62] Somerville demurred. He wanted the slower ships to take part, both because it would have an 'adverse effect' on them not to, and they would provide 'maximum insurance'. In addition, the voyage would provide valuable opportunities for fleet training.[63]

Given the great distances involved, the heavy ships would have to refuel twice during the mission, but there was no fleet-train capable of carrying this out whilst at sea. Accordingly, Somerville organized an alternative; a replenishment force, designated Task Force 67, with which he would rendezvous at Exmouth Gulf, on the north-west coast of Australia and about 600 miles from Java, where there was a USN submarine base. This force consisted of the modern Royal Fleet Auxiliary (RFA) tankers *Arndale*, *Echodale* and *Eaglesdale*, the older RFA tankers *Appleleaf* and *Pearleaf*, plus the stores and distilling ship *Bacchus*, the latter having a capacity of 250 tons per day.[64] With the 'County' class heavy cruiser *London*, the destroyers *Rotherham* and *Van Galen*, and the 'River' class frigate *Findhorn* as initial escort, Task Force 67 departed for Australia on Sunday 30 April.[65]

The composition of the carrier and battleship forces was much the same as for the Sabang attack. The latter, with Somerville again commanding in *Queen Elizabeth*, though now designated Task Force 65, departed Trincomalee on 6 May and rendezvoused at sea with the carriers under Power, now forming Task Force 66, the following day. The two forces reached Exmouth Gulf early on 15 May, after carrying out intensive training exercises during the voyage, and spent the rest of the day refuelling and replenishing. Vice Admiral

Kinkaid and Rear Admiral Christie were also there, and called on Somerville who was reported to be 'greatly impressed by the cooperation given him by U.S. authorities'.[66]

The fleet sailed from Exmouth Gulf on the evening of 16 May, timing the voyage so that it arrived at the flying-off position, around 90 miles from the south-west coast of Java, at daybreak the next morning. The distance to the target area was therefore about 180 miles, half of it over land which was enemy-held.

As per previous lessons learned, tactical command was passed to Moody for flying off the strike and the rest of Task Force 66 conformed to the movements of the carriers, forming a protective cordon around them. At 06:30 hours Task Force 66 started launching. The weather was, as Somerville had noted the previous day, 'gin clear' with only a light south-easterly wind and a few scattered clouds.[67] One Avenger from *Saratoga* had to land back on with engine trouble, whilst two from *Illustrious* ditched after taking off, their crews being rescued. The strike then comprised eleven Avengers, eighteen Dauntless and twenty-four Hellcats from *Saratoga*, with sixteen Avengers and sixteen Corsairs from *Illustrious*.[68] Once the aircraft had rendezvoused, they formed up into two strike groups. Force A was to target the *Machinefabriek Braat* (Braat Engineering Works) and the *Bataafse Petroleum Maatschappij* (Batavian Oil Company owned by Shell) refinery at Wonokromo. The former had been a heavy civil engineering concern converted by the occupiers for war production; the refinery produced aviation-quality fuel and was the only such installation on Java.[69] Force B was to hit the docks, harbour installations, floating docks, and any shipping in the commercial area of Surabaya harbour. Four fighters from each carrier were flown off to provide Combat Air Patrol.

Just as had been the case at Sabang, the attackers achieved tactical surprise. Force A swept in from south to north whilst Force B overflew the harbour area in the opposite direction. No fighter opposition was encountered, and two enemy aircraft that tried to get airborne were shot down, and anti-aircraft fire was initially weak though later described as 'considerable'.[70] One Avenger from *Saratoga* was however downed. Somerville summed up the observable damage:

> 10 merchant ships totalling 35,000 tons had been hit by bombs and one of these was seen to blow up; the oil refinery was completely destroyed,[71] two floating docks hit by bombs; the naval base was well strafed and the Braak [*sic*] engineering works probably entirely destroyed; 2 enemy aircraft were shot down and 19 destroyed on the ground whilst other were damaged.[72]

After landing-on aircraft, both task forces withdrew in close company at 08:50, heading to the south-west 'to avoid giving the impression to any shadowers that we were making for Exmouth Gulf'. Photographs of the raid taken by Clifton were dropped onto Somerville's flagship later that day which suggested that there were five undamaged submarines in the harbour. He noted that 'it would probably have paid to carry out a second strike, but by the time this was fully appreciated we were too far away from the target'. He added: 'I feel we must make a reasonable distance to the SW from land before dark in view of the vulnerability of the Fleet to attack at dusk or night. We require more practice still for our night barrages and of course have no night fighters to operate against such attacks.'[73]

It is evident that Japanese capabilities still worried Somerville. This was wise; it was only the inestimable benefit of hindsight that allowed the editor of his papers to conclude: 'It is now clear that at least from the autumn of 1943, the Japanese in the East Indies resembled a fireless dragon.'[74] The C-in-C did note in his report to MacArthur that 'no attempt appears to have been made to locate or shadow the Fleet after the attack although weather was clear and sighting was possible outside Radar range'.[75]

The Fleet refuelled and replenished from Task Force 67 at Exmouth Gulf on 18 May, on the evening of which *Saratoga* and her three destroyers parted company to return to the United States. This concluded what Somerville called 'a profitable and very happy association of Task Group 58.5 with the Eastern Fleet'.[76]

The Fleet departed for Ceylon on 19 May with a full programme of both day and night training exercises planned. Somerville, however, handed tactical command to Power the next day in order to give him, Moody and the Commodore in charge of the destroyers, Albert Poland, 'as much opportunity as possible to exercise independently whilst we are in waters free from submarines'.[77]

The return voyage was uneventful, despite unrealized worries that U-boats were waiting to attack, but upon his return on 28 May Somerville found a 'personal signal' from the Admiralty waiting. This passed on a request from Admiral Chester Nimitz, whose command was about to commence the massive Mariana and Palau Islands campaign, to the effect that he would 'like a continuance of operations by the Eastern Fleet against the Malayan Barrier in order to assist the Pacific Fleet by maintaining pressure'. Somerville noted that 'it is unfortunate that for some time we shall only have one carrier as this must of necessity limit the scope of our operations'.[78] Fleet carrier reinforcements, in the shape of *Victorious* and *Formidable*, did not arrive until early July though the former had been scheduled to join Somerville's command in May. Another problem was that the Avengers used during Operation Transom had been redeployed back to escort carriers for anti-submarine work and replaced aboard *Illustrious* with Barracudas. This seemingly retrograde step had been necessitated by the inability of the Barracuda to get airborne from a slow (circa 17–18 knots), short-decked escort carrier whilst also carrying a weapons load.[79]

Neither the lack of a second (or third) fleet carrier, nor the performance (or lack thereof) of the Barracuda, was of much relevance in terms of the initial operation carried out by the Eastern Fleet in pursuit of Nimitz's request. Designated Operation Councillor (10–11 June 1944), and under the command of Moody, it involved the *Illustrious* and the escort carrier *Atheling*, escorted by the *Dido* class light cruiser *Phoebe* and six destroyers, stationing themselves off Sabang. The object of the exercise was to elicit a reaction from the enemy by making them think that an invasion force was on the way and that a landing scheduled for 12 June had been aborted. To that end the submarine *Surf*, situated some 200 miles west of Sabang, broadcast signals simulating an escort force commander 'ordering his party back to harbour'.[80] As an operation it failed inasmuch as there was no Japanese response. One lesson learned was that it was impractical to operate a fleet and an escort carrier together due to the circa 12-knot disparity in their speeds.[81]

A more substantial operation was carried out by a portion of the Eastern Fleet, designated Force 60 under Vice Admiral Power, on 19–21 June. Operation Pedal was an air attack by *Illustrious*, accompanied by *Renown* and *Richelieu* with the 'Crown Colony' class light cruisers *Nigeria*, *Kenya* and *Ceylon*, the *Phoebe*, and the destroyers *Quality*, *Quickmatch*, *Quilliam*, *Racehorse*, *Raider*, *Relentless*, *Roebuck* and *Rotherham*, against Port Blair in the Andaman Islands. Two submarines, *Clyde* and *Tantivy*, were stationed to provide air-sea rescue.[82] It had been previously agreed between Somerville, Moody, and *Illustrious'* commander, Captain Charles Lambe, that for single carrier operations the number of fighters aboard would have to be increased at the expense of the strike aircraft.[83] Accordingly, aboard for the operation were three squadrons of fighters and only one of bombers; forty-two Corsairs and fifteen Barracudas.

Launching commenced at first light on 21 June from a point 95 miles west of Port Blair. With fifty-seven aircraft aboard *Illustrious* was full to capacity, and the first five aircraft had to be 'accelerated' (catapulted) off because of the lack of deck space to get up to speed.[84] Fifteen Barracudas, two of which had to later abort due to engine trouble, and sixteen Corsairs were tasked with attacking the harbour area and facilities around and about. A further eight Corsairs were flown off to attack two airfields close by Port Blair, whilst another eight maintained a Combat Air Patrol above the fleet.

The Corsairs tasked with attacking the airfields went in first, destroying two aircraft on the ground, but no Japanese fighters were observed at all. Despite intense light anti-aircraft fire they all returned, though with five damaged; one pilot had to bail out over the fleet. The Barracudas experienced heavy fire as they approached the target, but this ceased prior to them dropping. The barracks, power station, motor transport yard, seaplane base and radar stations were bombed and strafed but one was lost. According to Hobbs, ten out of the fifty-two bombs carried by the strike weren't delivered for one reason or another, which no doubt accounted for subsequent Japanese claims that little damage had been caused.[85] After recovering the aircraft, Task Force 60 withdrew westwards at high speed, though there was no attempt at pursuit by enemy forces. Somerville, after receiving Power's report, commented on how small the margins of error were when operating so many aircraft from one carrier:

> At one time there were 51 aircraft in the air and it was most fortunate that landing on was not delayed by a crash since otherwise some of the Barracudas would most certainly have had to land in the sea; tests of consumption once more indicated that the practical radius of the Barracuda is apparently not more than 125 miles.[86]

These matters notwithstanding, *Illustrious'* performance serves to demonstrate the great improvements that had been attained in terms of carrier operations in a short time.

The prospect of the Eastern Fleet landing weightier blows was greatly enhanced on 7 July when two further fleet carriers, *Victorious* and *Indomitable*, arrived in Ceylon.[87] However, the latter was deemed not yet ready to take part in active operations, so it was *Illustrious* and *Victorious* that sortied on 22 July as part of Task Force 62 to undertake Operation Crimson, a further attack on Sabang. This was not, however, to be an airstrike, but rather a sea bombardment of the target during which carrier aircraft would play an ancillary role; supressing enemy air attack and spotting for the big ships' gunfire.[88] Somerville led the mission from *Queen Elizabeth*, accompanied by the *Valiant*, *Richelieu* and *Renown*. The accompanying cruisers and destroyers were those that had taken part in the operation against Port Blair, with the addition of the 'County' class heavy cruiser *Cumberland* and the Dutch *Tromp*. Two submarines, *Tantalus* and *Templar*, were deployed to carry out the air-sea rescue role.

The Task Force started to leave Trincomalee at 15:15 hours on 22 July and approached Sabang during the night of 24/25 July when the carriers were detached, moving to an operating area some 35 miles west-north-west of the target before dawn. *Illustrious'* air group consisted of fifty-one aircraft, all Corsairs apart from nine Barracudas, whilst *Victorious* was loaded with thirty-nine Corsairs. At first light, approximately 05:30 hours, Rear Admiral Moody began flying off his aircraft; eighteen Corsairs from *Illustrious* and sixteen from *Victorious*. Sixteen of these, eight from each carrier, headed for Sabang, their targets being the airfields and a radar installation. The remainder formed a Combat Air Patrol over the rest of the fleet, which was moving inshore to commence firing.

Somerville noted that 'at 06:00, the pre-arranged time, we could see gun flashes from A/A guns and later on shell bursts in the sky as the Corsairs flew overhead'.[89] At 06:55 hours *Queen Elizabeth* opened up with her main armament, followed by *Valiant, Renown*, then *Richelieu*. The cruisers had opened fire some 30 seconds earlier. The action is perhaps best summarised by Somerville in a letter to his wife which he wrote on the day:

> ... I've wanted to bombard Sabang for some time past but so far it has always seemed that the air the Japs had available was a bit too much for us to compete with. However after our first tap at Sabang and then Sourabaya and Port Blair it seemed that we had over-estimated the Jap air strength so I felt justified in going in this time. It was a very carefully planned operation with everything timed to take place to the tick and everything went exactly according to plan ... We made a proper mess of Sabang by all accounts and I doubt if it will be much further use to the Japs as a Naval base.
>
> Certain of the Corsair pilots came on board Queen Elizabeth later and reported that a number of the Zekes[90] failed to open fire even when they were in a favourable position to do so; the Zekes can out-manoeuvre the Corsairs very easily but these Zekes appeared to be a very green lot and had it not been for the cover afforded by the cloud, the Corsairs think they might well have bagged the lot.[91]

Somerville's comments about the Japanese pilots being 'green' and that he had previously overestimated the Japanese 'air strength' are telling. The forays against Sabang, Sourabaya, Port Blair and then Sabang again had, as noted, been undertaken at the request of the Americans in an effort to distract the enemy from imminent offensive operations in the Central and Southwest Pacific Areas. They were, in truth, essentially ineffective in that regard and, in the grand scheme of things, may be regarded as tinkering on the perimeter; merely tweaking the tail of the Japanese dragon. That they were able to be undertaken at all, and that the enemy response was so inadequate, was because that dragon had, in Simpson's words, become 'fireless'. Or at least in the East Indies and Indian Ocean, for it was obvious from what direction the greatest threat loomed. To borrow a phrase from a different context: '. . . the least guarded points, in the Second World War at any rate, were almost invariably the least important points'.[92]

Quenching that fire in the naval context had been achieved by the US Pacific Fleet, and in particular its carrier component which had in 1944 just about reached its apotheosis in Mitscher's Fast Carrier Task Force (Task Force 58). Indeed on 19 June, the first day of the Battle of the Philippine

Sea (19–20 June 1944), Task Force 58 had 450 Hellcats operating from its four Task Groups, each of which contained four carriers.[93] The result of the largest carrier-to-carrier battle in history has come down to us as the 'Great Marianas Turkey Shoot', with Japanese carrier aviation playing the turkey rather than the dragon. It cost the IJN two fleet carriers and virtually the entire air strength of the Combined Fleet.[94]

Similarly, MacArthur's campaigns in the Southwest Pacific Area, particularly the ongoing Western New Guinea campaign of which the aforementioned Hollandia operation was the curtain-raiser, had a devastating effect on Japanese land-based aviation. Allied Intelligence had reported that there were 351 enemy aircraft stationed at three airfields around Hollandia where they were considered out of range of USAAF attack.[95] The commander of the Fifth Air Force in MacArthur's command, General George Kenney, pushed to get P-38 fighters modified for long-range missions so that they could accompany long-range B-24 heavy bombers.[96] Kenney sent sixty of these, with P-38 escort fighters, against Hollandia on 30 March. That, and follow-up raids, destroyed nearly all the operational Japanese aircraft: 'On April 3rd we completed the destruction of all the airplanes based at Hollandia. The photographs indicated a total number of 288 wrecked and burned-out aircraft.'[97] Morison says that these claims were on the 'modest side': 'after the airfields had been captured 340 wrecked aircraft were counted on and around the strips and an estimated 50 more had been shot down over the jungle, in which their remains were concealed.'[98]

Nevertheless, and despite it being a minor player, under Somerville's tutelage the Eastern Fleet had not only survived but had, in 1944, begun to grow into a force to be reckoned with. What might be done with its ever-growing capabilities was however a matter he was not to oversee; the bombardment of Sabang being, as he put it, 'my farewell party'.[99] On 23 August 1944 he was succeeded as Commander-in-Chief Eastern Fleet by Admiral Sir Bruce Fraser, the former Commander-in-Chief of the Home Fleet.

Chapter 13

Admirals in Collision[1]
(Generals and Politicians too)

The replacement of Somerville had first been mooted by the Admiralty in early 1944. Admiral Andrew Cunningham, the former C-in-C of the Mediterranean, who became First Sea Lord and Chief of the Naval Staff after the death of Dudley Pound in October 1943, explained the rationale in his memoirs:

> Some changes in the important naval commands were due at about this time. Before long the most important fleet would be that in the East, while the Home Fleet would decline in importance. Moreover the Admiralty representative in Washington, Admiral Sir Percy Noble, was shortly due to retire and it was necessary to find a suitable relief. The position was very important, and Noble had been most successful. He was popular and highly esteemed by his American colleagues, and his place was difficult to fill. Sir James Somerville seemed to be the very man . . .[2]

As Marder, Jacobsen and Horsefield point out, this arrangement made perfect sense from Cunningham's perspective. Noble, a former commander of Western Approaches, had been ideal to head the British Admiralty Delegation while the North Atlantic was the central zone of Anglo-American naval co-operation. However, by early 1944 the main naval scene was moving to the war with Japan; therefore Somerville's background was highly relevant. Also, and surely not incidentally, he would support Cunningham's strong desire for the Royal Navy to operate in the Pacific.[3] This was of course to cause ructions, of which more below. In any event, Somerville reluctantly accepted the appointment on 6 March; he was to write to Fraser two months later that '. . . the idea of the next job for which I am earmarked fills me with gloom and despondency. I would much sooner have command of a trawler.'[4] Neither was Churchill keen on the idea. His new-found admiration of Somerville, prompted by the April attack on Sabang, led him to question Cunningham and the First Lord, Alexander: 'Why do we want to make a change here at all? It seems to me that he knows the theatre, has right ideas about it, and is capable of daring action. Does he want to go to Washington and give up his fighting command?'[5] To quote Cunningham again: '. . . it was some time before he [Churchill] would agree to any change'.[6] Even then he had second thoughts after the Sourabaya attack: 'this idea of moving Admirals, when they are on the top of their form, from the theatres where they are acting with success, in order that they should dance on Admiral King in Washington, is, in my opinion, entirely wrong'.[7]

Emphasizing these points about Somerville's redeployment is of importance because of a controversy that later arose, the author of which was Admiral of the Fleet Earl Mountbatten of Burma as he had then become. With the rather lowlier rank of captain, but raised to being an acting-admiral, Mountbatten had been appointed to the position of Supreme Commander for the newly created South East Asia Command (SEAC); established on 15 November 1943. As Churchill put it: 'The appointment of an officer of the substantive rank of Captain RN to the Supreme Command of one of the main theatres of the war was an unusual step; but, having carefully prepared the ground beforehand, I was not surprised when the President agreed.'[8] Mountbatten had, according to Churchill, 'unique qualifications, in that he is intimately acquainted with all three branches of the Services, and also with amphibious operations'.[9]

It is not proposed to here delve deeply into the labyrinthine complexities attendant upon the command arrangements of SEAC, beyond how they impinged upon the Eastern Fleet and its Commander-in-Chief. Indeed, differences of opinion on what SEAC's strategy should be were summed up in a few words by the American General Everett Hughes in his diary entry for 13 April 1944: 'Something wrong in Burma! British want to go to Singapore, US to China.'[10] Indeed, SEAC was supposedly known by Americans to stand for 'Save England's Asian Colonies'.[11]

As has already been discussed, the Americans prioritised operations in northern Burma as a way of succouring Chiang's regime in China whilst the British, at least in Churchill and his Cabinet's, view saw the reconquest of their imperial possessions as being more important. This was to be achieved by amphibious operations in the Bay of Bengal, most notably Operation Culverin, an amphibious operation to occupy the northern tip of Sumatra which over time encompassed several variations on much the same theme. The Prime Minister, on his way to the Second Quebec Conference (12–16 September 1944), put it thus: 'Singapore must be redeemed and Malaya freed. . . . We had to regain on the field of battle our rightful possessions in the Far East, and not have them handed back to us at the peace table.'[12] Both involved the Eastern Fleet. The British were, however, divided, inasmuch as the Chiefs of Staff, and particularly Cunningham, rejected Churchill's view; the resources required for extensive amphibious operations in

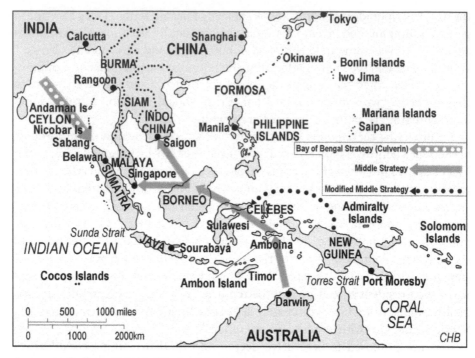

Strategic Options 1944. © Charles Blackwood.

The Eastern Fleet began to be reinforced and built up early in 1944, causing a tremendous war of words and ideas between Churchill and his advisers as to what it would be used for and future British strategy against Japan. The Prime Minister wanted to utilize it to support amphibious operations across the Bay of Bengal to recapture lost colonial possessions. The Chiefs of Staff, knowing that resources were not available for this and that the United States would not provide them, wanted the Eastern Fleet to operate in the Pacific alongside the American Fleet. They eventually compromised on the Middle Strategy, subsequently modified slightly, in which the Fleet would operate on the left flank of MacArthur's Southwest Pacific Area advance. Ultimately, all three of these strategic plans were, perforce, abandoned and the Eastern Fleet segued into the British Pacific Fleet.

the Bay of Bengal were simply not available, so therefore they wanted an alternative strategy: a reinforced Eastern Fleet to join the United States in the Pacific. However it was to be used, the issue that caused a breach between Somerville and Mountbatten was over who commanded it.

Discounting Nimitz, whose command was overwhelmingly American and almost exclusively naval, and Wilson (Eisenhower's Mediterranean successor), there were basically only two other Supreme Commanders on the (Western) Allied side at that time: Eisenhower and MacArthur. These very different men, with equally disparate command styles and structures, furnished models on which Mountbatten might base his command of SEAC. The important distinction between these two paradigms, as far as Somerville was concerned, was the role of the individual service commanders within the overall structure. Eisenhower's role was seen as that of chairman and co-ordinator of three distinct (Army, Navy, and Air) Commanders-in-Chief who led their respective services and planned their own operations as required. MacArthur's command functioned quite differently. He was in direct command of all land, sea and air forces, and each subordinate service carried out operations in accordance with plans drawn up by MacArthur and his staff. Somerville's position as he understood it at the time was laid out in a letter to his wife of 30 September 1943:

> You ask what Dickie has to do with [the] E[astern] F[leet]?[13] Well all that happens is that certain ships are placed under his orders for specific operations . . . Unless he tries to do a MacArthur, which I trust he won't, I think Dickie ought to do quite well. Anyhow I shall do my best to help him over any difficult stiles where possibly my experience may be of value.[14]

Unfortunately, from Somerville's perspective, Dickie did indeed try and 'do a MacArthur' and he was writing again to his a wife a month later stating that:

> D[ickie] is too much inclined to go into detail and furthermore to try and centralise the conduct of operations in his own hands. I've told him that any attempt to set up a MacArthur command is bound to end in failure . . .[15]

This feud, which is not too strong a term, escalated to the point where each admiral fired off messages to the Chiefs of Staff seeking clarification of what their respective roles and responsibilities were and whether or not the Eastern Fleet did, or did not, form part of SEAC. The matter grew wearisome in the extreme, with what can now only be judged as infantile bickering over, for example, whether or not Mountbatten had the right to visit individual ships of the Eastern Fleet, or whether he could only do so as a guest of Somerville. As the editor of his papers put it: 'The increasing differences between the two men overshadowed the remainder of Somerville's time in the Indian Ocean. It is not too much to say that at time he became obsessed with them, and their constant repetition in his papers becomes tedious.'[16] The conclusions reached by Marder, Jacobsen and Horsefield about the background to it all rings true; the Eastern Fleet was not 'actively engaged' so, 'not having the Japanese to fight, the Admirals fought one another'.[17]

More seriously, and paralleling and in many ways underlying these disagreements, there was a much larger row brewing between the Government, as represented by Churchill, the War Cabinet and Mountbatten on one side, and the

Chiefs of Staff on the other, over the correct British strategy to be pursued in the war against Japan. As already noted, there was a difference of opinion between these two bodies concerning what the Eastern Fleet, in particular, should be used for. What it boiled down to ultimately was that Churchill, and his civilian colleagues (or most of them), had a political purpose in mind; regaining Imperial possessions. Pursuing this policy, however, meant mounting significant amphibious operations across the Bay of Bengal, which is of course why the former head of Combined Operations, 'a complete triphibian', had been appointed.[18]

Churchill wrote to Mountbatten in early January 1944 exhorting him to plan and undertake such operations:

> The main thing for you to concentrate on is . . . CULVERIN. . . . Do not allow anything to take your eye off it. Here alone will you have the opportunity of organizing new fields in the world war, and here alone in the amphibious sphere will you have my aid.[19]

Churchill's rhetorical 'aid' was not enough. Mountbatten required resources and in an attempt to get them, and gain approval for major operations in South East Asia in general, in February 1944 he had despatched his American Chief of Staff, General Albert C. Wedemeyer, to London and Washington as head of what became known as the Axiom Mission. As if to demonstrate the inevitable intertwining of politics and war, Mountbatten's American Deputy Supreme Allied Commander, General Joseph 'Vinegar Joe' Stilwell, intervened. Upon discovering what Mountbatten was up to he despatched a mission of his own to Washington five days ahead of Wedemeyer. Its purpose was to 'checkmate the Limies'.[20] Stilwell, to be fair to him, was attempting to prevent any major deviation from basic US policy, which consistently sought to reinstate the Burma Road and build up forces and supplies in China. Given he wore multiple hats, being also Chief of Staff to Chiang Kai-shek and US commander in the China-Burma-India Theatre (including being responsible for all Lend-Lease supplies going to China), this was an unsurprising position. As Ritter points out, 'Stilwell agreed with that policy and sought to carry it out. Churchill and Mountbatten disagreed with that policy. That was the conflict in a nutshell.'[21]

There was a third policy which we shall come to in due course, but though the Axiom Mission visited London before going to Washington, it will be convenient to consider the reaction of the American Joint Chiefs of Staff first:

> The Joint Chiefs objected to CULVERIN because they believed that resources for it would not be available until after the defeat of Germany. Therefore, exploitation of a successful CULVERIN would

not reach Singapore before the middle of 1945 at the best. This date would be eight to ten months after U.S. forces were expected to have cut the Japanese line of communications to that area.[22]

There was no difference of opinion between the Joint Chiefs of Staff and the US Government. This radically differed from what was happening in London, which was rather disarmingly mentioned in the US Army's official history: 'In London the AXIOM Mission found that the British Chiefs of Staff and the War Cabinet had not settled on what British strategy in the Pacific war should be.'[23] In fact a 'mighty storm was brewing'.[24]

Churchill had been taken ill with pneumonia following the Cairo Conference (codenamed Sextant) of 22–26 November 1943 and had convalesced at Marrakesh, in French Morocco, before arriving back in London on 18 January.[25] This had not of course stopped him corresponding widely and there were many other matters with which he had to deal or in which he was greatly interested: for example, the amphibious landing at Anzio in Italy took place on 22 January 1944 and the Normandy Landings were scheduled for May. Despite it becoming quite clear at the Cairo Conference that Culverin could not be mounted through lack of resources, Churchill had not wavered in his ambition, as per his message to Mountbatten that resulted in the Axiom Mission.[26] In their final report on the Conference, the Combined Chiefs had agreed in principle on a document concerning an overall plan for the defeat of Japan which, in Churchill's words, 'contemplated the dispatch of a detachment of the British Fleet which was provisionally scheduled to become active in the Pacific in June 1944'. Both Roosevelt and Churchill initialled the document, but had no time 'to discuss these long-term schemes either with our own advisers or between ourselves'.[27]

Churchill was at Marrakesh when he received the first intimation that the Chiefs of Staff had begun work on developing the strategy he had initialled. He found himself 'immediately in disagreement' and 'thus arose the only considerable difference which I and the War Cabinet had with our trusted military colleagues'.[28]

General Sir Alan Brooke, the Chairman of the British Chiefs of Staff, was of the opinion that the project had to be tested by one essential question: 'what would it contribute to the shortening of the war against Japan?'[29] Since the answer, an opinion shared by all three Chiefs, was that it would contribute nothing and might even cause delays, then the stage was set for a major confrontation. Brooke's diary entry for 21 February sets this out:

A long Chiefs of Staff meeting . . . discussing Pacific strategy and deciding on a plan of action to tackle the PM to convince him that we cannot take the tip of Sumatra for him. We shall have very serious trouble with him over this.[30]

Brooke wrote to Wavell the following day about the 'dissension' amongst Allied leaders as to how to achieve the defeat of Japan, noting that '. . . the PM . . . still passionately in love with the tip of Sumatra'.[31] This 'passion', according to Brooke, was not entirely new. He traced 18 August 1943, whilst Churchill and the Chiefs were on their way to Quebec, as 'the first day on which Winston began to develop his affection for the northern tip of Sumatra. It became an obsession with him . . .'[32] Indeed, whilst at the Quebec Conference, and despite it being pointed out to him by Roosevelt (who believed that the direct route to Japan lay along the Burma Road to China and through China to Japan)[33] that operations in Sumatra at that time would be 'heading away from the main direction of advance' he continued to insist that it would be a 'great strategic blow' and the 'Torch of the Indian Ocean'.[34]

Another parallel he utilized was perhaps less fortunate: 'in its promise of decisive consequences; he claimed it compared with the Dardanelles operation of 1915'.[35] Lieutenant General Sir Henry Pownall, Mountbatten's Chief of Staff in SEAC, was unimpressed. He later noted:

> Winston has compared northern Sumatra to the Dardanelles, and did so proudly. The analogy may well be correct. A tempting objective that glittered so brightly that it was attempted without adequate resources, and therefore failed. In fact a typical Winstonian project.[36]

Churchill famously once said 'I have not become the King's First Minister in order to preside over the liquidation of the British Empire'.[37] Yet he knew all was not well, particularly with 'The Jewel in the Crown'.[38] Nevertheless he remained defiant and an avowed Imperialist, determined to fight for the continuation of Empire.[39] He certainly fought with the Chiefs of Staff over preserving the attack on Sumatra in particular and the liberation of British territory generally. Brooke's diary entry for 25 February shows the extent of the difference of opinion:

> I am quite exhausted after seven-and-a-half hours with Winston to-day, and most of that time engaged in heavy argument . . . At 12 noon the Chiefs of Staff met the P.M. and were kept till 1.45 p.m. He was still insisting on doing the North Sumatra operation and would not discuss any other. I had a series of heated discussions with him. Then a hurried lunch and at 3 p.m. we met again. This time he had packed the house against us, and was accompanied by Anthony Eden, Oliver Lyttelton and Attlee, in addition the whole of Dickie Mountbatten's Army, Naval and Air Force officers. . . . The whole party were against the Chiefs of Staff . . . Dickie chipped in and talked unadulterated nonsense and I lost my temper with him. It was a desperate meeting with no opportunity of discussing strategy on its merits. Thank God

I have now got Andrew Cunningham to support me. It makes all the difference from the days of poor old Dudley Pound . . . We argued from 3 p.m. to 5:30 p.m. I got very heated at times . . . Winston pretended that this was all a frame-up against his pet Sumatra operation and almost took it as a personal matter . . .[40]

Churchill was, though, fighting on too many fronts, and whilst he could, and did, continue contradicting the Chiefs of Staff he could not feasibly dismiss the concerns of the head of what was now unquestionably the dominant partner in the Western Alliance; President Roosevelt. Indeed, Ritter says that, seeing Culverin as a 'colonialist enterprise' (which of course it was), Roosevelt 'vetoed it'.[41] Not quite, but the President had telegraphed the Prime Minister on 24 February reiterating the American position in respect of Upper Burma:

I am gravely concerned over the recent trends in strategy that favour an operation toward Sumatra and Malaya in the future rather than face the immediate obstacles that confront us in Burma. I fail to see how an operation against Sumatra and Malaya, requiring tremendous resources and forces, can possibly be mounted until after the conclusion of the war in Europe. Lucrative as a successful 'Culverin' might be, there appears much more to be gained by employing all the resources we now have available in an all-out drive into Upper Burma, so that we can build up our air strength in China and ensure the essential support for our westward advance to the Formosa–China–Luzon area.[42]

This was not quite a veto because the Prime Minister was able to deflect the President by 'disingenuously' assuring him that 'nothing will be withdrawn or withheld from the operations in North Burma for the sake of Culverin'.[43] Resources would though have to be withdrawn from somewhere in order to carry it out, for whilst Wedemeyer's mission reckoned that undertaking Culverin would not require forces that weren't already in South East Asia, including the Eastern Fleet, it did concede that further resources would have to be temporarily assigned.

According to a minute compiled by Brigadier Ian Jacob, the Military Assistant Secretary to the War Cabinet, this requirement was huge: four fleet carriers, twenty-two escort carriers, twenty-three cruisers, sixty-five destroyers and twenty-two other escorts. The amphibious lift alone would require 142 cargo ships and more than 1,000 specialized landing craft.[44] This was certainly a massive over-estimate. Nevertheless, there would at least be some requirement for the specialized equipment necessary for amphibious warfare, and this was inevitably in short supply. The only possible source, unless they were to be withdrawn from

Europe which would jeopardise Overlord, was the Pacific. The reaction of the American administration, and perhaps Admiral King in particular, to any such request can only be imagined. That of course was where the American veto lay.

To return to the Chiefs of Staff battle, Churchill would not let the matter go and things had become serious. As Brooke recorded in his diary on 3 March pertaining to a 'very long' Chiefs of Staff meeting which had been 'cleared of secretaries':

> . . . I had to discuss the very difficult problem which is brewing up, and in which the PM is trying to frame up the War Cabinet against the Chiefs of Staff Committee. It is all about the future Pacific strategy, it looks very serious and may well lead to the resignation of the Chiefs of Staff Committee. I am shattered by the present condition of the PM. He has lost all balance and is in a very dangerous mood.[45]

The resignation of the Chiefs of Staff, their ultimate recourse if overruled, would, as Fraser pointed out, 'have been an intolerable blow to public confidence'.[46] Major General Sir Hastings Ismay, Churchill's Chief Staff Officer, Deputy Secretary (Military) to the War Cabinet, and an additional member of the Chiefs of Staff Committee (who 'embodied the formal and informal links between civil and military authority, betweeen the Minister of Defence and the Chiefs of Staff'), tried to smooth the matter over.[47]

> It seems absolutely certain that you and your Ministerial colleagues will not agree to the Pacific Strategy. On the other hand, the Chiefs of Staff . . . are extremely unlikely to retract the military opinions they have expressed . . . Nor can we exclude the possibility of resignation on the part of the latter. A breach of this kind, undesirable at any time, would be little short of catastrophic at the present juncture. . . .
>
> I suggest that you should call a meeting . . . of the Defence Committee next week to go exhaustively into the Indian Ocean and Pacific strategies. . . . It is just possible that agreement can be reached. If so, well and good. If not, would it not be possible and right for you to take the line that the issue cannot be decided on military grounds alone and that, apart from the military merits of the respective strategies, political considerations must be overriding? I cannot but think that the Chiefs of Staff would accept this decision with complete loyalty and would set to work at once to make the best possible plans for implementing it.[48]

Churchill indeed held a meeting, but it was definitely the case that no agreement could be reached. He was supported by Cabinet Ministers Clement Atlee (Deputy Prime Minister), Anthony Eden (Foreign Secretery), Oliver Lyttelton

(Minister of Production), and Lord Leathers (Minister of War Transport). Brooke recorded that the proceedings had 'Cunningham so wild with rage that he hardly dared to let himself speak'.

> I therefore had to do most of the arguing, and for 2½ hours from 10 p.m. to 12.30 a.m. I went at it hard, arguing with the PM and 4 Cabinet Ministers. The arguments of the latter were so puerile it made me ashamed to think that they were Cabinet Ministers. . . . I had little difficulty in dealing with any of the arguments they put forward.[49]

Churchill glossed over these issues in his memoirs, merely noting 'discussions with the Chiefs of Staff were long and sometimes tense'.[50] He did mention though how the arrival of the Japanese Fleet at Singapore, the presence of which had discomfited Somerville, created an 'unexpected event of the first importance' and the possibility of it entering the Bay of Bengal 'put a stop for the time being to Culverin or other amphibious adventures . . .'[51] It didn't, however, prevent the Prime Minister from attempting to find further justification for his favoured strategy. This involved writing, without informing any of the Chiefs of Staff, to Roosevelt:

> After the surrender of the Italian Fleet in September 1943 I was very keen on sending a detachment of our Fleet as quickly as possible to the Pacific, but when I opened this with Admiral King . . . I formed the impression that he did not need us very much . . . Accordingly, I should be very grateful if you could let me know whether there is any specific American operation in the Pacific . . . which would be hindered or prevented by the absence of a British Fleet detachment.[52]

The President advised on 13 March that there weren't any specific operations that would be adversely affected by the absence of a British Fleet Detachment. This was a reply that Churchill deemed 'conclusive', and so 'thus fortified' he felt it his 'duty to give a ruling'.[53]

> . . . it is in the interest of Britain to pursue what may be termed the 'Bay of Bengal Strategy', at any rate for the next twelve months. I therefore feel it my duty, as Prime Minister and Minister of Defence, to give the following rulings:
>
> (a) Unless unforeseen events occur, the Indian theatre and the Bay of Bengal will remain, until the summer of 1945, the centre of gravity for the British and Imperial war effort against Japan.
> (b) All preparations will be made for amphibious action across the Bay of Bengal against the Malay peninsula and the various island outposts by which it is defended, the ultimate objective being the reconquest of Singapore.

(c) A powerful British fleet will be built up, based on Ceylon, Addu Attoll and East Indian posts, under the shield of our strong shore-based aircraft. The fleet train for this Eastern Fleet must be developed as fast as possible . . .

(d) The plans of the South-East Asia Command for amphibious action across the Bay of Bengal shall be examined, corrected and improved with the desire of engaging the enemy as closely and as soon as possible.

(e) The reconnaissance mission to Australia shall be sent as soon as I have approved the personnel. They should report promptly . . . and propose measure for carrying the Eastern Fleet and its Fleet Train . . . into the South-West Pacific and basing it on Australian ports should we at any time wish to adopt that policy.

I should be very ready to discuss the above rulings with the Chiefs of Staff in order that we may be clear in our minds as to the line we are going to take in discussion with our American friends. Meanwhile, with this difference on long-term plans settled, we may bend our-selves to the tremendous and urgent tasks which are now so near . . .[54]

This was pretty much the course of action that Ismay had suggested, though it didn't quite go the full way of being a diktat; Churchill was too clever a politician for that. Adding that he was ready to discuss the rulings, and the nod in the strategic direction the Chiefs of Staff advocated with his final point had, to plunder modern phraseology, left him some wriggle room. He was certainly shrewd enough to know that the mass resignation of the Chiefs would have been a disaster for him with the potential to bring down the Cabinet.[55] It was, perhaps, an attempt to head off any such outcome, and divide them, which led him to send it to each Chief individually rather than collectively. Also note-worthy are the paragraphs omitted from the published version of his 'rulings'. These included:

I very much regret that the Chiefs of Staff should have proceeded so far in this matter and reached such settled conclusions upon it with-out in any way endeavouring to ascertain the views of the civil power under which they are serving.[56]

This was, in no uncertain terms, laying down the law about who was in charge. But that he was willing to address the professional heads of the three armed services in these terms, especially at the height of a war and with the crucial invasion of Western Europe looming, does not reflect at all well on the author. Indeed, it smacks of treating them as recalcitrant juniors.

Brooke's diary entry for 20 March exemplifies his frustration: 'One of the worst of Cabinet meetings with Winston in one of his worst moods . . . I cannot stick any more meetings like it! He has now produced an impossible document on the Pacific strategy in which he is overriding our opinions and our advice.'[57] The following day, the three Chiefs discussed 'how best to deal with Winston's last impossible document' with resignation again being mentioned.[58]

Though Churchill's 'impossible document' had been addressed to the Chiefs as individuals, they responded collectively and, perhaps more importantly, in a convincing but non-confrontational manner.

> We feel sure that there is still some misunderstanding as to our views and proposals, and we welcome the opportunity of a further discussion with you on the whole subject . . . We did our best to explain our views on long-term strategy for the war against Japan to you before Sextant [the Cairo Conference], but your other preoccupations, both before and after . . . precluded this. We were therefore at pains to ensure that the conclusions of the Combined Chiefs of Staff were couched in the most non-committal terms . . . [and only] approved in principle as a basis for further investigation and preparation, subject to final approval.[59]

Whilst this response avoided the head-on collision that had appeared imminent, it did not resolve the matter. Rather it put it off for another day, which nevertheless had the effect of taking some of the heat out of the conflict. There were no resignations on the one side, nor a final ultimatum on the other.

A further distraction had arrived on 12 March 1944 with the Japanese taking the offensive in Northern Burma. Though Churchill and Mountbatten, and indeed the Chiefs of Staff, were wary of land campaigns in such hostile territory, Lieutenant General Sir William Slim was preparing to undertake one: 'with landing craft and shipping unavailable, we should have to re-enter Burma overland . . .'[60] Choosing to fight a defensive campaign initially, so as to break the Japanese before launching his own offensive, the campaign around Imphal and Kohima lasted until July. The counter-offensive saw the Indian Army reach an 'apotheosis of glory'.[61]

Another factor was of course that even if Culverin had been adopted as the unanimous, unreserved and official policy of the British Government it could not have been carried out. As Slim had noted, landing craft and shipping were simply unavailable, and the infrastructure in India could not support both a land campaign and amphibious operations; it has been estimated that India's entire harbour system in 1944 had only the capacity of Southampton.[62]

There was very little that could be done about Indian infrastructure in the short term, but Churchill appealed personally to Roosevelt in an effort to increase British amphibious capability in the Indian Ocean. The indispensable equipment for carrying out seaborne assaults was the Landing Ship Tank (LST); a vessel capable of transporting large numbers of heavy tanks, artillery and personnel directly onto the landing beach. First used in large number during the invasion of Sicily in 1943, LSTs proved to be a transformative technical innovation essential for amphibious warfare, but there were never enough of them and the vast majority were built in the United States.[63] An overburdened Britain did not have the capabilities to produce the number it required as he told the President:

> A review of our requirements for amphibious operations against Japan clearly shows that LST will be the limiting factor. We are trying every expedient to increase our own output, but it appears inevitable that for operations in the spring of 1945 we shall have a shortage between 80 and 100 of these ships.
>
> I understand that on your present programme you will reach an output of 55 per month by June, and that thereafter your monthly rate drops to about 40. If you could see your way to maintain the monthly rate at 55, then by the 1st December the greater part of the shortage would be met.
>
> It is my earnest wish to operate against the Japanese as soon as our amphibious resources are released from the European theatre and I very much hope you will find it possible to meet this request.[64]

The response that arrived some nine days later was not reassuring:

> Our program has recently been increased . . . so that the drop you mention does not occur so soon. It is not possible further to accelerate or increase our program without interference with other programs which have already been reduced to the limit . . . the United States Chiefs of Staff believe that the combined needs for prosecuting the war against Japan can be met under present programs and that allocations should not be made until operations have been definitely decided upon.[65]

Churchill clearly resented Britain's dependence on, and thus loss of the power of decision to, America. He was to rail, ineffectually, at British impotence in the matter, and the consequences thereof, in May:

> The American method of trying to force particular policies by the withholding or giving of certain weapons, such as carrying [transport] airplanes or LSTs, in theatres where the command belongs by right of overwhelming numbers to us, must be objected to at the right time and strongly protested against.[66]

In truth it wouldn't have made an immediate difference if LSTs had been immediately available; the Eastern Fleet, right up until the time of Somerville's leave-taking, was incapable of much more than hit-and-run type actions. In any event, the imminence of the overwhelmingly important Operation Overlord, the operation to open the Second Front which Stalin had been promised would take place in May, was increasingly very much at the forefront of the British Government's concerns.

Notwithstanding this, the Commonwealth Prime Ministers' Conference was held in London between 1–16 May 1944, with Australia's John Curtin and General Thomas Blamey attending. The Australian Army's Commander-in-Chief, Blamey had been appointed Commander, Allied Land Forces, in the Southwest Pacific Area under MacArthur in 1942, though the latter seldom let him function as such.[67] According to Horner, when Blamey arrived he was greeted by Lieutenant General Edward Smart, the Australian Army Representative in London, who informed him that:

> . . . the position is now that all the [British] Services favour the use of Australia as a main base and the strategy that would go with it. . . . Winston Churchill was hard to convince and reluctant to make the approach to Australia. However, it is said that he is coming round to the Services view.[68]

This might have been a somewhat over-optimistic view, though discussion around the varying strategies that might, or could, apply were undertaken. That referred to by Smart was dubbed the Middle Strategy. This foresaw Australian and British forces conducting operations from Darwin, Australia, into the Netherlands East Indies (against Ambon (Amboina) Island, Sulawesi (Celebes), and Borneo) then on towards French Indochina and Malaya. Also considered was the Modified Middle Strategy, which started from northern New Guinea and bypassed Ambon.[69] Whether 'modified' or not, the Middle Strategy was essentially a proposal to operate on the left-flank of MacArthur's command.

Eventually, and after 'a good number of days' the British gave the Australians a detailed statement of what forces might be sent on the assumption that 'Germany was defeated by the end of 1944'. Brooke though 'felt constrained' to warn the Australians on 10 May that: 'It should be clearly understood that the statement does not imply any commitment or the adoption of any specific policy or plan of operation in the Pacific.' The problem for the Chiefs was that whilst they wanted Australia to begin development of bases, which would be needed if British forces were to operate in the Pacific, they were unable to give any firm commitment to Australia until such time as the Government, and Churchill in particular, came down on their side. The fact that the Prime Minister had though participated in discussions that allowed of alternatives to operations in the Bay of Bengal was perhaps an indication that he was indeed 'coming round to the Services view'. Even if that were the case, there were though many other difficulties. Brooke enumerated several on 18 May:

> . . . a long [Chiefs of Staff meeting] . . . to try and settle a final Pacific strategy to put up to the PM. The problem is full of difficulties, although the strategy is quite clear. . . . Winston is determined Mountbatten must be given some operation to carry out; Andrew Cunningham is equally determined that Mountbatten should not control the Eastern Fleet; Americans wish to gather all laurels connected with Pacific fighting, and Winston is equally determined that we should not be tied to the apron strings of the Americans![70]

Four days later, the Chiefs of Staff put a version of the Middle Strategy to Churchill, with Ambon Island as the first objective. They couched it in terms that were almost guaranteed to appeal to the Prime Minister, describing 'a substantial Imperial and Dominion contribution by forces under the command of their own British commanders'. To make it a truly joint British-American operation, they even proposed a change in the current command arrangements of the Southwest Pacific Area:

> At present General MacArthur . . . takes his instructions from the United States Joint Chiefs of Staff, and the British Chiefs of Staff have no say in the choice of his operations. Since it is one of our objects to ensure that the British Empire plays the greatest possible effective part in the operations for the defeat of Japan, we feel it is only right that the Command arrangements should be altered and that the South-West Pacific Area should become a theatre of joint responsibility, subordinate to the Combined Chiefs of Staff, so that we may share in the control of operations in that theatre . . . [and] that the British and Dominion forces should operate as a distinct Command with British Commanders under General MacArthur's supreme direction.[71]

If the memorandum had indeed been prepared with a view to appealing to its recipient then it seemed to have worked. Or at least Brooke thought so after a Chiefs of Staff meeting on the evening of 24 May: 'I think we have at last got him swung towards an Australian-based strategy as opposed to his old love, the Sumatra tip.'[72]

The Chiefs of Staff also had an opportunity to discuss their proposals with their American opposite numbers when the Joint Chiefs arrived in the UK on

8 June.[73] The main purpose of the visit was related to the Normandy Landings, which had taken place two days earlier, and to iron out an Anglo-American dispute which had arisen over Operation Anvil (to be renamed Dragoon on 1 August); the amphibious assault on France's Mediterranean coast.[74] After visiting the beachhead in France, which was still being contested by the defenders, the Combined Chiefs found time to discuss the Middle Strategy on 14 June: '. . . meeting with the American Chiefs of Staff in the afternoon . . . We discussed the Pacific and found that they were in agreement with a proposed strategy based on North-Western Australia and directed through Amboina towards Borneo.'[75]

There are two matters that stand out in respect of the Middle Strategy as proposed above. The first, and surely most important, was that whilst it moved the operational base from India to Australia and changed the axis of attack from west-east to south-north, it in no way changed the situation with regard to resources. Therefore, operations in furtherance of it would likely take even longer to build-up and execute than would be the case for Culverin.

The second relates to MacArthur, the Supreme Commander under whose auspices operations would be carried out. The existence of the proposed strategy was revealed to him by King in a message of 25 July 1944, in which he was informed that:

> The British might propose to extend the boundaries of the South East Asia Command to include most of the Netherlands East Indies where British forces might hope to operate after Southwest Pacific Area forces had moved on into the Philippines.[76]

The 'American Caesar's'[77] reaction, in a letter to King with a copy to Marshall of 5 August 1944, was predictable:

> I am completely opposed to this proposition . . . The British have contributed nothing to this campaign . . . They now propose to enter this theatre at the moment when victory clearly lies before us in order to reap the benefit of our successes. . . . Let the British operate in their own area against Burma, Malaya, Sumatra, and the east coast of Asia![78]

He wrote to Marshall five days later, pointing out that he intended to attack Borneo and the rest of the Netherlands East Indies with the exception of Sumatra as soon as possible from the direction of the Philippines. He had no objection to British participation, but they should operate 'under the command set-up and the strategic control that has been agreed upon and which has been in successful operation for so long'.[79] In other words, they must be under his Supreme Command. MacArthur need not have worried, for both parties to the dispute in Britain had cooled on the Middle Strategy very quickly, the Chiefs due to the delays and difficulties that it would inevitably entail, and Churchill because he had reverted to his original conception of operations to recover British imperial territory very much along lines that MacArthur would have approved.

The harsh reality of the situation was obvious to the Chiefs. If Britain was to meaningfully participate in the war with Japan, the only feasible way of doing so was by concentrating naval forces, a battlefleet, in the Pacific and operating alongside the US Navy. The advantages were obvious. Reinforcements that were no longer required in Europe were already being sent to build up the Eastern Fleet, and the shipping requirements needed for support were, relatively, modest compared with a large-scale amphibious campaign, though the notion would meet with strong opposition from Lord Leathers, the Minister of War Transport.[80] Also, bases in Australia, already being investigated in terms of the Middle Strategy, would be available.

It was not so obvious to Churchill and his colleagues, though the minds of the latter were changing, at least in the direction of the Middle Strategy. Eden recorded that at a meeting held on 6 July that the Chiefs were 'emphatic' that resources to mount Culverin were simply not available until after Germany had been defeated. However, 'W[inston] kept muttering that resources were available, but produced no evidence and ended up by accusing us all of trying to corner the Prime Minister or take it out of him or some such phrase . . . I called this "a deplorable evening".'.[81] Brooke too noted the disagreement, adding that it infuriated Churchill who became 'ruder and ruder'.[82]

Rudeness could not overcome reality however, and a further meeting on 14 July in which they were '. . . treated to the same old monologue of how much better it was to take the tip of Sumatra and then the Malay States and finally Singapore than it was to join the Americans and fight Japan close at home in the Pacific' underlined the fact that Churchill was becoming isolated.[83] Cunningham recorded his dissatisfaction:

> The attitude of mind of the politicians about this question is astonishing. They are obviously frightened of the Americans laying down the law as to what is to happen when Japan is defeated to the various islands, ports and other territories. This appears to be quite likely if the Americans are left to fight Japan by themselves. But they will not lift a finger to get a force into the Pacific; they prefer to hang about outside and recapture our own rubber trees. No decision of course though there are indications that the three ministers [Atlee, Eden, and Lyttelton] are starting to disagree with the PM.[84]

Eden and Atlee had indeed been convinced by the Chiefs' arguments, and were rejecting Churchill's as 'wishful thinking', as the Foreign Secretary recorded:

> 'Two hours of wishful thinking', Attlee called it on a slip to me and he was not far wrong. The Far Eastern war is going to be a problem for our people and what I like about [the] Chiefs of Staff plan is that it gives us the nucleus of an Imperial force at an early date and upon this we can build.[85]

Brooke too deprecated the fact that still no decision had been arrived at, and that they had to listen to 'the PM's futile and empty arguments . . . again and again'. Both Atlee and Eden were against Churchill, and eventually Brooke put the matter directly to him: '. . . one or other course must be selected at once . . . we cannot go on with this indecision. If the Government does not wish to accept our advice let them say so, but for Heaven's sake let us have a decision.' The Prime Minister stated he would think about it and would give a decision within a week.[86]

Brooke was right to argue in favour of a rapid decision. In fact it was probably too late in any event, for what the British leadership were arguing over was in danger of rapidly becoming a redundant exercise. The Americans were accelerating their campaign; the amphibious invasion of the island of Leyte, the first step in the liberation of the Philippines, was planned for the end of the year. MacArthur had stated that, after seizing the islands, 'the blockade that I will put across the line of supply between Japan and the Dutch East Indies will so strangle the Japanese Empire that it will have to surrender'.[87] This was hyperbole of course, but it was still fairly obvious what it meant for campaigns south of the Philippines; better to leave the Japanese garrisons there to 'wither on the vine'. The next stage in the American plan, as it stood at that time, was to land on Taiwan in early 1945. If the British were going to do anything by way of helping in this advance, then they would have to start doing it rapidly.

That Churchill's decision would not in fact be rapidly formulated was revealed when he stated that, before he arrived at any conclusions, matters would have to be discussed with Mountbatten. Brooke complained in his diary: 'he [Churchill] cannot understand strategy and argues the relative advantages of an attack on north Sumatra as opposed to one on Amboina, instead of discussing [the] relative merits of an attack on Japan based on India as opposed to one based on Australia.'[88]

Accordingly summoned, Mountbatten and Wedemeyer set off for London on 3 August and arrived on the evening of the following day. They were scheduled to hold discussions with the Chiefs the following Monday, 7 August, and then with Churchill on the mornings of the next two days. The hope was that a decision would be arrived at before the Wednesday evening, as the Prime Minister was leaving for a visit to the Italian front then.[89] Brooke and his fellow Chief of Staff, Marshal of the Royal Air Force Charles Portal, were to have accompanied him but could not go 'as we shall have to put his decision into effect'.[90]

The series of meetings held between Mountbatten and Wedemeyer on the one hand, and the Chiefs plus Churchill, Eden, Lyttelton and Atlee on the other, on 7 and 8 August failed to arrive at a definitive conclusion. Brooke recorded after the early session on the latter date that the Chiefs recommended 'the capture of Burma by a landing at Rangoon [Operation Vanguard] combined with a Pacific strategy of naval, air, and Dominion (Australian and New Zealand) forces operating from Australia'. Churchill, however, 'still hovers back to his tip of Sumatra and refuses to look at anything else'. The evening conference was 'if anything worse'. Churchill's arguments, he opined, 'were becoming puerile, for instance he upheld . . . that an attack on the tip of Sumatra would force a withdrawal of Japanese forces in northern Burma and would liquidate our commitment in that area'.[91] Cunningham echoed Brooke: 'No decisions were reached, in fact a thoroughly wasted day. What a drag on the wheel of war this man is. Everything is centralized in him with consequent indecision and waste of time before anything gets done.'[92] Churchill was indeed still pushing for Culverin and all that he saw flowing from it:

> If we could capture the Sumatra tip, we could soon master the air over the Malacca Straits, Malaya, and the Gulf of Siam, and we could strike direct at Singapore. . . . He felt that it was essential that we should have British troops in or near Singapore when Japan was defeated.[93]

Eden had already lent support to this latter point, by arguing earlier that '. . . it would be preferable for us to recapture our own territory than to play a minor role in the Pacific'.[94] Interestingly enough it was Mountbatten who, this time, pointed out that Churchill's idea for Sumatra was a non-starter. 'Considerable resources were required for Culverin, because there was no port in the Northern tip of Sumatra until Belawan was reached – 180 miles from the tip.' He went on to point out that given the requisite scale of resources Culverin could indeed be carried out, but that there was a caveat:

> . . . it should be remembered that when the operation had been examined a year ago the Japanese had not reinforced Burma. Since then they had put in four to five divisions which had made it impossible to release three Indian Divisions from Northern Burma as had originally been proposed . . . the reason he now recommended Vanguard was that he could take three divisions from Burma in order to put them into Burma at the South, whereas he could not afford to take these divisions and put them into Sumatra.[95]

However, the following day's meeting heralded a compromise, when the Chiefs drafted a conclusion on their South East Asia strategy based on the previous evening's work and presented it to Churchill, Atlee, Lyttelton, and Eden. Churchill had also produced a document which, as Brooke recorded, was 'not far off ours and I said so'. He suggested that Ismay should draft a third document 'combining our two papers', then adding, 'I told him privately that he was to draft it on our paper but with [the] PM's phraseology'.[96] That evening Brooke recorded 'we finally arrived at a policy for South East Asia'.[97]

Put basically, this policy had three components covering both the Bay of Bengal and the Pacific. The first was to 'contain the Japanese in Northern Burma'. This was a process already underway, the Fourteenth Army's victory in the Imphal-Kohima battle in June being a prelude to further advances.[98]

The second strand involved planning and preparing for Operation Vanguard, to which end proposals should be formulated for 'putting to the American Chiefs of Staff'. Carrying out the operation was a priority: 'Extreme efforts should be made . . . to launch this operation at the earliest moment whether Germany has surrendered or not.' In any event, 'plans and arrangements should be made forthwith' for moving four 'British Indian' and two 'British' divisions 'into the war against Japan' from the European theatre 'as soon as they can be spared'. No doubt at Churchill's insistence, Culverin was mentioned. 'If German organized resistance collapses early, it will be necessary to review the situation and decide between the operations against Rangoon and other operations, principally Culverin or a variant thereof . . .'[99] Thus was the Bay of Bengal dealt with. The Middle Strategy had though been relegated in favour of sending a battlefleet to the Pacific:

> The greatest offer of naval assistance should be made at once to the
> US Chiefs of Staff, it being impressed upon them that it is our desire
> to share with them in the main operations against the mainland of
> Japan or Formosa.[100]

Only if this offer were declined would the Middle Strategy be resurrected, in which case a 'British Empire Task Force under a British Commander, consisting of British, Australian, and New Zealand, land, sea and air forces, [would] operate under General MacArthur's supreme command'.[101] With this interminable issue at last settled, or apparently so, the Chiefs wrote to their opposite numbers in America apprising them of the decisions arrived at. Churchill, however, set in motion plans for a conference to discuss it, and other matters, with the President and his Joint Chiefs of Staff. He wrote to Roosevelt the same day:

> We have to settle the part the British Empire should take in the war
> against Japan after Germany's unconditional surrender. The situation

in Burma causes me much anxiety . . . It is impossible to resolve these thorny matters by correspondence and I am sure that, if we and the staffs were together, good working agreements could be reached.[102]

The meeting that ensued was thus arranged for Quebec (the Second Quebec Conference codenamed Octagon), Canada, on 12–16 September 1944.

Meanwhile, Somerville had been arranging to hand-over his command to Fraser, the latter having arrived in Ceylon on 22 August. They drove together to Geoffrey Layton's house where they had a 'short talk'.

He told me that he had not taken part in any of the discussions regarding future operations in this Theatre, but had been told we had made an offer of the Eastern Fleet to the US, to be used in the Pacific. . . . On the other hand General MacArthur was anxious to have a British Task Force in his area and this was backed up by Mr Curtin who also wished to see British Naval Forces based in Australia in order to counter balance to some extent American domination . . .[103]

The formal hauling up and down of flags signifying the transfer of command took place the next day, and the day after that Mountbatten returned and called on Somerville. He confirmed that the main units of the Eastern Fleet had been offered to the Americans, but was of the same opinion as Fraser in that Admiral King would refuse them a place in any attack on Japan proper. The Supreme Commander also offered that whereas the British could launch an amphibious attack using at most three divisions, the Americans now had the capability of throwing twenty divisions ashore. Any British participation could therefore only be token. They also discussed the likelihood of the Eastern Fleet coming under MacArthur's command and the command arrangements in that event. With regard to the amphibious attack on Rangoon (Operation Vanguard), Mountbatten stated that 'it must be fully staged and every effort made to ensure success'. Both men agreed that by the time an attack on Sumatra could be mounted 'we should be in a position to go straight to the Kra Peninsula [*sic*] or to any other points selected for the recapture of Malaya. He went on to add though that 'the PM still hankered after Culverin'.[104]

That the PM did indeed still hanker 'after Culverin', and considered the matter far from settled, became embarrassingly obvious during the journey to Canada aboard the great liner *Queen Mary* for the Quebec Conference. Brooke's diary reveals that he expected trouble: 'I am not looking forward to this journey and conference. Winston is still always set on capturing the tip of Sumatra . . .'[105] The Prime Minister had been unwell and therefore somewhat cantankerous, and on 9 September he sent them a written minute disagreeing with the notion that British troops should come under MacArthur: 'As is known I consider that all United Kingdom forces should operate across the Indian Ocean and not in the South-west Pacific.'[106] Brooke vented his feelings in his diary:

> . . . he now repudiates what we secured from him weeks ago and which we submitted to the Americans with his approval; namely the possible formation of a British Task Force under MacArthur. . . . The situation becomes quite impossible and I am at my wits' end as to what we are to do.[107]

He went on to add that 'we were to have met him this evening but he had started another temperature and had to remain in bed, cancelling an invitation for us to dine with him. I am afraid that he is definitely ill.' A meeting did take place the next day at noon, but Brooke again recorded his frustration at what he termed Churchill's 'absurdities' and 'nonsense'.[108]

As it happened, Brooke was to be most pleasantly surprised. On the morning of 13 September the first plenary meeting at Quebec was held. Churchill had with him the Chiefs of Staff, including Mountbatten's successor as Chief of Combined Operations Major General Robert Laycock, and Ismay. Also present was Field Marshal Sir John Dill, the Senior British Representative to the Combined Chiefs of Staff Committee. With Roosevelt were the Joint Chiefs, including Admiral William D Leahy, the President's Chief of Staff and Chairman of the Joint Chiefs. Churchill began the meeting prompted by Roosevelt, 'who asked me to open the discussion'.[109]

After a lengthy 'general survey of the war' the Prime Minister moved on to the campaigns against Japan. He noted that 'certain trouble-makers', who were tactfully left unnamed, had claimed that Britain 'would take no part in the war against Japan once Germany had been defeated'. This was not the case: 'The offer I now made was for the British main fleet to take part in the major operations against Japan under United States Supreme Command.' Roosevelt immediately intervened to say 'that the British Fleet was no sooner offered than accepted'.[110]

This came as something of a surprise. Indeed Cunningham, knowing that the offer of a Pacific battlefleet was being tabled to make a political point (Churchill had commented on 8 August that it would provide a valuable argument 'if we were at any time accused of not fulfilling our part as an Ally in the Pacific operations') had mused in his diary: 'He wants . . . to leave on record that the US refused the assistance of the British Fleet in the Pacific. He will be bitterly disappointed if they don't refuse!!!' [111]

Whether Churchill was 'bitterly disappointed' or not is unknown, but according to his subsequent account he 'cast back' a little later to 'ask for a definitive undertaking' on the matter:

> 'The offer of the British Fleet has been made' I repeated. 'Is it accepted?'
> 'Yes' said Mr Roosevelt.[112]

General Marshall's biographer quoted an unnamed 'irreverent British observer' who declared that the official minutes should read: 'At this point Admiral King was carried out.'[113] In fact, according to Buell, he merely 'glowered'.[114] Nevertheless, King, who was undoubtedly one of the 'trouble-makers' Churchill had avoided naming, attempted to row back on the arrangement at a subsequent Combined Chiefs' meeting. 'We had great trouble with King who lost his temper entirely', Brooke confided to his diary. 'He was determined if he could not to let British naval forces into Nimitz's command in the Central Pacific.'[115] Cunningham observed the same phenomenon, but was slightly more expansive about it:

> King flew into a rage. It couldn't be allowed there. He wouldn't have it, and so on. I called his attention to the President's acceptance of the Prime Minister's offer. He tried to make out that the acceptance didn't mean what it said . . . In fact King made an ass of himself and having the rest of the US COS against him had to give way to the fact that the fleet would operate in the central Pacific but with such bad grace.[116]

Indeed, such was King's fury that he had to be called to order by Leahy.[117] There was no doubt that King's position had been thoroughly rejected. Thus the Middle Strategy fell by the wayside and its Bay of Bengal counterpart likewise, or virtually so. The official records of the meetings mention Sumatra only twice, almost in passing and neither in the context of Culverin. In its place was an operation dubbed Dracula, a sea and airborne assault on Rangoon which would be carried out as and when the necessary resources became available from the European theatre.[118] The directive sent to Mountbatten read: 'The Combined Chiefs of Staff attach the greatest importance . . . to the execution of Operation DRACULA before the monsoon in 1945, with a target date of 15 March [1945].'[119]

Roosevelt's acceptance of a British Fleet in the Pacific, and the subsequent agreements reached by the Combined Chiefs, finally cleared up the plague of 'distraction, confusion and fundamental political differences' that had detained the British at the highest level over strategy.[120] There is, however, no definitive answer to the question of why Roosevelt, seemingly off the cuff, acted as he did. Hall remarks that the President's 'failure to leave a paper trail makes this question a difficult one to answer' but goes on to point out that it may have been related to 'a desire to prevent an anti-British backlash in the United States which could jeopardize post-war Anglo-American cooperation in the Far East and Europe'.[121] On the other hand, Kimball says that the President understood what motivated Churchill's offer, and quotes a remark (unreferenced) which he says was made to Henry Morgenthau, his Treasury Secretary: 'All they want is Singapore back.'[122]

Whatever the various and shifting motivations behind the matter, the end result was that the question about what the rapidly-reinforcing Eastern Fleet would actually do had now been answered. 'Cunningham's triumph' as his biographer noted, 'was complete.'[123] Examining the tortuous processes that led to this conclusion does however call to mind what Bismarck almost said: 'To retain respect for sausages and policies, one must not see them in the making.'[124]

Chapter 14

Final Operations

Somerville had begun planning further strikes for the Eastern Fleet despite knowing his tenure as C-in-C was drawing to a close. His diary entry for 3 August reveals that whilst there were several places that he deemed suitable, none of his plans could be implemented 'until we have some idea of what the strategy is to be in this theatre'. He went on to state: 'the cement works at Padang are, however, an exception and will be suitable for a carrier borne air strike but not for bombardment'.[1] Also on 3 August heavy reinforcement for the fleet arrived in the shape of the modern *King George V* class battleship *Howe*, the arrival of which proved opportune. He shortly lost the battleship *Valiant*, not to enemy action but through an accident whilst she was berthed in the 50,000-ton Admiralty Floating Dock 26 at Trincomalee for repairs. Through mistakes made whilst raising the dock on 8 August it had listed, broken its back and eventually sunk leaving *Valiant* badly damaged.[2]

It was *Howe* then that accompanied Task Force 64, comprising *Victorious*, *Indomitable*, the light cruisers *Ceylon* and *Kenya* and the destroyers *Raider*, *Rapid*, *Redoubt*, *Rocket* and *Rotherham*, when they left Trincomalee on 19 August to carry out Operation Banquet. To support the operation, in refuelling the destroyers and cruisers, the tanker *Easedale* escorted by *Tromp* had left Trincomalee two days previously so as to be in position on 22 August. Also in support was the submarine *Sea Rover*, which had left Trincomalee on 7 August for a war patrol scheduled to terminate at Exmouth Gulf, and was routed to the area to carry out air-sea rescue duties.

The Task Force commander was Rear Admiral Moody, and the primary targets were: the military airfield at Tabing some 3 miles to the north of Padang; Emmahaven (Emma Haven, Taluak Bayua) the port of Padang some 5 miles to the south of the city; and the Indaroeng Cement Works (*NV Portland Cement Maatschapij Padang*).

Having successfully refuelled, Task Force 64 arrived at the launch point off Padang early on the morning of 24 August. The weather was fine, but with only a slight wind which meant the carriers had to go to near maximum speed in order to get their aircraft aloft. This was particularly so in the case of the Barracudas, of which there were twenty-one aboard *Victorious* (plus twenty-eight Corsairs) and twenty-four (plus twenty-four Hellcats) on *Indomitable*. Though, as per

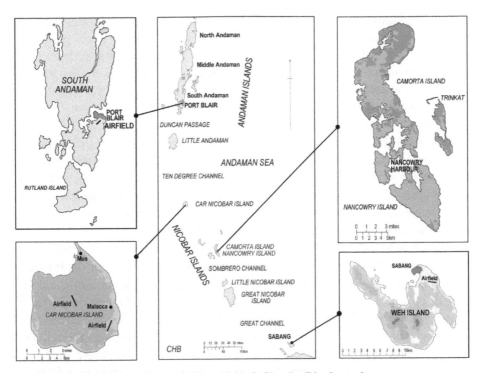

Final Operations of the Eastern Fleet 1944. © Charles Blackwood.
Details of the Eastern Fleet's main targets during its final operations under Somerville and Fraser.

past experience, the entire force was supposed to manoeuvre as a unit with, and around, the carriers, it was found that *Howe* had difficulty keeping up due to problems with fuel efficiency, or rather the lack thereof, and had to pull away.[3] The purpose of having a battleship accompany the Task Force was, at least to the carrier pilots, 'not quite clear. They [battleships] consumed huge amounts of fuel . . . equivalent probably to that of purchasing four new Corsairs!'[4]

Despite this problem the strike was successfully launched in two waves. The first, comprising ten Barracudas carrying 500lb bombs from each carrier and escorted by nineteen Corsairs, was on its way at about 06:00 hours. An hour or so later the second strike of twelve Barracudas, nine from *Victorious* and three from *Indomitable*, escorted by twelve more Corsairs, was launched. Because of Somerville's policy of avoiding reconnaissance, there was no prior knowledge that the port and airfield were pretty much empty. The Barracudas nevertheless attacked what they could, sinking the freighter *Shiretoko Maru* and damaging the *Senko Maru* and *Chisho Maru*.[5] The strike on the cement plant was more fruitful; production was severely curtailed for two months. Resistance had been minimal, though one Corsair from *Victorious* was hit by anti-aircraft fire and crashed into the sea with the pilot being killed. A Barracuda was also lost whilst trying to land back on *Indomitable* and its three-man crew perished. The Combat Air Patrol had nothing to do as no enemy aircraft appeared. Task Force 64 returned to Trincomalee on 27 August, somewhat later than anticipated.[6] The ongoing problems with *Howe*, and the fact that she was consuming fuel at a vastly accelerated rate, meant that the speed of the whole formation had to be reduced to prevent her running dry.

Fraser had been 'rather adverse' [*sic*] to taking up command of the Eastern Fleet 'until he was aware of how his fleet was to be used'.[7] The question had not been settled in August when he arrived. In September it had been, and both Cunningham and Fraser now knew that they had many lessons to learn from the US Navy, including the undertaking of multi-carrier operations and the requirements of a fleet train to sustain them for lengthy periods. As Simpson, Cunningham's biographer, put it, future operations in the Pacific '. . . came to be less about defeating Japan than about preparing the Royal Navy for the future'.[8]

That there was some way to go was demonstrated when Fraser took the fleet, now dubbed Task Force 63, to sea in order to carry out Operation Light; a two-day affair scheduled for 17–18 September. The composition of the force was essentially the same as it had been for Operation Banquet, though the 'County' class heavy cruiser *Cumberland* replaced *Ceylon* and there were two extra destroyers, *Racehorse* and *Relentless*. The submarine *Spirit* was detailed to provide the air-sea rescue facility. The carrier air groups were unchanged.

One important difference, however, was that the targets were on the east coast of Sumatra, so the attackers would have to cross the island, a distance of about 60 miles, before reaching them. The first day's task, termed 'Light A', involved a fighter sweep over Japanese airfields around Medan and its port at Belawan, which were 'expected to be full of Japanese fighter aircraft and troop carriers'.[9] A secondary objective was to attack shipping in Belawan harbour and the Deli River, and carry out photographic reconnaissance of Pangkalan Susu, some 35 miles along the coast to the north-west of Belawan.[10]

The morning of 17 September found Task Force 63 off Sumatra, but the weather was atrocious with thick cloud at low level, incessant heavy rain and little wind. Henry 'Hank' Hedlam, one of the pilots involved, explained the matter from his perspective:

> If the decision was taken to 'Go', it would mean that some sixty fighter aircraft . . . would take off and be milling around, just above the sea and below a very low cloud base and in bad visibility, trying to form up into the formation of a controlled and effective strike force. It was a scenario for disaster.[11]

Disaster, and the potential for it, was averted when the strike was aborted and the Task Force instead steamed some 280 miles to the north-west in preparation for the second day's operation. 'Light B' was an air strike on the workshops, locomotive depot and carriage shops at Sigli (Segli). This was an important facility on the *Atjeh Tram*, the 372-mile narrow-gauge railway linking the provincial capital Kutaraja (Koetaradja) to Medan.[12]

The weather was clear, though with low wind, on the morning of 18 September and twenty Barracudas were launched, ten from each carrier, with an escort of eight Hellcats and sixteen Corsairs. The attack was to be at dawn, which meant launching in the dark. One of the Barracuda pilots involved, Dunstan Hadley, later recorded his thoughts about how this would affect the flight deck crew: 'scrabbling about . . . amongst about 30 to 40 aeroplanes with their engines running would be no fun . . . at 05:00 hours'.[13]

In fact launching and forming these aircraft up took an inordinately long time, some 40 minutes, due to errors made on *Indomitable* where too many aircraft had been brought up at one time. Several had then to be returned below to create sufficient deck-length for the long take-off runs required by the Barracudas in low wind. Then of course those aircraft struck below had to be brought back up and launched in turn. One Barracuda ditched and three Corsairs had to return with engine trouble, but the raid was a success inasmuch as extensive damage was caused to the railway facilities. Each Barracuda carried either three 500lb bombs or two 500lb and two 250lb bombs. There was no enemy reaction other than some light anti-aircraft fire.

The performance of the Barracudas caused concern again on their return. The strike flew a circuitous route to the target in order to avoid giving away the position of the carriers, which were relatively close to the shore, before turning to approach Sigli from inland, delivering the attack, then flying back across the island.[14] Despite that Sumatra narrows considerably towards its northern tip, Sigli being about 60 miles from the west coast, the strike aircraft were very low on fuel as they made their landing approaches. This problem was exacerbated when positioning errors were made; the carriers got too close to each other. This in turn caused the aircraft approach circuits to overlap, and the further delays in sorting it out meant the Barracudas' fuel reserves became dangerously low. Fortunately all were landed-on safely, but it was a further demonstration that the Barracuda simply had an insufficient strike radius for operations in the Indian Ocean. Indeed, and according to the legendary Captain Eric 'Winkle' Brown, '. . . the Barracuda was the Royal Navy's albatross. Its performance was pathetic by contemporary standards . . .'[15]

In parallel with the raid on Sigli, two Hellcats equipped for photo-reconnaissance were despatched from *Indomitable* on a reconnaissance mission over Sabang and the Nicobar Islands to the north.[16] These mistakenly strafed *Spirit* as she was engaged in picking up the crew of the ditched Barracuda.[17]

Unsurprisingly, an intensive training programme was put into effect when the Task Force arrived back at Trincomalee. As one who was involved put it: 'The special training . . . was in the procedures of forming up into large groups of Hellcats and Corsairs to fly as a wing in support of the Avenger bombers. The purpose was to train and accustom six squadrons or more of aircraft to form up and formate together . . .'[18]

After some three weeks of training Task Force 63, under the command of Power, left Trincomalee on 15 October at 08:30 hours and headed eastward at 18 knots. The mission was to carry out attacks on the previously reconnoitred Nicobar Islands and Sabang. Termed Operation Millet, a three-day affair (17–20 October), it was designed to mislead the enemy into thinking that landings were imminent and was diversionary in intent; MacArthur's invasion of the Philippines commenced with amphibious landings on the island of Leyte on 20 October 1944.

The Task Force was divided into three Task Groups for the operation. Task Group 63.1 consisted of Power's flagship *Renown* plus the destroyers *Queenborough*, *Quiberon* and *Quilliam*. Task Group 63.2 was made up of the 'County' class heavy cruisers *London*, *Cumberland* and *Suffolk* and three destroyers; *Norman* (Australian), *Raider* and *Van Galen* (Dutch). The carriers formed Task Group 63.3, escorted by the light cruiser *Phoebe* and the destroyers *Wager*, *Wakeful*, *Wessex* and *Whelp*.[19] The submarines *Strongbow* and *Subtle* were deployed for air-sea rescue duties off Sabang and Nancowry respectively.

The destroyers and *Phoebe* refuelled from *Renown* and the heavy cruisers on the morning of 16 October, and at 06:00 hours on 17 October Task Group 63.3 was positioned around 15 nautical miles to the south-south-east of the island of Car Nicobar. This, the northernmost of the Nicobar Islands, was where the Japanese had constructed two airfields. One was located near the centre whilst the second, complete with a 3,000ft bitumen-surfaced runway, was close to the principal settlement of Malacca on the east coast.[20] Some thirty minutes later the carriers began flying off aircraft. *Indomitable* launched ten Barracudas with an escort of eight Hellcats to strike Nancowry (Nancowrie, Nankauri) harbour, located between the islands of Camorta (Kamorta) and Nancowry, around 45 nautical miles to the south. *Victorious* sent up twenty-seven Corsairs, eight of which joined the attack on Nancowry flying top-cover, whilst nineteen struck the airfields, plus their associated installations and anti-aircraft positions, on Car Nicobar. The airfields were successfully cratered and, temporarily at least, put out of action.

The approach of the Task Force had not gone unnoticed. A report sent that morning from the naval command in Singapore to the C-in-C Combined Fleet, reported that what appeared to be an enemy task force of eight ships was some 250 miles due south of Car Nicobar.[21] Despite this, surprise was achieved at both objectives, though there were few real targets at Nancowry Harbour. The Hellcats went in first to strafe the enemy gun positions ahead of the Barracudas, who followed up immediately after. The only sizeable vessel, the 830-ton collier *Ishikari Maru*, was sunk by a direct hit and the harbour installations were damaged. One Barracuda was lost during the strike, probably to ground fire. The Corsairs dropped down to strafe the area after the initial bombing, but two were lost to the increasing volume of anti-aircraft fire whilst three were damaged. The remaining aircraft were recovered safely, with the exception of a Hellcat which crashed whilst landing. This was achieved despite *Indomitable* mistaking her returning aircraft for enemy attackers and opening up with anti-aircraft fire. According to Hedlam:

> As we approached at some 4,000 feet bursts of flak appeared around us, but fortunately not close enough to hit us. . . . I called up to complain . . . they stopped before I could finish my abusive call.[22]

He later buttonholed the ship's Gunnery Officer and 'was as scathing to him as it is possible for a RNVR Sub Lieutenant to be to a Lieutenant Commander'. His 'parting shot' to the officer was to observe that 'as he had failed to hit aircraft flying straight and level and slowly at 4,000 feet, there was little hope of his chaps ever knocking down a fast attacking Jap'.[23]

Whilst the aircraft raided Nancowry Harbour, Task Groups 63.1 and 63.2 had begun a bombardment of Car Nicobar. *Renown* and her Group shot from the north-west whilst the heavy cruisers did the same from the south-east. The small size of the island, its total area being 49 square miles, rendered every part of it vulnerable to naval gunfire. Firing commenced at 08:00 hours and went on until 09:58 hours, when the destroyers had expended their ammunition allowance of 300 rounds each, with Hellcats from *Indomitable* spotting. There was no response from the enemy. Upon ceasing fire, Task Group 63.2 proceeded around the island to rendezvous with *Renown* and both Groups retired westward. An intercepted report sent to Combined Fleet headquarters in Japan stated that Car Nicobar had been bombarded by a fleet consisting of two carriers, two battleships, two cruisers and eight destroyers, supported by more than twenty aircraft. In addition, the harbour at Nancowry had been attacked by more than ten aircraft.[24]

Three ships of Task Group 63.2, *London*, *Norman* and *Van Galen* were detached from the main body at 18:00 hours to return to Car Nicobar and carry out a night bombardment. This object of the exercise being to mask the movement of the rest of Task Force 63 southwards in preparation for the attack on Sabang. Fire was opened early on 18 October at 01:28 hours on the north-west of the island, including the use of star shell, but this elicited no response. After around an hour the three ships ceased fire and retired westwards, shaping course to Trincomalee where they arrived on the evening of 19 October without re-joining the rest of the Task Force.

The Sabang attack had to be cancelled however due to bad weather; 18 October was 'a restless day' for the aircrews who had to 'be at readiness to take off should the weather improve'.[25] It failed to do so, and the decision was made to return to the Nicobar Islands and reprise the actions of the previous day. Accordingly a second bombardment of Car Nicobar was carried out on the morning of 19 October, and the air strikes were repeated. Hedlam, with tongue firmly in cheek no doubt, described these: 'strafing operations were carried out . . . on the well camouflaged shipping in and around the bays of Nancowry'.[26]

This time there was a response. Japan's Combined Fleet Headquarters had, as stated, been informed of the operations in the Nicobars. Given, however, the limited Allied forces employed there as against those now operating off the Philippines, and the relative unimportance of the islands when compared to the Philippines, it had been decided to leave the matter to local forces.[27] This meant the Third Air Army, the Supreme Army Air Command in the Southern Regions that controlled all Japanese air operations in South East Asia, which was headquartered in Singapore. That the Japanese were suffering from a desperate shortage of aircraft in the region was now demonstrated.

A number of hostile aircraft were detected on radar at 09:30 hours approaching from the east, but neither carriers' Combat Air Patrol was able to engage immediately. Indeed the formation was about 12 miles to the northeast of the carrier group before being intercepted 20 minutes later. The attackers comprised nine (some sources say twelve) Nakajima Ki-43 fighters of the First Field Reserve Air Unit, aircraft which were also capable of carrying a small bomb load.[28] For some 40 minutes, up until 10:30 hours, Corsairs and Hellcats engaged the Japanese in a dogfight, the end result being claims of six or seven enemy downed for the loss of two Corsairs and one Hellcat. One Japanese source maintains that there were an additional three aircraft, making twelve attackers in total, and that this trio carried out suicide attacks on the carriers. The same source claims eleven British aircraft were downed.[29] Combined Fleet Headquarters were also informed that the attackers had lost one carrier and one destroyer.[30] Such is the fog of war, for in fact Task Force 63 returned safely to Trincomalee on 21 October.

Operation Millet undoubtedly failed in its strategic object; the Japanese recognized that it was diversionary and concentrated instead on defending the Philippines.[31] In so doing they brought on a series of engagements that are collectively known as the Battle of Leyte Gulf; 'the biggest and most multi-faceted naval battle in all of history'.[32] In comparison with such an encounter the strikes on the Nicobars were, as General Albert Wedemeyer once termed outlying operations, mere 'periphery picking'.[33] Nevertheless it, and the other strikes carried out by the Eastern Fleet in 1944, definitely had value in allowing that Fleet valuable practice in real combat situations. This was otherwise unobtainable experience.

Another lesson concerned the Barracuda.[34] Although it had performed well during the Nicobar strikes, its relatively poor range and endurance had limited the choice of land-based targets. The attack on Sigli had demonstrated how fine the margins were, and increasing these could only be achieved by deploying carriers closer inshore, a tactic to be avoided wherever possible.[35] This was a previously-known problem, and since the only possible replacement was the American Avenger Cunningham had asked for more during the Quebec Conference. King replied that the US Navy was short of Avengers too, and that he: 'was not . . . optimistic with regard to availability of additional Avengers for at least another six months'.[36]

King's pessimism, if it can be called that, proved to be unfounded. The Eastern Fleet's Barracudas had all been replaced with Avengers by the end of November 1944.[37] 'These aircraft', as Hedlam put it, 'carried a bigger bomb load very much faster and much further than the Barracudas could do.'[38] Whilst that was indisputably the case, there was nevertheless a penalty to pay inasmuch as the Avenger couldn't accommodate British aerial torpedoes. Given that torpedoes are maritime weapons, and that 'the most effective way to sink a ship is to hole the hull and let the salt water flow in' is an eternal truism, then it followed that the Fleet was degrading its anti-ship, and especially armoured ship, capability.[39] This was though of lesser import than it might have been; the Battle of Leyte Gulf saw the Imperial Japanese Navy virtually eliminated.[40]

Operation Millet was also notable for being the first occasion when the carrier fighter aircraft tangled with Japanese land-based fighters. That the earlier actions had met with no opposition troubled Royal Marine Major Ronald 'Ronnie' Hay, one of the flight leaders on *Victorious*:

> . . . the younger pilots may develop a casual attitude to flying over this part of Japanese occupied territory which will certainly stand them in no stead when they are called upon to perform more hazardous operations.[41]

The Fleet Air Arm pilots had, though, been well trained under the 'Towers Scheme', and now they had had the opportunity to put that training into effect. To quote Whitby: 'The fighter boys were finally blooded.'[42] The experience gained by the Fleet in general would of course stand it in good stead when operations commenced in the Pacific, and in fact Operation Millet is also notable for being the last major action of the Eastern Fleet; on 22 November it was formally dissolved.

Two new commands arose in its place. Fraser hoisted his flag as Commander-in-Chief British Pacific Fleet (BPF), the core of which was formed from the armoured fleet carriers along with the *Howe*, whilst what remained was renamed the East Indies Fleet under the command of Vice Admiral (now promoted Admiral) Power.[43] This command, inheriting as it did the growing amphibious capability, was much more closely integrated with SEAC than the Eastern Fleet had been.[44]

Rear Admiral Moody, who had planned and executed the Eastern Fleet's carrier attacks, also stayed in the Indian Ocean becoming Flag Officer (Air) East Indies Station with promotion to Vice Admiral on 13 December 1944.[45] Command of the carriers in the Pacific was given instead to Rear Admiral Philip Vian, who admitted in his memoirs 'I was altogether inexperienced in the operation of a force of aircraft carriers . . .'[46] So quite why this change was made remains something of a mystery, though Vian was certainly a favourite of Cunningham.[47]

These final operations of the Eastern Fleet were essentially practice for operations in the Pacific, and as such they were advantageous. However, it was definitely the case that the BPF had an awful lot to learn from their American colleagues, and that this was to some extent a sore point. Fraser's deputy, who would actually command the BPF at sea whilst his Commander-in-Chief remained ashore, was Vice Admiral Bernard Rawlings. He ruffled feathers by remarking that, in terms of the BPF operating in the Pacific along American lines, 'we have to go back to school again'.[48]

The fact that the Royal Navy, which for so long had dominated the oceans of the world, did indeed have to go 'back to school' was unpalatable; incredibly so to some British officers.[49] Equally distasteful was that it would both have to learn from, and play second fiddle to, the United States Navy. These though were facts and, as the second President of the Republic had put it in 1770, 'facts are stubborn things'.[50]

Chapter 15

'. . . Not a Rolls Royce outfit.'

Apart from the brief and tragic tenure of Phillips at the very beginning, Layton's short period in charge immediately afterwards, and the three months with Fraser at the very end, the Eastern Fleet in its various manifestations was Somerville's command. Very few admirals can have had a more unenviable task than the one that faced James Somerville upon his arrival in Ceylon on 24 March 1942. On paper his Fleet looked substantial; five battleships and three aircraft carriers, plus supporting cruisers and destroyers. This was, in terms of numbers, the largest fleet assembled by the Royal Navy since the beginning of the war. However, and as we have seen, four of the battleships were effectively useless, and whilst two of the carriers were modern they were, as he later put it, without 'aircraft fit for sailors to fly in'.

Straight away he was faced with a Japanese incursion, 31 March – 10 April, into the Indian Ocean, with which he had to deal though knowing little of the enemy's intentions or capabilities. Even so, he was aware that here was a state of affairs fraught with danger: 'if the Japanese capture Ceylon and destroy the greater part of the Eastern Fleet then I admit the situation becomes really desperate.' The Japanese seemed, to their enemies and at that time, to be rolling out a stupendous plan of conquest with chilling precision, and whether this involved the invasion of Ceylon was unknown. It seemed all too possible, whilst it looked utterly to do anything to stop it. Indeed, by March 1942 Japan's war machine appeared, to those attempting to resist it, virtually invincible.

That it was far from that had yet to be demonstrated, and so it was fortunate then that Somerville's attempts to intercept and attack the Mobile Force (*Kido Butai*), based around five carriers, were abortive. Having said that, the radar-directed night-attack tactics he proposed to employ against them did offer the only realistic chance of inflicting heavy damage on his opponent, an opponent moreover whose striking power had not yet been fully revealed to him. Indeed, the possession of radar gave the British a huge potential advantage, particularly as the Japanese had no similar apparatus aboard any of their warships.[1] Though we are in the realm of speculation, it does though seem unlikely that in any such action all five of the enemy carriers would have been accounted for. If this be granted, then retribution the following day cannot be seriously doubted, and the destruction of the 'greater part of the Eastern Fleet' would likely have followed.

There can be little doubt that, as argued, Somerville possessed that 'ratcatcher's instinct for war' which made him cautious when necessary and bold as appropriate. His decision to move in 'the last direction in which the Japanese would expect us to proceed' in order to rescue the survivors from *Dorsetshire* and *Cornwall* is a fine example of the latter. Of course, by that time he had at least started to realize what he was up against, and concluded that 'dodging the enemy' was his chief object. He did of course succeed in that and recovered the survivors, as well as preserving the greater part of his command. Had he though, as per the subsequent accusation of his second-in-command, taken grave risks with the fleet?

The answer to that, with of course the inestimable benefit of hindsight, is a resounding 'yes'. On the other hand and given what he knew at the time, which is the only possible basis upon which to judge his actions, the response becomes a definite 'no'. As has been pointed out, the intelligence available to him indicated that the enemy force was broadly comparable, at least in size and composition, to his own. He didn't know just how far the Japanese had developed naval aviation, nor the extent of its ability to deliver 'shattering, blasting, overpowering force' upon any given target. Had he, then it is probable that he would have acted differently.

The reasons why the Eastern Fleet in particular, and the Royal Navy more generally, found itself in such a disadvantageous position have been explored. It is however worth reiterating that even if Somerville (or indeed anyone else) had been in command of all of the most modern battleships and aircraft carriers that Britain possessed, his chances would not have markedly altered. The navies of Britain and Japan had evolved differing philosophies and doctrines in respect to the use of carrier-based naval aircraft; the former as battlefleet support, the latter as a striking force in its own right. The Japanese had, moreover, equipped the striking force with weapons fitted to its role. More Royal Navy resources of the type then in existence could not have offset the capability gap between the two navies; the British simply did not have the requisite capabilities to withstand Japanese air-naval superiority.

Despite their seeming invincibility, there were, however, deficiencies in Japanese doctrine and tactics, particularly with respect to reconnaissance. The offloading of this duty to floatplanes launched from cruisers and battleships was undoubtedly a mistake. Somerville was also fortunate in that his opposite number over the period of the Indian Ocean raid was Nagumo Chuichi. He singularly failed to initiate comprehensive measures to search out the opponent he had been sent specifically to destroy, and undoubtedly made many errors in the deployment of his command. More than Somerville in any event. The Battle of

Midway, 4–7 June 1942, exposed Nagumo's limitations, changed the course of the war in the Pacific, and shattered the myth of Japanese naval invincibility.

Having lost the strategic initiative, and with the focus of the war moving decisively to the Central and Southwest Pacific Areas, the Indian Ocean became a theatre of secondary importance to Japan. Not so to the Allies, or at least in terms of the western portion of that ocean, for whom it remained vital in terms of sustaining operations in the Middle East, retaining access to oil and of succouring Russia via the Persian Corridor. That the Axis knew this just as well was made plain with the launching of anti-shipping campaigns. From the summer of 1942 the Eastern Fleet began to lose capital ships that were redeployed to other areas, mainly the Mediterranean, and became engaged instead in operations to defend vital sea lines of communication and stem shipping losses.

Dönitz, in line with his philosophy that it was immaterial where a ship was sunk, deployed significant resources to the Indian Ocean area in 1943. These were in search of easier pickings than were available in the 'war decisive' Atlantic where the U-boats were losing the battle. This more or less coincided with the Italian surrender of 8 September 1943 which to, a great extent, opened up the Mediterranean to Allied shipping and removed the necessity for routeing convoys around South Africa. Even so there were, from the German and Japanese submariners' point of view, still plenty of targets in the Indian Ocean and the base at Penang was utilized to take advantage of this. Somerville, as his biographer pointed out, had to try to make do with too little in attempts to plug the worst holes in the defences. One distinct advantage he had, which was not information in the public domain when that biography appeared, was Ultra intelligence. Despite there being a significant risk in doing so, Somerville used information thus obtained tactically; the sudden appearance of Allied naval and air forces, in remote areas of the Indian Ocean where U-boats were refuelling, had the inevitable effect of raising German suspicions that their communications had been compromised. This was a recurring theme throughout the war, but fortunately for the Allies several investigations came to broadly the same conclusion; the German naval cypher was secure and it was 'unimaginable' that the enemy could read it. Armed with knowledge of Ultra, it is possible to dismiss the charge of 'heresy' in respect to Somerville's revival of 'the hunting group' as a measure of anti-submarine warfare.

Definitely less creditable is his attitude towards Operational Research relating to unescorted convoys. Indeed, his quoted diary entry concerning 'a scientist making guesses' is suggestive of old-school, reactionary and even Luddite tendencies. Yet as has been noted, he was regarded as the 'foster father of naval radar' and was certainly one of the, if not *the*, most air-minded senior flag officers in the Royal Navy. These are hardly positions consistent with a

Colonel Blimp type, so his attitude to Operational Research would seem very much at variance with the norm. The entry was though written in January 1944, a time when Mountbatten was canvassing the introduction of an Operational Research Section into SEAC. This, as with most of the Supreme Commander's proposals, was almost guaranteed to raise Somerville's hackles.

The feud between the admirals has been lightly touched upon, and those who wish to peruse an extremely thorough account will find it in Jacobsen, Marder and Horsefield. These authors also repudiate the statements by Mountbatten which surfaced in 1980, a year after his death at the hands of the Provisional IRA, that he had reprimanded and ultimately sacked Somerville from his command. They somewhat diplomatically attribute these erroneous claims to Mountbatten's memory playing him false. They were made during the airing of a series of television programmes, entitled 'Lord Mountbatten Remembers,' broadcast on the BBC in November 1980, but which had been recorded in 1972. Also covered in one of the programmes was the 1956 Anglo–French Suez operation, where Mountbatten's memory once again played him false. Or perhaps not. According to Keith Kyle; 'To the ordinary fallibility of memory there has to be added, in the case of Mountbatten, a great man's well attested habit of improving the historical record.'[2] Indeed! He was neither the first, and certainly not the last, 'great man' to indulge in a modicum, and more, of historical revisionism.

Having said all that, there is no doubt that in their falling-out both men were at fault. Murphy made the point that 'Somerville had been planning Fleet strategy in the Mediterranean when Commander Mountbatten was training his boat crews to win the Fleet Regatta'.[3] Quite so, and there is plenty of evidence that Somerville resented Mountbatten's approach to Supreme Command, at least as he perceived it, and particularly with regards to which of them controlled the Eastern Fleet. He went so far as to accuse Mountbatten, in private, of wanting to 'establish himself as a sort of Hitler with everything under his personal control'.[4] He was nowhere near as extreme in communications with Cunningham and the Admiralty, but Ziegler characterises his behaviour as suggestive of 'an imbalance not far removed from paranoia'.[5] That is an exaggeration, but Somerville's deputy, Arthur Power, acknowledged that the disagreements had 'not shown James Somerville at his best'.[6] On the other hand, there is no doubt that Mountbatten did indeed seek to mould his command along the lines of MacArthur's autocratic model, rather than on Eisenhower's more collective approach.[7]

The issue was no doubt exacerbated due to the dispute, and consequent indecision, at the highest levels over strategy; debates over what the, now rapidly reinforcing, Eastern Fleet would be actually used for. Churchill, as has been shown, wanted amphibious operations conducted across the Bay of Bengal to recover lost colonial territory, and it was in pursuit of this that the 'complete triphibian' had been appointed. It was though a strategy impossible to realize; Churchill might have willed the end, but he couldn't will the means to achieve it. The required resources, most notably the Landing Ships Tank, were held by the United States who had better uses for them, and were antagonistic towards British colonialism anyway.[8] Churchill railed against this 'American method of trying to force particular policies by the withholding or giving of certain weapons' but was powerless to change it.

It was the eventual agreement on strategy that ultimately resolved the Somerville-Mountbatten dispute by totally removing the Eastern Fleet from the equation. In addition, Somerville's appointment to Washington separated the antagonists completely. Before he left though, and at long last, Somerville got to deploy the Eastern Fleet in offensive operations. The British carriers now had bigger, and better, 'hammers' in the shape of a large complement of American aircraft that were certainly 'fit for sailors to fly in', but they still needed to learn the latest techniques of carrier warfare. The various strikes on Sumatra and other targets in 1944 may well have been undertaken against a 'fireless dragon', but they were nevertheless essential training. Further education would take place in the Pacific, as per Rawlings and his 'back to school again' comment, but there the teachers would of course be American.

That the Royal Navy had become dependent on, and could only play second fiddle to, the United States Navy was not disputable. Even the irascible Vian conceded in his memoirs that 'there can be little doubt that the Americans are much quicker than we are at learning the lessons of war and applying them to their ships and their tactics'.[9] In the league table of offensive naval power the British now came a definite second, and that only because the new holder of the top spot had destroyed the only other contender. The British Pacific Fleet played an important role in the final part of the campaign against Japan, and was recognised as having done so, but it fought no naval engagements; there was, put basically, no enemy navy left to engage with.[10]

If the BPF was a success, and it was, then Somerville deserves some of the credit; he trained many of the ships and men who went on to serve with it. His *circa* two and a half years in command of the Eastern Fleet was though an onerous business. Forever starved of resources, and for the most part forced to make do with second best in terms of ships, he nevertheless successfully defended a huge, strategically vital, oceanic area over the period. He was admired, as James Forrestal, the Secretary of the US Navy, told him in 1945, as a 'fighting admiral'.[11] Yet, as has been shown, the Eastern Fleet during his tenure, and certainly in terms of major actions, did very little actual fighting. Only once did it come close to 'a good stand-up fight', but one that it was compelled to refuse before the event once the tactical and technical superiority of the *Kido Butai* was realized. Rather, it was forced to 'dodge the enemy' and hide in order to assume the mantle of a 'fleet in being'. In so doing it emulated the behaviour of the 'despicable' High Seas Fleet of 1914–18. Thus were Beatty's words comprehensively ingested.

In the larger context, the inability of the Eastern Fleet to deter or fight its enemy proclaimed that the age of European colonialism had passed. The young Lee Kuan Yew's declaration that the explosion demolishing the causeway to Singapore in 1942 heralded 'the end of the British Empire' proved entirely accurate.

This was very far from being Somerville's fault. He, being the man on the spot in more ways than one, was left to salvage what could be salvaged from two decades' worth of error and misjudgement on the part of the British Government, and Admiralty, in their various manifestations. Ultimately, he could do little more than hang on until Japan's strength was shattered by more powerful forces. That he achieved so much with 'a Ford, not a Rolls Royce outfit' is testament to his ability, character, and professionalism. He was arguably Britain's best, if probably least known, admiral of the Second World War.

Bibliographical Note

Given commercial constraints, driven by the need to keep page-count and thus publishing costs down, it was decided to omit a dedicated bibliography for this work. Those who wish to consult the sources have not been totally abandoned, however; full references may be found in the relevant endnotes. It can only be hoped that this departure from scholarly requisites will be understood, and forgiven, by readers.

Notes

Introduction

1. W. S. Chalmers (Rear Admiral), *The Life and Letters of David, Earl Beatty: Admiral of the Fleet, Viscount Borodale of Wexford, Baron Beatty of the North Sea and of Brooksby* (London: Hodder and Stoughton, 1951), p. 444.
2. *The Times.* 22 November 1918. The article was syndicated worldwide.
3. *Kaiser, Friedrich der Grosse, Kaiserin, Prinzregent Luitpold, König Albert, Grosser Kurfürst, Kronprinz Wilhelm, Bayern* and *Baden.* There were several capital ships of the High Seas Fleet missing from the array, the *Helgoland, Oldenburg, Ostfriesland* and *Thüringen* as well as *Nassau, Rheinland, Posen* and *Westfalen. Deutschland, Hannover, Schlesien* and *Schleswig-Holstein* were obsolete pre-dreadnoughts and unfit for front-line service. *König* was in dock. See: Holger Herwig, *'Luxury' Fleet: The Imperial German Navy 1888–1918* (London: George Allen & Unwin, 1980), p. 254.
4. 'Address delivered by Admiral Sir David Beatty on board HMS Lion, on 24th November, 1918, to the Officers and Men of the Lion and First Battle Cruiser Squadron'. Taken from: A Corbett-Smith, *The Seafarers* (London: Cassell and Company, 1919), pp. 270–2.
5. An article from the *Belfast Telegraph* of 25 November 1918 by Captain J. M. McCleery entitled; 'Fleet and the Armistice, RAF Officer's Graphic Story. A Belfast RAF officer on one of His Majesty's ships writes'. Reproduced in: Guy Warner, *World War One Aircraft Carrier Pioneer: The Story and Diaries of Jack McCleery RNAS RAF* (Barnsley: Pen & Sword Aviation, 2011), pp. 249–50.
6. Hugh Rodman: Rear Admiral United States Navy, *Yarns of a Kentucky Admiral* (Indianapolis: Bobbs-Merrill, 1928), pp. 288–9.
7. *The Times.* 22 November 1918.
8. 'Address delivered by Admiral Sir David Beatty on board HMS Lion, on 24th November, 1918, to the Officers and Men of the Lion and First Battle Cruiser Squadron'. Taken from: A Corbett-Smith, *The Seafarers* (London: Cassell and Company, 1919), pp. 270–2.
9. David Hobbs, *British Aircraft Carriers: Design, Development and Service Histories* (Barnsley: Seaforth, 2013), p. 44.
10. H. F. King, *Sopwith Aircraft 1912–1920* (London: Putnam, 1980), p. 188.
11. Richard Hough, *The Fleet that Had to Die* (London: Hamish Hamilton, 1958).

Chapter 1

1. See Chapter 1, 'Creating a Modern Navy', in David C. Evans and Mark R. Peattie, *Kaigun: Strategy, Tactics and Technology in the Imperial Japanese Navy, 1887–1941* (Annapolis MD: Naval Institute Press, 1997) for details of the process whereby RN traditions influenced the IJN. See also: Archibald Campbell Douglas, *Life of Admiral Sir*

Archibald Lucius Douglas, GCB, GCVO, Commander of the Legion of Honour, Order of the Rising Sun of Japan, Spanish Naval Order of Merit (Totnes; Mortimer Bros., 1938) for information on the head of the British Mission.

2. See: Timothy D. Saxon, Anglo-Japanese Naval Cooperation, 1914–1918'. Faculty Publications and Presentations. Paper 5. 2000. http://digitalcommons.liberty.edu/hist_fac_pubs/5

3. Colonel The Master of Sempill, 'The British Aviation Mission to the Imperial Japanese Navy (Extracts from a paper read before the Royal Aeronautical Society April 3, 1924)', in *Flight and Aircraft Engineer Magazine*, 10 April 1924, pp. 209–12. Unless otherwise stated, this is the source for Sempill's account of the Mission.

4. UK National Archives. Japan. Code 23 Files 193 (papers 2333 – end) – 199. FO 371/5358. Japanese Embassy to Foreign Office, No. 101, 6.10.1920. Air Ministry to Foreign Office, S.13449/S.6, 'Secret and Urgent'.

5. UK National Archives. Japan. Code 23 Files 193 (papers 2333 – end) – 199. FO 371/5358. 22.10.1920 'Minutes'.

6. The Admiralty's basic strategy for an eastern war emerged between 1919 and 1921, with the Plans Division compiling the first Eastern War Memorandum in 1920. See ADM 116/3124.

7. UK National Archives. Japan. Code 23 Files 193 (papers 2333 – end) – 199. FO 371/5358. Eliot, Tokyo No. 423, 13.11.20.

8. UK National Archives. Japan. Code 23 Files 348 (papers 3519 – end) – 499. FO 371/6693. Lampson 20.7.21. Japan. Code 23 Files 193 (papers 2333 – end) – 199. FO 371/5367. Japanese Embassy to Foreign Office No. 130, 7.12.20. Lampson 9.12.20, Wellesley 10.12.20.

9. 'Source: Reliable'. (13945.) 12 April 1921, Office of Naval Intelligence, *Monthly Information Bulletin Number 6, 15 June 1921* (Washington DC: Navy Department, 1921), p. 13.

10. UK National Archives. Japan. Code 23 Files 193 (papers 2333 – end) – 199. FO 371/5358. Eliot, Tokyo No. 423, 13.11.20. 23. Curzon 8.11.20, 15.11.20; Lampson 9.11.20; Foreign Office to Nagai, F 2761/193/23, 12.11.20; Nagai to Foreign Office, 25.11.20; Nagai to Curzon, 'Private', 30.11.20; Foreign Office to Nagai, F 3188/193/23, 22.11.20.

11. There are several substantial files in the UK National Archives (KV – Records of the Security Service; Japanese Intelligence Agents and Suspected Agents) on Sempill related to his undoubted espionage activities on behalf of Japan, both in the 1920s and later. His Service Record in respect of naval matters at the same institution (ADM 273/3/61 Admiralty: Royal Naval Air Service: Registers of Officers' Services) is, on the other hand, extremely thin. Commissioned as a 2nd Lieutenant in the RFC in August 1914, he gained his Aviator Certificate (number 922) in a Maurice Farman biplane at the Central Flying School (CFS), Upavon, on 29 September 1914 before rising to the rank of Captain and 'Flight Commander'. He was appointed an Instructor at the CFS on 6 August 1915 (*The London Gazette*, 3 September 1915, p. 8730), before transferring to the RNAS on 1 January 1916. 'Highly recommended for promotion', he became a temporary 'Squadron Commander' and then temporary 'Wing Commander' before being seconded to the Air Department. His RAF record (AIR 76/454/59) is slightly more expansive, but again nothing remarkable leaps out, though he was appointed Deputy Director for Air Technical Services, with the temporary rank of Colonel, at the Air Ministry on 1 April 1918 (*The London Gazette*, 2 April 1918, p. 4030). During his period of service there he sat on the 'Aerodynamics Sub-Committee' and 'Special Committee on the Electrification of Balloons'. (*Technical Report of the Advisory Committee for Aeronautics for the Year 1918–19. (With Appendices.) Vol I. General Questions, Airships and Model Aeroplane Research* (London: HMSO, 1922), p. 2).

12. The Air Force Cross was awarded to 'Officers and Warrant Officers for acts of courage or devotion to duty when flying, although not in active operations against the enemy'. See: *Supplement to The London Gazette*, 3 June 1918, p. 6533.

13. Frida H. Brackley (ed.), *Brackles: Memoirs of a Pioneer of Civil Aviation* (Chatham: W & J Mackay, 1952), p. 91. The life and achievements of Air Commodore Herbert George Brackley, naval aviator and pioneer of civil aviation.

14. UK National Archives. Japan. Code 23 / Code W23 File 150734-182383. FO 371/3823. Tokyo No. 274, 12.11.19 (Ley No. 21, 30.10.19).

15. John Ferris, 'A British "Unofficial" Aviation Mission and Japanese Naval Developments, 1919–1929', in *The Journal of Strategic Studies*, Vol. 5 Issue 3, 1982, p. 424.

16. According to Sempill's own account: 'Equipment was obtained from many firms such as Messrs. Armstrong-Whitworth Aircraft Company, Blackburn Aeroplane Company, Gloucestershire Aircraft Company, Supermarine Aviation Company, Vickers, Ltd., Rolls-Royce, Ltd., Napier and Son, Ltd., Geo. Parnall and Co., Short Bros., A. V. Roe, Ltd., Disposals Company, Nobel Industries, Ltd., Monarch Engineering Company, Butchers, Yorkshire Steel Company, Metal Air Screws, Ltd., etc.. etc.'

17. In 1914 it was common for pilots to be allowed to go solo after no more than an hour's tuition. The results were devastating: of the 14,000 British pilots killed during the War, 8,000 died in training accidents. In 1916, Major Robert Smith-Barry RFC was given command of a flying school at the Grange Airfield in Hampshire. His new 'Gosport System' utilized competent instructors, a standard training aircraft with enhanced dual-control and the 'Gosport tube' (a rubber speaking-tube worn on the pilot's helmet allowing verbal communication between pupil and instructor), revolutionized pilot training. His system was adopted worldwide, leading to him being credited by the head of the Royal Flying Corps, Lord Trenchard, as 'the man who taught the air forces of the world to fly'. See: Frank D. Tredrey, *Pioneer Pilot: The Great Smith-Barry Who Taught the World to Fly* (London: Peter Davies, 1976).

18. See: David C. Evans and Mark R. Peattie, *Kaigun: Strategy, Tactics and Technology in the Imperial Japanese Navy, 1887–1941* (Annapolis MD: Naval Institute Press, 1997), pp. 180–1. Kathrin Milanovich, '*Hosho*: The First Aircraft Carrier of the Imperial Japanese Navy' in John Jordan (ed.) and Stephen Dent (asst. ed.), *Warship 2008* (London: Conway, 2008), pp. 9–11.

19. Ikuhiko Hata and Yasuho Izawa, *Japanese Naval Aces and Fighter Units in World War II* (Annapolis MD: Naval Institute Press, 1989), p. 17.

20. Frida H. Brackley (ed.), *Brackles: Memoirs of a Pioneer of Civil Aviation* (Chatham: W & J Mackay, 1952), pp. 116, 124.

21. Frida H. Brackley (ed.), *Brackles: Memoirs of a Pioneer of Civil Aviation* (Chatham: W & J Mackay, 1952), pp. 174–5.

22. That Sempill introduced this device to Japan is, even if nothing else is, prima facie evidence that he was revealing militarily sensitive information. Batchelor's patent (No. 17,082) for 'Optical Apparatus for use in connection with aircraft' was applied for on 4 December 1915 and accepted on 30 July 1916 but 'withheld from publication' at that time. Indeed, authorization for publication was not to be granted until 3 March 1923. The original patent can be viewed online at the European Patent Office (EPO) website (https://www.epo.org/index.html). Patent Number: GB191517082 (A).

23. 'Captain and Mrs Sempill [Captain IJN was the Colonel's equivalent attached rank] return to England at the end of the year but several technical members will be staying on – Armament Officer, Design Officer, Engineer Officer and Rigging Officer; also John

Redmond and two or three other warrant officers. I shall be responsible for all flying operations and experimental work.' Letter of 25 April 1922 from Herbert George Brackley to Frida Helen Mond. Frida H. Brackley (ed.), *Brackles: Memoirs of a Pioneer of Civil Aviation* (Chatham: W & J Mackay, 1952), p. 135.

24. John Ferris, 'A British "Unofficial" Aviation Mission and Japanese Naval Developments, 1919–1929', in *The Journal of Strategic Studies*, Vol. 5 Issue 3, 1982, pp. 426, 429.

25. Letter of 28 February 1922 from Herbert George Brackley to Frida Helen Mond. Frida H. Brackley (ed.), *Brackles: Memoirs of a Pioneer of Civil Aviation* (Chatham: W & J Mackay, 1952), pp. 132–3.

26. Memorandum (Special Study in England) of 4 July 1922 from Rear Admiral Tajiri Tadatsugu IJN Commanding Kasumi-Ga-Uru [Kasumigaura] Aerial Training Station to Lieut.-Commander Brackley, (Attd.) IJN. Reproduced in Frida H. Brackley (ed.), *Brackles: Memoirs of a Pioneer of Civil Aviation* (Chatham: W & J Mackay, 1952), p. 146.

27. Commander Ohzeki Takamaro to Herbert George Brackley 7 July 1922. Reproduced in Frida H. Brackley (ed.), *Brackles: Memoirs of a Pioneer of Civil Aviation* (Chatham: W & J Mackay, 1952), p. 147.

28. Kathrin Milanovich, '*Hosho*: The First Aircraft Carrier of the Imperial Japanese Navy', in John Jordan (ed.) and Stephen Dent (asst. ed.), *Warship 2008* (London: Conway Maritime Press, 2008), pp. 16–17.

29. The world's first fighter aeroplane designed specifically for carrier operations. Robert C. Mikesh and Shorzoe Abe, *Japanese Aircraft 1910–1941* (Annapolis MD: Naval Institute Press, 1990), p. 161.

30. On 19 June 1920, the Ministry of Labour reported that there were circa 167,000 unemployed ex-servicemen receiving benefits. See: UK National Archives, CAB 241107, CP 1493, ff. 343–44. 'The Training and Resettlement of Ex-Servicemen', Memorandum by the Minister of Labour [Thomas James Macnamara], I9 June 1920.

31. Navy Type 10 Carrier Torpedo Aircraft or 1MT1N.

32. Navy Type 13 Carrier-Borne Attack Aircraft or B1M.

33. Navy Type 10 Carrier Reconnaissance Aircraft or 2MR. The Type 10 aircraft date from 1921; the Type 13 from 1924. The numbers relate to the 10th and 13th years of Taisho, the name of the era ruled by Emperor Yoshihito.

34. See: *Flight and Aircraft Engineer*, 10 March 1921, p. 179. *Flight Magazine*, 6 March 1924, p. 136. *Malaya Tribune*, 7 May 1921, p. 2. *The Straits Times*, 9 March 1921, p. 9. For much useful information see also: http://britishaviation-ptp.com/index.html. Short Brothers also provided assistance to the US Navy; they sold them the patent for a carrier arrestor system in 1923. See: AIR 5/489. DCAS to DNI (Steel to Hotham) S. 12764, 27.8.23; Air Ministry to Admiralty S.12764/S.6, 8.10.23.

35. Frida H. Brackley (ed.), *Brackles: Memoirs of a Pioneer of Civil Aviation* (Chatham: W & J Mackay, 1952), p. 176. See also: Kathrin Milanovich, '*Hosho*: The First Aircraft Carrier of the Imperial Japanese Navy', in John Jordan (ed.) and Stephen Dent (asst. ed.), *Warship 2008* (London: Conway Maritime Press, 2008), p. 16.

36. General Sanagi Sadamu JASDF (Ret.). Quoted in: Lieutenant Commander Michael Bryant Hughes USN, 'Japan's Air Power Options: The Employment of Military Aviation in the Post-War Era. A Thesis Presented to the Faculty of the Fletcher School of Law and Diplomacy, Tufts University, in partial fulfilment of the requirements for the Degree Doctor of Philosophy'. August 16, 1972, p. 117, n. 11. Available at: https://archive.org/stream/japansairpowerop00hugh/japansairpowerop00hugh_djvu.txt Sanagi, who had been on the Operations Section of the Imperial Japanese Navy Staff and has been described

as an 'air operations mastermind', was in a position to know. See: John Prados, 'Japan's Sea Lords in the South Pacific' in *Naval History*, Vol. 26 Issue 5, October 2012, p. 52. Also: Major Gilbert M. Billings Jr., 'Japan's Air Self Defense Force', in *Air University Review: The Professional Journal of the United States Air Force*, Vol. XVI, No. 5 July–August 1965, p. 71.

37. Mark R Peattie, *Sunburst: The Rise of Japanese Naval Air Power 1909–1941* (Annapolis MD: Naval Institute Press, 2001), p. 19.

38. Geoffrey Till, 'Adopting the Aircraft Carrier: The British, American and Japanese Case Studies', in Williamson R. Murray and Allan R. Millett (eds), *Military Innovation in the Interwar Period* (Cambridge: Cambridge University Press, 1998), p. 197.

39. The agreement in December 1921 on the Four Powers Treaty at the Washington Conference rendered the Alliance obsolete, though it did not officially terminate until all the parties ratified the treaty in August 1923. There is much scholarly disputation as to the wisdom, on Britain's part, of terminating the alliance. It is though surely unarguable that Germany's defeat in 1918 removed its raison d'être. For a discussion on the matter see: Antony Best, 'The "Ghost" of The Anglo-Japanese Alliance: An Examination into Historical Myth-Making', in *The Historical Journal*, 49, 3 (2006), pp. 811–31.

40. Arthur J. Marder, *Old Friends, New Enemies: The Royal Navy and the Imperial Japanese Navy; Strategic Illusions, 1936–1941* (Oxford: Clarendon Press, 1981), p. 336.

41. UK National Archives. KV – Records of the Security Service; Japanese Intelligence Agents and Suspected Agents KV 2/871. Payne to Alexander, 9 January 1923. The 'Tosu' referred to may have been Japan's Naval Attaché in London: Rear Admiral Tosu Tamaki. The servant Naval Rating, if indeed he was the latter, was Kazu Masuda aged 23. Document 297A in the Sempill file.

42. UK National Archives. KV – Records of the Security Service; Japanese Intelligence Agents and Suspected Agents KV 2/871. Copy of telegram dated 26 December 1922 from Tosu, Paris, to Vice-Minister of Marine, Tokyo. Received 6 January 1923.

43. Desmond Young, *Rutland of Jutland* (London: Cassels, 1963). The sortie of Flight Lieutenant F. J. Rutland and his observer, Assistant Paymaster G. S. Trewin, was aborted prematurely when the engine failed. The reconnaissance was in any event greatly hindered by low cloud cover. Rutland recalled that: 'On sighting the enemy it was very hard to tell what they were and so I had to close to within a mile and a half at a height of 1,000 feet. They then opened fire on me with anti-aircraft and other guns, my height enabling them to use their anti torpedo armament.' H. W. Fawcett and G. W. W. Hooper, *The Fighting at Jutland: The Personal Experiences of Sixty Officers and Men of the British Fleet* (Glasgow: Maclure, MacDonald, 1921), p. 13.

44. Arthur J. Marder, *From the Dreadnought to Scapa Flow: Volume IV 1917, Year of Crisis* (Barnsley: Seaforth, 2014), p. 13.

45. UK National Archives. KV – Records of the Security Service; Japanese Intelligence Agents and Suspected Agents. KV 2/339; Frederick Joseph RUTLAND. Major George Joseph Ball, 'Notes on the Case of Squadron Leader Rutland, RAF'. August 1924. Document 221a. Ball is an interesting, though murky, character who progressed from undertaking intelligence work for MI5 in the 1920s to doing much the same for the Conservative Party from 1927 until the fall of Neville Chamberlain. He may have had a hand in the infamous Zinoviev letter of 1924 and was certainly close to members of the Right Club, the main object of which was, in the words of the founder, 'to oppose and expose the activities of Organized Jewry'. He later served on the Second World War

Swinton Committee which dealt with 'Fifth Column activities and other cognate matters'. As a member Ball may have protected 'fellow travellers of the right' from detention. See: A. W. Brian Simpson, *In the Highest Degree Odious: Detention Without Trial in Wartime Britain* (Oxford: Clarendon Press, 1992), pp. 186–8. R. B. Cockett, 'Ball, Chamberlain and Truth' in *The Historical Journal*, Vol. 33, Issue 1, 1990, pp. 131–42. Martin Pugh, *Hurrah For The Blackshirts!: Fascists and Fascism in Britain Between the Wars* (London: Random House, 2006), p. 267. Richard Griffiths, *Patriotism Perverted: Captain Ramsay, the Right Club and English Anti-Semitism, 1939–40* (London: Constable, 1998), p. 32. Richard Cockett, *Twilight of Truth: Chamberlain, Appeasement and the Manipulation of the Press* (London: Weidenfeld and Nicolson, 1989), pp. 9–10. W. S. Churchill. HC Debates. 15 August 1940, Volume 364. Cc 957–64.

46. Which has the annotation 'Volume 1 presumed destroyed' written on the cover. UK National Archives. KV – Records of the Security Service; Japanese Intelligence Agents and Suspected Agents KV 2/871. PF 37,966 Volume 2. Rutland, Frederick Joseph.

47. UK National Archives. KV – Records of the Security Service; Japanese Intelligence Agents and Suspected Agents. KV 2/339; Frederick Joseph RUTLAND. Anonymous note which, from the contents, appears to have come from the British Embassy in Tokyo. Document 225a.

48. UK National Archives. KV – Records of the Security Service; Japanese Intelligence Agents and Suspected Agents. KV 2/339; Frederick Joseph RUTLAND. 'Extract from a letter sent to the Admiralty from the British Naval Attaché, Tokyo, dated 20.11.25'. Document 230a.

49. Royle was Britain's Naval Attaché at the Tokyo Embassy between 1924 and 1927. His service records are at the UK National Archives: ADM 196/50/3, ADM 196/126/114, ADM 196/143/596, ADM 196/91/141. Royle, Guy Charles Cecil, Service Record.

50. UK National Archives. KV – Records of the Security Service; Japanese Intelligence Agents and Suspected Agents. KV 2/339; Frederick Joseph RUTLAND. 'Extract from a letter sent to the Admiralty from the British Naval Attaché, Tokyo, dated 20.11.25'. Document 230a.

51. *The London Gazette*, 18 September 1923, p. 6279.

52. UK National Archives. KV – Records of the Security Service; Japanese Intelligence Agents and Suspected Agents. KV 2/339; Frederick Joseph RUTLAND. Letter [Colonel Piggott to Major Ball] from British Embassy, Tokyo. Document 229a. For general information on Piggott's time in Japan see: Major-General F. S. G. Piggott, *Broken Thread* (Aldershot; Gale & Polden, 1950).

53. UK National Archives. KV – Records of the Security Service; Japanese Intelligence Agents and Suspected Agents. KV 2/339; Frederick Joseph RUTLAND. Major George Joseph Ball, 'Notes on the Case of Squadron Leader Rutland, RAF'. August 1924. Document 221a.

54. A. G. Denniston, 'The Government Code and Cypher School Between the Wars', in *Intelligence and National Security*, Vol. 1, Issue 1, 1986, pp. 48–70. John Johnson, *The Evolution of British Sigint, 1653–1939* (London: HMSO, 1997).

55. UK National Archives. KV – Records of the Security Service; Japanese Intelligence Agents and Suspected Agents. KV 2/339; Frederick Joseph RUTLAND. From Air Ministry. Document 232a.

56. Following the Great War and right through until 1939, the Air Ministry intelligence organization fell on very hard times and was reduced to a mere remnant consisting of

under forty officers. Sebastian Cox, 'The Organization and Sources of RAF Intelligence', in *Air Intelligence Symposium: Bracknell Paper No 7* (Bracknell; Royal Air Force Historical Society and the Royal Air Force Staff College, 1997), p. 6.

57. UK National Archives. KV – Records of the Security Service; Japanese Intelligence Agents and Suspected Agents KV 2/871. 'Memorandum for Air Ministry by MI5'. November 1924, p. 2.

58. UK National Archives. KV – Records of the Security Service; Japanese Intelligence Agents and Suspected Agents KV 2/871. 'Note prepared by Major Ball for DSI to take to Sir Geoffrey Salmond', p. 2. For Salmond see: Anne Baker, *From Biplane to Spitfire: The Life of Air Chief Marshal Sir Geoffrey Salmond* (Barnsley: Leo Cooper, 2003).

59. See: 'Capt. Keep, of "Westlands," Injured', in *Flight: The Aircraft Engineer and Airships*, 15 May 1924, p. 280. Also: Derek N. James, *Westland Aircraft Since 1915* (London: Putnam, 1991), pp. 101–2.

60. UK National Archives. KV – Records of the Security Service; Japanese Intelligence Agents and Suspected Agents KV 2/871. 'Notes re. Conference with Admiralty, Air Ministry, Foreign Office and Department of Trade re. Greece'. Dated 25.03.1926. Document 542a.

61. See: Quincy Wright, *Mandates under the League of Nations* (Chicago; University of Chicago Press, 1930).

62. Major Earl H. Ellis USMC, *Advanced Base Operations in Micronesia* [Fleet Marine Force Reference Publication (FMFRP) 12–46. Department of the Navy – Headquarters US Marine Corps] (Washington DC: US Government Printing Office, 1992), p. 29. For American strategy in a war with Japan see: Edward S. Miller, *War Plan Orange: The U.S. Strategy to Defeat Japan 1897–1945* (Indianapolis, MD: Naval Institute Press, 2007).

63. John R. Ferris, 'Student and Master: The United Kingdom, Japan, Airpower and the Fall of Singapore, 1920–1941', in Brian Farrell and Sandy Hunter (eds), *A Great Betrayal?: The Fall of Singapore Revisited* (Singapore: Marshall Cavendish, 2009), p. 80.

64. The Navy Type 15 for example, which first flew in 1925, was based on the Felixstowe F5. Likewise, the Navy Type 89, which saw its maiden flight in 1930, had its origins in the Supermarine Southampton. See: Robert C. Mikesh and Shorzoe Abe, *Japanese Aircraft 1910–1941* (London: Putnam, 1990).

65. 'When [the Second World War] came, the Fleet Air Arm was at least ten years behind the developments in the American and Japanese fleets'. Arthur J. Marder, *From the Dardanelles to Oran: Studies of the Royal Navy in War and Peace 1915–1940* (Barnsley: Seaforth Publishing, 2015), p. 56.

Chapter 2

1. Ian Hamill, *Strategic Illusion: The Singapore Strategy and the Defence of Australia and New Zealand, 1919–1942* (Singapore: Singapore University Press, 1981), p. 42.

2. The 'Two Power Standard', first adopted in 1889, called for the Royal Navy to be as strong as the world's next two largest navies combined. In 1903 this was stated by the then First Lord of the Admiralty, the Earl of Selborne, as also meaning a 'real margin' over and above the pair of inferior fleets and further clarified in 1908 by Herbert Asquith as meaning 'a preponderance of 10 per cent over the combined strengths in capital ships of the two next strongest Powers, whatever those Powers may be and wherever they may be situated'. See: *Hansard*, House of Commons Debates, 26 May 1909, Volume 5, ccl277–325. D. G. Boyce (ed.), *The Crisis of British Power: The Imperial and Naval Papers of the Second Earl of Selborne, 1895–1910* (London: The Historians' Press, 1990), pp. 154–5.

3. J. Wormell, *The Management of the National Debt of the United Kingdom, 1900–32* (London: Routledge, 2000), p. 732. C. H. Feinstein, *National Income, Expenditure and Output of the United Kingdom, 1855–1965* (Cambridge: Cambridge University Press, 1972), Table 4.

4. Josephus Daniels, *Annual Report of the Secretary of the Navy, 1916* (Washington DC: Government Printing Office, 1916).

5. Arthur S. Link (ed.), *The Papers of Woodrow Wilson*, 69 Volumes (Princeton NJ: Princeton University Press, 1966–1994), January-May, 1916, Vol. 36, p. 120.

6. Kenneth J. Hagan, *This People's Navy: The Making of American Sea Power* (New York: Free Press, 1991), p. 273.

7. Ian Nish, *Japanese Foreign Policy, 1869–1942* (London: Routledge & Keegan Paul, 1977), p. 290.

8. G. A. H. Gordon, 'The British Navy, 1918–1945', in Keith Neilson and Elizabeth Jane Errington (eds), *Navies and Global Defence: Theories and Strategy* (Westport CT: Praeger, 1995), p. 162. Inbal Rose, *Conservatism and Foreign Policy during the Lloyd George Coalition 1918–1922* (Abingdon UK: Taylor & Francis, 1999), pp. 169–70.

9. Jellicoe also visited India, New Zealand and Canada to advise on naval defence

10. Report of Admiral of the Fleet Viscount Jellicoe of Scapa G.C.B. O.M. G.C.V.O. on Naval Mission to the Commonwealth of Australia (May-August 1919). Four Volumes. Vol. I, p. 1.

11. Report of Admiral of the Fleet Viscount Jellicoe of Scapa G.C.B. O.M. G.C.V.O. on Naval Mission to the Commonwealth of Australia (May-August 1919). Four Volumes. Vol. I, p. 5.

12. UK National Archives CAB 23/29 (Original Reference CC 1 (22)-22 (22), 10 January – 29 March 1922). 'Conclusions of a Meeting of the Cabinet held at 10 Downing Street on Friday, 17 February, 1922 at 5:30 pm', p. 134.

13. Erik Goldstein, 'The Evolution of British Diplomatic Strategy for the Washington Conference', in Erik Goldstein (ed.), *The Washington Conference 1921–22: Naval Rivalry, East Asian Stability and the Road to Pearl Harbor* (London: Frank Cass, 1994), p. 14. One of a planned class of four battlecruisers, *Hood* of the projected 'Admiral' class, was commissioned in 1920 – she was to be Britain's last completed battlecruiser. Mounting a main armament of eight 15in (381mm) guns and displacing some 46,000 tonnes, *Hood* was, at 860ft 6in (262.3m) in length, the largest capital ship in the world at the time of her commissioning.

14. Richard Worth, *Fleets of World War II* (Cambridge MA: Da Capo, 2001), p. 93; Ian Johnston and Rob McAuley, *The Battleships* (Osceola WI: MBI, 2001), p. 113.

15. Opening Speech by General Smuts in *The Summary of Proceedings and Documents of The Conference Of Prime Ministers and Representatives of the United Kingdom, the Dominions and India held in June, July, And August, 1921, at London* (London: HMSO, 1921), p. 27.

16. The Admiralty's first Eastern War Memorandum was prepared by the Plans Division in 1920 [ADM 116/3124]; new editions were issued in 1923 [ADM 116/3124], 1924 [ADM 116/3125], 1931 [ADM 116/3118], 1933 [ADM 116/3475] and 1937 [ADM 116/4393]. Early memoranda covering the 'Passage of the Fleet to the Far East', can be found in ADM 116/3125 [dated 17.3.25.] and in ADM 116/3123 [dated June 1925, revised May 1927]. Beginning in 1933 this information was incorporated directly into the Eastern War Memoranda.

17. Report of Admiral of the Fleet Viscount Jellicoe of Scapa G.C.B. O.M. G.C.V.O. on Naval Mission to the Commonwealth of Australia (May-August 1919). Four Volumes. Vol. I, p. 24. As the American diplomat and journalist Nicholas Roosevelt was to put it: 'Singapore guards the western gateway of the Pacific. Situated at the extreme south-eastern corner of Asia, where the tongue of the Malay Peninsula protrudes into the East

Indies, it is so favored by geography that ships plying between Suez and Japan as well as between India and Australia must pass within a mile of it. Off Singapore the waters of the Indian Ocean, the China Sea and the Java Sea meet. Like Panama, Gibraltar and Suez, it is one of the great focal points for shipping, where geography forces far-flung lines of communication to converge'. Nicholas Roosevelt, 'The Strategy of Singapore', in *Foreign Affairs*, January 1929, p. 321.

18. 'An Appreciation of the Value of Singapore to Australia'. A document in the Australian Archives; Series: A981/1; Item: DEF 331 Pt. 2. Title: Defence Singapore, p. 1. This document is undated, but its contents reveal it was written in 1936.

19. 'An Appreciation of the Value of Singapore to Australia'. A document in the Australian Archives; Series: A981/1; Item: DEF 331 Pt. 2. Title: Defence Singapore, pp. 1–2.

20. Admiral Sir Herbert Richmond, *Statesmen and Sea Power* (Oxford: Clarendon, 1947), p. 328. Less well known is his similar statement (on p. 129 of the same book) that '. . . responsibilities in two oceans cannot be defended with a one-ocean sea power'. The canon of literature on the Singapore Naval Base and associated strategy is massive. Personal favourites include: Ian Hamill, *Strategic Illusion: The Singapore Strategy and the Defence of Australia and New Zealand, 1919–1942* (Singapore: Singapore University Press, 1981); Brian Farrell and Sandy Hunter (eds), *Sixty Years On: The Fall of Singapore Revisited* (Singapore: Eastern Universities Press, 2002); and W. David MacIntyre, *The Rise and Fall of the Singapore Naval Base* (Hamden CT: Archon, 1979).

21. The East Indies Station was a Royal Navy command which encompassed the Indian Ocean, with bases at Colombo, Trincomalee, Bombay, Basra and Aden. In 1924–5 it consisted of 'a squadron of three cruisers and a few small ships'. See: Arthur J. Marder, *Portrait of an Admiral: The Life and Papers of Sir Herbert Richmond* (London: Jonathan Cape, 1952), p. 27.

22. War Memorandum 1923, February 1923, ADM 116/3124.

23. Richmond to Haldane, 16.4.24., Lord Haldane of Cloan Papers, Vol. 5916, National Library of Scotland.

24. War Memorandum (Eastern), 29.7.24, ADM 116/3125.

25. Richmond to Admiralty, 13.4.25., ADM 116/3125.

26. Commander Russell Grenfell, *Sea Power in the Next War* (London: Geoffrey Bles, 1938), p. 165.

27. Stephen Roskill, *Admiral of the Fleet Earl Beatty: The Last Naval Hero – An Intimate Biography* (London: Collins, 1980), p. 307.

28. Hansard, House of Commons Debates, 5th series, Vol. 126, 2300–01.

29. Warren G Harding, Inaugural Address, March 4, 1921 at 'The American Presidency Project'. http://www.presidency.ucsb.edu/ws/index.php?pid=25833

30. https://www.gpo.gov/fdsys/pkg/GPO-CRECB-1921-pt2-v61/pdf/GPO-CRECB-1921-pt2-v61-21-1.pdf

31. 'Letter of the Secretary to the Treasury Relative to Internal Revenue Laws' of 30 April 1921 in: Internal-Revenue Hearings Before The Committee On Finance, United States Senate Sixty-Seventh Congress First Session, On The Proposed Revenue Act Of 1921 May 9–27 1921 (Washington; Government Printing Office, 1921), p. 8. See also: Philip H. Love, *Andrew W. Mellon: The Man and His Work* (Whitefish MT: Kessinger, 2003), p. 47.

32. William R. Braisted, 'The Evolution of the United States Navy's Strategic Assessments in the Pacific, 1919–31', in Erik Goldstein (ed.), *The Washington Conference 1921–22: Naval*

Rivalry, East Asian Stability and the Road to Pearl Harbor (London: Frank Cass, 1994), p. 103. There was also, from the British point of view, the worry that a war between the United States and Japan might well find Australia, Canada and New Zealand aligned with the Americans, while Britain was allied with Japan. Lord Esher had raised this point in a memo of 21 January 1910. UK National Archives. Cab. 4/3/1.

33. UK National Archives. ADM 116/1774, 'Memorandum for the Cabinet. Navy Estimates and Naval Policy,' dated 13 February 1920.

34. Hughes had resigned as an associate justice of the Supreme Court in order to campaign, unsuccessfully, against Wilson in the 1916 presidential election. He was, following his term under Harding and, after 1923, Coolidge, to go on to have a distinguished legal career as Chief Justice of the Supreme Court following his appointment to the post by Herbert Hoover in 1930. See: Betty Glad, *Charles Evans Hughes and the Illusions of Innocence: A Study in American Diplomacy* (Urbana IL: University of Illinois Press, 1966); Robert Sobel, *Biographical Directory of the United States Executive Branch, 1774–1989* (New York: Greenwood Press, 1990), pp. 187–8.

35. The Jellicoe Report had been widely discussed in the Japanese media. See, for example, the *Asahi Shimbun*, 29 October 1919, p. 2.

36. Sadao Asada, *Ryotaisenkan no Nichi-Bei Kankei: Kaigun to Seisaku Kettei Katei [Japanese-American Relations between the Wars: Naval Policy and Decision-Making Process]* (Tokyo: University of Tokyo Press, 1993), pp. 78–9. Ian Hamill, *Strategic Illusion: The Singapore Strategy and the Defence of Australia and New Zealand, 1919–1942* (Singapore: Singapore University Press, 1981), p. 46.

37. Niall A. Palmer, *The Twenties in America: Politics and History* (Edinburgh: Edinburgh University Press, 2006), p. 77.

38. William H. Honan, *Bywater: The Man who Invented the Pacific War* (London: Macdonald, 1990), p. 90; See also Erik Goldstein, 'The Evolution of British Diplomatic Strategy for the Washington Conference', in Erik Goldstein (ed.), *The Washington Conference 1921–22: Naval Rivalry, East Asian Stability and the Road to Pearl Harbor* (London: Frank Cass, 1994), pp. 28–9.

39. Mark Sullivan, *The Great Adventure at Washington* (Garden City, NY: Doubleday, Page, 1922), p. 27.

40. Allen W. Dulles, *The Craft of Intelligence* (New York: Harper & Row, 1963), p. 62. Interestingly, Yardley was to later state that the impetus for the Conference came from Lord Curzon, the British Foreign Secretary. 'The first telegram we deciphered which pointed definitely to the opening of a Pacific Conference between the Great Powers to settle disputes in the Far East was telegram No. 813, dated July 5, 1921, from the Japanese Ambassador in London to his home government in Tokio [*sic*]. The Japanese Ambassador and Lord Curzon were discussing the Anglo-Japanese Alliance that was of such tremendous concern to the United States. Lord Curzon suggested that if Japan, America and Great Britain would agree, they might open a Pacific Conference and discuss pending questions. Lord Curzon wished first confidentially to obtain the Japanese views, after which he could communicate with the American Ambassador. He expressed the hope that China, France and the countries of South America would also participate.' Herbert O. Yardley, *The American Black Chamber* (Laguna Hills CA: Aegean Park, 1931), p. 283. For a biography of Yardley see: David Kahn, *The Reader of Gentlemen's Mail: Herbert O Yardley and the Birth of American Codebreaking* (New Haven CT: Yale University Press, 2004).

41. 'Treaty between Japan and China for the Settlement of Outstanding Questions Relative to Shantung', in *The American Journal of International Law*, Vol. 16, No. 2, Supplement: Official Documents (Apr., 1922), pp. 84–94.

42. For an excellent account of the Washington Naval Conference and its context and consequences see Chapter 2 of: Herbert P. LePore, *The Politics and Failure of Naval Disarmament 1919–1939: The Phantom Peace* (Lewiston NY: Edwin Mellen Press, 2003). For the actual text of the Treaties see: Charles I. Bevans (ed.), 'Limitation of Naval Armament (Five-Power Treaty or Washington Treaty)', in *Treaties and Other International Agreements of the United States of America 1776–1949: Volume 2 Multilateral 1918–1930* (Washington DC: US Government Printing Office, 1969), pp. 351–80.

43. See: Admiral Mark Kerr, 'Foolery of Singapore', in *The Singapore Free Press and Mercantile Advertiser*, 23 June 1923, p.7. 'Singapore Base. Sir Percy Scott Antagonistic. Government Not Decided. The proposal to construct a naval base at Singapore is warmly opposed by Admiral Sir Percy Scott', in *The Advertiser* (Adelaide) 12 Mar 1924, p. 9.

44. James Neidpath has convincingly argued that the strategy was right for the circumstances of the 1920s. James Neidpath, *The Singapore Naval Base and the Defence of Britain's Eastern Empire, 1919–1941* (Oxford: Clarendon Press, 1981).

45. Though they had to scrap the older, 13.5in-gunned *Thunderer*, *King George V*, *Ajax* and *Centurion*.

46. Norman Polmar, *Aircraft Carriers: A History of Carrier Aviation and its Influence on World Events. Vol. 1, 1909–1945* (Washington DC: Potomac Books, 2006), pp. 57–60. The US Navy converted the uncompleted battlecruisers *Lexington* (launched October 1925, commissioned December 1927) and *Saratoga* (launched April 1925, commissioned November 1927). The Japanese did the same to their still-building battlecruisers *Akagi* (launched April 1925, commissioned March 1927) and *Amagi* (damaged beyond repair by an earthquake whilst on the slipway in September 1923 and scrapped). The total tonnage for aircraft carriers in terms of standard displacement was 135,000 tons for the US and UK and 81,000 tons for Japan. Individual carrier tonnage was limited to 27,000 tons standard displacement. However, any of the Contracting Powers could, provided that its total tonnage allowance was not exceeded, build two aircraft carriers of not more than 33,000 tons standard displacement and use for this purpose any two of their ships, whether constructed or in course of construction, which would otherwise be scrapped. Charles I. Bevans (ed.), 'Limitation of Naval Armament (Five-Power Treaty or Washington Treaty)', in *Treaties and Other International Agreements of the United States of America 1776–1949: Volume 2 Multilateral 1918–1930* (Washington DC: US Government Printing Office, 1969), p. 354.

47. Captain Russell Grenfell RN, *Main Fleet to Singapore* (New York: Macmillan, 1952), p. 216.

48. Ian Hamill, *Strategic Illusion: The Singapore Strategy and the Defence of Australia and New Zealand, 1919–1942* (Singapore: Singapore University Press, 1981), p. 58.

Chapter 3

1. Raymond H. Fredette, *The Sky on Fire: The First Battle of Britain 1917–1918* (Tuscaloosa, AL: University of Alabama Press, 2006). Christopher Cole and E. F. Cheesman, *The Air Defence of Great Britain 1914–1918* (London: Putnam, 1984). Neil Hanson, *First Blitz: The Secret German Plan to Raze London to the Ground in 1918* (London: Corgi, 2009). For the memorial to the children of Upper North Street School, see: https://www.historicengland.org.uk/listing/the-list/list-entry/1065215

2. H. A. Jones, *The War In The Air: Being the Story of the Part Played in the Great War by the Royal Air Force*, Vol. V [History of the Great War based on Official Documents by Direction of The Historical Section of the Committee of Imperial Defence] (Oxford: Clarendon, 1935), p. 38.

3. UK National Archives. CAB/24/22. 'Committee on Air Organization and Home Defence against Air Raids (2nd Report)' dated 17 August 1917, p. 4.

4. Office of Naval Intelligence, *Monthly Information Bulletin. Number 1–1920* (Washington DC: Navy Department, 1920), pp. 31–2.

5. S. W. Roskill (ed.), *Documents Relating to the Naval Air Service, Volume I* (London: Navy Records Society, 1969), p. xiv. 'Additional Reports of Gunnery Committee 24 June 1916', in B. M. Ranft (ed.), *The Beatty Papers* (London: Naval Records Society, 1989), No. 173, 1:359. He did have some high-calibre support in this. Rear Admiral Murray Sueter, one of the founders of the RNAS, Commodore Godfrey Paine, latterly Fifth Sea Lord responsible for all naval aviation and Commander Charles Samson, an early RNAS pioneer and the first person to fly an aircraft from a moving ship, were also in favour of the establishment of an independent air force. See: John Abbatiello, *Anti-Submarine Warfare in World War I: British Naval Aviation and the Defeat of the U-Boats* (New York: Routledge, 2006), p. 36.

6. Anthony J. Cumming, *The Battle for Britain: Interservice Rivalry Between the Royal Air Force and Royal Navy, 1909–1940* (Annapolis, MD: Naval Institute Press, 2015), p. 43. Andrew Boyle, *Trenchard: Man of Vision* (London: Collins, 1962).

7. H. A. Jones, *The War in The Air: Being the Story of the Part Played in the Great War by the Royal Air Force*, Vol. VI [History of the Great War based on Official Documents by Direction of The Historical Section of the Committee of Imperial Defence] (Oxford: Clarendon, 1937), p. 13.

8. https://www.rafmuseum.org.uk/london/whats-going-on/news/read-the-smuts-report/

9. H. A. Jones, *The War in The Air: Being the Story of the Part Played in the Great War by the Royal Air Force*, Vol. V [History of the Great War based on Official Documents by Direction of The Historical Section of the Committee of Imperial Defence] (Oxford: Clarendon, 1935), p. 42.

10. UK National Archives. AIR 6; Air Board and Air Ministry, Air Council: Minutes and Memoranda etc. Air 6/16 Minutes of Meetings of the Air Board and Air Council Precis No. 84, 'Order of the Air Council for the Transferring and Attaching Officers and Men to the Air Force'. See also: (The) Air Ministry, *The King's Regulations and Orders for the Royal Air Force, 1918* (London: HMSO, 1918).

11. The nascent Air Ministry was beset by disputes and infighting, most particularly between Trenchard and Rothermere. Indeed, both Trenchard and Rothermere, as well as the latter's deputy, Lieutenant-General Sir David Henderson, had all resigned by the end of April 1918. Richard Bourne, *Lords of Fleet Street: The Harmsworth Dynasty* (London: Routledge, 1990), pp. 87–8.

12. C. Cronin, *Royal Navy Shipboard Aircraft Developments 1912–1931* (Tonbridge: Air-Britain, Ltd., 1990), p. 61.

13. National Maritime Museum, Greenwich, London. 'Grand Fleet Battle Instructions' – 1 January 1918. Beatty Papers, NMM/BTY/7/4/1.

14. UK National Archives. ADM 1/8549/13, 'Appreciation of British Naval Effort, RNAS. Aircraft Operations, Part 1'.

15. Imperial War Museum, London. 'Royal Air Force State of Personnel and Materiel Readiness' dated 1 December 1918, Phillimore Papers, IWM 66/9/1. See also: Arthur Hezlet, *Aircraft and Seapower* (London: Cox and Wyman, 1970), p. 104.

16. S. W. Roskill (ed.), *Documents Relating to the Naval Air Service, Volume I* (London: Navy Records Society, 1969), p. 609.

17. For the political side of the Admiralty see: G. H. Bennett, *The Royal Navy in the Age of Austerity 1919–22: Naval and Foreign Policy under Lloyd George* (London: Bloomsbury, 2016).

18. Geoffrey Till, *Air Power and the Royal Navy 1914–1945: A Historical Survey* (London: Janes, 1979), pp. 32–40.

19. Bernard Fergusson (ed.), *The Business of War: The War Narrative of Major General Sir John Kennedy* (London: Hutchinson, 1957), p. 7.

20. © Sir Terry Pratchett.

21. S. W. Roskill, *The War at Sea 1939–1945: Volume I The Defensive* (London: HMSO, 1954), p. 31.

22. *Ark Royal* was followed by the four ships of the *Illustrious* class (*Illustrious, Formidable* and *Victorious* plus their slightly upgraded sister *Indomitable*)', laid down in 1937 and launched in 1939–40 and the two *Implacable* class vessels (*Implacable* and *Indefatigable*) laid down in 1939 but not completed until 1944.

23. David Lloyd George, *War Memoirs of David Lloyd George* (London: Odhams, 1938). Vol. I, p. 687.

24. UK National Archives. ADM 116/2771. 'Rear Admiral (Air) – appointment etc'. Minute by Captain Edward O Cochrane, Director of Training and Staff Duties, 7 July 1930. Admiralty instructions to Henderson, 11 June 1931.

25. Churchill Archives Centre, The Papers of Stephen Roskill, ROSK/7/48. Naval Policy between the Wars, vol I, 1919–39: source files: naval aviation 1925–29. Minute C. E. 119/27 dated 17 February 1927 by Sir Charles Walker [Walker was a career civil servant who served for two years as 'Jacky' Fisher's private secretary and ultimately rose to become Deputy Secretary of the Admiralty. His memoirs, *Thirty-Six Years at the Admiralty* (London: Lincoln Williams, 1933), are of interest]. See also: Eric Grove, 'The Naval Aviation Controversy 1919–1939', in Peter Hore (ed.), *Dreadnought to Daring: 100 Years of Comment, Controversy and Debate in The Naval Review* (Barnsley: Seaforth, 2012), p. 118.

26. Norman Friedman, *British Carrier Aviation: The Evolution of The Ships and Their Aircraft* (Annapolis, MD: Naval Institute Press, 1988), p. 158.

27. Stephen Roskill, *Naval Policy Between the Wars II: The Period of Reluctant Rearmament 1930–1939* (Barnsley: Seaforth, 2016), p. 207. The Imperial Japanese Navy numbered ten flag officers who were former aviators in 1941. The USN had thirteen, plus one Marine Corps General, who were former pilots and a further two that had been observers. The Royal Navy had none during the course of the Second World War. Norman Polmar, *Aircraft Carriers: A History of Carrier Aviation and its Influence on World Events Volume I* (Washington, DC: Potomac Books, 2006), pp. 142–3.

28. UK National Archives. ADM 186/560. C B 3003/26 [C B = Confidential Book – Classified Admiralty Publication]. 'Progress of Fleet Air Arm up to 30 Sept 1926'. 1927. ADM 186/561. 'C B 3003/32 '.Progress in the Fleet Air Arm, 1932'. Admiralty, Naval Staff, Naval Air Division, dated June 1933. ADM 186/562. C. B. 3003/34.

'Progress in the Fleet Air Arm, 1934'. Admiralty, Naval Staff, Naval Air Division, dated April 1934.

29. Thomas C. Hone, Norman Friedman and Mark D. Mandeles, *Innovation in Carrier Aviation: Newport Paper Thirty-Seven* (Newport, RI: Naval War College Press, 2011), p. 45.
30. UK National Archives. ADM 239/261. 'Fighting Instructions'. '1939–1941'.
31. Norman Friedman, *Fighters Over the Fleet: Naval Air Defence from Biplanes to the Cold War* (Barnsley: Seaforth, 2016.), p. 74.
32. For *Spearfish*'s ordeal and escape see: Geirr H. Haarr, *No Room for Mistakes: British and Allied Submarine Warfare 1939–1940* (Barnsley: Pen & Sword, 2015), pp. 110–12. Also: The Obituary of Commander John Eaden in *The Daily Telegraph*, 07 May 2007. https://www.telegraph.co.uk/news/obituaries/1550780/Commander-John-Eaden.html
33. UK National Archives. ADM 199/393 – Home Fleet War Diaries 1939–41. No. 37. Despatch from Commander in Chief, Home Fleet, to Secretary of Admiralty, 15 April 1940. Torpedo and air attacks on HMS Ark Royal, 14 and 26 September 1939, pp. 13–14. Unless otherwise stated, this is the source used for this section of the work.
34. Christopher Mann, *British Policy and Strategy towards Norway, 1941–45* (London: Palgrave Macmillan, 2012), p. 107. Patrick Dalzel-Job, *Arctic Snow to Dust of Normandy: The Extraordinary Wartime Exploits of a Naval Special Agent* (Barnsley: Pen and Sword, 2003), p. 58.
35. Jean-Denis G. G. Lepage, *Aircraft of the Luftwaffe, 1935–1945: An Illustrated Guide* (Jefferson, NC: McFarland, 2009), p. 325.
36. The pilot made a controlled landing on the water. The crew were captured a short while later by the British destroyer *Somali*. See: Peter C. Smith, *Skua! The Royal Navy's Dive-Bomber* (Barnsley: Pen & Sword, 2006), p. 73.
37. The Type 79Y was the first operational radar system deployed by the Royal Navy. Requiring separate transmitting and receiving antenna, it utilized a frequency of 38–42 MHz and had a power output of 20 kW. Aircraft flying at 30,000ft could be detected at 120 miles, though the range dropped to 70 miles for those at 10,000ft. A set was installed aboard *Rodney* in October 1938. H. W. Pout, 'Weapon Direction in the Royal Navy 1939–45', in F. A. Kingsley (ed.), *The Applications of Radar and other Electronic Systems in the Royal Navy in World War 2* (London: Palgrave Macmillan, 1995), pp. xxi, 10–11, 40.
38. These aircraft were part of I/KG 30 (*Kampfgeschwader* 30) a recently formed anti-shipping unit based on the island of Sylt off the north German coast.
39. Cajus Bekker, *Angriffshöhe 4000: Die deutsche Luftwaffe im Zweiten Weltkrieg* (München: Wilhelm Heyne, 1972), pp. 92–3. SC (*Sprengbombe-Cylindrisch*) 500; a thin-cased general-purpose bomb weighing 500kg.
40. For a perspective from those aboard the target see: William Jameson, *Ark Royal: The Life of an Aircraft Carrier at War 1939–41* (Penzance; Periscope, 2004), pp. 28–31.
41. Cajus Bekker, *Angriffshöhe 4000: Die deutsche Luftwaffe im Zweiten Weltkrieg* (München: Wilhelm Heyne, 1972), p. 91.
42. First Lord to First Sea Lord and DCNS dated 29.IX.39. Quoted in Winston S. Churchill, *The Gathering Storm* (London: Cassell & Co., 1948), p. 579.
43. UK National Archives. ADM 199/393 – Home Fleet War Diaries 1939–41. No. 37. Despatch from Commander in Chief, Home Fleet, to Secretary of Admiralty, 15 April 1940. Torpedo and air attacks on HMS Ark Royal, 14 and 26 September 1939, p. 13.
44. Heinz J. Nowarra, *Die Ju 88 und ihre Folgemuster* (Stuttgart: Motorbuch, 1987), p. 87.

45. William Jameson, *Ark Royal: The Life of an Aircraft Carrier at War 1939–41* (Penzance: Periscope, 2004.), p. 191.
46. A point emphasized by Haarr: Geirr H. Haarr, *The Gathering Storm: The Naval War in Northern Europe September 1939 – April 1940* (Barnsley: Seaforth, 2012), p. 235.
47. Kenneth Poolman, *Ark Royal* (London: William Kimber, 1956), p. 34.
48. Clark G. Reynolds, *The Fast Carriers: The Forging of an Air Navy* (Annapolis, MD: Naval Institute Press, 2013), p. 126.
49. And taken from the following accounts: Tim Slessor, 'The Tragedy of HMS Glorious', in *The RUSI Journal*, Vol. 144, 1999, Issue 1, pp. 68–74. James Levy, 'The Inglorious End of The Glorious: The Release of the Findings of the Board of Enquiry into the loss of HMS Glorious', in *The Mariner's Mirror*, 2002, 86:3, pp. 302–09. Vernon W Howland, 'The Loss of HMS Glorious: An Analysis of the Action', in *Warship International*, No. 1, 1994, pp. 47–62. 'Report from Board of Inquiry to Commander-in-Chief, Rosyth. 22 June 1940' reproduced in: Ben Jones (ed.), *The Fleet Air Arm in the Second World War Volume 1, 1939–1941: Norway, the Mediterranean and the Bismarck* (London: Routledge, 2012). John Winton, *Carrier Glorious: The Life and Death of an Aircraft Carrier* (London: Cassell, 1986). Philip Weir, 'HMS Glorious: History of a Controversy', on the *History Today* website, published 8 June 2015: https://www.historytoday.com/philip-weir/hms-glorious-history-controversy
50. Petty Officer Dick Leggott, a Gladiator pilot aboard HMS *Glorious*. Max Arthur, *Lost Voices of the Royal Navy* (London: Hodder & Stoughton, 2005), pp. 250–4. Leggott's testimony also appeared in 'Secret History' (a long-running British television documentary series) *The Tragedy of HMS Glorious*, broadcast by on Channel 4 on 30 June 1997.
51. As one online blogger commented: 'You have to be a real moron to be surprised by a BATTLESHIP in good weather when you're the one with the carrier'. 'Saphroneth' on 30 May 2014 at https://www.alternatehistory.com/forum/threads/wi-the-bpf-engaged-yamato.316220/
52. Air Chief Marshal Sir Kenneth Brian Boyd Cross, then Squadron Leader Kenneth 'Bing' Cross, a Hurricane pilot aboard *Glorious*. Cross was one of only three officers and forty-one other ranks rescued out of the three ships' companies. 'Secret History' (a long-running British television documentary series) *The Tragedy of HMS Glorious*, broadcast by on Channel 4 on 30 June 1997.
53. See: Chapter 7, 'Killing the *Königsberg*', in Peter C. Smith, *Skua! The Royal Navy's Dive-Bomber* (Barnsley: Pen & Sword, 2006), pp. 81–97. http://www.forgottenairfields.com/united-kingdom/scotland/orkney-and-shetland/hatston-s886.html
54. Some authorities class them as battlecruisers.
55. See: Arthur Marder, *From the Dardanelles to Oran: Studies of the Royal Navy in War and Peace 1915–1940* (Barnsley: Seaforth Publishing, 2015). David Brown, *The Road to Oran: Anglo-French Naval Relations September 1939–July 1940* (London: Frank Cass, 2004). David W. Wragg, *Sink the French! At War with Our Ally–1940* (Barnsley: Pen and Sword, 2007). Hervé Coutau-Bégarie and Claude Huan, *Mers el-Kébir (1940): La rupture franco-britannique* (Paris: Economica, 1994). Robert Dumas, *Les cuirassés Dunkerque et Strasbourg* (Nantes: Marines Édition, 2001).
56. Arthur Marder, *From the Dardanelles to Oran: Studies of the Royal Navy in War and Peace 1915–1940* (Barnsley: Seaforth Publishing, 2015), p. 255.
57. Jack Greene and Alessandro Massignani, *The Naval War in the Mediterranean, 1940–1943* (Newbury; Chatham, 1998), p. 60.

58. Arthur Marder, *From the Dardanelles to Oran: Studies of the Royal Navy in War and Peace 1915–1940* (Barnsley: Seaforth Publishing, 2015), pp. 256–8. John Jordan and Robert Dumas, *French Battleships 1922–1956* (Annapolis, MD: Naval Institute Press, 2009), pp. 78–89.

59. Robert Dumas, *Le cuirassé Jean Bart 1939–1970* (Nantes: Marine Éditions, 2001). See also Chapter 6 of John Jordan and Robert Dumas, *French Battleships 1922–1956* (Annapolis, MD: Naval Institute Press, 2009), pp. 152–62.

60. Tasked to cooperate with the French Navy in hunting German shipping, *Hermes* had been based at Dakar since October 1939. She was ordered to leave on 29 June and begin a blockade of the port following a declaration of allegiance to the Vichy Government by the colonial authorities.

61. For details of the various manoeuvrings, both naval and political, occasioned by this sortie see Chapter 6, 'The Cruise of the *Richelieu*, 25–26 June', in David Brown, *The Road to Oran: Anglo-French Naval Relations September 1939–July 1940* (London: Frank Cass, 2004), pp. 119–28.

62. Quoted in: Jonathan Sutherland and Diane Canwell, *Vichy Air Force at War: The French Air Force that Fought the Allies in World War II* (Barnsley: Pen & Sword, 2011), p. 23.

63. Naval Staff History Second World War, *Battle Summaries No. 3 and 20: Naval Operations Off Dakar July–September 1940* (London: HMSO, 1959), p. 22.

64. UK National Archives. ADM 1/10835. RN OFFICERS (71): 'Attack on French warship RICHELIEU and ships at Dakar: appointment of Captain R F J Onslow HMS HERMES as Acting Rear Admiral for operation'. Robert Dumas, *Le cuirasse Richelieu 1935–1968* (Bourg-en-Bresse: Marines Éditions et Réalisations, 1992).

65. For details on the development of the techniques and technology of air-dropping torpedoes see: UK National Archives. AVIA 8/335. 'Aircraft torpedoes: drum control gear: design and tests'. 1937–1938. UK National Archives. AVIA 16/31. 'Attempts to improve the anti-roll effect on torpedoes in air of parallel drum control gear'. 1938. UK National Archives. AVIA 16/37. 'Further experiments on attempts to improve the anti-roll effect on torpedoes in air of parallel drum control gear'. 1938. UK National Archives. ADM 204/275. 'Torpedo control in air by fixed rudders and drum control gear'. 1939. W. A. Harrison, 'Running Straight and True: Torpedo and Delivery Tactics', in *Swordfish: The Fleet Air Arm's Versatile, Long Serving, Legendary 'Stringbag'* [Aeroplane Icons Magazine] (Cudham; Kelsey, no date), p. 56. Roger Hayward, 'British Air-Dropped Depth Charges and Anti-Ship Torpedoes' in the *Royal Air Force Historical Society Journal*, No. 45, 2009, pp. 128, 130.

66. Roger Branfill-Cook, *Torpedo: The Complete History of the World's Most Revolutionary Naval Weapon* (Barnsley: Seaforth, 2014), p. 239.

67. Naval Staff History Second World War, *Battle Summaries No. 3 and 20: Naval Operations Off Dakar July–September 1940* (London: HMSO, 1959), p. 22.

68. Angelo N. Caravaggio, 'The Attack at Taranto: Tactical Success, Operational Failure', in *Naval War College Review*, Summer 2006, Vol. 59, No. 3, p. 112.

69. His 'highly reliable informant' was 'an officer on Ramsay's staff'. Arthur Marder, *From the Dardanelles to Oran: Studies of the Royal Navy in War and Peace 1915–1940* (Barnsley: Seaforth Publishing, 2015), p. 102. n 82. A. J. Smithers, *Taranto 1940: A Glorious Episode* (London: Leo Cooper, 1995), p. 58.

70. Lyster was appointed to the command on 19 August 1940.

71. Viscount Cunningham of Hyndhope, *A Sailor's Odyssey: The Autobiography of Admiral of the Fleet Viscount Cunningham of Hyndhope* (New York: Dutton, 1951), p. 273.

72. The reconstructed First World War battleships *Conte di Cavour, Giulio Cesare, Andrea Doria* and *Caio Duilio*, plus the two modern ships *Littorio* and *Vittorio Veneto*. A sister of the latter pair, *Roma*, was incomplete.
73. An excellent map detailing these defences can be found in: Angus Konstam, *Taranto 1940: The Fleet Air Arm's precursor to Pearl Harbor* (Oxford: Osprey, 2015), p. 32. See also: Giorgio Giorgerini, *La guerra italiana sul mare: La Marina tra vittoria e sconfitta 1940–1943* (Milano: Mondadori, 2002), pp. 218–19.
74. The basic principle of radar had been demonstrated by Guglielmo Marconi in 1933. This was followed in 1935 by a report from the engineer Ugo Tiberio, which led to the forming of a research group at Livorno Naval Academy the following year. This was, however, poorly supported and financed until the Battle of Cape Matapan of 27–29 March 1941. This cost the Italian Navy the loss of three cruisers, two destroyers and 2,300 men and highlighted the fact that without a radar capability they were practically helpless during the hours of darkness. The resulting impetus, together with a sharing of similar German apparatus, led to the development of a seagoing radar set named *Gufo* (Owl), of which fifty were ordered. Serious difficulties were though found in the manufacturing process and the first sets were only installed in 1942. See: Professor M. Calamia and Captain R. Palandri, 'The History of the Italian Radio Detector Telemetro', in Russell Burns (ed.), *Radar development to 1945* (London: Peter Peregrinus, 1988), pp. 97–105. Ugo Tiberio, 'Some Historical Data Concerning the First Italian Naval Radar', in *IEEE Transactions on Aerospace and Electronic Systems*, Vol. 5, No. 5 September 1979, pp. 733–5. Ugo Tiberio, 'Ricordo del primo Radar navale italiano', in *Rivista Marittima*, No. 12 December 1976, p. 17. Francesco Baroni, *La guerra dei radar: il suicidio dell'Italia 1935/1943* (Milano: Greco & Greco, 2007).
75. Giorgio Cobolli, *Gli aerofonisti ciechi durante la seconda guerra mondiale* (Roma: Unione Italiana Ciechi, 1993). See also: Military Intelligence Service, *TME 30-420: Handbook on the Italian Military Forces* (Washington DC: War Department, 1943), p. 236.
76. Giuseppe Fioravanzo (Compilatore), *La Marina italiana nella seconda guerra mondiale: Volume II La guerra nel Mediterraneo: Le azioni navali: Tomo I, dal 10 giugno 1940 al 31 marzo 1941* (Roma: Ufficio Storico Marina Militare, 1959), p. 247. Piero Baroni, *La guerra dei radar: il suicidio dell'Italia 1935/1943* (Milano: Greco & Greco, 2007), p. 97.
77. Taken from: 'Fleet Air Arm Operations against Taranto on 11 November 1940'. From a Despatch submitted to The Lords Commissioners of the Admiralty on the 16 January 1941, by Admiral Sir Andrew B. Cunningham, Commander-in-Chief, Mediterranean. Published in a *Supplement to The London Gazette*, Tuesday 22 July 1947, p. 3472.
78. G. A. Titterton, *The Royal Navy and the Mediterranean Volume II: November 1940-December 1941* (London: Whitehall History Publishing with Frank Cass, 2002), p. 11.
79. Michael Simpson, *A Life of Admiral of the Fleet Andrew Cunningham: A Twentieth-Century Naval Leader* (London: Frank Cass, 2004), p. 74.
80. Ciano's diary entry dated 12 November 1940 read: 'A black day. The British, without warning, have attacked the Italian fleet at anchor in Taranto and have sunk the dreadnought *Cavour* and seriously damaged the battleships *Littorio* and *Duilio*. These ships will remain out of the fight for many months.' Galeazzo Ciano and Hugh Gibson (ed.) (V Umberto Coletti-Perucca, trans.), *The Ciano Diaries 1939–1943: The Complete, Unabridged Diaries of Count Galeazzo Ciano, Italian Minister of Foreign Affairs, 1936–1943* (Garden City, NY: Garden City, 1947), p. 310.

81. Viscount Cunningham of Hyndhope, *A Sailor's Odyssey: The Autobiography of Admiral of the Fleet Viscount Cunningham of Hyndhope* (New York: Dutton, 1951), p. 286.
82. 'La disfatta subita senza combattere dalla marina italiana, nella notte dell' 11 e 12 novembre 1940, decise le sorti della guerra tra l'Italia e la Grand Bretagna. Taranto fu la Trafalgar italiana'. ['The defeat suffered without fighting by the Italian navy, on the night of 11 and 12 November 1940, decided the fate of the war between Italy and Great Britain. Taranto was the Italian Trafalgar'.] Antonino Trizzino, *Navi e poltrone* (Milano: Longanesi, 1953), p. 28.
83. Angelo N. Caravaggio, 'The Attack at Taranto: Tactical Success, Operational Failure', in *The Naval War College Review*, Vol. 59, No 3 Summer 2006, pp. 103–27.
84. James J Sadkovich, *The Italian Navy in World War II* (Westport, CT: Greenwood, 1994), p. 94.
85. Both were eventually repaired. '*Valiant* occupied Alexandria's floating dry dock until April 1942, when it moved to Durban, South Africa, to continue repairs and refit. The battleship returned to service with the Eastern Fleet in August 1942. *Queen Elizabeth* emerged from dock on 27 June 1942 and sailed to Norfolk, Virginia, for permanent repairs. Her first fleet operations occurred in January 1944.' See: Vincent P O'Hara and Enrico Cernuschi, 'Frogmen against a Fleet: The Italian Attack on Alexandria 18/19 December 1941', in *Naval War College Review*, Vol. 68, Number 3, Summer, 2015, p. 131. The fact that they had been disabled was effectively disguised: 'Admiral Cunningham C-in-C Mediterranean, directed that the ceremony of Colours, with Guard and Band and himself attending, would be carried out as usual on board his Flagship, HMS *Queen Elizabeth* following the devastating attack by Italian human torpedoes. The hope was that the world would think the battleship was undamaged and the Royal Navy was still supreme'. Richard Compton-Hall, *The Underwater War 1939–1945* (Poole: Blandford, 1982), p. 133.
86. *Ark Royal* by *U-81* on 14 November; *Barham* by *U-331* on 25 November.
87. ASV (Air to Surface Vessel) Mark II Radar could detect large ships up to 90 miles ahead, but became virtually useless at very short range. This was so because it transmitted a pulse powerful enough to damage the receiver. This was avoided by the expedient of automatically shutting off the receiver for a fraction of a second as the pulse was transmitted. It followed that signals that were returned during this period, that is those bounced back from objects within about three-quarters of a mile, were not detected. The British had ordered 4,000 sets in the spring of 1940, but production was delayed. Alan Beyerchen, 'From Radio to Radar: Interwar Military Adaptation to Technological Change in Germany, the United Kingdom and the United States', in Williamson Murray and Alan R. Millet (eds), *Military Innovation in the Interwar Period* (Cambridge: Cambridge University Press, 1998), p. 294–5.
88. For a 'forensic analysis' of the damage caused see: William Jurens, William H. Garzke Jr. and Robert O. Dulin Jr., John Roberts and Richard Fiske, 'A Marine Forensic Analysis of HMS *Hood* and DKM *Bismarck*', in *Transactions of the Society of Naval Architects and Marine Engineers*, Vol. 110, 2002, pp. 115–53. The information was obtained from a survey of the wreck-site carried out in July 2001.
89. The classic account of the hunt for and destruction of, *Bismarck* is Ludovic Kennedy's *Pursuit: The Sinking of the Bismarck* (London: William Collins, 1974). More recent treatments include: Niklas Zetterling and Michael Tamelander, *Bismarck: The Final Days of Germany's Greatest Battleship* (Havertown, PA: Casemate, 2011) and Angus Konstam, *The Bismarck 1941: Hunting Germany's Greatest Battleship* (Oxford: Osprey, 2011). For an account from the German side see: Burkard Baron von Mullenheim-Rechberg and

Jack Sweetman (trans.), *Battleship Bismarck: A Survivor's Story* (Annapolis, MD: US Naval Institute Press, 2002). See also: UK National Archives. AIR 20/1329. BISMARCK: 'Reports on Sinking'. April 1941 – January 1942. UK National Archives. ADM 199/1188. Pursuit and destruction of German battleship BISMARCK. 1941–1942.

90. Ships sunk in harbours or shallow water are, generally, salvable. Those in deep water generally not.

91. The Type 91 had a warhead that weighed in at either 149.5kg or 205kg dependant on model. See: Patrick Mahoney and Martin Middlebrook, *The Sinking of the Prince of Wales & Repulse: The End of the Battleship Era* (Barnsley: Pen & Sword, 2014), p. 162.

92. Winston S. Churchill, *The Second World War: Volume III The Grand Alliance* (Boston: Houghton Mifflin, 1950), p. 286.

Chapter 4

1. B. H. Liddell Hart, *A History of the World War 1914 -1918* (London: Faber, 1934), p. 357.
2. Books devoted exclusively to the sinking of the *Prince of Wales* and *Repulse* include the following (there are many larger works that also deal with the event in detail): Admiralty Historical Section, *Battle Summary No. 14 (revised): Loss of HM Ships Prince of Wales and Repulse 10th December 1941* (London: Admiralty Historical Section, 1953); Bernard Ash, *Someone had Blundered: The Story of the 'Repulse' and the 'Prince of Wales'* (Garden City, NY: Doubleday, 1961); Geoffrey Bennett, *The Loss of the Prince of Wales & Repulse* (Annapolis, MD: Naval Institute Press, 1973); Richard Hough, *The Hunting of Force Z* (London: William Collins, 1963); Rod Macdonald, *Force Z Shipwrecks of the South China Sea: HMS Repulse and HMS Prince of Wales* (Dunbeath: Whittles Publishing, 2013); Stephen Martin, *Scapegoat: The Death of Prince of Wales and Repulse* (Barnsley: Pen & Sword Maritime, 2014); Martin Middlebrook and Patrick Mahoney, *Battleship: The Loss of the Prince of Wales and the Repulse* (London: Allen Lane, 1977); Arthur Nicholson, *Hostages to Fortune: Winston Churchill and the Loss of the Prince of Wales and Repulse* (Stroud: Sutton, 2005). There are also several monographs, one of the most informative being: William Jurens, William H. Garzke Jr. and Robert O. Dulin Jr., 'Death of a Battleship. The Loss of HMS Prince of Wales, 10 December 1941: A Marine Forensic Analysis of the Sinking' (National Harbor, MD: Society of Naval Architects and Marine Engineers, International Marine Forensics Symposium, 2012). Available from: https://www.pacificwrecks.com/ships/hms/prince_of_wales/death-of-a-battleship-2012-update.pdf
3. Winston S. Churchill, *The Second World War: Volume III The Grand Alliance* (Boston: Houghton Mifflin, 1950), p. 551.
4. Submarine and surface-launched torpedoes were larger and heavier than their aerial counterparts.
5. Admiralty Historical Section, *Battle Summary No. 14 (revised): Loss of HM Ships Prince of Wales and Repulse 10th December 1941* (London: Admiralty Historical Section, 1953), p. 4.
6. Andrew Boyd, *The Royal Navy in Eastern Waters: Linchpin of Victory 1935–1942* (Barnsley: Seaforth, 2017), pp. 321–3.
7. Quoted in: John Burton, *Fortnight of Infamy: The Collapse of Allied Airpower West of Pearl Harbor* (Annapolis, MD: Naval Institute Press, 2006), p. 96.
8. Post-war interrogation of Captain Sonokawa Kameo, commanding officer of the *Genzan* Air Group. United States Strategic Bombing Survey [Pacific] Naval Analysis Division, *Interrogations of Japanese Officials Volume 2* (Washington, D.C.: Naval Analysis Division, 1946), p. 333.

9. Yoichi Hirama, 'Japanese Naval Preparations for World War II', in *Naval War College Review*, Vol. 44 No. 2 Spring 1991, pp. 78–9. See also: Osamu Tagaya, *Mitsubishi Type 1 Rikko 'Betty' Units of World War 2* (Oxford: Osprey, 2001).

10. Force G initially comprised just *Prince of Wales* (plus two destroyers), until the rendezvous with *Repulse* off Ceylon on 29 November 1941.

11. Martin Middlebrook and Patrick Mahoney, *Battleship: The Loss of the Prince of Wales and the Repulse* (London: Allen Lane, 1977), p. 106. Cartwright was one of the two attendees still living at the time the authors were researching their book. The other was Lieutenant Richard Dyer of *Tenedos*.

12. Admiralty Historical Section, *Battle Summary No. 14 (revised): Loss of HM Ships Prince of Wales and Repulse 10th December 1941* (London: Admiralty Historical Section, 1953), p. 8.

13. Admiralty Historical Section, *Battle Summary No. 14 (revised): Loss of HM Ships Prince of Wales and Repulse 10th December 1941* (London: Admiralty Historical Section, 1953), p. 31.

14. Air Chief Marshal Sir Robert Brooke-Popham Commander-in-Chief in the Far East, 'Operations in The Far East, From 17th October 1940 to 27th December 1941: A Despatch Submitted to the British Chiefs of Staff on 28th May, 1942'. Published as a Supplement to *The London Gazette* of Tuesday, the 20th of January 1948, p. 557.

15. Douglas Gillison, *Royal Australian Air Force, 1939–1942* (Canberra: Australian War Memorial, 1962), pp. 145, 204–5.

16. The Commander-in-Chief, Far East, Air Vice-Marshal Sir Robert Brooke-Popham, is claimed to have argued that 'we can get on all right with Buffaloes out here, but they haven't got the speed for England. Let England have the Super-Spitfires and the Hyper-Hurricanes. Buffaloes are good enough for Malaya.' James Leasor, *Singapore: The Battle that Changed the World* (London: Hodder and Stoughton, 1968), p. 161. See also: Douglas Gillison, *Royal Australian Air Force 1939–1942* (Canberra: Australian War Memorial, 1962), pp. 151–2, 170–1.

17. Steve Eather, *Flying Squadrons of the Australian Defence Force* (Weston Creek, ACT: Aerospace, 1995), pp. 108–9.

18. S. W. Roskill, *The War at Sea 1939–1945: Volume I The Defensive* (London: HMSO, 1954), p. 564. Based on a post-action report by Captain of the Fleet Leonard H. Bell, now in the UK National Archives. ADM 199/1149. 'Loss of HM Ships PRINCE OF WALES and REPULSE'. 1941–1942.

19. Arthur J. Marder, *Old Friends, New Enemies: The Royal Navy and the Imperial Japanese Navy, Volume 1: Strategic Illusions, 1936–1941* (Oxford: Oxford University Press, 1981), p. 385. For the belief that Phillips 'was inclined to scoff at the air menace and advocated facing it with anti-aircraft fire alone' see: David Hamer, *Bombers versus Battleships: The Struggle Between Ships and Aircraft for the Control of the Surface of the Sea* (Indianapolis, MD: Naval Institute Press, 1998), p. 119.

20. An observation on 'our intelligence at that time' (i.e. 1941) on Japanese capabilities by Captain of the Fleet Leonard H. Bell. Quoted in Arthur J. Marder, *Old Friends, New Enemies: The Royal Navy and the Imperial Japanese Navy, Volume 1: Strategic Illusions, 1936–1941* (Oxford: Oxford University Press, 1981), pp. 416–17.

21. T. J. Cain and A. V. Sellwood, *HMS Electra* (London: Frederick Muller, 1959), pp. 168–9.

22. Norman Friedman, *Naval Anti-Aircraft Guns and Gunnery* (Barnsley: Seaforth, 2013), p. 196.

23. Norman Friedman, *Naval Anti-Aircraft Guns and Gunnery* (Barnsley: Seaforth, 2013), p. 82.
24. Geoffrey Shakespeare, *Let Candles be Brought In* (London: Macdonald, 1949), p. 176. The de Havilland DH.82B Queen Bee was a remote-controlled target drone first produced in 1935 in response to an Air Ministry request for an inexpensive, expendable (but reusable) radio-controlled target drone for anti-aircraft gunnery practice. Although intended to operate without a pilot the Queen Bee had a cockpit and a full set of manual flying controls for ferry and test purposes. Under radio control the Queen Bee's flying controls were restricted to the rudder and elevator with the ailerons locked in a neutral position. Additional controls were fitted to operate the ignition and throttle. Radio control was effected through a simple rotary telephone dial, each number representing a specific function such as left, right, close or open throttle and so on. These signals operated pneumatic servos in a compartment behind the cockpit, which received air from a small wind turbine powered compressor mounted on the left side of the fuselage just behind the engine. Robin Braithwaite, 'The Queen of Bees', in *Light Aviation* magazine, June 2012, pp. 50–3.
25. Corelli Barnett, *Engage The Enemy More Closely: The Royal Navy In The Second World War* (New York: Norton, 1991), pp. 46–9.
26. Viscount Cunningham of Hyndhope, *A Sailor's Odyssey: The Autobiography of Admiral of the Fleet Viscount Cunningham of Hyndhope* (New York: Dutton, 1951), p. 259.
27. Viscount Cunningham of Hyndhope, *A Sailor's Odyssey: The Autobiography of Admiral of the Fleet Viscount Cunningham of Hyndhope* (New York: Dutton, 1951), p. 270.
28. Norman Friedman, *Naval Anti-Aircraft Guns and Gunnery* (Barnsley: Seaforth, 2013), pp. 25, 182.
29. Norman Friedman, *Naval Anti-Aircraft Guns and Gunnery* (Barnsley: Seaforth, 2013), p. 91.
30. At a trial of the fuse in August 1942 four rounds brought down three drones; 'this was so far beyond anything possible in anti-aircraft fire that observers were astounded'. Frederik Nebeker, *Dawn of the Electronic Age: Electrical Technologies in the Shaping of the Modern World, 1914 to 1945* (Hoboken, NJ: John Wiley, 2009), p. 439.
31. Outclassed that is by the United States Navy's Mk 37. The Japanese pre-war system, officially adopted in 1934, was though adjudged to have been 'broadly equivalent' to the American. Friedman also argues that the overall performance of the German anti-aircraft control system was 'apparently poor' and that the Italian Navy relied on 'barrage fire'. Norman Friedman, *Naval Anti-Aircraft Guns and Gunnery* (Barnsley: Seaforth, 2013), pp. 145, 163, 166–7, 208.
32. Kevin Denlay, 'An Overview of Expedition "Job 74" which carried Explorers Club Flag #118 to the Wrecks of HMS Prince of Wales and HMS Repulse, South China Sea, May 13-May 25 2007', pp. 6–7, 9–10. Available at: https://explorers.org/flag_reports/Flag_118_-_Kevin_Denlay_-_Update.pdf
33. William Jurens, William H. Garzke Jr. and Robert O Dulin Jr., 'Death of a Battleship. The Loss of HMS Prince of Wales, 10 December 1941: A Marine Forensic Analysis of the Sinking' (National Harbor, MD: Society of Naval Architects and Marine Engineers, International Marine Forensics Symposium, 2012), p. 41.
34. William Jurens, William H. Garzke Jr. and Robert O Dulin Jr., 'Death of a Battleship. The Loss of HMS Prince of Wales, 10 December 1941: A Marine Forensic Analysis of the Sinking' (National Harbor, MD: Society of Naval Architects and Marine Engineers, International Marine Forensics Symposium, 2012), p. 44.

35. Martin Stephen, *Scapegoat: The Death of Prince of Wales and Repulse* (Barnsley: Pen & Sword, 2014), p. 173. The Japanese Type 91 Model 1 torpedo, which dated from 1931, ran at 42 knots and was fitted with a 150kg warhead. The Model 2, first manufactured in November 1941, had an uprated warhead weighing 205kg. US Strategic Bombing Survey Military Analysis Division, *Japanese Air Weapons and Tactics* (Washington DC: Government Printing Office), pp. 55–6. It had taken four submarine-launched torpedoes, each with a warhead weighing 280kg, to sink the battleship *Royal Oak* on 14 October 1939 and three to do the same to *Barham* on 25 November 1941. Daniel Morgan and Bruce Taylor, *U-Boat Attack Logs: A Complete Record of Warship Sinkings from Original Sources 1939–1945* (Barnsley: Seaforth, 2011).
36. For a discussion of the development of underwater protection see: D. K. Brown, *Nelson to Vanguard: Warship Design and Development 1923–1945* (Barnsley: Seaforth, 2006), pp. 22–4.
37. Richard Hough, *The Hunting of Force Z* (London: William Collins, 1963), p. 147.
38. A couple spring readily to mind. Vice Admiral Maximilian Graf von Spee, who made a huge tactical error in approaching an unreconnoitred Port Stanley on 8 December 1914 and paid for it with his life and the loss of his command. Also Vice Admiral Sir George Tryon, who ordered his squadron to attempt an impossible manoeuvre on 22 June 1893 which then failed spectacularly. He went down with his flagship, as did 358 of her crew.
39. Arthur J. Marder, *Old Friends, New Enemies: The Royal Navy and the Imperial Japanese Navy, Volume 1: Strategic Illusions, 1936–1941* (Oxford: Oxford University Press, 1981), p. 81.
40. '. . . in war, as in every calling, he who wills the end must also understand and will the means'. Alfred T. Mahan, *Lessons of the War with Spain and Other Articles* (Boston: Little, Brown and Company, 1899), p. 18.
41. Andrew Boyd, *The Royal Navy in Eastern Waters: Linchpin of Victory 1935–1942* (Barnsley: Seaforth, 2017), p. 301.
42. Martin Stephen, *Scapegoat: The Death of Prince of Wales and Repulse* (Barnsley: Pen & Sword Maritime, 2014), pp. 70–2.
43. Arthur Bryant, *The Turn of the Tide, 1939–1943: A Study Based on the Diaries and Autobiographical Notes of Field Marshal The Viscount Alanbrooke* (London: Collins, 1957), p. 271.
44. Sumio Hatano and Sadao Asada, 'The Japanese Decision to Move South (1939–1941)', in Robert Boyce and Esmonde M. Robertson (eds), *Paths to War: New Essays on the Origins of the Second World War* (New York: St. Martin's Press, 1989); J. Charles Schencking, 'The Imperial Japanese Navy and the Constructed Consciousness of a South Seas Destiny, 1872–1921', in *Modern Asian Studies*, Vol. 33, No. 4, 1999, pp. 769–96. Some authorities have also cited the '*Automedon* Incident' as a cause behind the Japanese decision. This occurred on the 11 November 1940 when the German commerce raider *Atlantis* stopped and captured SS *Automedon* in the Indian Ocean some 250 nautical miles north-west of Sumatra. She was a British freighter carrying, amongst other things, a weighted bag containing a copy of the British War Cabinet Minutes of 8 August 1940. These included the Chiefs-of-Staff report on the defence of Singapore and the Far East in the event of a Japanese attack (August 1940 COS Far Eastern Appreciation (available at: http://filestore.nationalarchives.gov.uk/pdfs/small/cab-66-10-wp-40-302-33.pdf). The document was in transit to the Commander-in-Chief in Singapore, Sir Robert Brooke-Popham. The entire bag should have been jettisoned, but wasn't and so was seized by the Germans who

handed the report to the Japanese. The import of the appreciation was that Singapore and
Malaya could never survive a concerted attack by Japan and that no fleet could be despatched: 'Our general policy must be to play for time, cede nothing until we must and build
up our defences as soon as we can.' How much it actually influenced Japanese policy is a
matter of conjecture and dispute. See: James Rusbridger, 'The Sinking of the *Automedon*,
the Capture of the *Nankin*: New Light on Two Intelligence Disasters in World War II', in
Encounter, May 1985, Vol. LXIV, No. 5, pp. 9–12. Eiji Seki, *Mrs Ferguson's Tea-Set, Japan
and The Second World War: The Global Consequences Following Germany's Sinking of the
SS Automedon in 1940* (Folkestone: Global Oriental, 2007).

45. Thomas C. Hart, *War in the Pacific; End of the Asiatic Fleet: The Classified Report of
Admiral Thomas C. Hart* (Staunton, VA: Clarion, 2013), p. 46.
46. Richard Hough, *The Hunting of Force Z* (London: William Collins, 1963), p. 124,
47. The Captain Cook Graving Dock at Sydney was not officially opened until 24 March 1945.
48. Winston S. Churchill, *The Second World War: Volume III The Grand Alliance* (Boston:
Houghton Mifflin, 1950), p. 483.
49. *Prince of Wales* had required maintenance work on her distillers almost immediately
on arrival.
50. Winston S. Churchill, *The Second World War: Volume III The Grand Alliance* (Boston:
Houghton Mifflin, 1950), p. 484.
51. Arthur J. Marder, *Old Friends, New Enemies: The Royal Navy and the Imperial Japanese
Navy, Volume 1: Strategic Illusions, 1936–1941* (Oxford: Oxford University Press, 1981),
pp. 452, 462, 511, 512, 518 n. 50.
52. Martin Middlebrook and Patrick Mahoney, *Battleship: The Loss of the Prince of Wales and
the Repulse* (London: Allen Lane, 1977), p. 290. Whitworth has Chuichi Nagumo saying
something similar to his fellow officers aboard *Akagi* before the Pearl Harbor attack.
Sam H. Whitworth, *Chariots of Wrath: Engines, Aviation & Equitation* (Scarborough;
Farthings, 2016), pp. 50, 483.
53. Arthur J. Marder, *Old Friends, New Enemies: The Royal Navy and the Imperial Japanese
Navy, Volume 1: Strategic Illusions, 1936–1941* (Oxford: Oxford University Press, 1981),
p. 494 n. 5. Forbes-Sempill succeeded his father in 1934 and became the 19th Baron
Sempill, inheriting Craigievar Castle, Aberdeenshire. He rejoined the Royal Navy in 1939
and was assigned to the Admiralty where he worked in the Department of Air Material.
Suspicions over Sempill were aroused in June 1940 when MI5 intercepted messages
referring to payments being made to him by the Japanese Government. He denied the
allegations and said he had not received payments from an 'improper quarter'. He told the
Admiralty Board that the money had stopped on the outbreak of war. However, telephone
taps revealed that he maintained contact with the Japanese. A year later he again came to
the attention of the security services and Churchill ordered he be employed elsewhere in
the Admiralty. He was moved to a post in the North of Scotland in order not to provoke a
scandal via a prosecution. See: Antony Best, 'Lord Sempill (1893–1965) and Japan, 1921–
41', in Hugh Cortazzi (ed.), *Britain and Japan: Biographical Portraits, Volume 4* (London:
Routledge, 2002), pp. 375–82. 'Rutland of Jutland' had continued to work in in Japan
until 1932, when he moved to the United States with his family. The US Office of Naval
Intelligence concluded that he was an agent working for Japan and kept a close eye on
him. He returned to the UK in October 1941 and was interned under Defence Regulation
18B, which allowed for the indefinite detention of British nationals suspected of enemy
sympathies. He was released in late 1943 and some six years later committed suicide.

See: Ken Kotani, *Japanese Intelligence in World War II* (Oxford: Osprey, 2009), pp. 82–6. Nigel West, *Historical Dictionary of Naval Intelligence* (Lanham, MD: Scarecrow Press, 2010), pp. 267–8.

54. Air Chief Marshal Sir Robert Brooke-Popham Commander-in-Chief in the Far East, 'Operations in The Far East, From 17th October 1940 to 27th December 1941: A Despatch Submitted to the British Chiefs of Staff on 28th May 1942'. Published as a Supplement to *The London Gazette* of Tuesday, the 20th of January 1948, p. 536.

55. Winston S. Churchill, *The Second World War: Volume III The Grand Alliance* (Boston: Houghton Mifflin, 1950), p. 377.

56. UK National Archives. CAB 105/20. The principal telegrams relating to operation in the Far East, December 4 – December 25, 1941. Chiefs of Staff to Vice Admiral Sir Geoffrey Layton, 17 December 1941.

57. Richard A Stewart, *Sunrise at Abadan: The British and Soviet Invasion of Iran, 1941* (New York: Praeger, 1988).

58. James Bamberg, *The History of the British Petroleum Company: Volume 2; The Anglo-Iranian Years, 1928–1954* (Cambridge: Cambridge University Press, 1994), p. 218.

59. Henry Longhurst, *Adventure in Oil: The Story of British Petroleum* (London: Sidgwick and Jackson, 1959), pp. 106–8.

60. Ashley Jackson, *Persian Gulf Command: A History of the Second World War in Iran and Iraq* (New Haven, CT: Yale University Press, 2018), pp. 294–315. See also: Winston S. Churchill, *The Second World War: Volume III The Grand Alliance* (Boston: Houghton Mifflin, 1950), pp. 377–84. Department of Military Art and Engineering, *The War in North Africa: Part I: Operations in Egypt and Libya* (West Point, NY: United States Military Academy, 1951), p. 2. Harold E. Raugh Jr., *Wavell in the Middle East 1939–1941: A Study in Generalship* (Norman, OK: University of Oklahoma Press, 2013), p. 61. D. J. Payton-Smith, *Oil: A Study of War-Time Policy and Administration* (London: HMSO, 1971).

61. Srinath Raghavan, *India's War: The Making of Modern South Asia, 1939–1945* (London: Penguin, 2016) Kindle Edition Location 1298–9.

62. Andrew Gordon, 'The Admiralty and Imperial Overstretch 1902–1941', in *The Journal of Strategic Studies*, 17:22 March 1994, pp. 80–1.

63. See: Keith Bird, *Erich Raeder: Admiral of the Third Reich* (Annapolis, MD: Naval Institute Press, 2013), pp. 170–3. The Raeder quote is in Arthur J. Marder, Mark Jacobsen and John Horsfield, *Old Friends, New Enemies: The Royal Navy and the Imperial Japanese Navy. Volume II: The Pacific War 1942–1945* (Oxford: Clarendon, 1990), p. 81. See also the relevant portions of John W. M. Chapman (ed. and trans.), *The Price of Admiralty: The War Diary of the German Naval Attaché in Japan, 1939–1943: Volume 4, 10 September 1941–31 January 1942* (Ripe: Saltire Press 1989).

Chapter 5

1. S. W. Roskill, *The War at Sea 1939–1945: Volume I The Defensive* (London: HMSO, 1954), p. 562.

2. UK National Archives. CAB 105/20. 'The principal telegrams relating to operation in the Far East: 4 – 25 December 1941'. Messages from Layton to the Admiralty dated 13 December and 15 December 1941.

3. UK National Archives. CAB/80/60. War Cabinet. Chiefs of Staff Committee. Memoranda. 'Future British Naval Strategy', 14 December 1941.

4. The fifth, *Royal Oak*, had been sunk by a submarine at Scapa Flow on 14 October 1939.
5. It is tempting to view it as a Freudian slip; Diego Suarez (now Antsiranana) would have made an excellent base. A city in the north-east of Madagascar, its eponymous bay is a natural feature that stretches for some 20km (12.5 miles) north to south along the coast. There was already a first-class naval base there, but it belonged to (Vichy) France. It was largely to forestall any Japanese attempt at seizing this vital strategic point that Operation Ironclad, the British invasion of Madagascar, was undertaken on 5 May 1942. Fighting lasted until 6 November. See: John Grehan, *Churchill's Secret Invasion: Britain's First Large Scale Combined Operations Offensive 1942* (Barnsley: Pen and Sword, 2013).
6. UK National Archives. CAB 105/20. 'The principal telegrams relating to operation in the Far East' 4 – 25 December 1941. Admiralty to Layton 17 December.
7. UK National Archives. ADM 116/4877. 'Anglo/US co-operation in European, Atlantic and Pacific theatres of war: strategic and tactical planning and provision of lease/lend supplies'. Admiralty Telegram 523 dated 13 May 1941 to C-in-C Home Fleet.
8. The scale of the success was hidden and because the perpetrators of the attack were captured the Italians never learned what had been achieved. The *Regia Marina* were thus deceived into thinking their opponents still possessed a battlefleet.
9. When the British rearguard retreated to Singapore Island on 27 January 1942 they demolished part of the causeway connecting it to the mainland. According to the later account of a young Singaporean student at Raffles College named Lee Kuan Yew – who was to become independent Singapore's first Prime Minister and founding father – the college principal asked what the explosion meant. Lee replied. 'That is the end of the British Empire'. Christopher Bayly and Tim Harper, *Forgotten Armies: The Fall of British Asia, 1941–1945* (Cambridge, MA: Belknap, 2005), p. 130. See also: Prasenjit K. Basu, *Asia Reborn: A Continent Rises from the Ravages of Colonialism and War to a New Dynamism* (New Delhi: Aleph, 2017).
10. A Joint Chiefs of Staff (JCS) directive approved by President Roosevelt on 30 March 1942 divided the Pacific into three operational theatres: the North Pacific Area (NPA), Central Pacific Area (CPA) and South Pacific Area (SPA). The South Pacific Area included every Pacific Ocean Area landmass south of the equator and included New Zealand. The commander of the South Pacific Area was initially Vice Admiral Robert L. Ghormley, then after October 1942, Admiral William F. Halsey. See: Alan Rems, *South Pacific Cauldron: World War II's Great Forgotten Battlegrounds* (Annapolis, MD: Naval Institute Press, 2014).
11. There is a vast body of work on MacArthur and his command. See, for example: Peter J. Dean, *MacArthur's Coalition: US and Australian Operations in the Southwest Pacific Area, 1942–1945* (Lawrence, KS: University Press of Kansas, 2018); Walter R. Borneman, *MacArthur at War: World War II in the Pacific* (New York: Little, Brown, 2016); Joan Beaumont (ed.), *Australia's War 1939–45* (St. Leonards, NSW: Allen & Unwin, 1996).
12. Alan D Zimm, *Attack on Pearl Harbor: Strategy, Combat, Myths, Deceptions* (Havertown, PA: Casemate, 2011), p. 366. It also more or less compelled the US Navy to operate as a fleet based on carrier aviation, something it would develop to a previously undreamt-of level. In addition, it united the entire American nation against the attackers, shattering Japan's hope that a compromise peace, which would allow it to keep some of its conquests, was achievable.
13. Captain A. T. Mahan, *The Influence of Sea Power upon History 1660–1783* (Boston: Little Brown, 1890), p. 25.

14. Richard Hough, *The Fleet that Had to Die* (London: Hamish Hamilton, 1958).
15. Donald Macintyre, *Fighting Admiral: The life of Admiral of the Fleet Sir James Somerville* (London: Evans Brothers, 1961), p. 169.
16. Donald Macintyre, *Fighting Admiral: The life of Admiral of the Fleet Sir James Somerville* (London: Evans Brothers, 1961), pp. 177–8.
17. Stephen Roskill, *Naval Policy Between the Wars II: The Period of Reluctant Rearmament 1930–1939* (Barnsley: Seaforth, 2016), p. 123.
18. Michael Simpson (ed.), *The Somerville Papers: Selections from the Private and Official Correspondence of Admiral of the Fleet Sir James Somerville, GCB, GBE, DSO* (London: Scolar, 1995), p. 4.
19. Donald Macintyre, *Fighting Admiral: The life of Admiral of the Fleet Sir James Somerville* (London: Evans Brothers, 1961), p. 14.
20. J. F. Coates, 'The Origins and Development of Radar in the Royal Navy, 1939–1945, with Particular Reference to Decimetric Gunnery Equipments', in F. A. Kingsley (ed.), *The Development of Radar Equipments for the Royal Navy, 1935–45* (London: Macmillan, 1995), p. 30.
21. Sir Robert Watson-Watt, *Three Steps to Victory: A Personal Account by Radar's Greatest Pioneer* (London: Odhams, 1957), p. 304. See also: R. Hanbury Brown, 'Robert Watson-Watt, the Father of Radar', in *The Engineering Science and Educational Journal*, Vol. 3 No. 1, February 1994.
22. For the evident 'distress of the British Admiral and his principal officers' pertaining to Mers-el-Kebir see: Winston S. Churchill, *Their Finest Hour* (London: Cassell & Co., 1949), p. 201. Somerville's signals concerning his part in the Dudley North Affair are in, 'Part Two. The Story of Dudley North: Was Justice Done?', in Arthur J. Marder, *Operation Menace: The Dakar Expedition and the Dudley North Affair* (Barnsley: Seaforth, 2016).
23. Andrew Gordon, *The Rules of the Game: Jutland and British Naval Command* (London: John Murray, 1996), p. 597. For the origins of the term see: Andrew Gordon, 'Ratcatchers and Regulators at the Battle of Jutland', in Gary Sheffield and Geoffrey Till (eds), *The Challenges of High Command: The British Experience* (Houndmills: Palgrave Macmillan, 2003), p. 26. Gordon postulates that 'regulators' are successful in ascending a hierarchy in peacetime, but in wartime, under dynamic, stressful, complex and confusing combat situations, they tend to fail. On the other hand, 'ratcatchers' are comfortable with uncertainty and ambiguity, ready to exercise initiative when appropriate and thus tend to thrive under combat conditions.
24. He had written to his fellow 'fighting admiral' Andrew Cunningham on 4 October 1941 relating his misgivings about the appointment of Phillips and his team to 'that Far East Party' which contained 'no one with sea experience in this war'. Similar reservations were expressed in another message of 20 October about the 'Pocket Napoleon': 'All the tricks to learn and no solid sea experience to fall back on. They ought to have someone who knows his stuff . . .'. Michael Simpson (ed.), *The Somerville Papers: Selections from the Private and Official Correspondence of Admiral of the Fleet Sir James Somerville, GCB, GBE, DSO* (London: Scolar, 1995), pp. 323, 328.
25. Stephen Roskill, *Naval Policy Between the Wars Volume 2: The Period of Reluctant Rearmament, 1930–1939* (Annapolis, MD: Naval Institute Press, 1976).
26. Ian Buxton and Ian Johnston, *The Battleship Builders: Constructing and Arming British Capital Ships* (Barnsley: Seaforth, 2013), pp. 44–7.

27. Edmund S. Wong, *The Sea Takes No Prisoners: The Men and Ships of the Royal Navy in the Second World War* (Brighton: Uniform Press, 2018). The technical shortcomings referred to were by no means confined to the 'R' class. The subject of Admiralty neglect of the engineering branch during the interwar years, which led to a much wider malaise merely typified by the example in question, is relatively unknown. It is, alas, a somewhat sorry tale which, according to Christopher M. Bell, amounted to 'two decades of cautious and reluctant experimentation' in democratisation. Christopher M. Bell, 'The King's English and the Security of the Empire: Class, Social Mobility and Democratization in the British Naval Officer Corps, 1918–1939', in *The Journal of British Studies*, Vol. 48, No. 3, July 2009, pp. 695–716. See also Louis Le Bailly, *The Man Around the Engine: Life Below the Waterline* (Emsworth: Kenneth Mason, 1990), pp. 49–50. Le Bailly is bitterly critical of the Royal Navy's treatment of its engineer officers and amongst many other examples of British ineptitude in the technical context, he relates stories of the British Pacific Fleet in 1945. Supposed to operate alongside its American allies, it could keep its vessels at sea for eight days at a time. For the US Navy the period was 90 days. Eventually the BPF compromised on 20 days. Obituary, Vice Admiral Sir Louis Le Bailly, in *The Times*, 8 October 2010. See also: Oliver Johnson, 'Class Warfare and the Selborne Scheme: The Royal Navy's Battle over Technology and Social Hierarchy', in *The Mariner's Mirror*, Vol. 100, Issue 4, November 2014, pp. 422–33. For a rather more anodyne account see: Geoffrey Penn, *Up Funnel, Down Screw! The Story of the Naval Engineer* (London: Hollis & Carter, 1955). In another work, however, Penn comments that the Admiralty's purpose 'was clearly to revert the engineer from the military branch to his old position where he could never succeed to the command of ships or operational units'. Geoffrey Penn, *HMS Thunderer: The story of the Royal Naval Engineering College, Keyham and Manadon* (Emsworth: Kenneth Mason, 1984), p. 73.

28. An unmodernized *Queen Elizabeth* class battleship, small aircraft carrier and modern *Dido* class light cruiser respectively. From an entry in Somerville's pocket diary dated 17 February 1942. Michael Simpson (ed.), *The Somerville Papers: Selections from the Private and Official Correspondence of Admiral of the Fleet Sir James Somerville, GCB, GBE, DSO* (London: Scolar, 1995), p. 385.

29. G. A. H. Gordon, *British Seapower and Procurement between the Wars: A Reappraisal of Rearmament* (Annapolis, MD: Naval Institute Press, 1988), p. 110. David Hobbs, *British Aircraft Carriers: Design, Development and Service Histories* (Barnsley: Seaforth, 2013), p. 83.

30. Norman Friedman, *British Carrier Aviation: The Evolution of The Ships and Their Aircraft* (Annapolis, MD: Naval Institute Press, 1988), p. 160.

31. 'The offensive power of modern battleships is out of all proportion to their defensive power. Never was the disproportion so marked. If you want to make a true picture in your mind of a battle between great modern ironclad ships you must not think of it as if it were two men in armour striking at each other with heavy swords. It is more like a battle between two egg-shells striking each other with hammers.' From Winston Churchill's House of Commons speech on the Naval Estimates of 17 March 1914. Reported in *The Times*, 18 March 1914. Quoted in: F. B. Czarnomski, *The Wisdom of Winston Churchill: Being a Selection of Aphorisms, Reflections, Precepts, Maxims, Epigrams, Paradoxes and Opinions from his Parliamentary and Public speeches, 1900–1955* (London: George Allen & Unwin, 1956), p. 42. Quoted in part in Richard M. Langworth, *Churchill By Himself: The Definitive Collection of Quotations* (London: Ebury, 2008), p. 227. As one British

commentator put it in respect of the Battle of Jutland; 'unfortunately for us their egg-shells proved very tough and their hammers uncomfortably accurate'. 'Clinker', 'Reflections and Suggestions', in *The Naval Review*, Vol. XIX, No. 4, November 1931, p. 653.

32. David Hobbs, *British Aircraft Carriers: Design, Development & Service Histories* (Barnsley: Seaforth, 2013), pp. 85–8.

33. Captain Arthur William La Touche Bisset was commanding officer of *Formidable* from August 1940 to August 1942.

34. Letter to his wife, 17–25 February 1942 and extracts from his 'Pocket Diary' in: Michael Simpson (ed.), *The Somerville Papers: Selections from the Private and Official Correspondence of Admiral of the Fleet Sir James Somerville, GCB, GBE, DSO* (London: Scolar, 1995), pp. 386–7. See also his report to the Admiralty of 2 March 1942 in the same book; p. 389.

35. See: W. A. Harrison, *Fairey Albacore: Warpaint Series No. 52* (Luton; Warpaint Books, no date).

36. Captain Eric 'Winkle' Brown, *Wings on My Sleeve* (London: Arthur Barker, 1961), p. 44. The Fulmars were two-seat escort fighters rather than interceptors.

37. Glen Phillips, *Grumman F4F Wildcat Including Grumman Martlet Mks. I-VI: Warpaint Series No. 9* (Husborne Crawley: Hall Park Books, no date). For the Fulmar see: David Brown, *Aircraft Profile 254: Fairey Fulmar Mks I & II* (Windsor: Profile, 1973).

38. See: Chapter 18 of Jeffrey Cox, *Rising Sun, Falling Skies: The Disastrous Java Sea Campaign of World War II* (Oxford: Osprey 2014). The Netherlands East Indies (NEI) encompassed a huge swath of maritime territory across the south-west Pacific Ocean, stretching from the eastern end of the island of Sumatra to the western half of New Guinea (the eastern half was Portuguese). It included the major islands of Java and Timor, most of southern Borneo, the Celebes and hundreds of smaller islands in between. With a population reckoned to total some 60 million, only some 250,000 of which were European, the NEI produced some 29 per cent of global rubber production, 20 per cent of the world's tin and 97 per cent of its quinine. It also had substantial oilfields. See: Marc Lohnstein, *Royal Netherlands East Indies Army 1936–42* (Oxford: Osprey, 2018). See: 'The Forgotten Campaign: The Dutch East Indies Campaign 1941–1942' at: https://dutcheastindies. webs.com/index.html

39. The Battle of Sunda Strait, fought on the night of 28 February–1 March, for example. See: W. G. Winslow, *The Ghost That Died at Sunda Strait* (Annapolis, MD: Naval Institute Press, 1984).

40. Antony Best, 'Constructing an image: British Intelligence and Whitehall's perception of Japan, 1931–1939', in *Intelligence and National Security*, Vol. 11, No. 3, July 1996, p. 413. It wasn't just the British. According to a French report that was handed to the Netherlands Foreign Secretary in June 1939, the Japanese navy 'has lived 30 years on the reputation that it gained in the war against Russia'. Ger Teitler and Kurt W. Radtke (eds), *A Dutch Spy in China: Reports on the First Phase of the Sino-Japanese War (1937–1939)* (Leiden: Brill, 1999), p. 46. The spy in question was Colonel Henri Johan Diederick De Fremery.

41. Arthur J. Marder, *Old Friends, New Enemies: The Royal Navy and the Imperial Japanese Navy, Volume 1: Strategic Illusions, 1936–1941* (Oxford: Oxford University Press, 1981), p. 353.

42. See, for example, Chapter 3, 'Image and accident: intelligence and the origins of the Second World War, 1933–1941', in John Robert Ferris, *Intelligence and Strategy: Selected Essays* (Abingdon: Routledge, 2005), pp. 99–137.

43. Quoted in: Christopher M. Bell, 'The Royal Navy, War Planning and Intelligence Assessments of Japan, 1921–1941', in Peter Jackson and Jennifer Siegel (eds), *Intelligence and Statecraft: The Use and Limits of Intelligence in International Society* (Westport, CT: Praeger, 2005), p. 154.

44. Samuel Eliot Morison, *History of United States Naval Operations in World War II, Volume III: The Rising Sun in the Pacific, 1931–April 1942* (Boston: Little, Brown, 1948), p. 338. See also: Peter Brune, *The Spell Broken. Exploding The Myth of Japanese Invincibility. Milne Bay To Buna Sanananda 1942* (St Leonards, NSW: Allen & Unwin, 1998).

45. Mitsuo Fuchida and Masatake Okumina with Clarke H. Kawakami and Roger Pineau (eds), *Midway: The Battle That Doomed Japan, the Japanese Navy's Story* (Annapolis, MD: Naval Institute Press, 1955), p. 283.

46. Letter to his wife, 1 March 1942 in: Michael Simpson (ed.), *The Somerville Papers: Selections from the Private and Official Correspondence of Admiral of the Fleet Sir James Somerville, GCB, GBE, DSO* (London: Scolar, 1995), p. 388.

47. Somerville to his wife, 14 March 1942. In Michael Simpson (ed.), *The Somerville Papers: Selections from the Private and Official Correspondence of Admiral of the Fleet Sir James Somerville, GCB, GBE, DSO* (London: Scolar, 1995), p. 394.

48. Admiralty Historical Section, *Battle Summary No. 15: Naval Operations off Ceylon 29th March To 10th April, 1942* (London: Admiralty Historical Section, 1943), p. 2. Curiously, in *The Somerville Papers* this is given as 28 March 1942. This is undoubtedly a typographical error. The C-in-C Ceylon, Admiral Layton also has the date as 26 March 1942. See: Admiralty War Diaries of World War 2: Eastern Theatre Operations, the Diaries of Admiral Layton, C-in-C, China Station – November 1941 to March 1942. Transcribed by Don Kindell. https://www.naval-history.net/xDKWD-EF1941ChinaStation.htm

49. Pocket diary entry, 28 March 1942. In Michael Simpson (ed.), *The Somerville Papers: Selections from the Private and Official Correspondence of Admiral of the Fleet Sir James Somerville, GCB, GBE, DSO* (London: Scolar, 1995), p. 396.

50. Anonymous, 'Now It Can Be Told! How Royal Marines Hacked a Base From Jungle', in *The War Illustrated*, Vol. 9, No. 214, 31 August 1945, pp. 268–9. Peter Doling, *From Port T to RAF Gan: An Illustrated History of the British Military Bases at Addu Atoll in the Maldive Islands 1941–76* (Bognor Regis; Woodfield, 2003). UK National Archives. CAB 80/33/46. Addu Atoll. Defence Plan for base at: Memorandum by Ad Hoc Sub-Committee on the Defence Arrangements for the Indian Ocean Area covering. 29 January 1942.

51. 'It was a place that on appearance alone would give a travel-agent a rush of adjectives to the head: white coral beaches, waving palms, a cobalt sea changing to jade-green inshore and a sun like an ultra-violet-ray lamp. The reality was rather different. The sea inside the lagoon was tepid and brackish; the white beaches were floored with chinks of coral as jagged as a kitchen knife that cut one's skin to ribbons and started sores it took months to heal. The heat was inescapable and the flies stuck to one's skin like limpets.' Hugh Popham, *Sea Flight: The Wartime Memoirs of a Fleet Air Arm Pilot* (Barnsley: Seaforth, 2010), pp. 101–2.

52. Brownfield Family History Web Site: http://www.sandylane.plus.com/brownfieldline/Leslie_Newton_Brownfield.pdf

53. David Hobbs, *British Aircraft Carriers: Design, Development & Service Histories* (Barnsley: Seaforth, 2013), p. 100.

54. Commander R. 'Mike' Crosley, *They Gave me a Seafire* (Barnsley: Pen & Sword Aviation, 2014), p. 43.
55. UK National Archives. AVIA 46/136. Naval aircraft type biographies 1936–4. 4. Fleet Air Arm Aircraft: General Notes. Supply of Grumman Martlet Fighters. Fighter Aircraft for The Fleet Air Arm. Minute from First Lord of the Admiralty to the Prime Minister, 6 December 1941.
56. Henry 'Hank' Adlam: *On and Off the Flight Deck: Reflections of a Naval Fighter Pilot in World War II* (Barnsley: Pen & Sword Aviation, 2007) Kindle Edition. Location 1820. For the Sea Hurricane more generally see: Tony O'Toole, Martin Derry and Neil Robinson, *Hawker Hurricane and Sea Hurricane* (Barnsley: Pen and Sword Aviation, 2014), pp. 31–5.
57. Somerville to his wife, 1 April 1942. In Michael Simpson (ed.), *The Somerville Papers: Selections from the Private and Official Correspondence of Admiral of the Fleet Sir James Somerville, GCB, GBE, DSO* (London: Scolar, 1995), p. 398.
58. For details see: Ross Watton, *Anatomy of the Ship: The Battleship Warspite* (Annapolis, MD: Naval Institute Press, 2002) and Iain Ballantyne, *Warspite: From Jutland Hero to Cold War Warrior* (Barnsley: Pen and Sword, 2010).
59. Pocket diary entry, 29 March 1942. In Michael Simpson (ed.), *The Somerville Papers: Selections from the Private and Official Correspondence of Admiral of the Fleet Sir James Somerville, GCB, GBE, DSO* (London: Scolar, 1995), p. 397.
60. From a paper written for Arthur Marder by Vice Admiral Sir Kaye Edden, dated 24 February 1977. In The Papers of Admiral Sir James Somerville, SMVL 8/15, at Churchill College, Cambridge.

Chapter 6

1. Admiralty Historical Section, *Battle Summary No. 15: Naval Operations off Ceylon 29th March To 10th April, 1942* (London: Admiralty Historical Section, 1943), p. 2.
2. F. H. Hinsley, E. E. Thomas, C. F. G. Ransom and R. C. Knight, *British Intelligence in The Second World War: Volume I* (London: HMSO, 1979), p. 20.
3. Admiralty Historical Section, *Battle Summary No. 15: Naval Operations off Ceylon 29th March To 10th April, 1942* (London: Admiralty Historical Section, 1943), p. 2.
4. Somerville Pocket Diary entry for 29 March. In Michael Simpson (ed.), *The Somerville Papers: Selections from the Private and Official Correspondence of Admiral of the Fleet Sir James Somerville, GCB, GBE, DSO* (London: Scolar, 1995), p. 397.
5. Michael Smith, *The Emperor's Codes: The Breaking of Japan's Secret Ciphers* (Harmondsworth: Penguin, 2002), p. 129.
6. John Prados, *Combined Fleet Decoded: The Secret History of American Intelligence and the Japanese Navy in World War II* (New York: Random House, 1995), p. 274.
7. '. . . strategic empathy: the ability to think like [an] opponent. Strategic empathy is the skill of stepping out of our own heads and into the minds of others.' Zachary Shore, *A Sense of the Enemy: The High Stakes History of Reading Your Enemy's Mind* (New York: Oxford University Press, 2014), p. 2.
8. Rob Stuart, 'Leonard Birchall and The Japanese Raid on Colombo', in the *Canadian Military Journal*, Winter 2006–2007, p. 67. Stuart's source is given as: T. W. Melnyk, *Canadian Flying Operations in South East Asia 1941–1945* (Ottawa: Authority of the Minister of National Defence, 1976), p. 16. The numbers of operational aircraft are confirmed in Admiralty Historical Section, *Battle Summary No. 15: Naval Operations off Ceylon 29th March To 10th April, 1942* (London: Admiralty Historical Section, 1943), p. 2.

9. Alexander Kiralfy, 'Watch Japanese Air Power', in *Foreign Affairs: An American Quarterly Review*, Vol. 23, Issue 1, October 1944, p. 72.

10. Gordon Wallace, *Carrier Observer* (Shrewsbury: Airlife, 1993), pp. 58, 66. Wallace was an observer serving with 831 Squadron aboard *Indomitable* at the time.

11. DoD News Briefing – Secretary Rumsfeld and Gen. Myers. Presenter: Secretary of Defense Donald H Rumsfeld, February 12, 2002 11:30 AM EDT. http://archive.defense.gov/Transcripts/Transcript.aspx?TranscriptID=2636

12. Though a modernized *Kongo* with guns able to elevate to 43 degrees would have out-ranged an unmodernized 'R' class by a considerable margin; 38,770 yards (35,450m) to 28,000 yards (25,600m). There was also a substantial speed difference between the two types: 30.5 knots and 21 knots (theoretically) respectively. In addition, the British vessels had relatively thin deck armour, so would have been vulnerable to the type of plunging fire that featured in a long-range gunnery duel. Only in weight of shot, 1,938lbs (879kg) to 1,485lbs (673.5kg) per gun (both types had eight-gun main batteries), were the 'R' class at all superior. Ian Sturton (ed.), *Conway's Battleships: The Definitive Visual Reference to the World's All-Big-Gun Ships* (Annapolis, MD: Naval Institute Press, 2008).

13. 'At 0100, 31st March, Japanese submarine patrols were reported on an arc 360 miles from Colombo between the bearings of 090° and 140°. The Commander-in-Chief came to the conclusion that these were intended for the double purpose of providing reconnaissance and of serving as a screen through which their Ceylon raiding force would withdraw after the attack. An Albacore from the Formidable was flown ashore to request the Deputy Commander-in-Chief to arrange a patrol from 090° to 110°, in addition to the Catalina patrols [already] mentioned.' Admiralty Historical Section, *Battle Summary No. 15: Naval Operations off Ceylon 29th March To 10th April, 1942* (London: Admiralty Historical Section, 1943), p. 3.

14. Nelson's 'Trafalgar Memorandum' of 9 October 1805. Quoted in: John Charnock, *Biographical Memoirs of Lord Viscount Nelson: With Observations Critical and Explanatory* (Newburyport, MA: Thomas & Whipple, 1806), p. 292.

15. Atsushi Oi, 'The Japanese Navy in 1941', in Donald M. Goldstein and Katherine V. Dillon (eds), *The Pacific War Papers: Japanese Documents of World War II* (Washington, DC: Potomac Books, 2004), p. 21.

16. Sun Wenzhu, 'From Auxiliary to Weapon: Japan and Britain's Changing Understanding of the Naval Tactical Role of Aircraft, 1910–1929', in *The Journal of the Graduate School of Asia-Pacific Studies* (Waseda University), Number 30, August 2015, p. 99.

17. Jisaburo Ozawa, 'Development of the Japanese Navy's Operational Concept against America', in Donald M. Goldstein and Katherine V. Dillon (eds), *The Pacific War Papers: Japanese Documents of World War II* (Washington, DC: Potomac Books, 2004), pp. 74–5.

18. Probably the best book on the subject is: Mark R. Peattie, *Sunburst: The Rise of Japanese Naval Air Power, 1909–1941* (Annapolis, MD: Naval Institute Press, 2001).

19. The Combined Fleet was Japan's principal naval force. Almost synonymous with the navy afloat, the vast majority of naval vessels came under its command.

20. H. Agawa, *The Reluctant Admiral: Yamamoto and the Imperial Navy* (Tokyo: Kodansha International, 1979), pp. 92–3.

21. Ronald H. Carpenter, *Rhetoric in Martial Deliberations and Decision Making: Cases and Consequences* (Columbia, SC: University of South Carolina Press, 2004), p. 134.

22. Mark Peattie, *Sunburst: The Rise of Japanese Naval Air Power, 1909–1941* (Annapolis, MD: Naval Institute Press, 2001), pp. 248–9.

23. This section, unless otherwise stated, is based on: Jonathan Parshall and Michael Wenger, 'Pearl Harbor's Overlooked Answer', in *Naval History Magazine*, Vol. 25, Number 6, December 2011, pp. 16–21.

24. Gordon W Prange, *At Dawn We Slept: The Untold Story of Pearl Harbor* (New York: McGraw-Hill, 1981), p. 18.

25. Donald M. Goldstein, Katherine V. Dillon and J. Michael Wenger, *The Way It Was: Pearl Harbor, the Original Photographs* (London: Brassey's, 1995), p. 2.

26. Mark Peattie, *Sunburst: The Rise of Japanese Naval Air Power, 1909–1941* (Annapolis, MD: Naval Institute Press, 2001), p. 159.

27. Gordon W. Prange, *At Dawn We Slept: The Untold Story of Pearl Harbor* (New York: McGraw-Hill, 1981), p. 110.

28. Nor was his Chief of Staff, Rear Admiral Kusaka Ryunosuke, an aviator. See: Norman Polmar, *Aircraft Carriers: A History of Carrier Aviation and Its Influence on World Events Vol. 1, 1909–1945* (Washington, DC: Potomac, 2006), p. 142.

29. Clark Reynolds, *The Fast Carriers: The Forging of an Air Navy* (Annapolis, MD: Naval Institute Press, 1968), p. 9.

30. 'Through January and February desperate efforts were made to ship material, including airplanes, to Java, as well as to fly planes to that area.' Richard M. Leighton and Robert W. Coakley, *United States Army in World War II. The War Department: Global Logistics and Strategy 1940–1943* (Washington, DC: Center Of Military History United States Army, 1995), p. 170.

31. For the aircraft types used at that period see: Jonathan Parshall and Anthony Tully, *Shattered Sword: The Untold Story of the Battle of Midway* (Dulles, VA: Potomac, 2005), p. 78.

32. M. F. Hawkins, *The Nakajima B5N "Kate"* (Windsor: Profile, 1966).

33. Peter C. Smith, *Aichi D3A1/2 Val* (Marlborough: Crowood, 1999).

34. Captain Eric 'Winkle' Brown, *Wings on My Sleeve* (Shrewsbury: Airlife, 1978), p. 226. See also: Peter C. Smith, *Mitsubishi Zero: Japan's Legendary Fighter* (Barnsley: Pen & Sword Aviation, 2015).

35. For the latest scholarship on the raid see: Dr Tom Lewis and Peter Ingman, *Carrier Attack Darwin 1942: The Complete Guide to Australia's own Pearl Harbor* (Kent Town, SA; Avonmore, 2013).

36. Richard M. Leighton and Robert W. Coakley, *United States Army in World War II. The War Department: Global Logistics and Strategy 1940–1943* (Washington, DC: Center Of Military History United States Army, 1995), pp. 170–1.

37. For detailed information on these, see: Stefan Dramiński, *The Japanese Aircraft Carrier Akagi* (Lublin; Kagero, 2017); Miroslaw Skwiot, *The Japanese Aircraft Carriers Soryu and Hiryu* (Lublin: Kagero, 2015); Mark Stille, *Imperial Japanese Navy Aircraft Carriers 1921–45* (Oxford: Osprey, 2005).

38. For various totals see: Chapter 8, 'Le temps des victoires, décembre 1941-mai 1942', in Michel Ledet, *Samouraï sur Porte-Avions* (Le Vigen: Éditions Lela, 2006); Jonathan Parshall and Anthony Tully, *Shattered Sword: The Untold Story of the Battle of Midway* (Dulles, VA: Potomac, 2005); Mark Stille, *USN Carriers vs IJN Carriers: The Pacific 1942* (Oxford: Osprey, 2007).

39. For example; Harold J. Goldberg, *D-Day in the Pacific: The Battle of Saipan* (Bloomington, IN: Indiana University Press, 2007), p. 20. H. P. Willmott, *The Great Crusade: A New Complete History of the Second World War, Revised Edition* (Washington, DC: Potomac, 2008), p. 181.

40. Vice Admiral Sir Arthur Hezlet, *Aircraft and Seapower* (New York: Stein and Day, 1970), p. 126.
41. 'Report of Proceedings of Eastern Fleet 29 March to 13 April 1942' at: https://www.naval-history.net/xDKWD-EF1942-Introduction.htm Macintyre says that the four battleships of Force B '. . . had to call up every horse-power they could muster to make eighteen knots through the water'. Donald Macintyre, *Fighting Admiral: The life of Admiral of the Fleet Sir James Somerville* (London: Evans Brothers, 1961), p. 185. Wallace states that 15 knots '. . . was the most that the old "Rs" could manage'. Gordon Wallace, *Carrier Observer* (Shrewsbury: Airlife, 1993), p. 64.
42. Gordon Wallace, *Carrier Observer* (Shrewsbury: Airlife, 1993), p. 66.
43. 'There is less danger in fearing too much than too little'. Sir Francis Walsingham in a letter to William Cecil of December 1568. Stephen Budiansky, *Her Majesty's Spymaster: Elizabeth I, Sir Francis Walsingham and the Birth of Modern Espionage* (New York: Viking, 2005), p. 71.
44. Winston S. Churchill, *The World Crisis 1911–1918* (London: Odhams, 1938) Two Volume Edition, Vol. 2, p. 1015.
45. Dated 1 April to his wife; 1–3 April 1942. In Michael Simpson (ed.), *The Somerville Papers: Selections from the Private and Official Correspondence of Admiral of the Fleet Sir James Somerville, GCB, GBE, DSO* (London: Scolar, 1995), p. 398.
46. Gordon Wallace, *Carrier Observer* (Shrewsbury: Airlife, 1993), p. 66.
47. Dated 2 April to his wife; 1–3 April 1942. In Michael Simpson (ed.), *The Somerville Papers: Selections from the Private and Official Correspondence of Admiral of the Fleet Sir James Somerville, GCB, GBE, DSO* (London: Scolar, 1995), p. 398.
48. Donald Macintyre, *Fighting Admiral: The life of Admiral of the Fleet Sir James Somerville* (London: Evans Brothers, 1961), p. 187.
49. Report of Proceedings of Eastern Fleet 29 March to 13 April 1942' at: https://www.naval-history.net/xDKWD-EF1942-Introduction.htm
50. 272mph (438kmh) as against 161mph (259kmh).
51. Gordon Wallace, *Carrier Observer* (Shrewsbury: Airlife, 1993), p. 66.
52. *Cornwall* to resume her refit; *Dorsetshire* to escort a troop convoy; *Hermes* and *Vampire* in preparation for a proposed operation to invade Madagascar. Donald Macintyre, *Fighting Admiral: The life of Admiral of the Fleet Sir James Somerville* (London: Evans Brothers, 1961).
53. Gordon Wallace, *Carrier Observer* (Shrewsbury: Airlife, 1993), p. 67.
54. Donald Macintyre, *Fighting Admiral: The life of Admiral of the Fleet Sir James Somerville* (London: Evans Brothers, 1961), p. 188.
55. Rob Stuart, 'Leonard Birchall and the Japanese Raid on Colombo', in *The Canadian Military Journal*, Vol. 7, No. 4, Winter 2006–2007, p. 68.
56. The lead ship was *Akagi*, with the cruisers *Tone* and *Chikuma* roughly abreast on each beam. Immediately astern of the flagship were *Soryu* and *Hiryu*, then the four battleships *Hiei, Kirishima, Haruna* and *Kongo*, with *Shokaku* and *Zuikaku* bringing up the rear. The fleet was screened at all points by the destroyers See: http://dreadnoughtproject.org/friends/dickson/IJN%201942%20Carrier%20Formations.pdf for disposition diagrams taken from Jiro Kimata, *Nihon kubo senshi* [*The History of Japanese Carrier Operations*] (Tokyo: Tosho Shuppansha, 1977).
57. David L. Bashow, 'Four Gallant Airmen: Clifford Mackay McEwen, Raymond Collishaw, Leonard Joseph Birchall and Robert Wendell McNair', in Colonel Bernd Horn (ed.),

Intrepid Warriors: Perspectives on Canadian Military Leaders (Toronto; Dundern Group and Canadian Defence Academy, 2007), p. 177.

58. Encoding, or rather enciphering, a message involved the use of a mechanical encryption system called SYKO. Developed and used by the RAF, it consisted of lists that were moved by hand to disclose letters or numbers beneath them, whereby a plaintext letter could be represented by a large number of different cypher letters or numerals. The cipher, held on SYKO cards, was changed daily, but poor practice meant that combinations of them were often repeated after a brief time. This had led to the breaking of the cipher by the Italians in the Mediterranean. Vincent P. O'Hara and Enrico Cernuschi, 'The Other Ultra: Signal Intelligence and the Battle to Supply Rommel's Attack toward Suez', in *Naval War College Review*, Summer 2013, Vol. 66, No. 3, p. 121. The US patent for the SYKO apparatus can be found at: https://patentimages.storage.googleapis.com/92/2e/46/737d9db6eec180/US2270137.pdf A copy of the manual for operating the machine is online at: http://www.jproc.ca/crypto/syko_manual.pdf

59. Rob Stuart, 'Leonard Birchall and the Japanese Raid on Colombo', in *The Canadian Military Journal*, Vol. 7, No. 4, Winter 2006–2007, p. 69.

60. Birchall and several of his crew survived both being shot down and subsequent Japanese internment. See: https://www.telegraph.co.uk/news/obituaries/1472001/Air-Commodore-Leonard-Birchall.html

61. Andrew Boyd, *The Royal Navy in Eastern Waters: Linchpin of Victory 1935–1942* (Barnsley: Seaforth, 2017), p. 370.

62. Dated 4 April to his wife; 4–6 April 1942. In Michael Simpson (ed.), *The Somerville Papers: Selections from the Private and Official Correspondence of Admiral of the Fleet Sir James Somerville, GCB, GBE, DSO* (London: Scolar, 1995), p. 399.

63. Robert Stuart, 'Air Raid Colombo, 5 April 1942: The Fully Expected Surprise Attack', in *The Royal Canadian Air Force Journal*, Vol. 3, No. 4, Fall 2014, p. 37. Admiralty Historical Section, *Battle Summary No. 15: Naval Operations off Ceylon 29th March To 10th April, 1942* (London: Admiralty Historical Section, 1943), p. 6. Ernest Cable, 'The Measure of a Leader: Squadron Leader L.J. Birchall (The Saviour of Ceylon)', in W. A. March (ed.), *Sic Itur Ad Astra: Canadian Aerospace Power Studies, Volume 1 Historical Aspects of Air Force Leadership*, p. 20. Available from http://publications.gc.ca/collections/collection_2010/forces/D4 7-1-2009-eng.pdf

64. Admiralty Historical Section, *Battle Summary No. 15: Naval Operations off Ceylon 29th March To 10th April, 1942* (London: Admiralty Historical Section, 1943), p. 5.

65. Report of Proceedings of Eastern Fleet 29 March to 13 April 1942' at: https://www.naval-history.net/xDKWD-EF1942-Introduction.htm

66. Donald Macintyre, *Fighting Admiral: The life of Admiral of the Fleet Sir James Somerville* (London: Evans Brothers, 1961), p. 189.

67. Admiralty Historical Section, *Battle Summary No. 15: Naval Operations off Ceylon 29th March To 10th April, 1942* (London: Admiralty Historical Section, 1943), p. 6. n. 5.

68. Jonathan Parshall and Anthony Tully, *Shattered Sword: The Untold Story of the Battle of Midway* (Dulles, VA: Potomac, 2005), p. 108. See also: Mitsuo Fuchida and Masatake Okumiya, *Midway: The Battle That Doomed Japan, The Japanese Navy's Story* (Annapolis, MD: Naval Institute Press, 2001), p. 180.

69. Mark R. Peattie, *Sunburst: The Rise of Japanese Naval Air Power 1909–1941* (Annapolis MD: Naval Institute Press, 2001), pp. 49–50, 153–4. Waldemar Goralski and Grzegorz Nowak, *Japanese Heavy Cruiser Tone* (Lublin: Kagero, 2012). Nagumo had a total of

twenty-three floatplanes aboard his cruisers and battleships as follows: Light Cruiser *Abukuma*: one Kawanishi E7K: Range: 1,105 miles (1779km). Heavy Cruisers *Tone* and *Chikuma*: one Kawanishi E7K; three Nakajima E8N: Range: 558 miles (904km); one Aichi E13A: Range: 1,300 miles (2,100km) aboard each vessel. Battleships *Kongo*, *Haruna*, *Kirishima* and *Hiei*: three Nakajima E8N aboard each vessel. Information from: Robert Stuart, 'State of the Art: The Japanese Attacks on *Hermes, Vampire, Hollyhock, Athelstane, British Sergeant* and *Norviken*, 9 April 1942', 2018. Available from: http://www.combinedfleet.com/articles.htm

70. A Kawanishi E7K. See: http://www.combinedfleet.com/tone_t.htm 'the E7K . . . had a very respectable range (over 1,000 nm), making it perfectly usable for long-range scouting missions'. Jonathan Parshall and Anthony Tully, *Shattered Sword: The Untold Story of the Battle of Midway* (Dulles, VA: Potomac, 2005), p. 539, n. 50.

71. Captain Augustus Agar, *Footprints In The Sea* (London: Evans Brothers, 1959), p. 306.

72. Arthur J. Marder, Mark Jacobsen and John Horsefield, *Old Friends New Enemies, the Royal Navy and the Imperial Japanese Navy Volume II: The Pacific War, 1942–1945* (Oxford: Clarendon, 1990), p. 129.

73. Admiralty Historical Section, *Battle Summary No. 15: Naval Operations off Ceylon 29th March To 10th April, 1942* (London: Admiralty Historical Section, 1943), p. 7.

74. John Prados, *Combined Fleet Decoded: The Secret History of American Intelligence and the Japanese Navy in World War II* (New York: Random House, 1995), p. 540. See also: Mark R. Peattie, *Sunburst: The Rise of Japanese Naval Air Power 1909–1941* (Annapolis MD: Naval Institute Press, 2001), p. 41. Sources differ, but Marder et al put the number of strike aircraft at fifty-three. Arthur J. Marder, Mark Jacobsen and John Horsefield, *Old Friends New Enemies, the Royal Navy and the Imperial Japanese Navy Volume II: The Pacific War, 1942–1945* (Oxford: Clarendon, 1990), p. 131.

75. Peter C. Smith, *Fist from the Sky: Japan's Dive-bomber Ace of World War II* (Mechanicsburg, PA: Stackpole, 2006), pp. 193–4. Masatake Okumiya and Jiro Horikoshi with Martin Caidin, *Zero: The Story of Japan's Air War in the Pacific – As Seen by the Enemy* (New York: Ballantine Books, 1956), pp. 150–1.

76. Admiralty Historical Section, *Battle Summary No. 15: Naval Operations off Ceylon 29th March To 10th April, 1942* (London: Admiralty Historical Section, 1943), p. 7.

77. Peter C. Smith, *Fist from the Sky: Japan's Dive-bomber Ace of World War II* (Mechanicsburg, PA: Stackpole, 2006), p. 155. Marder et al put the percentage at 'nearly 87 per cent'. Arthur J. Marder, Mark Jacobsen and John Horsefield, *Old Friends New Enemies, the Royal Navy and the Imperial Japanese Navy Volume II: The Pacific War, 1942–1945* (Oxford: Clarendon, 1990), p. 131.

78. Admiralty Historical Section, *Battle Summary No. 15: Naval Operations off Ceylon 29th March To 10th April, 1942* (London: Admiralty Historical Section, 1943), p. 11.

79. Andrew Boyd, *The Royal Navy in Eastern Waters: Linchpin of Victory 1935–1942* (Barnsley: Seaforth, 2017), p. 372. Wallace says that there was a tannoy broadcast at 13:45 hours stating that 'enemy aircraft were on the radar screen at the extreme range of 84 miles'. Gordon Wallace, *Carrier Observer* (Shrewsbury: Airlife, 1993), p. 68.

80. Hugh Popham, *Sea Flight: A Fleet Air Arm Pilot's Story* (London: William Kimber, 1954), pp. 103–4. For the obituary of Hugh Henry Home Popham, aviator, writer and poet, see: https://www.independent.co.uk/incoming/obituary-hugh-popham-5609673.html

81. Dated 6 April 'at sea' to his wife; 4–6 April 1942. In Michael Simpson (ed.), *The Somerville Papers: Selections from the Private and Official Correspondence of Admiral of the Fleet Sir James Somerville, GCB, GBE, DSO* (London: Scolar, 1995), p. 401. Admiralty Historical

Section, *Battle Summary No. 15: Naval Operations off Ceylon 29th March To 10th April, 1942* (London: Admiralty Historical Section, 1943), p. 11.

82. Gordon Wallace, *Carrier Observer* (Shrewsbury: Airlife, 1993), p.68.

83. From one of the Albacores at 16:00 hours and Colombo at 17:00 hours. Dated 6 April 'at sea' to his wife; 4–6 April 1942. In Michael Simpson (ed.), *The Somerville Papers: Selections from the Private and Official Correspondence of Admiral of the Fleet Sir James Somerville, GCB, GBE, DSO* (London: Scolar, 1995), p. 401. Admiralty Historical Section, *Battle Summary No. 15: Naval Operations off Ceylon 29th March To 10th April, 1942* (London: Admiralty Historical Section, 1943), p. 11.

84. Admiralty Historical Section, *Battle Summary No. 15: Naval Operations off Ceylon 29th March To 10th April, 1942* (London: Admiralty Historical Section, 1943), p. 11.

85. Admiralty Historical Section, *Battle Summary No. 15: Naval Operations off Ceylon 29th March To 10th April, 1942* (London: Admiralty Historical Section, 1943), p. 11. Report of Proceedings of Eastern Fleet 29 March to 13 April 1942' at: https://www.naval-history.net/xDKWD-EF1942-Introduction.htm

86. Extract from Commodore Edwards's Diary. 6 April 1942. In Michael Simpson (ed.), *The Somerville Papers: Selections from the Private and Official Correspondence of Admiral of the Fleet Sir James Somerville, GCB, GBE, DSO* (London: Scolar, 1995), p. 401.

87. Dated 6 April 'at sea' to his wife; 4–6 April 1942. In Michael Simpson (ed.), *The Somerville Papers: Selections from the Private and Official Correspondence of Admiral of the Fleet Sir James Somerville, GCB, GBE, DSO* (London: Scolar, 1995), p. 401.

88. Andrew Boyd, *The Royal Navy in Eastern Waters: Linchpin of Victory 1935–1942* (Barnsley: Seaforth, 2017), p. 372. The figure was of course an underestimate, but the British still believed it to be 'about 70' in 1943. See: Admiralty Historical Section, *Battle Summary No. 15: Naval Operations off Ceylon 29th March To 10th April, 1942* (London: Admiralty Historical Section, 1943), p. 6.

89. Dated 6 April 'at sea' to his wife; 4–6 April 1942. In Michael Simpson (ed.), *The Somerville Papers: Selections from the Private and Official Correspondence of Admiral of the Fleet Sir James Somerville, GCB, GBE, DSO* (London: Scolar, 1995), p. 401.

90. Dated 6 April 'at sea' to his wife; 4–6 April 1942. In Michael Simpson (ed.), *The Somerville Papers: Selections from the Private and Official Correspondence of Admiral of the Fleet Sir James Somerville, GCB, GBE, DSO* (London: Scolar, 1995), p. 401.

91. Sunil S. Amrith, *Crossing the Bay of Bengal: The Furies of Nature and the Fortunes of Migrants* (Cambridge, MA: Harvard University Press, 2013), p. 197.

92. Field Marshal The Viscount Wavell, 'Operations In Eastern Theatre, Based On India, From March 1942 To December 31, 1942', in *The Supplement To The London Gazette Of Wednesday, 18 September, 1946*, pp. 4664–6. By way of comparison, the attacks on the vessels comprising the Arctic Convoy PQ-17 (27 June–10 July 1942) occasioned the loss of twenty-four merchantmen; gross weight some 130,000 tons. This was, according to Churchill, 'one of the most melancholy naval episodes in the whole of the war'. Michael G. Walling, *Forgotten Sacrifice: The Arctic Convoys of World War II* (Oxford: Osprey, 2012), pp. 153–170.

93. Somerville, quoted in: Arthur J. Marder, Mark Jacobsen and John Horsefield, *Old Friends New Enemies, the Royal Navy and the Imperial Japanese Navy Volume II: The Pacific War, 1942–1945* (Oxford: Clarendon, 1990), p. 131.

94. Nineteen officers and 215 ratings were lost from *Dorsetshire* and 10 officers and 180 ratings from *Cornwall*. Admiralty Historical Section, *Battle Summary No. 15: Naval Operations*

off Ceylon 29th March To 10th April, 1942 (London: Admiralty Historical Section, 1943), p. 10.

95. Andrew Boyd, *The Royal Navy in Eastern Waters: Linchpin of Victory 1935–1942* (Barnsley: Seaforth, 2017), p. 492, n. 159.

96. Extract from Commodore Edwards's Diary. 6 April 1942. In Michael Simpson (ed.), *The Somerville Papers: Selections from the Private and Official Correspondence of Admiral of the Fleet Sir James Somerville, GCB, GBE, DSO* (London: Scolar, 1995), p. 401. Admiralty Historical Section, *Battle Summary No. 15: Naval Operations off Ceylon 29th March To 10th April, 1942* (London: Admiralty Historical Section, 1943), p. 12.

97. Signal of 8 April to the Admiralty. In Michael Simpson (ed.), *The Somerville Papers: Selections from the Private and Official Correspondence of Admiral of the Fleet Sir James Somerville, GCB, GBE, DSO* (London: Scolar, 1995), p. 404.

98. Dated 7 April to his wife. In Michael Simpson (ed.), *The Somerville Papers: Selections from the Private and Official Correspondence of Admiral of the Fleet Sir James Somerville, GCB, GBE, DSO* (London: Scolar, 1995), p. 402.

99. Admiralty Historical Section, *Battle Summary No. 15: Naval Operations off Ceylon 29th March To 10th April, 1942* (London: Admiralty Historical Section, 1943), p. 12.

100. Admiralty Hydrographic Department, *West Coast of India Pilot* (London: The Hydrographer of the Navy, 1961), p. 69.

101. Admiralty Historical Section, *Battle Summary No. 15: Naval Operations off Ceylon 29th March To 10th April, 1942* (London: Admiralty Historical Section, 1943), p. 12.

102. Dated 9 April to his wife. In Michael Simpson (ed.), *The Somerville Papers: Selections from the Private and Official Correspondence of Admiral of the Fleet Sir James Somerville, GCB, GBE, DSO* (London: Scolar, 1995), p. 405.

103. Quoted in: Arthur J. Marder, Mark Jacobsen and John Horsefield, *Old Friends New Enemies, the Royal Navy and the Imperial Japanese Navy Volume II: The Pacific War, 1942–1945* (Oxford: Clarendon, 1990), p. 133. Willis wrote nothing for publication and has very little in the way of biography beyond an entry in T. A. Heathcote, *The British Admirals of the Fleet 1734–1995: A Biographical Dictionary* (Barnsley: Leo Cooper, 2002), pp. 263–4. His private papers are in the Imperial War Museum Department of Documents and the Churchill Archives Centre, Churchill College, Cambridge (Papers of Admiral Sir Algernon U Willis; Reference GBR/0014/WLLS). In the former collection is a 100-page typescript memoir, pages 30–50 of which deal with his time as Deputy C-in-C of the Eastern Fleet. Marder et al, used this memoir as their source.

104. To the Admiralty. HMS *Warspite* 8 April 1942. In Michael Simpson (ed.), *The Somerville Papers: Selections from the Private and Official Correspondence of Admiral of the Fleet Sir James Somerville, GCB, GBE, DSO* (London: Scolar, 1995), p. 403.

105. Winston S. Churchill, *The Second World War: Volume I The Gathering Storm* (London: The Reprint Society, 1952), p. 377.

106. Admiralty Historical Section, *Battle Summary No. 15: Naval Operations off Ceylon 29th March To 10th April, 1942* (London: Admiralty Historical Section, 1943), p. 12.

107. Irene S. van Dongen, 'Mombasa in the Land and Sea Exchanges of East Africa' ('Mombasas Rolle Im Land-Und Seehandel Ostafrikas'), in *Erdkunde: Archive for Scientific Geography*, Vol. 17, No. 1/2, 1963, pp. 31–3.

108. To the Admiralty. HMS *Warspite* 8 April 1942. In Michael Simpson (ed.), *The Somerville Papers: Selections from the Private and Official Correspondence of Admiral of the Fleet Sir James Somerville, GCB, GBE, DSO* (London: Scolar, 1995), p. 403.

109. Report of Proceedings of Eastern Fleet 29 March to 13 April 1942' at: https://www.naval-history.net/xDKWD-EF1942-Introduction.htm

110. Donald Macintyre, *Fighting Admiral: The life of Admiral of the Fleet Sir James Somerville* (London: Evans Brothers, 1961), p. 195.

111. Admiralty Historical Section, *Battle Summary No. 15: Naval Operations off Ceylon 29th March To 10th April, 1942* (London: Admiralty Historical Section, 1943), p. 13.

112. *Sumatra* had been sent to the Netherlands East Indies in 1940. Whilst undergoing a refit in early 1942 the Japanese had invaded so, capable of only 15 knots, she had voyaged to Ceylon. Donald A. Bertke, Gordon Smith and Don Kindell, *World War II Sea War Volume 5: Air Raid Pearl Harbor. This Is Not a Drill. Day to Day Naval Actions December 1941 through March 1942* (Dayton, OH: Bertke, 2013), p. 317.

113. Lt. Cdr. Geoffrey B. Mason RN (Rtd), *Service Histories of Royal Navy Warships in World War 2: HMS Erebus – Erebus-class 15in gun Monitor*, 2003. At: http://www.naval-history.net/xGM-Chrono-03Mon-Erebus.htm

114. The best and most thorough account of the 9 April attack on Trincomalee is by Stuart: Robert Stuart, '91 Bombs: The Japanese Attack on Trincomalee' (2017). Available from: http://www.combinedfleet.com/articles.htm Stuart's work forms the basis of this section unless otherwise stated. The remaining naval vessels comprised one mine-sweeping trawler, two mine-sweeping tugs, two barrage/gate vessels and a boom defence tender.

115. Admiralty Historical Section, *Battle Summary No. 15: Naval Operations off Ceylon 29th March To 10th April, 1942* (London: Admiralty Historical Section, 1943), p. 13, n. 4.

116. British aircraft losses: one Catalina, one Fulmar and nine Hurricanes. Also three Albacores and one Walrus (aboard *Sagaing* as deck cargo), plus the seven Swordfish, four Fulmars and two Albacores destroyed in the China Bay attack.

117. Director of Naval Construction, *HM Ships Damaged or Sunk by Enemy Action, 3rd Sept. 1939 To 2nd Sept. 1945* (London: Admiralty, 1952), p. 26.

118. '. . . two direct hits were sustained, one, near the funnel, was thought to have exploded in or near the after magazine. HOLLYHOCK immediately blew up, disintegrated and sank within 45 seconds'. Director of Naval Construction, *HM Ships Damaged or Sunk by Enemy Action, 3rd Sept. 1939 To 2nd Sept. 1945* (London: Admiralty, 1952), p. 352.

119. For information on *Norviken* see: http://www.warsailors.com/singleships/norviken.html

120. For information on *Vita* see: http://www.poheritage.com/Upload/Mimsy/Media/factsheet/94890VITA-1914pdf.pdf

121. Surgeon Commander J. L. S. Coulter, *The Royal Naval Medical Service, Volume I: Administration* (London: HMSO, 1954), p. 111.

122. UK National Archives: CAB/66/23/34. War Cabinet Weekly Resume (No. 136) of the Naval, Military and Air Situation from 0700 April 2nd to 0700 April 9th 1942, p. 8.

123. Wing Commander W. W. Russell, *Forgotten Skies: The Story of the Air Forces in India and Burma* (London: Hutchinson, 1946), pp. 33–4.

124. Bryn Evans, *Air Battle for Burma: Allied Pilots' Fight for Supremacy* (Barnsley: Pen & Sword, 2016), p. 70.

125. To the Admiralty. 11 April 1942. In Michael Simpson (ed.), *The Somerville Papers: Selections from the Private and Official Correspondence of Admiral of the Fleet Sir James Somerville, GCB, GBE, DSO* (London: Scolar, 1995), p. 406. See also: Arthur J. Marder, Mark Jacobsen and John Horsefield, *Old Friends New Enemies, the Royal Navy and the Imperial Japanese Navy Volume II: The Pacific War, 1942–1945* (Oxford: Clarendon, 1990), pp. 117–18.

126. Paul S. Dull, *A Battle History of the Imperial Japanese Navy, 1941- 1945* (Annapolis, MD: Naval Institute Press, 1978), p. 110. Malcolm Murfett, *Naval Warfare 1919–45: An Operational History of the Volatile War at Sea* (London: Routledge, 2009), p. 162.

Chapter 7

1. C-in-C, Ceylon, in: Admiralty Historical Section, *Battle Summary No. 15: Naval Operations off Ceylon 29th March To 10th April, 1942* (London: Admiralty Historical Section, 1943), pp. 17–18.
2. 'The composition of the enemy force is uncertain, but it seems likely that the force operating south of Ceylon on 5th April consisted of three battleships, four aircraft carriers (probably the *Zuikaku, Shokaku, Ryujo* and *Soryu*) with at least two cruisers and six destroyers. On 7th or 8th April this force was joined by the carrier *Akagi*, which had been operating against shipping in the Bay of Bengal on 6th April and possibly other cruisers and destroyers.' Admiralty Historical Section, *Battle Summary No. 15: Naval Operations off Ceylon 29th March To 10th April, 1942* (London: Admiralty Historical Section, 1943), p. 17.
3. Dated 6 April 'at sea' to his wife; 4–6 April 1942. In Michael Simpson (ed.), *The Somerville Papers: Selections from the Private and Official Correspondence of Admiral of the Fleet Sir James Somerville, GCB, GBE, DSO* (London: Scolar, 1995), p. 401.
4. For matters pertaining to Roskill's 'official historian' status see: Barry Gough, *Historical Dreadnoughts: Arthur Marder, Stephen Roskill and Battles for Naval History* (Barnsley: Seaforth, 2010), p. 134. A career naval officer, Roskill served in the Royal New Zealand Navy from 1941, becoming executive officer of the light cruiser *Leander*. Whilst serving in the Solomon Islands he fought in the Battle of Kolombangara, an unsuccessful effort to interdict Japanese reinforcements sent to Vila, on the south-eastern shore of Kolombangara Island, from Rabaul, on the night of 12/13 July 1943. For details of his career see: http://www.unithistories.com/officers/RN_officersR3.html
5. Captain S. W. Roskill, *The War at Sea 1939–45: Volume II, The Period of Balance* (London: HMSO, 1956), pp. 31–2.
6. Vice Admiral Sir Arthur Hezlet, *Aircraft and Seapower* (New York: Stein and Day, 1970), p. 126.
7. Colin White, 'The Nelson Touch: The Evolution of Nelson's Tactics at Trafalgar', in the *Journal for Maritime Research*, Vol. 7, No. 1, 2011, pp. 123–39. To be fair, the IJN, as an organization, also failed to completely grasp at that time that what they had achieved with the creation of the *Kido Butai* was transformative. Most of the leaders clung to the belief, one necessarily of long standing, that battleship-centred fleets wielded the greatest power. It was only after their catastrophic defeat in the Battle of Midway, at the hands of USN carrier aircraft, that the IJN began to acknowledge the fact with the designation of a carrier force as the reorganized Third Fleet. Conversely, the United States Navy was very quick to understand there had been a step-change and move towards the 'Air Navy' concept that had long been advocated by several of its senior officers. It probably helped that they no longer had any battleships left in the Pacific; the Pearl Harbor strike had seen to that. Naoko Sajima and Kyochi Tachikawa, *Japanese Sea Power: A Maritime Nation's Struggle for Identity* (Canberra, ACT: Sea Power Centre–Australia, 2009), p. 48. Minoru Nomura, *Nihon kaigun no rekishi* (Tokyo: Yoshikawa Kōbunkan, 2002), p. 203.
8. For a discussion of this see: Dallas Woodbury Isom, *Midway Inquest: Why the Japanese Lost the Battle of Midway* (Bloomington, IN: Indiana University Press, 2007), p. 367, n. 20.

9. Mark R. Peattie, *Sunburst: The Rise of Japanese Naval Air Power 1909–1941* (Annapolis MD: Naval Institute Press, 2001), pp. 49–50. See also: Alan D. Zimm, *Attack on Pearl Harbor: Strategy, Combat, Myths, Deceptions* (Havertown, PA: Casemate, 2011), p. 92.

10. Malcolm Murfett, *Naval Warfare 1919–45: An Operational History of the Volatile War at Sea* (London: Routledge, 2009), pp. 137, 491.

11. Parshall and Tully conclude that he 'valued conformity and obedience over creativity or personal initiative'. Jonathan Parshall and Anthony Tully, *Shattered Sword: The Untold Story of the Battle of Midway* (Dulles, VA: Potomac, 2005), pp. 408–9.

12. Fleet Admiral Chester W. Nimitz and E. B. Potter, *Triumph in the Pacific: The Navy's Struggle Against Japan* (Englewood Cliffs, NJ: Prentice-Hall, 1963), p. 8.

13. Australia's Prime Minister, John Curtin, put it thus in a broadcast to the 'people of America' on 20 March 1942: 'Without any inhibitions of any kind, I make it quite clear that Australia looks to America, free of any pangs as to our traditional links or kinship with the United Kingdom.' See: Sally Warhaft (ed.), *Well May We Say . . . The Speeches that Made Australia* (Melbourne; Black, 2004), p. 101.

14. Admiral G. A. Ballard, *Rulers of the Indian Ocean* (London: Duckworth, 1927), pp. 310–11. Though he is pretty much forgotten now, Ballard was the originator of a blockade scheme, the *Système Ballard*, that was originally conceived as being of utility against France. It was later found to be equally applicable to Germany. See: Shawn T. Grimes, *Strategy and War Planning in the British Navy, 1887–1918* (Woodbridge: Boydell, 2012), pp. 30–3, 36.

15. See Chapter 43 of S. K. Kirpalani, *Fifty Years with the British* (Hyderabad: Disha, 1993).

16. Srinath Raghavan, *India's War: World War II and the Making of Modern South Asia* (New York: Basic, 2016), p. 256.

17. The British Library, London, Oriental and India Office Collection, L/WS/1/1247, Viceroy of India [Lord Linlithgow] telegram to [Leo Amery] Secretary of State for India [and Burma], 11 September 42.

18. Christopher Bayly, 'The Nation Within: British India at War 1939–1947', in the *British Academy Review*, Issue 8, 2005, p. 16. Available online at: https://www.thebritishacademy.ac.uk/sites/default/files/06-bayly.pdf The full text of this lecture was published in 'Proceedings of the British Academy', Vol. 125, 2003 Lectures and can be found via www.proc.britac.ac.uk For the Quit India movement see: Shachi Chakravarty, *Quit India Movement: A Study* (Delhi: New Century Publications, 2002); V. T. Patil, *Gandhi, Nehru and the Quit India Movement: A Study in the Dynamics of a Mass Movement* (Delhi: BR Publishing, 1984).

19. Srinath Raghavan, *India's War: World War II and the Making of Modern South Asia* (New York: Basic, 2016), pp. 268–9. See also: Indivar Kamtekar, 'The Shiver of 1942', in *Studies in History*, Vol. 18, No. 1, February 2002, pp. 81–102.

20. Alan Warren, *Burma 1942: The Road from Rangoon to Mandalay* (London: Continuum, 2011).

21. Srinath Raghavan, *India's War: World War II and the Making of Modern South Asia* (New York: Basic, 2016), p. 403.

22. He did however 'propose to continue work on the 16-inch gun mountings and guns for *Lion*. Modification of the original design of the ship is now, however, essential and as this will delay the laying down by perhaps a year, I do not include *Lion* in this year's programme.' UK National Archives. CAB/66/24/3. 'New Construction Programme, 1942: Memorandum by the First Lord of the Admiralty' dated 21 April 1942, pp. 3–4. The *Lion* class were to comprise six larger and improved versions of the *King George V* class with main batteries of nine 16in guns. The first two vessels, *Lion* and *Temeraire*,

were ordered in February 1939 but none of them were ever completed. See: Ian Johnston and Ian Buxton, *The Battleship Builders: Constructing and Arming British Capital Ships* (Barnsley: Seaforth, 2013), pp. 43–7.

23. UK National Archives. CAB/66/24/3. 'New Construction Programme, 1942: Memorandum by the First Lord of the Admiralty' dated 21 April 1942, pp. 3–4.

24. Guy Robbins, *The Aircraft Carrier Story 1908–1945* (London: Cassell, 2001), p. 91. See also: Neil McCart, *The Colossus-Class Aircraft Carriers 1944–1972* (Cheltenham: Fan, 2002).

25. Layton to The Admiralty, 9 April 1942. In Michael Simpson (ed.), *The Somerville Papers: Selections from the Private and Official Correspondence of Admiral of the Fleet Sir James Somerville, GCB, GBE, DSO* (London: Scolar, 1995), pp. 404–5.

26. Somerville to Wavell. 21 April 1942. In Michael Simpson (ed.), *The Somerville Papers: Selections from the Private and Official Correspondence of Admiral of the Fleet Sir James Somerville, GCB, GBE, DSO* (London: Scolar, 1995), p. 413.

27. As has been noted, the Aichi D3A, once it had shed its bomb load, could successfully compete with a Fulmar.

28. Then equipped with nine Sea Hurricanes on *Indomitable*. J. D. Brown and David Hobbs (ed.), *Carrier Operations in World War II* (Barnsley: Seaforth, 2009), p. 72.

29. To the Admiralty. 29 April 1942. In Michael Simpson (ed.), *The Somerville Papers: Selections from the Private and Official Correspondence of Admiral of the Fleet Sir James Somerville, GCB, GBE, DSO* (London: Scolar, 1995), p. 415. Also p. 415. n 2.

30. Pound to Somerville. 1 May 1942. In Michael Simpson (ed.), *The Somerville Papers: Selections from the Private and Official Correspondence of Admiral of the Fleet Sir James Somerville, GCB, GBE, DSO* (London: Scolar, 1995), p. 415.

31. Somerville to Pound. 2 May 1942. In Michael Simpson (ed.), *The Somerville Papers: Selections from the Private and Official Correspondence of Admiral of the Fleet Sir James Somerville, GCB, GBE, DSO* (London: Scolar, 1995), pp. 415–16.

32. Phil Keith, *Stay the Rising Sun: The True Story of USS Lexington, Her Valiant Crew and Changing the Course of World War II* (Minneapolis, MN: Zenith, 2015), p. viii. Roy A. Grossnick, *United States Naval Aviation 1910–1995* (Washington, DC: Naval Historical Center Department of the Navy, 1997), p. 122. The quote appears in Clark G. Reynolds, *The Fast Carriers: The Forging of an Air Navy* (Annapolis, MD: Naval Institute Press, 1968), p. 305. For Bernhard's position vis à vis Spruance see the same work, p. 91.

33. Somerville Pocket Diary entry for 11 April. In Michael Simpson (ed.), *The Somerville Papers: Selections from the Private and Official Correspondence of Admiral of the Fleet Sir James Somerville, GCB, GBE, DSO* (London: Scolar, 1995), p. 409.

34. See: Samuel Eliot Morison, *History of United States Naval Operations in World War II Volume IV: Coral Sea, Midway and Submarine Actions: May 1942–August 1942* (Boston, MA: Little, Brown, 1949). For a shorter version see: Richard Freeman, *Coral Sea 1942: Turning the Tide* (London: Endeavour, 2013).

35. The Japanese plan for invading Port Moresby in New Guinea, from where its land-based planes could dominate northern Australia, was thwarted.

36. John B. Lundstrom, *The First South Pacific Campaign: Pacific Fleet Strategy, December 1941–June 1942* (Annapolis, MD: US Naval Institute Press, 1976), p. 151.

37. John B. Lundstrom, *The First South Pacific Campaign: Pacific Fleet Strategy, December 1941-June 1942* (Annapolis, MD: US Naval Institute Press, 1976), pp. 175–6.
38. See: Martin Thomas, 'Imperial Backwater or Strategic Outpost? The British Takeover of Vichy Madagascar, 1942', in *The Historical Journal*, Vol. 39, No. 4, December 1996.
39. Admiralty Historical Section, *Battle Summary No. 16: Naval Operations at The Capture of Diego Suarez, May, 1942* (London: Admiralty Historical Section, 1943), p. 31.

Chapter 8

1.   Burkhart Mueller-Hillebrand, *Germany and Its Allies in World War II: A Record of Axis Collaboration Problems* (Frederick, MY: University Publications of America, 1980), p. 28.
2.   For the various intelligence indications see Chapter 2 of: John Grehan, *Churchill's Secret Invasion: Britain's First Large Scale Combined Operations Offensive 1942* (Barnsley: Pen and Sword, 2013), pp. 18–29.
3.   The Dakar Expedition, dubbed Operation Menace, took place on 23–25 September 1940. It was an attempt by British and Free French forces under General Charles de Gaulle to capture and occupy Dakar in French West Africa and displace the Vichy French administration then in place. The entire affair was badly bodged and ended in abject failure, during the course of which the battleship *Resolution* was torpedoed by the submarine *Bévéziers* and badly damaged. See: Arthur J. Marder, *Operation Menace: The Dakar Expedition and the Dudley North Affair* (Barnsley: Seaforth, 2016).
4.   Martin Thomas, 'Imperial Backwater or Strategic Outpost? The British Takeover of Vichy Madagascar, 1942', in *The Historical Journal*, Vol. 39, No. 4, December 1996, p. 1059.
5.   Admiralty Historical Section, *Battle Summary No. 16: Naval Operations at The Capture of Diego Suarez, May, 1942* (London: Admiralty Historical Section, 1943), p. 32.
6.   Admiralty Historical Section, *Battle Summary No. 16: Naval Operations at The Capture of Diego Suarez, May, 1942* (London: Admiralty Historical Section, 1943), p. 34.
7.   Winston S. Churchill, *The Second World War Volume IV: The Hinge of Fate* (London: Cassell, 1950), p. 199.
8.   Admiralty Historical Section, *Battle Summary No. 16: Naval Operations at The Capture of Diego Suarez, May, 1942* (London: Admiralty Historical Section, 1943), p. 37. n. 1. To Admiral Dudley North. 27 May 1942. In Michael Simpson (ed.), *The Somerville Papers: Selections from the Private and Official Correspondence of Admiral of the Fleet Sir James Somerville, GCB, GBE, DSO* (London: Scolar, 1995), p. 421.
9.   Martin Thomas, 'Imperial Backwater or Strategic Outpost? The British Takeover of Vichy Madagascar, 1942', in *The Historical Journal*, Vol. 39, No. 4, December 1996, p. 1060.
10. John Grehan, *Churchill's Secret Invasion: Britain's First Large Scale Combined Operations Offensive 1942* (Barnsley: Pen and Sword, 2013), p 47.
11. Somerville Pocket Diary entry for 5 May. In Michael Simpson (ed.), *The Somerville Papers: Selections from the Private and Official Correspondence of Admiral of the Fleet Sir James Somerville, GCB, GBE, DSO* (London: Scolar, 1995), p. 417.
12. John Grehan, *Churchill's Secret Invasion: Britain's First Large Scale Combined Operations Offensive 1942* (Barnsley: Pen and Sword, 2013), p 49.
13. John Grehan, *Churchill's Secret Invasion: Britain's First Large Scale Combined Operations Offensive 1942* (Barnsley: Pen and Sword, 2013), p 48.

14. Admiralty Historical Section, *Battle Summary No. 16: Naval Operations at The Capture of Diego Suarez, May, 1942* (London: Admiralty Historical Section, 1943), p. 35.
15. John Grehan, *Churchill's Secret Invasion: Britain's First Large Scale Combined Operations Offensive 1942* (Barnsley: Pen and Sword, 2013), pp. 84–6, 166. Donald A. Bertke, Gordon Smith and Don Kindell, *World War II Sea War Volume 6: The Allies Halt the Axis Advance Day-to-Day Naval Actions April 1942 through August 1941* (Dayton, OH: Bertke, 2014), p. 158. All of the *Redoubtable* class: thirty-one boats constructed in three series between 1928 to 1937. They displaced 2,082 tons submerged and had a maximum range of 10,000 miles at 10 knots surfaced. Submerged endurance was 60 hours at 2 knots. Armament consisted of 11 torpedo tubes, seven in trainable, external, mounts, one 100mm gun. Geirr H. Haarr, *No Room for Mistakes: British and Allied Submarine Warfare 1939–1940* (Barnsley: Seaforth, 2015), p. 239.
16. Grand Admiral Karl Dönitz, in: Edward P. Von der Porten, *The German Navy in World War II* (New York: Thomas Y Crowell, 1969), p. v. There were darker reasons according to Bernd Martin: 'Hitler made all of his decisions, before and during the war, according to his conviction that the "German master race" had to find its way to world power on its own, without the help of the "yellow" race. Only as long as there was nothing concretely planned between Germany and the Far Eastern Empire did Hitler welcome Japan as his associate . . .' Bernd Martin, *Japan and Germany in the Modern World* (Providence, RI: Berghahn, 1995), p. 194.
17. Hans-Joachim Krug, Yôichi Hirama, Berthold J. Sander-Nagashima and Axel Niestlé, *Reluctant Allies: German-Japanese Naval Relations in World War II* (Annapolis, MD: Naval Institute Press, 2001), p. 52. Evert Kleynhans, '"Good Hunting:" German Submarine Offensives and South African Countermeasures off the South African Coast during the Second World War, 1942–1945', in *Scientia Militaria: South African Journal of Military Studies*, Vol. 44, No. 1, 2016, p. 172.
18. John Grehan, *Churchill's Secret Invasion: Britain's First Large Scale Combined Operations Offensive 1942* (Barnsley: Pen and Sword, 2013), p. 30.
19. Dorr Carpenter and Norman Polmar, *Submarines of the Imperial Japanese Navy* (London: Conway Maritime, 1986), p. 22.
20. Admiralty Historical Section, *Battle Summary No. 16: Naval Operations at The Capture of Diego Suarez, May, 1942* (London: Admiralty Historical Section, 1943), p. 52.
21. Peggy Warner and Sadao Seno, *The Coffin Boats: Japanese Midget Submarine Operations in the Second World War* (Barnsley: Leo Cooper, 1986), p. 152.
22. Carl Boyd and Akihiko Yoshida, *The Japanese Submarine Force and World War II* (Annapolis, MD: Bluejacket, 2002), p. 89.
23. Admiralty Historical Section, *Battle Summary No. 16: Naval Operations at The Capture of Diego Suarez, May, 1942* (London: Admiralty Historical Section, 1943), pp. 52–3. Peggy Warner and Sadao Seno, *The Coffin Boats: Japanese Midget Submarine Operations in the Second World War* (Barnsley: Leo Cooper, 1986). The attack at Diego Suarez is comprehensively covered in Chapter 11.
24. 'Told *Duncan* and *Active* to leave us and go to Diego. Danks [Acting Vice Admiral Victor Hilary Danckwerts, Somerville's shore-based Chief of Staff] ordered the [Dutch destroyer] *Jan van Galen* to go there. Told the 'L's ['L' class destroyers] to come on so as to [Rendezvous] with us'. Somerville Pocket Diary entry for 31 May. In Michael Simpson (ed.), *The Somerville Papers: Selections from the Private and Official Correspondence of Admiral of the Fleet Sir James Somerville, GCB, GBE, DSO* (London: Scolar, 1995), p. 423.

25. Carl Boyd and Akihiko Yoshida, *The Japanese Submarine Force and World War II* (Annapolis, MD: Bluejacket, 2002), p. 90.
26. Evert Kleynhans, '"Good Hunting:" German Submarine Offensives and South African Countermeasures off the South African Coast during the Second World War, 1942–1945', in *Scientia Militaria: South African Journal of Military Studies*, Vol. 44, No. 1, 2016, p. 172.
27. L. C. F. Turner, H. R. Gordon-Cumming and J. E. Betzler, *War in The Southern Oceans 1939–1945* (Cape Town: Oxford University Press, 1961), pp. 116–17, 136, 137, 139, 141. H. J. Martin and N. D. Orpen, *South Africa at War: Military and Industrial Organization and Operations in Connection with the Conduct of the War, 1939–1943: South African Forces World War II Volume VII* (Cape Town: Purnell, 1979), pp. 178–80.
28. Somerville Pocket Diary entry for 6 June. In Michael Simpson (ed.), *The Somerville Papers: Selections from the Private and Official Correspondence of Admiral of the Fleet Sir James Somerville, GCB, GBE, DSO* (London: Scolar, 1995), p. 423.
29. John Grehan, *Churchill's Secret Invasion: Britain's First Large Scale Combined Operations Offensive 1942* (Barnsley: Pen and Sword, 2013), p. 101.
30. The literature on the Battle of Midway is vast, which is entirely proportional to its importance. One personal favourite, even though perhaps somewhat dated, is: Samuel Eliot Morison, *History of United States Naval Operations in World War II Volume IV: Coral Sea, Midway and Submarine Actions: May 1942-August 1942* (Boston, MA: Little, Brown, 1949).
31. Churchill to Pound. 10 June 1942. In Michael Simpson (ed.), *The Somerville Papers: Selections from the Private and Official Correspondence of Admiral of the Fleet Sir James Somerville, GCB, GBE, DSO* (London: Scolar, 1995), p. 424.
32. Prime Minister to General Ismay, for Chief of Staff Committee. 1 June 1942. In Winston S. Churchill, *The Second World War Volume IV: The Hinge of Fate* (London: Cassell, 1950), p. 775.
33. Pound to Alexander. 6 June 1942. In Michael Simpson (ed.), *The Somerville Papers: Selections from the Private and Official Correspondence of Admiral of the Fleet Sir James Somerville, GCB, GBE, DSO* (London: Scolar, 1995), p. 408.
34. Pound to Churchill. 10 June 1942. In Michael Simpson (ed.), *The Somerville Papers: Selections from the Private and Official Correspondence of Admiral of the Fleet Sir James Somerville, GCB, GBE, DSO* (London: Scolar, 1995), pp. 424–5.
35. Somerville to Pound. 29 June 1942. In Michael Simpson (ed.), *The Somerville Papers: Selections from the Private and Official Correspondence of Admiral of the Fleet Sir James Somerville, GCB, GBE, DSO* (London: Scolar, 1995), p. 428.
36. Somerville to Pound. 29 June 1942. In Michael Simpson (ed.), *The Somerville Papers: Selections from the Private and Official Correspondence of Admiral of the Fleet Sir James Somerville, GCB, GBE, DSO* (London: Scolar, 1995), pp. 428–9.
37. Ian Cameron, *Wings of the Morning: The British Fleet Air Arm in World War II* (London: Hodder & Stoughton, 1962), p. 16.
38. UK National Archives. AVIA 46/136. 'Fleet Air Arm aircraft: General Notes'. Interview with Commodore Matthew Slattery, Chief Naval Representative at the Ministry of Aircraft Production, 25 June 1943. Slattery had been a Flight Commander aboard *Courageous* and Staff Officer (Operations) to Rear Admiral Aircraft Carriers. He'd also served as Chief Staff Officer to Commodore-in-Charge Naval Air Stations (Eastern Stations) at HMS *Kipanga* in Kenya. See: http://www.unithistories.com/officers/RN_officersS2.html
39. UK National Archives. ADM 239/198. 'Naval Aircraft Progress and Operations: Periodical Summaries'. No. 4: Up to 25 Dec. 1941.

40. UK National Archives. ADM 239/195. 'Naval Aircraft Progress and Operations: Periodical Summaries'. No. 1: Up to 20 September 1940.
41. UK National Archives. ADM 239/197. 'Naval Aircraft Progress and Operations: Periodical Summaries'. No. 3: Up to 13 July 1941.
42. 'On January 10, 1941, law, H.R. 1776, – popularly called the "Lend-Lease Bill" – was introduced into Congress. The Chief Executive under the proposed act could provide for the production of weapons, munitions, aircraft and ships. He was authorized to secure the necessary machinery, tools, materials and supplies for their manufacture, repair, servicing, or operation. And he was given power to transfer weapons and tools as well as farming and industrial machines and articles to any country whose defense he deemed "vital to the defense of the United States".' The War Department, *How Shall Lend-Lease Accounts be Settled?* (Washington, DC: The American Historical Association, 1945), p. 3. 'The burning question was not about the right to sell American arms to Britain in its time of dire need (that was already allowed), but rather how Britain was to pay for them when its supply of dollars was vanishing. The answer embodied in Lend-Lease was for the American government to purchase the entire output of arms and "lend" appropriate portions of it to countries fighting the dictators.' Waldo H Heinrichs Jr, 'Waldo H Heinrichs, George D Aiken and the Lend Lease Debate of 1941', in *Vermont History*, Vol. 69, Summer/Fall 2001, p. 268.
43. 'As Chief of the bureau of Aeronautics he organized the Navy's mass production program for all types of planes, increasing the total naval aircraft from 2,000 to more than 39,000 during his tenure of office. . . . In the training program, started during his administration, total personnel assigned to Naval Aviation reached approximately three quarters of a million'. http://www.freedomdocuments.com/Towers.html For a fine biography see: Clark G. Reynolds, *Admiral John H Towers: The Struggle for Naval Air Supremacy* (Annapolis, MD: Naval Institute Press, 1991).
44. Gilbert S. Guinn and G. H. Bennett, *British Naval Aviation in World War II: The US Navy and Anglo-American Relations* (London: Tauris, 2007), p. 21.
45. Message from Commander Richard Smeeton of the British Air Commission, Washington, to Ministry of Aircraft Production, 30 December 1941. UK National Archives. CAB 122/142. 'Allocation of F4 Single-Seat Fighters to the Royal Navy'. 1941–1942.
46. Barrett Tillman, *Warbird Tech Series Volume 4: Vought F4U Corsair* (North Branch, MN: Speciality, 2001), pp. 83–7. James D'Angina, *Vought F4U Corsair* (Oxford: Osprey, 2014), p. 23.
47. Will Iredale, *The Kamikaze Hunters: Fighting for the Pacific* (New York: Pegasus, 2016), p. 107.
48. See Chapter 5 of: Barrett Tillman, *Corsair: The F4U in World War II and Korea* (Annapolis, MD: Naval Institute Press, 2014).
49. Telegram from the British Aircraft Commission to the Ministry of Aircraft Production, 6 January 1942. UK National Archives. CAB 122/142. 'Allocation of F4 Single-Seat Fighters to the Royal Navy'. 1941–1942.
50. UK National Archives. ADM 239/197. 'Naval Aircraft Progress and Operations: Periodical Summaries'. No. 3: Up to 13 July 1941.
51. Alexander to Churchill. 15 May 1942. In Michael Simpson (ed.), *The Somerville Papers: Selections from the Private and Official Correspondence of Admiral of the Fleet Sir James Somerville, GCB, GBE, DSO* (London: Scolar, 1995), p. 419.

52. Alexander to Churchill. 15 May 1942. In Michael Simpson (ed.), *The Somerville Papers: Selections from the Private and Official Correspondence of Admiral of the Fleet Sir James Somerville, GCB, GBE, DSO* (London: Scolar, 1995), p. 419.
53. For 'some of the problems' associated with the Seafire see: Commander R. 'Mike' Crosley DSC RN, *They Gave me a Seafire* (Barnsley: Pen & Sword, 2014), pp. 233–46. For a more general, though encyclopaedic, account see: David Brown, *The Seafire: The Spitfire That Went to Sea* (Annapolis, MD: Naval Institute Press, 1989).
54. UK National Archives. ADM 239/200. 'Naval Aircraft Progress and Operations: Periodical Summaries'. No. 6: Up to 31 Dec. 1942. The Fairey Firefly resembled its predecessor, the Fulmar, in appearance but was much more capable. Even so, it couldn't match American high-performance single-seat fighters. It was used in multiple roles following its combat debut on 17 July 1944; flying from *Indefatigable* and *Formidable*, Fireflys took part in Operation Mascot, a strike on Germany's *Tirpitz*, then located in Kaafjord, northern Norway. Its stablemate, the Barracuda, was the monoplane successor to the Albacore and the first British all-metal dive- and torpedo-bomber. Entering service, in 1943 it has been described as 'an aircraft of contradictions'. It was not as capable as its US equivalent, the Grumman Avenger. W. A. Harrison, *Fairey Firefly in Action* (Carrollton, TX: Squadron Signal, 2006); Matthew Willis, *The Fairey Barracuda* (Petersfield; MMP, 2017).
55. Michael Simpson (ed.), *The Somerville Papers: Selections from the Private and Official Correspondence of Admiral of the Fleet Sir James Somerville, GCB, GBE, DSO* (London: Scolar, 1995), p. 364.

Chapter 9

1. An extract from a poem in: Rudyard Kipling, *Sea Warfare* (Garden City, NY: Doubleday, Page, 1917), p. 46.
2. Arakawa Kenichi, 'The Maritime Transport War: Emphasizing a Strategy to the Enemy Sea Lines of Communication (SLOCs)', in *NIDS [National Institute for Defense Studies] Security Reports*, No. 3, March 2002, pp. 109–10.
3. Peter Padfield, *Dönitz: The Last Führer* (London: Panther, 1985), p. 324.
4. Grand Admiral Karl Doenitz (Trans. by R. H. Stevens in collaboration with David Woodward), *Memoirs: Ten Years and Twenty Days* (London: Weidenfeld & Nicolson, 1959), pp. 228–9.
5. The literature on the Battle of the Atlantic is huge. Personal favourites include: W. J. R. Gardner, *Decoding History: The Battle of the Atlantic and Ultra* (Houndmills: Macmillan, 1999); Jonathan Dimbleby, *The Battle of the Atlantic: How the Allies Won the War* (Oxford: Oxford University Press, 2016); David Fairbank White, *Bitter Ocean: The Battle of the Atlantic, 1939–1945* (New York: Simon & Schuster, 2007); Dan van der Vat, *The Atlantic Campaign: The Great Struggle at Sea 1939–1945* (London: Grafton, 1990); John Terraine, *Business in Great Waters: The U-Boat Wars 1916–1945* (London: Mandarin, 1990). Also useful and informative, though perhaps rather dated, is: Rear Admiral W. S. Chalmers, *Max Horton and the Western Approaches: A Biography of Admiral Sir Max Kennedy Horton* (London: Hodder & Stoughton, 1957).
6. David Miller, *Command Decisions: Langsdorff and the Battle of the River Plate* (Barnsley: Pen & Sword Maritime, 2013), p. 96. S. D. Waters, *Official History of New Zealand in the Second World War 1939–45: The Royal New Zealand Navy* (Wellington: Department of Internal Affairs War History Branch, 1956), p. 35.

7. Gerhard Koop and Klaus-Peter Schmolke, *Pocket Battleships of the Deutschland Class: Deutschland/Lutzow, Admiral Scheer and Admiral Graf Spee* (Barnsley: Seaforth, 2014), p. 124. Jürgen Rohwer, *Chronology of the War at Sea, 1939–1945: The Naval History of World War Two* (Annapolis, MD: Naval Institute Press, 2005), p. 59. For an authoritative account of the voyage of the *Admiral Scheer* see: Jochen Brennecke and Theodor Krancke, *Schwerer Kreuzer Admiral Scheer: Die Legendäre Kaperfahrt 1940/41* (Rastatt: Moewig Bei Ullstein, 1995).
8. Jürgen Rohwer, *Chronology of the War at Sea, 1939–1945: The Naval History of World War Two* (Annapolis, MD: Naval Institute Press, 2005), p. 6.
9. Terence Cole, *The Loss of HMAS Sydney II: Volume I* (Canberra: Department of Defence, 2009), p. 112.
10. See Chapter 3.
11. 'Enemy Action on the Australian Station 1939–45'. Available at: http://clik.dva.gov.au/history-library/part-1-military-history/ch-2-world-war-ii/s-7-australian-station/enemy-action-australian-station-1939-45
12. See the three-volume work: Terence Cole, *The Loss of HMAS Sydney II* (Canberra: Department of Defence, 2009). For the auxiliary cruisers more generally, see: August Karl Muggenthaler, *German Raiders of World War II: The First Complete History of Germany's Ocean Marauders – The Last of a Great Era of Naval Warfare* (Englewood Cliffs, NJ: Prentice-Hall, 1977). Stephen Robinson, *False Flags: Disguised German Raiders of World War II* (Dunedin: Exisle, 2016).
13. Lawrence Paterson, *Hitler's Grey Wolves: U-Boats in the Indian Ocean* (Barnsley: Frontline, 2016) Kindle Edition. Loc. 276–77.
14. Giorgio Giorgerini, *Uomini sul fondo: Storia del sommergibilismo italiano dalle origini a oggi* (Milano; Mondadori, 2002), p. 407.
15. The Italians had established a submarine base at Bordeaux (known by the acronym BETASOM) on 1 September 1940. See: Maurizio Brescia, *Mussolini's Navy: A Reference Guide to the Regia Marina 1930–1945* (Barnsley: Seaforth, 2012), p. 55.
16. Erminio Bagnasco, *I sommergibili della Seconda Guerra Mondiale* (Parma: Ermanno Albertelli, 1973), pp. 215–22. For naval operations in the Red Sea area in general see: Pier Filippo Lupinacci e Aldo Cocchia, *La Marina Italiana nella Seconda Guerra Mondiale Volume X: Le operazioni in Africa Orientale* (Roma: Ufficio Storico della Marina Militare, 1961).
17. Eric C. Rust, 'Type IXC U-Boats: Technical Data', in Theodore Savas (ed.), *Hunt and Kill: U-505 and the Battle of the Atlantic* (New York: Savas Beatie, 2004), pp. 221–3.
18. 'South Africa was unique amongst the British Dominions in that it not only faced the threat of external aggression, but also had to combat a serious threat to its internal security posed by a number or pro-Nazi, anti-British and predominantly right-wing Afrikaner groups. Chief amongst these was the Afrikaner Broederbond and the *Ossewabrandwag* (OB).' In other words, 'South Africa was – at least until mid-1943 – forced to fight a war on two fronts, potentially the most dangerous being those subversive elements within her own borders, the "enemy from within".' Kent Fedorowich, 'German Espionage and British Counter-Intelligence in South Africa and Mozambique, 1939–1944', in *The Historical Journal*, Vol. 48, No. 1, March 2005, p. 211. The *Ossewabrandwag* (Ox-wagon Sentinel) were led by Dr Hans van Rensburg and held fervent pro-Nazi and anti-British beliefs. Formed in Bloemfontein on 4 February 1939 by pro-German Afrikaners, it fiercely opposed South African participation in the war against Germany. At its peak in 1941, membership was estimated at 300,000 and included a military wing known as *Stormjaers* (Storm Troopers).

The latter were responsible for various violent plots, including one to blow up Durban graving dock. OB members collected, amongst other intelligence, information on the South African Expeditionary Force that sailed for Madagascar in April 1942. See: George Cloete Visser, *OB: Traitors or Patriots?* (Johannesburg: Macmillan, 1977) and Kent Fedorowich, 'German Espionage and British Counter-Intelligence in South Africa and Mozambique, 1939–1944', in *The Historical Journal*, Vol. 48, No. 1, March 2005, pp. 209–230. For how information was passed to Germany, see: UK National Archives. KV 2/761. 'TROMPKE Organization for German Espionage in South Africa'. Paul Trompke was the German Consul General in Lourenço Marques, capital of Portuguese East Africa (*Africa Oriental Portuguesa*, now Mozambique), during the Second World War. From his Consulate an Abwehr officer, Luitpold Werz, controlled the German Intelligence network operating to South Africa. See also: F. H. Hinsley and C. A. G. Simkins, *British Intelligence in the Second World War: Volume 4* (London: HMSO, 1990), pp. 167–8.

19. Lawrence Paterson, *Hitler's Grey Wolves: U-Boats in the Indian Ocean* (Barnsley: Frontline, 2016) Kindle Edition. Loc. 622–24.

20. F. H. Hinsley, E. E. Thomas, C. F. G. Ransom and R. C. Knight, *British Intelligence in the Second World War: Volume 2* (London: HMSO, 1981), p. 166.

21. Lawrence Paterson, *Hitler's Grey Wolves: U-Boats in the Indian Ocean* (Barnsley: Frontline, 2016) Kindle Edition. Loc. 631–32.

22. August Karl Muggenthaler, *German Raiders of World War II: The First Complete History of Germany's Ocean Marauders – The Last of a Great Era of Naval Warfare* (Englewood Cliffs, NJ: Prentice-Hall, 1977), pp. 117–18.

23. Richard Woodman, *The Real Cruel Sea: The Merchant Navy in the Battle of the Atlantic 1939–1943* (Barnsley: Pen & Sword Maritime, 2013), p. 391. For a first-hand account of the rescue and indeed the entire voyage of *Atlantis*, see: Ulrich Mohr and A. V. Sellwood, *Ship 16: The Story of the Secret German Raider Atlantis* (New York: John Day, 1956).

24. Hugh Sebag-Montefiore, *Enigma: The Battle For The Code* (New York: John Wiley & Sons, 2001), p. 179.

25. The first Type XIV U-tanker was launched in September 1940 and became operational in March 1942. See: John F. White, *The Milk Cows: The U-Boat Tankers at War 1941–1945* (Barnsley: Pen & Sword, 2012). 'The submarine tankers . . . provided the attack submarines with fuel, spare parts, food, clothing, ammunition, torpedoes, water, medical care and equipment and crew replacements. In effect, a submarine tanker enabled the attack submarines to double the length of time they remained on patrol.' Edward P. Von der Porten, *The German Navy in World War II* (New York: Thomas Y Crowell, 1969), pp. 179–80.

26. Hugh Sebag-Montefiore, *Enigma: The Battle For The Code* (New York: John Wiley & Sons, 2001), p. 179. The third ship mentioned was *Kota Pinang*, which had been sunk on 4 October 1941 whilst some 700 nautical miles west of Spain. For a general view of German codebreaking, see: Heinz Bonatz, *Seekrieg im Äther: Die Leistungen der MarineFunkaufklärung 1939–1945* (Herford: E S Mittler, 1981).

27. David Kahn, *Seizing the Enigma: The Race to Break the German U-Boat Codes, 1939–1943* (London: Arrow, 1996), p. 213. See also: R. A. Ratcliff, 'Searching for Security: The German Investigations into Enigma's Security', in *Intelligence and National Security*, Vol. 14, Issue 1, 1999, pp. 146–67.

28. Lawrence Paterson, *Hitler's Grey Wolves: U-Boats in the Indian Ocean* (Barnsley: Frontline, 2016) Kindle Edition. Loc. 638–40.

29. Lawrence Paterson, *Hitler's Grey Wolves: U-Boats in the Indian Ocean* (Barnsley: Frontline, 2016) Kindle Edition. Loc. 653–62. For an explanation of the Kriegsmarine's Naval Grid Reference System (*Gradnetzmeldeverfahren*) see: Ralph Erskine, 'The German Naval Grid in World War II', in *Cryptologia*, Vol. 16, Issue 1, 1992, pp. 39–51.

30. Evert Kleynhans, '"Good Hunting:" German Submarine Offensives and South African Countermeasures off the South African Coast during the Second World War, 1942–1945', in *Scientia Militaria: South African Journal of Military Studies*, Vol. 44, No. 1, 2016, p. 173.

31. Position 05° 05' S and 11° 38' W according to Gudmundur Helgason. See: https://uboat.net/ops/laconia.htm. Dönitz later stated that the position was 4° 52' S and 11° 26' W. Grand Admiral Karl Doenitz (Trans. by R. H. Stevens in collaboration with David Woodward), *Memoirs: Ten Years and Twenty Days* (London: Weidenfeld & Nicolson, 1959), p. 257.

32. G. H. Bennett, 'The 1942 *Laconia* Order: The Murder of Shipwrecked Survivors and the Allied Pursuit of Justice 1945–46', in *Law, Crime and History*, Vol. 1, No. 1, 2011, p. 17.

33. Contrary to wartime propaganda, German submariners did not routinely massacre shipwrecked crews. There is an apocryphal quote of Churchill's that encapsulates such disinformation quite neatly: 'Enemy submarines are to be called U-boats. Allied underwater craft are submarines. U-boats are those dastardly villains who sink our ships, while submarines are those gallant and noble craft which sink theirs.'

34. Grand Admiral Karl Doenitz (Trans. by R. H. Stevens in collaboration with David Woodward), *Memoirs: Ten Years and Twenty Days* (London: Weidenfeld & Nicolson, 1959), p. 263. For the *Laconia* Incident and its aftermath in general, see: Hans-Joachim Röll, *Korvettenkapitän Werner Hartenstein: Mit U 156 auf Feindfahrt und der Fall „Laconia"* (Würzburg: Flechsig, 2011), pp. 83–131. Jim McLoughlin with David Gibb, *One Common Enemy: The Laconia Incident: A Survivor's Memoir* (Kent Town, SA: Wakefield, 2006). Frederick Grossmith, *The Sinking of the Laconia: A Tragedy in the Battle of the Atlantic* (Donington; Paul Watkins, 1994). G. H. Bennett, 'The 1942 *Laconia* Order: The Murder of Shipwrecked Survivors and the Allied Pursuit of Justice 1945–46', in *Law, Crime and History*, Vol. 1, No. 1, 2011, pp. 16–34. Maurer Maurer and Lawrence J. Paszek, 'Origin of the *Laconia* Order', in *Royal United Services Institution Journal*, Vol. 109, Issue 636, 1964, pp. 338–44.

35. Evert Kleynhans, '"Good Hunting:" German Submarine Offensives and South African Countermeasures off the South African Coast during the Second World War, 1942–1945', in *Scientia Militaria: South African Journal of Military Studies*, Vol. 44, No. 1, 2016, p. 174.

36. 'The cryptanalysts learned that the four-letter indicators for regular U-boat messages were the same as the three-letter indicators for weather messages that same day except for an extra letter. Thus, once a daily key was found for a weather message, the fourth rotor had to be tested only in twenty-six positions to find the full four letter key. This gave Hut 8 little difficulty.' David Kahn, *Seizing the Enigma: The Race to Break the German U-Boat Codes, 1939–1943* (London: Arrow, 1996), p. 227. Led initially by Alan Turing, Hut 8 was the section at Bletchley Park that attacked Kriegsmarine Enigma messages.

37. Jack Copeland, 'Enigma', in B. Jack Copeland (ed.), *The Essential Turing: Seminal Writings in Computing, Logic, Philosophy, Artificial Intelligence and Artificial Life plus The Secrets of Enigma* (Oxford: Clarendon, 2004), pp. 343–4.

38. Evert Kleynhans, '"Good Hunting:" German Submarine Offensives and South African Countermeasures off the South African Coast during the Second World War, 1942–1945',

in *Scientia Militaria: South African Journal of Military Studies*, Vol. 44, No. 1, 2016, p. 174. See also: 'Report of Proceedings of Eastern Fleet 10 October to 6 November 1942' at: https://www.naval-history.net/xDKWD-EF1942-Introduction.htm. The former states 14 the latter 13.

39. Arthur J. Marder, Mark Jacobsen and John Horsefield, *Old Friends New Enemies, the Royal Navy and the Imperial Japanese Navy Volume II: The Pacific War, 1942–1945* (Oxford: Clarendon, 1990), p. 206.

40. H. F. Joslen, *Orders of Battle. United Kingdom and Colonial Formations and Units in the Second World War 1939–1945: Volume I* (London: HMSO, 1960), pp. 276–7.

41. 'In response to a request late in September, the Admiralty, with the concurrence of the Netherlands naval authorities, detached *Jacob van Heemskerck* and the destroyers *Van Galen* and *Tjerk Hiddes* from the Eastern Fleet in October, as soon as they could be spared from the Madagascar operations, for service in the South-West Pacific Area. They reached Fremantle on 25th October . . .' G. Hermon Gill, *Australia in the War of 1939–1945, Series Two, Navy, Volume II: Royal Australian Navy, 1942–1945* (Canberra: Australian War Memorial, 1968), p. 190.

42. 'Report of Proceedings of Eastern Fleet 10 October to 6 November 1942' at: https://www.naval-history.net/xDKWD-EF1942-Introduction.htm

43. Somerville Pocket Diary entry for 11 October 1942. In Michael Simpson (ed.), *The Somerville Papers: Selections from the Private and Official Correspondence of Admiral of the Fleet Sir James Somerville, GCB, GBE, DSO* (London: Scolar, 1995), p. 443.

44. To his wife. 11 October 1942. In Michael Simpson (ed.), *The Somerville Papers: Selections from the Private and Official Correspondence of Admiral of the Fleet Sir James Somerville, GCB, GBE, DSO* (London: Scolar, 1995), p. 443.

45. Somerville Pocket Diary entry for 13 October 1942. In Michael Simpson (ed.), *The Somerville Papers: Selections from the Private and Official Correspondence of Admiral of the Fleet Sir James Somerville, GCB, GBE, DSO* (London: Scolar, 1995), p. 443. 'Report of Proceedings of Eastern Fleet 10 October to 6 November 1942' at: https://www.naval-history.net/xDKWD-EF1942-Introduction.htm

46. Major General S. Woodburn Kirby with Captain C. T. Addis, Colonel J. F. Meiklejohn (succeeded by Brigadier M. R. Roberts), Colonel G. T. Wards and Air Vice Marshal N. L. Desoer, *History of the Second World War: The War Against Japan Volume II: India's Most Dangerous Hour* (London: HMSO, 1958), pp. 236–8.

47. Graham Dunlop, *Military Economics, Culture and Logistics in the Burma Campaign, 1942–1945* (Abingdon: Routledge, 2016), p. 2.

48. Guadalcanal marked the Allied transition from defensive to offensive operations. Afterwards they had the strategic initiative. Samuel Eliot Morison, *History of United States Naval Operations in World War II Volume V: The Struggle for Guadalcanal: August 1942–February 1943* (Boston, MA: Little, Brown, 1949).

49. Churchill to Pound. *Circa* 12 July 1942. In Michael Simpson (ed.), *The Somerville Papers: Selections from the Private and Official Correspondence of Admiral of the Fleet Sir James Somerville, GCB, GBE, DSO* (London: Scolar, 1995), p. 432. Somerville had only two aircraft carriers because *Indomitable* had been detached for Operation Pedestal, the fighting through of a convoy to Malta over the period 3–15 August 1942. During the operation *Indomitable* was hit by two 500kg bombs on 12 August, causing damage that required her to withdraw for repairs to the United States. See: Peter C. Smith, *Pedestal: The Convoy That Saved Malta* (Manchester: Crecy, 2002).

50. On 11 July 1942 these were reported as: twelve Martlets, twelve Fulmars and sixteen Albacores aboard *Formidable*; sixteen Martlets, six Fulmars and eighteen Swordfish aboard *Illustrious*. Pound to Churchill. 11 July 1942. See: Pound to Churchill. 11 July 1942. In: Michael Simpson (ed.), *The Somerville Papers: Selections from the Private and Official Correspondence of Admiral of the Fleet Sir James Somerville, GCB, GBE, DSO* (London: Scolar, 1995), p. 432.

51. To Joan Bright Astley. 11 August 1942. In Michael Simpson (ed.), *The Somerville Papers: Selections from the Private and Official Correspondence of Admiral of the Fleet Sir James Somerville, GCB, GBE, DSO* (London: Scolar, 1995), p. 437. Joan Bright Astley 'ran the Commander-in-Chief's Special Information Centre in the War Office and knew absolutely everybody who was anybody in the British war effort'. Thaddeus Holt, *The Deceivers: Allied Military Deception in the Second World War* (New York: Lisa Drew/ Scribner, 2004), p. 292.

52. These form a range along the whole western coast, dividing the island into two unequal parts; a narrow western strip and a wider eastern section.

53. Donald Macintyre, *Fighting Admiral: The Life of Admiral of the Fleet Sir James Somerville* (London: Evans Brothers, 1961), p. 209.

54. 'With the enactment of the Indian Navy (Discipline) Act of 1934, the Royal Indian Navy was formally inaugurated at a historic ceremony at Bombay on October 2, 1934. . . . The British Government, after considerable discussion with the Government of India agreed in January 1938 that India should undertake local naval defence of Indian ports, as well as maintain a Squadron of a minimum of 6 modern escort vessels for co-operation with the Royal Navy in the defence of India.' Rear Admiral K. Sridharan, *A Maritime History Of India* (New Delhi: Publications Division, Ministry Of Information And Broadcasting, Government Of India, 1982), pp. 273–4.

55. Ministry of Defence, *War with Japan: The Campaigns in the Solomons and New Guinea* (London: HMSO, 1995), p. 24. Operation Stab is covered in this work on pp. 23–5 and, unless indicated otherwise, it forms the basis for this section. See also: G. Hermon Gill, *Australia in the War of 1939–1945, Series Two, Navy, Volume II: Royal Australian Navy, 1942–1945* (Canberra: Australian War Memorial, 1968), pp. 126–7. See also: Report of Proceedings of Eastern Fleet 10 October to 6 November 1942' at: https://www.naval-history.net/xDKWD-EF1942-Introduction.htm

56. The Submarines of the Royal Netherlands Navy 1906–2005 http://www.dutchsubma-rines.com/boats/boat_o23.htm

57. To his wife. 31 July 1942. In: Michael Simpson (ed.), *The Somerville Papers: Selections from the Private and Official Correspondence of Admiral of the Fleet Sir James Somerville, GCB, GBE, DSO* (London: Scolar, 1995), pp. 436–7.

58. The Central Executive Administration, under Dr Ba Maw as Chief Administrator, was established by the Japanese military on 1 August 1942. Maung Maung, *Burma in the Family of Nations* (Amsterdam; Djambatan, 1956), p. 96. As Ba Maw put it: 'A new era began in Burma on August 1, 1942, with the coming into force of a Japanese military order called "The Organization of the Government". The order set up a Burmese government to function within the wider framework of a military administration.' Ba Maw, *Breakthrough in Burma: Memoirs of a Revolution, 1939–1946* (New Haven, CT: Yale University Press, 1968), p. 261.

59. For the development of naval IFF technology at that time see: J. S. Shayler, 'The Royal Navy and IFF – Identification Friend or Foe, 1935–45', in F. A. Kingsley (ed.),

The Development of Radar Equipments for the Royal Navy, 1935–45 (Houndmills: Macmillan, 1995), pp. 279–81.

60. Christopher F. Shores, *Air War for Burma: The Allied Air Forces Fight Back in South-East Asia 1942–1945* (London: Grub Street, 2005), p. 19.

61. Eric W. Osborne, 'Navy, Royal', in Stanley Sandler (ed.), *World War II in the Pacific: An Encyclopaedia* (New York: Garland, 2001), p. 728.

62. The Japanese Navy used a variant of the Zero, the Nakajima A6M2-N, as a float-fighter. See: James D'Angina, *Mitsubishi A6M Zero* (Oxford: Osprey, 2016), pp. 28–9. Peter C. Smith, *Mitsubishi Zero: Japan's Legendary Fighter* (Barnsley: Pen & Sword Aviation, 2015), pp. 56–7.

63. Report of Proceedings of Eastern Fleet 10 October to 6 November 1942' at: https://www.naval-history.net/xDKWD-EF1942-Introduction.htm

64. Somerville Pocket Diary entry for 5 August 1942. In Michael Simpson (ed.), *The Somerville Papers: Selections from the Private and Official Correspondence of Admiral of the Fleet Sir James Somerville, GCB, GBE, DSO* (London: Scolar, 1995), p. 438.

65. S. W. Roskill, *The War at Sea 1939–1945 Volume II: The Period of Balance* (London: HMSO, 1956), p. 223.

66. Arthur J. Marder, Mark Jacobsen and John Horsefield, *Old Friends New Enemies, the Royal Navy and the Imperial Japanese Navy Volume II: The Pacific War, 1942–1945* (Oxford: Clarendon, 1990), p. 193.

67. Edward P. von der Porten, *The German Navy in World War II* (New York: Thomas Y Crowell, 1969), p. 118.

68. For a detailed account of the action see: Clay Blair, *Hitler's U-Boat War Volume II: The Hunted 1942–45* (London: Cassell, 2000), p. 74. See also: G. Hermon Gill, *Australia in the War of 1939–1945, Series Two, Navy, Volume II: Royal Australian Navy, 1942–1945* (Canberra: Australian War Memorial, 1968), pp. 208–10.

69. Ian Uys, *Survivors of Africa's Oceans* (Minneapolis, MN: Fortress, 1993), p. 84.

70. Bill Bizley, 'U-Boats off Natal: The Local Ocean War, 1942–1944', in *Natalia: Journal of the Natal Society Foundation*, Issue Number 23/24, December 1993/94, p. 87.

71. Navy Department, Office of The Chief of Naval Operations, Washington. Final Report – G/Serial 34, Report On The Interrogation of Survivors from *U-177*, Sunk 6 February 1944, pp. 62–63. http://www.uboatarchive.net/*U-177*A/*U-177*INT.htm

72. Dean Crawford, *Shark* (London: Reaktion, 2008), p. 60. See also Chapter 10 of: Joseph B. Healy, *Unspeakable Horror: The Deadliest Shark Attacks in Maritime History* (New York: Skyhorse, 2017). According to the report of the US Interrogation conducted in 1944 of the surviving crew members of *U-177*, they were ordered at the end of the patrol to sign a pledge to the effect that the *Nova Scotia* incident would not be mentioned under any circumstances. Navy Department, Office of The Chief of Naval Operations, Washington. Final Report – G/Serial 34, Report On The Interrogation of Survivors from *U-177*, Sunk 6 February 1944, p. 63. http://www.uboatarchive.net/*U-177*A/*U-177*INT.htm

73. Ian Uys, *Survivors of Africa's Oceans* (Minneapolis, MN: Fortress, 1993), p. 100.

74. Bill Bizley, 'U-Boats off Natal: The Local Ocean War, 1942–1944', in *Natalia: Journal of the Natal Society Foundation*, Issue Number 23/24, December 1993/94, p. 78. LCF Turner, HR Gordon-Cumming and J. E. Betzler, *War in The Southern Oceans 1939–1945* (Cape Town: Oxford University Press, 1961), p. 199. Unsurprisingly there is a substantial body of literature in Italian on the loss of *Nova Scotia*. See for example: Valeria Isacchini, *L'onda gridava forte: Il caso della Nova Scotia e di altro fuoco amico su civili italiani* (Milano: Ugo Mursia, 2008).

75. S. W. Roskill, *The War at Sea 1939–1945 Volume II: The Period of Balance* (London: HMSO, 1956), p. 486.
76. Janie Malherbe, *Port Natal: A Pioneer Story* (Cape Town: Howard Timmins, 1965), p. 210. For Ernst and Janie Malherbe see: Ernst Gideon Malherbe papers. Campbell Collections, University of KwaZulu-Natal. http://campbell.ukzn.ac.za/?q=node/47878 Also: E. G. Malherbe, *Never a Dull Moment* (Cape Town: Timmins, 1981), p. 383.
77. 'White South African society was polarised on the war issue. The opposition held anti-British sentiments and was against participating in another of Britain's wars. Afrikaner society was further divided over a militant approach vis-à-vis a parliamentary approach to oppose the war.' A. M. Fokkens, 'Afrikaner Unrest Within South Africa During the Second World War and the Measures Taken to Suppress It', in the *Journal for Contemporary History*, Vol. 37, Issue 2, Dec 2012, p. 127. Consider also: 'Traditional government policy in South African was that only whites should serve in combatant roles in the armed forces. The spectre of blacks trained to use firearms roused white fears about the security of the racially organized state.' Louis Grundlingh, 'The Recruitment of South African Blacks for Participation in the Second World War', in David Killingray and Richard Rathbone (eds), *Africa and the Second World War* (London: Palgrave Macmillan, 1986), p. 181.
78. George Cloete Visser, *OB: Traitors or Patriots?* (Johannesburg; Macmillan, 1977), p. 116.
79. Kent Fedorowich, 'German Espionage and British Counter-Intelligence in South Africa and Mozambique, 1939–1944', in *The Historical Journal*, Vol. 48, No. 1 (2005), pp. 224–5. The enemy were also fed false information. See for example: Thadeus Holt, *The Deceivers: Allied Military Deception in the Second World War* (New York: Skyhorse, 2007), pp. 389–90.
80. Bill Bizley, 'U-Boats off Natal: The Local Ocean War, 1942–1944', in *Natalia: Journal of the Natal Society Foundation*, Issue Number 23/24, December 1993/94, p. 81.
81. Evert Kleynhans, '"Good Hunting:" German Submarine Offensives and South African Countermeasures off the South African Coast during the Second World War, 1942–1945', in *Scientia Militaria: South African Journal of Military Studies*, Vol. 44, No. 1, 2016, p. 179.
82. Evert Kleynhans, '"Good Hunting:" German Submarine Offensives and South African Countermeasures off the South African Coast during the Second World War, 1942–1945', in *Scientia Militaria: South African Journal of Military Studies*, Vol. 44, No. 1, 2016, p. 179.
83. 'Report of Proceedings of Eastern Fleet 10 October to 6 November 1942' at: https://www.naval-history.net/xDKWD-EF1942-Introduction.htm
84. Arthur J. Marder, Mark Jacobsen and John Horsefield, *Old Friends New Enemies, the Royal Navy and the Imperial Japanese Navy Volume II: The Pacific War, 1942–1945* (Oxford: Clarendon, 1990), p. 195.
85. Nicholas Rankin, *Churchill's Wizards: The British Genius for Deception, 1914–1945* (London: Faber and Faber, 2008), p. 178.
86. M. R. D. Foot and J. M. Langley, *MI9: The British Secret Service that Fostered Escape and Evasion 1939–1945 and Its American Counterpart* (London: Bodley Head, 1979), p. 88. For a detailed account of 'A Force' see: Whitney T, Bendeck, *'A' Force: The Origins of British Deception in the Second World War* (Annapolis, MD: Naval Institute Press, 2013).
87. Thaddeus Holt, *The Deceivers: Allied Military Deception in the Second World War* (New York: Skyhorse, 2007), p. 389.

Chapter 10

1. Somerville Pocket Diary entry for 19 August 1942. In Michael Simpson (ed.), *The Somerville Papers: Selections from the Private and Official Correspondence of Admiral of the Fleet Sir James Somerville, GCB, GBE, DSO* (London: Scolar, 1995), p. 438.
2. S. W. Roskill, *The War at Sea 1939–1945 Volume II: The Period of Balance* (London: HMSO, 1956), p. 486.
3. Evert Kleynhans, '"Good Hunting:" German Submarine Offensives and South African Countermeasures off the South African Coast during the Second World War, 1942–1945', in *Scientia Militaria: South African Journal of Military Studies*, Vol. 44, No. 1, 2016, p. 176.
4. Maurizio Brescia, *Mussolini s Navy: A Reference Guide to the Regia Marina 1930–1945* (Barnsley: Seaforth, 2012), p. 170.
5. Christian Lamb, *I Only Joined for the Hat: Redoubtable Wrens at War; Their Trials, Tribulations and Triumphs* (London: Bene Factum, 2007), p. 17. Ian S. Menzies, *We Fought Them on the Seas: Seven Years in the Royal Navy* (North Reading, MA: Cheshire, 2012), pp. 187–8. Richard Woodman, *The Real Cruel Sea: The Merchant Navy in the Battle of the Atlantic 1939–1943* (Barnsley: Pen & Sword, 2013), pp. 637–8.
6. Anti-submarine trawlers were, as the name suggests, fishing boats converted for naval use. Following experience in the Great War, the British maintained a number of trawlers in peacetime and were able to quickly requisition large numbers on the outbreak of hostilities in 1939. Small and elderly trawlers were converted to minesweepers, whilst newer and larger vessels were adapted for anti-submarine use. These, though lightly armed gunwise, generally a single 4in gun and a small number of machine guns, were fitted with ASDIC (SONAR) and could carry 40–50 depth charges. According to uboat.net, these trawlers sank six U-boats during the Second World War: *U-111*, *U-343*, *U-452*, *U-551*, *U-731* and *U-732*. See: Geirr H. Haarr, *The Gathering Storm: The Naval War in Northern Europe September 1939 – April 1940* (Barnsley: Seaforth, 2012), p. 94. George Franklin, *Britain's Anti-submarine Capability 1919–1939* (Abingdon: Routledge, 2014), pp. 44–6. For a first-hand account of service aboard one of these vessels see: Colin Warwick, *Really Not Required* (Edinburgh: Pentland, 1997). For the U-boat losses see: https://uboat.net/allies/ships/trawlers.htm
7. On 1 September 1939 the SAAF had mustered 173 permanent officers, 35 cadet officers and 1,664 other ranks. Leaving aside totally obsolete types dating back in some cases to the 1920s, it could deploy six Hurricane Mk Is, one Fairey Battle light bomber and one Bristol Blenheim bomber. It had also co-opted eighteen German-made Ju 86s owned by South African Airways. These were utilized as bombers and maritime patrol aircraft until 1942, supplemented in the latter role, from 1940 onwards, by British Avro Ansons. They were replaced by US-built Lockheed Venturas. SAAF Coastal Command aircraft attacked twenty-six submarines during the course of the war. André Wessels, 'The South African Air Force, 1920–2012: A Review of its History and an Indication of its Cultural Heritage', in *Scientia Militaria*, Vol. 40, No. 3, 2012, pp. 226–7. H. Potgieter and W. Steenkamp, *Aircraft of the South African Air Force* (Cape Town: Struik, 1981), p. 21.
8. S. W. Roskill, *The War at Sea 1939–1945 Volume II: The Period of Balance* (London: HMSO, 1956), pp. 269–70.
9. Evert Kleynhans, '"Good Hunting:" German Submarine Offensives and South African Countermeasures off the South African Coast during the Second World War, 1942–1945',

in *Scientia Militaria: South African Journal of Military Studies*, Vol. 44, No. 1, 2016, p. 176.

10. Entry for 03.03.43 at 14:00 hours, in: Jerry Mason and Ken Dunn (trans.), *Kriegstagebuch U-160: 4th War Patrol*. Available online at: http://uboatarchive.net/*U-160*/KTB160-4.htm

11. Bill Bizley, 'U-Boats off Natal: The Local Ocean War, 1942–1944', in *Natalia: Journal of the Natal Society Foundation*, Issue Number 23/24, December 1993/94, p. 91.

12. Entry for 03.03.43 at 23:20 hours, in: Jerry Mason and Ken Dunn (trans.), *Kriegstagebuch U-160: 4th War Patrol*. Available online at: http://uboatarchive.net/*U-160*/KTB160-4.htm

13. Entry for 04.03.43 at 02:41 hours, in: Jerry Mason and Ken Dunn (trans.), *Kriegstagebuch U-160: 4th War Patrol*. Available online at: http://uboatarchive.net/*U-160*/KTB160-4. htm, in: Jerry Mason and Ken Dunn (Trans.), *Kriegstagebuch U-160: 4th War Patrol*. Available online at: http://uboatarchive.net/*U-160*/KTB160-4.htm

14. Kenneth Wynn, *U-boat Operations of the Second World War Volume I: Career Histories, U 1 – U 510* (London: Chatham, 1998), p. 124. For the fate of this convoy in general see: L. C. F. Turner, H.R. Gordon-Cumming and J. E. Betzler, *War in The Southern Oceans 1939–1945* (Cape Town: Oxford University Press, 1961), pp. 210–12.

15. Prime Minister to First Lord and First Sea Lord, 5 March 1943. In: Winston S. Churchill, *The Second World War Volume IV: The Hinge of Fate* (London: Cassell, 1950), p. 832.

16. Arthur J. Marder, Mark Jacobsen and John Horsefield, *Old Friends New Enemies, the Royal Navy and the Imperial Japanese Navy Volume II: The Pacific War, 1942–1945* (Oxford: Clarendon, 1990), p. 206.

17. L. C. F. Turner, H. R. Gordon-Cumming and J. E. Betzler, *War in The Southern Oceans 1939–1945* (Cape Town: Oxford University Press, 1961), p. 202.

18. Bill Bizley, 'U-Boats off Natal: The Local Ocean War, 1942–1944', in *Natalia: Journal of the Natal Society Foundation*, Issue Number 23/24, December 1993/94, p. 92.

19. For differing perspectives on Portuguese India, which included Goa, Daman, Diu, Dadra and Nagar Haveli, see: S. S. Desai, *Goa, Daman and Diu, Dadra and Nagar Haveli* (New Delhi: Publications Division, Ministry of Information and Broadcasting, Government of India, 1976) and Luís Forjaz Trigueiros, *Portuguese India To-day* (Lisboa; Agência Geral do Ultramar, 1956).

20. See Chapter 1 *'Atlantis: "Under Ten Flags"'* and Chapter 5 *'Pinguin: The First Casualty'* in: James P. Duffy, *Hitler's Secret Pirate Fleet: The Deadliest Ships of World War II* (Lincoln, NE: University of Nebraska Press, 2005), pp. 1–34, 105–24.

21. UK National Archives. WO 106/3685. General A. P. Wavell: Cables. 21627 Cipher 23/12. 'Personal for CIGS from General Wavell' 24.12.41.

22. Joaquim da Costa Leite, 'Neutrality by Agreement: Portugal and the British Alliance in World War II', in the *American University International Law Review*, Vol. 14, Issue 1, pp. 185–99.

23. UK National Archives. CAB 79/16/33. 'Chiefs of Staff Committee; Minutes of Meeting Held on Wednesday 24 December 1941 at 10.30 am'. 'Goa'.

24. UK National Archives. WO 208/760. 'Relations with Portuguese Goa' 1939–1943 September. Letter [C1432X] from the 'Offices of the War Cabinet' to R M Makins of the Foreign Office dated 25 December 1941. Portuguese Timor (*Timor Português*) consisted of the eastern half of the island of Timor, plus the enclave of Oecusse in the western portion of Dutch Timor; the latter forming a part of the Netherlands East Indies. Australian and Dutch forces moved into the Portuguese territory on 17 December 1941 in order, as was claimed, to pre-empt a Japanese invasion. The Portuguese Government made

vociferous protests at this incursion, hence the 'delicate situation' referred to. See: Clinton Fernandes, 'Two Tales of Timor', in Craig Stockings (ed.), *Zombie Myths of Australian Military History* (Sydney: New South, 2010), pp. 216–22. Henry P Frei, 'Japan's reluctant decision to occupy Portuguese Timor, 1 January 1942–20 February 1942', in *Australian Historical Studies*, Vol. 27, Issue 107, 1996, pp. 281–302. Robert Lee, 'Crisis in a Backwater: 1941 in Portuguese Timor', in *Lusotopie: Lusophonies asiatiques, Asiatiques en lusophonies*, No. 7, 2000, pp. 175–89. It is fair to say that the Portuguese had not heavily invested in the colony. According to one source: 'On the eve of World War II the capital, Dili, had no electricity and no town water supply; there were no paved roads, no telephone services (other than to the houses and offices of senior officials) and not even a wharf for cargo handling.' James Dunn, *Timor: A People Betrayed* (Milton, QLD: Jacaranda Press, 1983), p. 21.

25. UK National Archives. CAB 66/35/7. War Cabinet Weekly Resume (No. 184) of the Naval, Military and Air Situation from 0700 March 4th, to 0700 March 11th, 1943. 11 March 1943, p. 4.

26. James Leasor, *Boarding Party: The Last Charge of the Calcutta Light Horse* (London: Heinemann 1978).

27. James Leasor, *The Sea Wolves* (London: Corgi, 1980).

28. https://www.imdb.com/title/tt0081470/releaseinfo?ref_=tt_dt_dt

29. The Special Operations Executive (SOE) was a secret British Second World War organization formed in 1940 to conduct espionage, sabotage and reconnaissance in occupied Europe against the Axis powers. A separate special operations organization in India was established in May 1941. See: Richard Duckett, *The Special Operations Executive (SOE) in Burma: Jungle Warfare and Intelligence Gathering in WWII* (London: I B Tauris, 2017).

30. 'The Auxiliary Force (India), organized under the Auxiliary Force Act, 1920, is confined to persons of British extraction. Enrolment is voluntary, but entails periodical training extending to 64 hours annually for infantry and 80 hours for other arms. The force, which comprises all arms, is liable to be called out or embodied for local service within strictly defined limits.' M. Epstein (ed.), *The Statesman's Year-Book: Statistical and Historical Annual of the States of the World for the Year 1940* (London: Macmillan, 1940), p. 123.

31. Lieutenant Colonel A. A. Mains (IA Ret.), 'The Auxiliary Force (India)' in the *Journal of the Society for Army Historical Research*, Vol. 61, No. 247, Autumn 1983, p. 160.

32. Lieutenant Colonel Lewis Henry Owain Pugh, aged 35 in 1943, was a Welshman from Glandovey (Glandyfi) in Cardiganshire (Ceredigion). See: PUGH, LEWIS HENRY OWAIN (1907–1981), soldier; in Y Bywgraffiadur Cymreig – The Dictionary of Welsh Biography. Available online at: https://biography.wales/article/s8-PUGH-OWA-1907

33. David Miller, *Special Forces Operations in South-East Asia 1941–1945: Minerva, Baldhead and Longshanks/Creek* (Barnsley: Pen & Sword, 2015), p. 128.

34. James Leasor, *The Sea Wolves* (London: Corgi, 1980), p. 31.

35. James Leasor, *The Sea Wolves* (London: Corgi, 1980), p. 57.

36. James Leasor, *The Sea Wolves* (London: Corgi, 1980), pp. 50–2.

37. Though Leasor gives no date for this, subsequent research has shown the journey to have taken place on 17 December 1942. David Miller, *Special Forces Operations in South-East Asia 1941–1945: Minerva, Baldhead and Longshanks/Creek* (Barnsley: Pen & Sword, 2015), p. 133.

38. James Leasor, *The Sea Wolves* (London: Corgi, 1980), p. 70.

39. James Leasor, *The Sea Wolves* (London: Corgi, 1980), p. 225.

40. Richard Duckett, *The Special Operations Executive (SOE) in Burma: Jungle Warfare and Intelligence Gathering in WWII* (London: I B Tauris, 2017), p. 73.
41. James Leasor, *The Sea Wolves* (London: Corgi, 1980), p. 103.
42. James Leasor, *The Sea Wolves* (London: Corgi, 1980), p. 108. See also: Dwight Jon Zimmerman, 'Operation Creek: Going to War on a River Barge, Part 2', in *Defense Media Network* online magazine, August 12, 2013. Available online at: https://www.defenseme-dianetwork.com/stories/operation-creek-going-to-war-on-a-river-barge/
43. David Miller, *Special Forces Operations in South-East Asia 1941–1945: Minerva, Baldhead and Longshanks/Creek* (Barnsley: Pen & Sword, 2015), p. 142.
44. David Gorman, 'A Glandyfi Sea Wolf: Major General Lewis Owain Pugh, Cymerau', in *The Ego*, July/Gorffennaf 2018, p. 70.
45. Savio Correia, 'Blitzkrieg in the Backyard: Goa's tryst with WW II' in *O Heraldo*, 11 March 2018. Available online at: https://www.heraldgoa.in/Review/Voice-Of-Opinion/Blitzkrieg-in-the-Backyard-Goa%E2%80%99s-tryst-with-WW-II/128016. html Gefallene der DDG-"Hansa" im WK2 http://www.ddg-hansa.de/content/ddg-hansa_frachter/ddg-hansa_wk2/gefallene_wk2.pdf
46. Robert Barr Smith, 'The Daring Calcutta Light Horse Raid', on *Warfare History Network*, November 30, 2015. Available online at: https://warfarehistorynetwork.com/daily/wwii/the-daring-calcutta-light-horse-raid/ Leasor says destroyed: James Leasor, *The Sea Wolves* (London: Corgi, 1980), p. 199.
47. Dwight Jon Zimmerman, 'Operation Creek: Going to War on a River Barge, Part 2', in *Defense Media Network* online magazine, August 12, 2013. Available online at: https://www.defensemedianetwork.com/stories/operation-creek-going-to-war-on-a-river-barge/
48. Miller explains the confusion regarding code names: 'Longshanks' was the name allocated to the operation in London and was used between SOE there and SOE India. 'Creek' was the designation used within India. Confusingly, the single word broadcast from Phoebe to denote the successful completion of 'Operation Creek' was 'Longshanks'. David Miller, *Special Forces Operations in South-East Asia 1941–1945: Minerva, Baldhead and Longshanks/Creek* (Barnsley: Pen & Sword, 2015), pp. 130, 167.
49. The line 'Lo, all our pomp of yesterday/Is one with Nineveh and Tyre!' appears in Kipling's 1897 poem *Recessional*. See: https://www.poetryfoundation.org/poems/46780/recessional
50. A Committee of Light Horsemen, *Calcutta Light Horse AF(I), 1759–1881–1947* (Aldershot; Gale & Polden, 1957), p. 90.
51. The phrase originates in the poem *Gerontion* by T. S. Eliot. Michael Holzman, *James Jesus Angleton, the CIA and the Craft of Counterintelligence* (Amherst, MA: University of Massachusetts Press, 2008), p. 320.
52. Owen Matthews, *An Impeccable Spy: Richard Sorge, Stalin's Master Agent* (London: Bloomsbury, 2019). This was known in 1978; the existence of 'the Sorge Spy Ring' had been revealed in 1952. See: Major General Charles A. Willoughby, *Shanghai Conspiracy: The Sorge Spy Ring: Moscow, Shanghai, Tokyo, San Francisco, New York* (New York: E P Dutton, 1952).
53. Gavin Stewart's name does not appear in the 'Acknowledgments' section of Leasor's book.
54. Unless otherwise stated, the information on Koch in this section comes from an 'unpublished memoir' written by Pugh and forwarded to Miller by his family. This however 'ends abruptly' on the night before the kidnapping referred to by Leasor. David Miller, *Special Forces Operations in South-East Asia 1941–1945: Minerva, Baldhead and Longshanks/Creek* (Barnsley: Pen & Sword, 2015), pp. xiii, 131–3, 207 n. 106.

55. Bruno Henrique Manfrim Cruz, 'Uma Missão em Goa', in *Revista De Villegagnon*, Ano V, Número 5, 2010, pp. 70–5.

56. David Miller, *Special Forces Operations in South-East Asia 1941–1945: Minerva, Baldhead and Longshanks/Creek* (Barnsley: Pen & Sword, 2015), p. 132. Bremner had complained previously of the freedom of movement, within the confines of the colony, granted to the ships' crews by the Goan authorities. The Governor was however 'not very much inclined to make a major intervention, even though he was sensitive to the economic difficulties of the crew members'. José António Barreiros, *O Espião Alemão em Goa* (Alfragide; Oficina do Livro, 2011), p. 36 n 9.

57. Martin Moynihan, 'Sir Olaf Caroe', in *Asian Affairs*, Vol. 28, Issue 3, 1997, p. 349.

58. Quoted in: Selma Carvalho, 'The Letters of C E U Bremner: Same Old Tired Prejudices', in Selma Carvalho (ed.), *The Brave New World of Goan Writing 2018: Anthology* (Mumbai: Bombaykala, 2018), p. 199.

59. James Onley, *Britain and the Gulf Shaikhdoms, 1820–1971: The Politics of Protection* (Doha; Georgetown University School of Foreign Service in Qatar, 2009), p. 4. The Protectorates under the Residency were : Bahrain; Muscat and Oman; Kuwait; Qatar; and what became the United Arab Emirates but were then known as the Trucial States. See: Tancred Bradshaw, *The End of Empire in the Gulf: From Trucial States to United Arab Emirates* (London; I B Tauris, 2019).

60. Quoted in: Selma Carvalho, 'The Letters of C E U Bremner: Same Old Tired Prejudices', in Selma Carvalho (ed.), *The Brave New World of Goan Writing 2018: Anthology* (Mumbai: Bombaykala, 2018), p. 188.

61. Quoted in: Selma Carvalho, 'The Letters of C E U Bremner: Same Old Tired Prejudices', in Selma Carvalho (ed.), *The Brave New World of Goan Writing 2018: Anthology* (Mumbai: Bombaykala, 2018), p. 188.

62. Adam von Trott zu Solz, who effectively ran the Special Bureau for India (*Sonderreferat Indien*) set up at the behest of Subhas Chandra Bose, opined that a communication link via between Bose and his followers in India might be possible via Goa. Jan Kuhlmann, *Subhas Chandra Bose und die Indienpolitik der Achsenmächte* (Berlin: Hans Schiler, 2003), p. 164. Bose promoted armed struggle against the British in collaboration with Germany and Japan and was considered either a traitor or a freedom fighter according to perspective. Sugata Bose, *His Majesty's Opponent: Subhas Chandra Bose and India's Struggle against Empire (New Haven, CT: Harvard University Press, 2011)*.

63. UK National Archives. HS 1/230, 'Operations: LONGSHANK and CREEK; miscellaneous dated 1943–1945'. Report from B/B 128 (Pugh) to B/B 100 (McKenzie) dated 15 March 1943. Quoted in: David Miller, *Special Forces Operations in South-East Asia 1941–1945: Minerva, Baldhead and Longshanks/Creek* (Barnsley: Pen & Sword, 2015), pp. 133–4.

64. Dr P. P. (Prakashchandra Pandurang) Shirodkar was an historian, a prolific author and former head of the Directorate of Archives, Archaeology and Museum of Goa. A former editor of *Colloquium*, the research journal of the Goa Institute of Historical and Cultural Research, he was also the executive editor at the *Goa Gazetter*. See: Pratima Achrekar, 'Honouring a Historian', in *O Heraldo-The Voice of Goa*, 31 October 2015. Available online at: https://www.heraldgoa.in/Cafe/Honouring-a-Historian/95170.html

65. P. P. Shirodkar, 'World War II: German Master Spy and Ships in Goa I', in *Colloquium, Journal of Goa Institute of Historical and Cultural Research*, Vol. 2, No. 2, July-December 1979, p. 24.

66. P. P. Shirodkar, *Goa's Struggle for Freedom* (Delhi: Ajanta, 1988), p. 19.

67. The manuscript is in the British Library: India Office Records and Private Paper. MSS Eur F226/4. 1936–1943. Anne Bremner, 'India during the British Raj: Recollections of Kathiawar, Quetta, Goa'. See also: Anne Bremner, 'A Segunda Guerra Mundial em Goa: o manuscrito de Anne Bremner', in Filipa Lowndes Vicente, *Entre Dois Impérios: Viajantes Britânicos em Goa (1800–1940)* (Lisboa: Tinta da China, 2015), pp. 169–85. Claude Bremner died in April 1965 in Dorking, Surrey. Anne Bremner died in May 2002 in Sudbury, Suffolk. See: http://www.brebner.com/uploads/bre19834.pdf

68. Anne Bremner, 'A Segunda Guerra Mundial em Goa: o manuscrito de Anne Bremner', in Filipa Lowndes Vicente, *Entre Dois Impérios: Viajantes Britânicos em Goa (1800–1940)* (Lisboa: Tinta da China, 2015), p. 181.

69. David Miller, *Special Forces Operations in South-East Asia 1941–1945: Minerva, Baldhead and Longshanks/Creek* (Barnsley: Pen & Sword, 2015), p. 135.

70. David Miller, *Special Forces Operations in South-East Asia 1941–1945: Minerva, Baldhead and Longshanks/Creek* (Barnsley: Pen & Sword, 2015), pp. 135–7.

71. James Leasor, *The Sea Wolves* (London: Corgi, 1980), p. 70.

72. Rear Admiral Satyindra Singh, *Blueprint to Bluewater: The Indian Navy, 1951–65* (New Delhi: Lancer, 1992), p. 411.

73. See: 'Deutsche Vertretung für Portugiesich-Indien', in Fritz Berber, *Jahrbuch für Auswärtige Politik: 1939* (Berlin: August Gross, 1939), p. 418. Subject: Enquiry from the Swiss Legation London, whether objection would be raised to the Consul General for Switzerland at Bombay Taking Charge of German Interest at Goa. 2. Refusal to allow the Swiss C.G. at Bombay Taking Charge of German Interest at Goa. File No: Progs., Nos. 63-W, 1940 (Secret) WAR 1940.

74. Anne Bremner, 'A Segunda Guerra Mundial em Goa: o manuscrito de Anne Bremner', in Filipa Lowndes Vicente, *Entre Dois Impérios: Viajantes Britânicos em Goa (1800–1940)* (Lisboa: Tinta da China, 2015), p. 181.

75. James Leasor, *Boarding Party: The Last Action of the Calcutta Light Horse* (London: William Heinemann, 1978), p. 223.

76. https://uboat.net/boats/successes/u160/html

77. James Leasor, *Boarding Party: The Last Action of the Calcutta Light Horse* (London: William Heinemann, 1978), p. 223.

78. Bill Bizley, 'U-Boats off Natal: The Local Ocean War, 1942–1944', in *Natalia: Journal of the Natal Society Foundation*, Issue Number 23/24, December 1993/94, p. 93.

79. James Leasor, *The Sea Wolves* (New York: Bantam, 1980), p. 23. That the British had cracked the wartime German ciphers, the 'Ultra Secret', had been publicly revealed in 1974. F. W. Winterbotham, *The Ultra Secret* (London: Weidenfeld and Nicolson, 1974).

80. Joel Greenberg, 'The Enigma Machine', in B. Jack Copeland, Jonathan Bowen, Mark Sprevak, Robin Wilson and others, *The Turing Guide* (Oxford: Oxford University Press, 2017), p. 86.

81. Anne Bremner, 'A Segunda Guerra Mundial em Goa: o manuscrito de Anne Bremner', in Filipa Lowndes Vicente, *Entre Dois Impérios: Viajantes Britânicos em Goa (1800–1940)* (Lisboa: Tinta da China, 2015), p. 183.

82. David Miller, *Special Forces Operations in South-East Asia 1941–1945: Minerva, Baldhead and Longshanks/Creek* (Barnsley: Pen & Sword, 2015), p. 178. Indeed, logic dictates that if there were concealed radio apparatus aboard *Ehrenfels* then it would have had to be installed before the war. This of course raises the question as to why; why would radio apparatus and, presumably, an Enigma machine, be secretly installed in a merchant vessel, even one that would have undoubtedly converted into an excellent auxiliary cruiser?

83. The Portuguese authorities declined to accept that any attack had taken place at all: 'The subsequent inquiry conducted by the Portuguese Navy and the trial of the crew members held in the local court, both concluded that the attack alleged never occurred and was a mere invention to justify the sinking of the ships, following a political altercation between the crews. Also, the Governor General of Goa, Colonel José Cabral, had, on the night of the incident, telegraphed a message to the Ministry of the Colonies in Lisbon, which was then passed on to Prime Minister Oliveira Salazar, stating that the story of the British attack was, in fact, not true.' Editorial synopsis of: José António Barreiros, *O Espião Alemão em Goa* (Alfragide; Oficina do Livro, 2012).

84. James Leasor, *The Sea Wolves* (London: Corgi, 1980), pp. 77, 150.

85. Anne Bremner, 'A Segunda Guerra Mundial em Goa: o manuscrito de Anne Bremner', in Filipa Lowndes Vicente, *Entre Dois Impérios: Viajantes Britânicos em Goa (1800–1940)* (Lisboa; Tinta da China, 2015), p. 184.

Chapter 11

1. Winston S. Churchill, *The Second World War Volume IV: The Hinge of Fate* (London: Cassell, 1950), p. 536.

2. Simon Sebag Montefiore, *Stalin: The Court of the Red Tsar* (London: Phoenix, 2004), p. 452.

3. Nigel Hamilton, *Commander in Chief: FDR's Battle with Churchill, 1943* (Boston, MA: Houghton Mifflin Harcourt, 2016.), pp. 127–9.

4. David Rigby, *Allied Master Strategists: The Combined Chiefs of Staff in World War II* (Annapolis, MD: Naval Institute Press, 2012), p. i.

5. King was the only individual to hold both these positions. As one of his biographers put it: 'It made King the most powerful naval officer in the history of the United States'. Thomas B. Buell, *Master of Sea Power: A Biography of Fleet Admiral Ernest J King* (Annapolis, MD: Naval Institute Press, 1995), p. 179.

6. All the documentation relating to the Casablanca Conference was published by the US Department of State as *Foreign Relations of the United States, The Conferences at Washington, 1941–1942 and Casablanca, 1943* (Washington DC: US Government Printing Office, 1968). This comprehensive work has now been digitised and is available at: https://history.state.gov/historicaldocuments/frus1941-43/comp3 The minutes of the meeting in question are available at: https://history.state.gov/historicaldocuments/frus1941-43/d336 and are the source for references in this section unless otherwise stated.

7. Bisheshwar Prasad (ed.), *Official History of the Indian Armed Forces in the Second World War 1939–45: The Reconquest of Burma Volume I* (Delhi: Combined Inter-Services Historical Section (India & Pakistan), 1958), p. 1. Maurice Matloff, *United States Army in World War: The War Department: Strategic Planning for Coalition Warfare 1943–1944* (Washington DC: Center Of Military History United States Army, 1994), p. 34.

8. Thomas B. Buell, *Master of Sea Power: A Biography of Fleet Admiral Ernest J King* (Annapolis, MD: Naval Institute Press, 1995), p. 277. 'The Nationalists maintained some 4 million troops in China throughout the war, helping to tie down some half a million or more Japanese soldiers who could otherwise have been transferred elsewhere. The Communists maintained a guerrilla campaign that prevented the Japanese from gaining control of large parts of northern China, tying down troops and resources.' Rana Mitter, *Forgotten Ally: China's World War II, 1937–1945* (Boston, MA: Houghton Mifflin Harcourt, 2013), p. 379.

9. Bisheshwar Prasad (ed.), *Official History of the Indian Armed Forces in the Second World War 1939–45: The Reconquest of Burma Volume I* (Delhi: Combined Inter-Services Historical Section (India & Pakistan), 1958), p. 3.
10. Various, *The Imperial Gazetteer of India: Volume XXII, Samadhiala To Singhana* (Oxford: Clarendon, 1908), p. 244.
11. John D. Plating, *The Hump: America's Strategy for Keeping China in World War II* (College Station, TX: Texas A&M University, 2011), p. 1. See also: Leo J. Daugherty III, *The Allied Resupply Effort in the China-Burma-India Theater During World War II* (Jefferson, NC: McFarland, 2008).
12. This physiological metaphor was coined by Chennault: Claire Lee Chennault and Robert Hotz (ed.), *Way of a Fighter: The Memoirs of Claire Lee Chennault* (New York: G P Putnam's Sons, 1949), p. 207.
13. Kaushik Roy, *Sepoys Against the Rising Sun: The Indian Army in Far East and South-East Asia, 1941–45* (Leiden: Brill, 2016), p. 256.
14. For 'First Arakan' see: Adrian Fort, *Archibald Wavell: The Life and Times of an Imperial Servant* (London: Jonathan Cape, 2009), pp. 312–17; Kaushik Roy, *Sepoys Against the Rising Sun: The Indian Army in Far East and South-East Asia, 1941–45* (Leiden: Brill, 2016), pp. 261–2.
15. Winston S. Churchill, *The Second World War Volume IV: The Hinge of Fate* (London: Cassell, 1950), p. 702. Slim demonstrated that the analogy was false. The Japanese had no organic aptitude for jungle warfare; their successes were based on training. Once Allied forces had received appropriate training they fought with great success. As he was to later write: 'we had by degrees become better in the jungle than the Japanese'. Field Marshal Sir William Slim, *Defeat into Victory* (London: Reprint Society, 1957), p. 361.
16. Maurice Matloff, *United States Army in World War: The War Department: Strategic Planning for Coalition Warfare 1943–1944* (Washington DC: Center Of Military History United States Army, 1994), p. 34.
17. For biographies of Chiang see: Jay Taylor, *The Generalissimo: Chiang Kai-shek and the Struggle for Modern China* (Cambridge, MA: Belknap, 2009); Jonathan Fenby, *Generalissimo: Chiang Kai-shek and the China He Lost* (London: Simon & Schuster, 2003).
18. 'The success of operations in Burma depended not only on the strength of Allied naval forces in the Indian Ocean, but on the simultaneous coordination of naval action with land operations.' Quoted in: Ronald Ian Heiferman, *The Cairo Conference of 1943: Roosevelt, Churchill, Chiang Kai-shek and Madame Chiang* (Jefferson, NC: McFarland, 2011), p. 73.
19. Yoshihiko Futamatsu, Peter N. Davies (ed.) and Ewart Escritt (trans.), *Across the Three Pagodas Pass: The Story of the Thai-Burma Railway* (Folkestone: Renaissance, 2013). Gavan McCormack and Hank Nelson (eds), *The Burma-Thailand Railway: Memory and History* (St Leonards, NSW: Allen & Unwin, 1993). A map of the route can be found at: https://anzacportal.dva.gov.au/history/conflicts/burma-thailand-railway-and-hellfire-pass/events/building-hellfire-pass/map-burma
20. Arthur J. Marder, Mark Jacobsen and John Horsefield, *Old Friends New Enemies, the Royal Navy and the Imperial Japanese Navy Volume II: The Pacific War, 1942–1945* (Oxford: Clarendon, 1990), p. 204.
21. Arthur J. Marder, Mark Jacobsen and John Horsefield, *Old Friends New Enemies, the Royal Navy and the Imperial Japanese Navy Volume II: The Pacific War, 1942–1945* (Oxford: Clarendon, 1990), p. 220.

22. Jeremy Black, 'Midway and the Indian Ocean', in *Naval War College Review*, Vol. 62, No. 4, Autumn 2009, p. 136.
23. https://history.state.gov/historicaldocuments/frus1941-43/d336
24. John D. Alden and Craig R. McDonald, *United States and Allied Submarine Successes* (Jefferson, NC: McFarland, 2009), pp. 8–9.
25. See: 'Chapter XIX, The Far East: January–September 1943' in Vice Admiral Sir Arthur Hezlet, *British and Allied Submarine Operations in World War II, Volume 1* (Gosport: Royal Navy Submarine Museum, 2001). Available online at: https://www.rnsubmus-friends.org.uk/hezlet/volume1/volume1.htm
26. The German light cruiser *Emden* had carried out an audacious raid on George Town harbour on 28 October 1914. During the course of this the Russian light cruiser *Zhemchug* and the French destroyer *Mosquet* were sunk. Charles Stephenson, *The Siege of Tsingtau: The German-Japanese War 1914* (Barnsley: Pen & Sword, 2017), p. 117.
27. Marcus Langdon, *George Town's Historic Commercial & Civic Precincts* (George Town: George Town World Heritage, undated), pp. 6–7.
28. Sidney F. Mashbir, Allied Translator and Interpreter Section, South-west Pacific Area. Report on information gained from five prisoners from a German submarine, U-168, sunk off Java on 5 October 1944. Dated 26 March 1945, pp. 7–8. Available online at: http://www.uboatarchive.net/U-168A/U-168INT.htm
29. Dennis Gunton, *The Penang Submarines: Penang and Submarine Operations 1942–45* (Penang: City Council of George Town, 1970), p. 2.
30. Dennis Gunton, *The Penang Submarines: Penang and Submarine Operations 1942–45* (Penang: City Council of George Town, 1970), p. 15.
31. Jochen Brennecke, *Haie im Paradies: Der Deutsche U-Boot-Krieg in Asiens Gewässern 1943–45* (Herford: Koehler, 1967), pp. 87–8.
32. Francesco Mattesini, 'I sommergibili da trasporto di "BETASOM" e la cessione di sommergibili tedeschi tipo VII C 42 alla Marina Italiana: l'ultima missione del sommergibile Ammiraglio Cagni e le conclusioni della guerra oceanica' p. 63. Available from: https://independent.academia.edu/FrancescoMattesini
33. Jochen Brennecke, *Haie im Paradies: Der Deutsche U-Boot-Krieg in Asiens Gewässern 1943–45* (Herford: Koehler, 1967), pp. 48–9. See also: http://www.uboataces.com/articles-fareast-boats3.shtml
34. Jochen Brennecke, *Haie im Paradies: Der Deutsche U-Boot-Krieg in Asiens Gewässern 1943–45* (Herford: Koehler, 1967), p. 55.
35. Dönitz had, somewhat bizarrely, remarked in 1942 that 'the U-boat has no more to fear from aircraft than a mole from a crow'. Quoted in: C. H. Waddington, *O R in World War 2: Operational Research against the U-boat* (London: Elek, 1973), p. 31.
36. The only book-length work dealing with Horton remains W. S. Chalmers, *Max Horton and the Western Approaches* (London: Hodder & Stoughton, 1957). There is added piquancy to the story in that Horton's mother was Jewish. According to Nazi racial laws, this 'Jewish blood' categorized him as being a Jewish *Mischling* (half-breed) of the first degree. In other words, Dönitz, a convinced Nazi and devotee of his 'beloved Führer' (who named him as his successor), was bested by an opponent he would have regarded as sub-human (*Untermensch*). See: Charles Stephenson 'The "Pirate", the Battle of the Atlantic and the Maelog Lake Hotel', in T. T. M. Hale (ed.), *Rhosneigr: People & Places* (Sheffield: Rhosneigr Publishing, 2017), pp. 27–38. For Walker see: Alan Burn, *The Fighting Captain: The Story of Frederic Walker RN CB DSO & the Battle of the Atlantic* (Barnsley: Pen & Sword, 2006).

37. Horst H. Geerken, *Hitlers Griff nach Asien: Das Dritte Reich und Niederländisch-Indien. Aufbau deutscher Marinestu?tzpunkte Eine Dokumentation, Band I* (Norderstedt: BoD-Books on Demand, 2015), pp. 319–20.

38. Clay Blair, *Hitler's U-Boat War Volume II: The Hunted 1942–45* (London: Cassell, 2000), pp. 775–6. Ashley Jackson, *War and Empire in Mauritius and the Indian Ocean* (Houndmills: Palgrave, 2001), p. 45.

39. Jochen Brennecke, *Haie im Paradies: Der Deutsche U-Boot-Krieg in Asiens Gewässern 1943–45* (Herford: Koehler, 1967), p. 56. Arthur J. Marder, Mark Jacobsen and John Horsefield, *Old Friends New Enemies, the Royal Navy and the Imperial Japanese Navy Volume II: The Pacific War, 1942–1945* (Oxford: Clarendon, 1990), p. 210. David Kohnen, 'The Cruise of U-188: Special Intelligence and the "Liquidation" of Group Monsoon, 1943–1944', in Marcus Faulkner and Christopher M. Bell (eds), *Decision in the Atlantic: The Allies and the Longest Campaign of the Second World War* (Lexington, KY: Andarta, 2019), p. 269.

40. Elena Agarossi and Harvey Ferguson II (trans.), *A Nation Collapses: The Italian Surrender of September 1943* (Cambridge: University Press, 2006).

41. Vincent O'Hara and Enrico Cernuschi, *Dark Navy: The Italian Regia Marina and the Armistice of 8 September 1943* (Ann Arbor, MI: Nimble Books, 2009), p. 3.

42. Vincent O'Hara and Enrico Cernuschi, *Dark Navy: The Italian Regia Marina and the Armistice of 8 September 1943* (Ann Arbor, MI: Nimble Books, 2009), p. 3.

43. See: Vincent O'Hara, *Torch: North Africa and the Allied Path to Victory* (Annapolis, MD: Naval Institute Press, 2015).

44. Arthur J. Marder, Mark Jacobsen and John Horsefield, *Old Friends New Enemies, the Royal Navy and the Imperial Japanese Navy Volume II: The Pacific War, 1942–1945* (Oxford: Clarendon, 1990), p. 263.

45. Lawrence Paterson, *Hitler's Grey Wolves: U-Boats in the Indian Ocean* (Barnsley: Frontline, 2016) Kindle Edition. Loc. 1759.

46. Somerville Pocket Diary entry for 10 April. In Michael Simpson (ed.), *The Somerville Papers: Selections from the Private and Official Correspondence of Admiral of the Fleet Sir James Somerville, GCB, GBE, DSO* (London: Scolar, 1995), p. 457. Donald Macintyre, *Fighting Admiral: The life of Admiral of the Fleet Sir James Somerville* (London: Evans Brothers, 1961), p. 228.

47. Winston S. Churchill, *The Second World War: Volume IV The Hinge of Fate* (London: The Reprint Society, 1953), p. 630.

48. An island just off the Burma coast, situated about 70 miles south of Akyab.

49. Somerville to Royle 17 July 1943. In Michael Simpson (ed.), *The Somerville Papers: Selections from the Private and Official Correspondence of Admiral of the Fleet Sir James Somerville, GCB, GBE, DSO* (London: Scolar, 1995), p. 462.

50. Maurice Matloff, *United States Army in World War: The War Department: Strategic Planning for Coalition Warfare 1943–1944* (Washington DC: Center Of Military History United States Army, 1994), p. 31.

51. Winston S. Churchill, *The Second World War: Volume IV: The Hinge of Fate* (London: Reprint Society, 1953), p. 632.

52. Combined Chiefs of Staff Minutes, Conclusions of the Minutes of the 90th and 91st Meetings May 21, 1943, 10:30 a.m. in: Department of State, *Foreign Relations of the United States: Conferences at Washington and Quebec, 1943* (Washington DC: US Government Printing Office, 1970), p. 148. Available online at: https://history.state.gov/historicaldocuments/frus1943/d57

53. *The London Gazette*, 13 August 1943, p. 3653.
54. Grace Person Hayes, *The History of the Joint Chiefs of Staff in World War II: The War Against Japan* (Annapolis, MD: Naval Institute Press, 1982), p. 401. See also: Christopher Baxter, 'In Pursuit of a Pacific Strategy: British Planning for the Defeat of Japan, 1943–45', in *Diplomacy & Statecraft*, Vol. 15, Issue 2, 2004, pp. 253–77.
55. 'As long as Tirpitz is in being it is essential to have two ships of King George V class available to work in company. . . . In order to have two King George V's available at all times it is necessary to have three of that class in home waters, to allow for one being damaged by torpedo, bomb, or mine or refitting . . . It is considered that the third ship can be in Force H at Gibraltar and that all three ships need not be at Scapa.' First Sea Lord to Prime Minister, 28 August 1941. Churchill had railed at this unwelcome advice: 'The fact that the Admiralty consider that three K.G.V.s must be used to contain Tirpitz is a serious reflection upon the design of our latest ships, which, through being under-gunned and weakened by hangars in the middle of their citadels, are evidently judged unfit to fight their opposite number in a single-ship action. . . . How foolish they would be to send her out, when by staying where she is she contains the three strongest and newest battleships we have and rules the Baltic as well!' Prime Minister to First Sea Lord, 29 August 1941. In: Winston S. Churchill, *The Second World War: Volume III: The Grand Alliance* (London: Reprint Society, 1952), pp. 669, 671.
56. John Ehrman, *History of the Second World War: Grand Strategy, Volume V, August 1943-September 1944* (London: HMSO, 1956), p. 139.
57. Arthur Bryant, *The Turn of the Tide: A Study Based on the Diaries and Autobiographical Notes of Field Marshal The Viscount Alanbrooke* (London: Collins, 1957), pp. 623–4.
58. Philip Ziegler, *Mountbatten: The Official Biography* (London: Collins, 1985), p. 220.
59. Lawrence Paterson, *Hitler's Grey Wolves: U-Boats in the Indian Ocean* (Barnsley: Frontline, 2016) Kindle Edition. Loc. 1908.
60. Four modern destroyers, two 'Q' class, *Quadrant* and *Quickmatch* (Australian) and two 'R' class, *Roebuck* and *Relentless*; four 'Flower' class anti-submarine corvettes, *Jasmine, Nigella, Rockrose* and *Thyme*; and two 'River' class anti-submarine frigates, *Derg* and *Tay*. Eastern Fleet War Diary, September 1943. http://www.naval-history.net/xDKWD-EF1943b.htm See also: Michael Simpson (ed.), *The Somerville Papers: Selections from the Private and Official Correspondence of Admiral of the Fleet Sir James Somerville, GCB, GBE, DSO* (London: Scolar, 1995), p. 474.
61. The *Shoreham* class sloop *Falmouth*; two armed yachts, *Maid Marion* and *Virginia*; three 'Flower' class corvettes, *Freesia, Fritillary* and *Tulip*; and three ex-US Coast Guard Cutters, *Banff, Lulworth* and *Landguard*. Eastern Fleet War Diary, September 1943. http://www.naval-history.net/xDKWD-EF1943b.htm See also: Michael Simpson (ed.), *The Somerville Papers: Selections from the Private and Official Correspondence of Admiral of the Fleet Sir James Somerville, GCB, GBE, DSO* (London: Scolar, 1995), p. 474.
62. Five Australian-designed, built and manned *Bathurst* class corvettes: *Cairns, Cessnock, Geraldton, Lismore* and *Wollongong*. Eastern Fleet War Diary, September 1943. http://www.naval-history.net/xDKWD-EF1943b.htm See also: Michael Simpson (ed.), *The Somerville Papers: Selections from the Private and Official Correspondence of Admiral of the Fleet Sir James Somerville, GCB, GBE, DSO* (London: Scolar, 1995), p. 474.
63. David Kohnen, 'The Cruise of U-188: Special Intelligence and the "Liquidation" of Group Monsoon, 1943–1944', in Marcus Faulkner and Christopher M. Bell (eds), *Decision in the Atlantic: The Allies and the Longest Campaign of the Second World War* (Lexington, KY: Andarta, 2019), p. 270.

64. Arthur J. Marder, Mark Jacobsen and John Horsefield, *Old Friends New Enemies, the Royal Navy and the Imperial Japanese Navy Volume II: The Pacific War, 1942–1945* (Oxford: Clarendon, 1990), p. 208.

65. Operational Research, 'a term first coined in 1938', can be defined as 'a descriptive term for the application of science to military operations in order to improve them'. See the History of The OR [Operational Research] Society at: https://www.theorsociety.com/who-we-are/history-of-the-or-society/

66. Arthur J. Marder, Mark Jacobsen and John Horsefield, *Old Friends New Enemies, the Royal Navy and the Imperial Japanese Navy Volume II: The Pacific War, 1942–1945* (Oxford: Clarendon, 1990), p. 253.

67. Desk Diary entry for 7 February 1944. In Michael Simpson (ed.), *The Somerville Papers: Selections from the Private and Official Correspondence of Admiral of the Fleet Sir James Somerville, GCB, GBE, DSO* (London: Scolar, 1995), p. 511.

68. UK National Archives. ADM 205/1. 'Committee of Imperial Defence. Chiefs of Staff Sub-Committee. Acceleration of defence programme 1939. Loss of HMS ROYAL OAK, etc'. February 1939 – February 1940. 'The Submarine Campaign'. In 1939 Vice-Admiral Sir Hugh Binney chaired an Admiralty Committee tasked with investigating problems and generating ideas which might be of use to the Naval Staff. 'The Submarine Campaign' was produced in September 1939.

69. Captain S. W. Roskill, *The War at Sea 1939–45: Volume III, The Offensive, Part 1, 1st June 1943- 31st May 1944* (London: HMSO, 1960), p. 348.

70. Lawrence Paterson, *Hitler's Grey Wolves: U-Boats in the Indian Ocean* (Barnsley: Frontline, 2016) Kindle Edition. Loc. 1908.

71. National Security Agency/National Cryptologic Museum, Special Research History (SRH) SRH-008: Battle of the Atlantic, Vol. II: 'U-Boat Operations – December 1942 to May 1942 including German U-boats and raiders in the Indian and Pacific Oceans', pp. 216–17. Available online at: https://www.ibiblio.org/hyperwar/ETO/Ultra/SRH-008/SRH008-14.html

72. Lawrence Paterson, *Hitler's Grey Wolves: U-Boats in the Indian Ocean* (Barnsley: Frontline, 2016) Kindle Edition. Loc. 1976.

73. German torpedoes used the letter G, followed by a number which indicated its length (7m) and a letter for its method of propulsion: e=electric. David Miller, *U-Boats: The Illustrated History of the Raiders of the Deep* (Washington DC: Brasseys, 2000), pp. 86–7.

74. Eberhard Rössler, *Die Torpedos der deutschen U-Boote* (Hamburg: Mittler, 2005), p. 69. See also: Anthony Newpower, *Iron Men and Tin Fish: The Race to Build a Better Torpedo during World War II* (Westport, CT: Praeger, 2006), p. 38.

75. Lawrence Paterson, *Hitler's Grey Wolves: U-Boats in the Indian Ocean* (Barnsley: Frontline, 2016) Kindle Edition. Locs. 1908, 1968.

76. Lawrence Paterson, *Hitler's Grey Wolves: U-Boats in the Indian Ocean* (Barnsley: Frontline, 2016) Kindle Edition. Loc 1983. The manifold problems encountered in attempting to operate German submarines in Asia are detailed in 'Deutsche U-Boote in asiatischen Gewässern', which forms Chapter 25 of: Jochen Brennecke, *Jäger-Gejagte: Deutsche U-Boote 1939–1945* (Herford: Koehler, 1956), pp. 306–14.

77. Commander C R Sanders USNR (Trans.), *War Diary: German Naval Staff Operations Division, Part A, Volume 47, July 1943* (Washington DC: Department of the Navy, Office of the Chief of Naval Operations, Naval History Division, 1958), p. 9.

78. Interrogation report of Günter Schmidt. Admiralty Naval Intelligence Division, C B 04051 (90), U 533 Interrogation of Survivors December, 1943, p. 8. Available at: http://www.uboatarchive.net/U-470A/U-470-533INT.htm

79. Jochen Brennecke, *Haie im Paradies: Der Deutsche U-Boot-Krieg in Asiens Gewässern 1943–45* (Herford: Koehler, 1967), pp. 83, 84, 94. Horst H. Geerken, *Hitlers Griff nach Asien: Das Dritte Reich und Niederländisch-Indien. Aufbau deutscher Marinestu?tzpunkte Eine Dokumentation, Band I* (Norderstedt: BoD-Books on Demand, 2015), p. 316.

80. Ashley Jackson, *War and Empire in Mauritius and the Indian Ocean* (Houndmills: Palgrave, 2001), p. 45.

81. Major-General S. Woodburn Kirby, Captain C. T. Addis, Brigadier M. R. Roberts, Colonel G. T. Wards and Air Vice-Marshal N. L. Desoer, *History of the Second World War: The War Against Japan, Volume III: The Decisive Battles* (London: HMSO, 1961) Kindle Edition, Locs. 7427–7434.

82. Quoted in: Arthur J. Marder, Mark Jacobsen and John Horsefield, *Old Friends New Enemies, the Royal Navy and the Imperial Japanese Navy Volume II: The Pacific War, 1942–1945* (Oxford: Clarendon, 1990), p. 293. n. 55.

83. Arthur J. Marder, Mark Jacobsen and John Horsefield, *Old Friends New Enemies, the Royal Navy and the Imperial Japanese Navy Volume II: The Pacific War, 1942–1945* (Oxford: Clarendon, 1990), p. 251.

84. Richard M. Leighton, 'US Merchant Shipping and the British Import Crisis', in Kent Roberts Greenfield (ed.), *Command Decisions* (Washington DC: Office of the Chief of Military History Department of the Army, 1960), p. 206.

85. Lance Brennan, Les Heathcote and Anton Lucas, 'War and Famine around the Indian Ocean during the Second World War', in Michael Schwartz, Howard Harris and Debra R. Comer (eds), *Ethics in the Global South: Research in Ethical Issues in Organizations, Volume 18* (Bingley: Emerald, 2017), pp. 5–6.

86. Lance Brennan, Les Heathcote and Anton Lucas, 'War and Famine around the Indian Ocean during the Second World War', in Michael Schwartz, Howard Harris and Debra R. Comer (eds), *Ethics in the Global South: Research in Ethical Issues in Organizations, Volume 18* (Bingley: Emerald, 2017), p. 63.

87. Madhusree Mukerjee, *Churchill's Secret War: The British Empire and the Ravaging of India during World War II* (Philadelphia, PA: Basic, 2011), p. 209.

88. Wavell to Secretary of State for India and Prime Minister, 9 February 1944. In: Penderel Moon (ed.), *Wavell: The Viceroy's Journal* (London: Oxford University Press, 1973), pp. 54–5.

89. Sugata Bose, 'Starvation amidst Plenty: The making of Famine in Bengal, Honan and Tonkin, 1942–1945', in *Modern Asian Studies*, Vol. 24, No. 4, October 1990, p. 701.

90. Scholars differ somewhat on the number of famine-related deaths. Sen puts it at 'around 3 million'. Greenough calculates it as being higher, between 3.5 and 3.8 million. Amartya Sen, *Poverty and Famines: An Essay on Entitlement and Deprivation* (Oxford: Clarendon, 1981), p. 215. Paul R. Greenough, *Prosperity and Misery in Modern Bengal: The Famine of 1943–44* (New York: Oxford University Press, 1982), pp. 299–309.

91. Memorandum by the Secretary of State [Cordell Hull] to President Roosevelt, Washington, May 31, 1944. Department of State, *Foreign Relations of the United States: Diplomatic Papers, 1944, The Near East, South Asia, And Africa, The Far East, Volume V* (Washington DC: US Government Printing Office, 1965), p. 273. Available online at: https://history.state.gov/historicaldocuments/frus1944v05/d281

92. Amartya Sen, *Poverty and Famines: An Essay on Entitlement and Deprivation* (Oxford: Clarendon, 1981), p. 78.
93. Kevin Smith, *Conflict over Convoys: Anglo-American Logistics Diplomacy in the Second World War* (Cambridge: Cambridge University Press, 1996), p. 157.
94. Amery to Wavell, 17 February. Quoted in David Whittington, 'An Imperialist at Bay: Leo Amery at The India Office, 1940–1945'. A thesis submitted in part fulfilment of the requirements of the University of the West of England, Bristol, for the Degree of Doctor of Philosophy, p. 291. Available from: http://eprints.uwe.ac.uk/26374

Chapter 12

1. Vice Admiral Eastern Fleet, War Diary: 15 December 1943 to 31 January 1944. Available from: https://www.naval-history.net/xDKWD-EF1943Dec-Apr1944.htm?_sm_au_=iVVVr3sMTsF2S3fF
2. David Hobbs, *British Aircraft Carriers: Design, Development and Service Histories* (Barnsley: Seaforth, 2013), pp. 225–9. *Unicorn* provided air cover for the Allied landings at Salerno, Italy, in early September 1943. See: Edgar Hibbert, *The Versatile Air Repair Ship HMS Unicorn* (Ilfracombe: Stockwell, 2006).
3. Viscount Cunningham of Hyndhope, *A Sailor's Odyssey: The Autobiography of Admiral of the Fleet Viscount Cunningham of Hyndhope* (New York: Dutton, 1951), p. 527.
4. Major-General S. Woodburn Kirby, Captain C. T. Addis, Brigadier M. R. Roberts, Colonel G. T. Wards and Air Vice-Marshal N. L. Desoer, *History of the Second World War: The War Against Japan, Volume III: The Decisive Battles* (London: HMSO, 1961) Kindle Edition, Loc. 7453.
5. Dieter Jung, Martin Maass, Berndt Wenzel, Arno Abendroth and Norbert Kelling, *Tanker und Versorger der deutschen Flotte 1900–1980* (Stuttgart; Motorbuch, 1981).
6. David Kohnen, 'The Cruise of U-188: Special Intelligence and the "Liquidation" of Group Monsoon, 1943–1944', in Marcus Faulkner and Christopher M. Bell (eds), *Decision in the Atlantic: The Allies and the Longest Campaign of the Second World War* (Lexington, KY: Andarta, 2019), p. 276.
7. UK National Archives. ADM 199/1388. Eastern Fleet: War Diaries, 1944. A. D. Read, Rear Admiral Commanding Fourth Cruiser Squadron to Commander-in-Chief, Eastern Fleet. 18 February 1944. No. 40S/03B. 'Report on Operation 'Canned', p. 4.
8. Günther Hessler, *The U-boat War in the Atlantic, 1939–1945, Volume III* [three volumes in one]: *June 1943–May 1945* (London: HMSO, 1989), p. 61. Hessler wrote the work at the behest of the British Admiralty between 1947–1951. *Charlotte Schlieman* was sunk at a position roughly some 1,000 miles east of Mauritius, about 1,600 miles from Madagascar and about 2,400 miles from Australia.
9. National Security Agency/National Cryptologic Museum, Special Research History (SRH) SRH-008: 'Battle of the Atlantic, Vol. II: U-boat operations in the Indian Ocean and the Far East', p. 237. Available online at: https://www.ibiblio.org/hyperwar/ETO/Ultra/SRH-008/SRH008-14.html
10. As well as the destroyers, the escort consisted of the *Hawkins* class heavy cruiser *Hawkins*, the *Banff* class sloops *Lulworth* and *Sennen* (formerly the US 'Lake' class Coastguard cutters *Chelan* and *Champlain* respectively) and the 'Flower' class corvette *Honesty*.
11. Somerville Desk Diary entry 14 February 1944. In Michael Simpson (ed.), *The Somerville Papers: Selections from the Private and Official Correspondence of Admiral of the Fleet Sir James Somerville, GCB, GBE, DSO* (London: Scolar, 1995), p. 516.

12. 'The simplest text is often the most revealing and the . . . list of female nurses killed . . . tells the reader a very great deal. It serves as a reminder that even though the war at sea was a predominantly male enterprise, several hundred women were killed as a result of naval action between 1939 and 1945.' G. H. Bennett, 'Women and the Battle of the Atlantic 1939–45: Contemporary Texts, Propaganda and Life Writing', in Angela K. Smith (ed.), *Gender and Warfare in the Twentieth Century: Textual Representations* (Manchester: Manchester University, 2004), p. 111. The best account of the episode is undoubtedly: Brian James Crabb, *Passage to Destiny. The Sinking of the S.S. Khedive Ismail in the Sea War against Japan* (Stamford: Paul Watkins, 1997).

13. David Kohnen, 'The Cruise of U-188: Special Intelligence and the "Liquidation" of Group Monsoon, 1943–1944', in Marcus Faulkner and Christopher M Bell (eds), *Decision in the Atlantic: The Allies and the Longest Campaign of the Second World War* (Lexington, KY: Andarta, 2019), p. 276.

14. Ronald Lewin, *Ultra Goes to War* (New York: McGraw-Hill, 1978), p. 212.

15. John Winton, *Ultra at Sea: How Breaking the Nazi Code Affected Allied Naval Strategy During World War II* (New York: William Morrow, 1988), p. 195. David Syrett (ed.), *The Battle of the Atlantic and Signals Intelligence: U-Boat Situations and Trends, 1941–1945* (Aldershot: Ashgate, 2002), p. 261. The Allied development of airborne radar and the successes aircraft so equipped had against U-boats in nocturnal transit across the Bay of Biscay in June 1942, had led the Germans to develop a radar-detection device named Metox (known to the Allies as German Search Receiver or GSR). This, which as the name suggests detected the output of the Mark II radar sets, was relatively simple and highly successful; by September 1942 most U-boats were equipped with Metox. Successful aerial attacks diminished in number. Allied technological progress was, however, relentless and new, improved radar equipment was put into operational service in early 1943. Dubbed Mark III, it operated on a wavelength that didn't register on the Metox detector; the number of successful attacks increased greatly. This convinced the Germans that Allied aircraft were using some new detection device, which indeed they were, but for a number of reasons they jumped to the conclusion that it was the Metox itself that was being homed in on. The result, as *Leutnant zur See* Herbert Werner aboard *U-230* recalled, 'had a greater impact on our lives than any since the beginning of the Allied offensive'. He was referring to the message received on 3 August 1943 from U-boat Headquarters: 'All U-Boats. Attention. All U-Boats. Shut off Metox at once. Enemy is capable of intercepting. Keep radio silence until further notice.' See: Martin W. Bowman, *Deep Sea Hunters: RAF Coastal Command and the War against the U-Boats and the German Navy 1939–1945* (Barnsley: Pen & Sword, 2014), pp. 58, 80 n. 24. Don E. Gordon, *Electronic Warfare: Element of Strategy and Multiplier of Combat Power* (New York: Pergamon, 1981), pp. 69–70. Philip M. Morse and George E. Kimball, *Methods of Operations Research* (Mineola, NY: Dover, 2003), p. 96. Azriel Lorberp, *Misguided Weapons: Technological Failure and Surprise on the Battlefield* (Washington DC: Potomac, 2002), p. 121. Herbert A. Werner, *Iron Coffins: A Personal Account of the German U-boat Battles of World War II* (New York: Holt, Rinehart and Winston, 1969), p. 152.

16. Major-General S. Woodburn Kirby, Captain C. T. Addis, Brigadier M. R. Roberts, Colonel G. T. Wards and Air Vice-Marshal N. L. Desoer, *History of the Second World War: The War Against Japan, Volume III: The Decisive Battles* (London: HMSO, 1961) Kindle Edition, Loc. 7473.

17. US Intelligence identified the battleships *Nagato*, *Kongo*, *Haruna*, *Yamashiro*, *Fuso*, *Hyuga* and *Ise*, plus the carriers *Shokaku* and *Zuikaku*. Arthur J. Marder, Mark Jacobsen and John Horsefield, *Old Friends New Enemies, the Royal Navy and the Imperial Japanese Navy Volume II: The Pacific War, 1942–1945* (Oxford: Clarendon, 1990), p. 286. Somerville Desk Diary entry 22 and 23 February 1944'. In Michael Simpson (ed.), *The Somerville Papers: Selections from the Private and Official Correspondence of Admiral of the Fleet Sir James Somerville, GCB, GBE, DSO* (London: Scolar, 1995), pp. 518–19.

18. Somerville Desk Diary entry 22 February 1944. In Michael Simpson (ed.), *The Somerville Papers: Selections from the Private and Official Correspondence of Admiral of the Fleet Sir James Somerville, GCB, GBE, DSO* (London: Scolar, 1995), p. 519.

19. W. J. Hudson, Barbara Kelly, Ashton Robinson and Wendy Way (eds), *Documents on Australian Foreign Policy, 1937–49, Volume VII* (Canberra: Australian Government Publishing Service), p. 143.

20. W. J. Hudson, Barbara Kelly, Ashton Robinson and Wendy Way (eds), *Documents on Australian Foreign Policy, 1937–49, Volume VII* (Canberra: Australian Government Publishing Service), p. 143. See also: Churchill Archives Centre, Churchill College, Cambridge. CHAR 20: Official: Prime Minister, 1940–1945. CHAR 20/158 Churchill to Prime Ministers of Australia and New Zealand 3 March 1944. The various British deliberations around the matter are contained in: UK National Archives. PREM 3/164/1 'Move of Japanese fleet to Singapore' February-April 1944. See also: Geoffrey Till, 'Churchill, Strategy and the Fall of Singapore', in Brian P. Farrell (ed.), *Churchill and the Lion City: Shaping Modern Singapore* (Singapore: NUS, 2011), p. 97.

21. Samuel Eliot Morison, *History of United States Naval Operations in World War II Volume 7: Aleutians, Gilberts and Marshalls, June 1942 – April 1944* (Boston, MA: Little, Brown, 1951), p. 315. The three Task Groups were made up of: TG 58.1: *Enterprise* (CV-6), *Yorktown* (CV-10) and *Belleau Wood* (CVL-24); TG 58.2: *Essex* (CV-9), *Intrepid* (CV-11) and *Cabot* (CVL-28); and TG 58.3: *Bunker Hill* (CV-17), *Monterey* (CVL-26) and *Cowpens* (CVL-25). See pp. 315–32 of Morison for a full account of the operation.

22. Somerville Desk Diary entry 24 February 1944. In Michael Simpson (ed.), *The Somerville Papers: Selections from the Private and Official Correspondence of Admiral of the Fleet Sir James Somerville, GCB, GBE, DSO* (London: Scolar, 1995), p. 521.

23. See: 'CHAPTER XXV, The Build Up of British Submarines in the Far East: January – September 1944', in Vice Admiral Sir Arthur Hezlet, *British and Allied Submarine Operations in World War II, Volume 1* (Gosport: Royal Navy Submarine Museum, 2001). Available online at: https://www.rnsubmusfriends.org.uk/hezlet/volume1/volume1.htm

24. Somerville Desk Diary entry 25 February 1944. In Michael Simpson (ed.), *The Somerville Papers: Selections from the Private and Official Correspondence of Admiral of the Fleet Sir James Somerville, GCB, GBE, DSO* (London: Scolar, 1995), p. 521.

25. George E. Melton, *Darlan: Admiral and Statesman of France 1881–1942* (Westport, CT: Praeger, 1998), pp. 189–222.

26. Somerville Desk Diary entry 10 March 1944. In Michael Simpson (ed.), *The Somerville Papers: Selections from the Private and Official Correspondence of Admiral of the Fleet Sir James Somerville, GCB, GBE, DSO* (London: Scolar, 1995), p. 528. A PWSS was a Port War Signal Station. It was via one of these installations that the movements of all shipping in and out of a harbour were monitored and controlled. For the *Richelieu* see: Robert Dumas, *Le cuirasse Richelieu 1935–1968* (Bourg-en-Bresse: Marines Éditions & Réalisations, 1992), pp. 37, 50. John Jordan and Robert Dumas, *French Battleships 1922–1956* (Barnsley: Seaforth, 2009), p. 192.

27. The genesis of the idea came in a memorandum of 7 September 1943 written by the admiral. Following the unseating of *Il Duce*, de Courten had been appointed Minister of the Navy in the government of *Maresciallo d'Italia* Pietro Badoglio. His missive proposed that the Allies should be approached and offered the use of the three modern battleships of the *Littorio* (or *Vittorio Veneto*) class, *Vittorio Veneto*, *Roma* and *Italia* (the latter being the renamed *Littorio*), for use against Japan in the Far East. Whilst the armistice with Italy had brought the fleet into play as a political factor, the question of actually utilizing two of these fast battleships, with Italian crews, was seriously contemplated by the Allies. That there were only two to consider came about because the third, *Roma*, had been sent to the bottom on 9 September 1943 in the Strait of Bonifacio between Sardinia and Corsica. The Germans, rather emulating the British at Mers-el-Kébir three years earlier, sent the Luftwaffe to attack their former ally; *Roma* was hit by two 'Fritz-X' guided anti-ship glide bombs and sank after her magazines exploded. *Italia/Littorio* was also hit but survived. The offer was, however, ultimately rejected, with practical grounds being the reason most often quoted. Francesco Mattesini, 'L'armistizio dell'8 settembre 1943, parte 1', in *Bollettino d'Archivio dell'Ufficio Storico della Marina Militare*, giugno 1993, pp. 57–8. See also: Francesco Mattesini, 'Da Cobelligeranti ad Alleati?: La Regia Marina e la dichiarazione di guerra al Giappone', in Antonio Nacca (Progetto grafico e realizzazione), *Rimland: Storia Militare di una Penisola Eurasiatica, Tomo II: Suez* (Roma: Società Italiana di Storia Militare, 2019), pp. 447–62. Raffaele de Courten, *Le memorie dell'Ammiraglio De Courten (1943–1946)* (Roma: Ufficio Storico della Marina Militare, 1993). Ermingo Bagnasco and Augusto de Toro, *The Littorio Class: Italy's Last and Largest Battleships* (Barnsley: Seaforth, 2011), p. 270. Martin J. Bollinger, *Warriors and Wizards: The Development and Defeat of Radio-Controlled Glide Bombs of the Third Reich* (Annapolis, MD: Naval Institute Press, 2010), p. 30.
28. Barbara Stahura, *USS Saratoga: CV-3 & CVA/CV-60* (Paducah, KY: Turner, 2003), p. 23.
29. Ian Cameron, *Wings of the Morning: The British Fleet Air Arm in World War II* (New York: Morrow, 1963), p. 256.
30. Somerville Desk Diary entry 15 March 1944. In Michael Simpson (ed.), *The Somerville Papers: Selections from the Private and Official Correspondence of Admiral of the Fleet Sir James Somerville, GCB, GBE, DSO* (London: Scolar, 1995), p. 530.
31. John Fry, *USS Saratoga CV-3: An Illustrated History of the Legendary Aircraft Carrier 1927–1946* (Atglen, PA: Schiffer, 1996), p. 137.
32. Clark G. Reynolds, *The Fast Carriers: The Forging of an Air Navy* (Annapolis, MD: Naval Institute Press, 2013), p. 308.
33. Clark G. Reynolds, *The Fast Carriers: The Forging of an Air Navy* (Annapolis, MD: Naval Institute Press, 2013), p. 308.
34. Clark G. Reynolds, *The Fast Carriers: The Forging of an Air Navy* (Annapolis, MD: Naval Institute Press, 2013), p. 308. This was not the first time that RN and USN carriers, in particular *Saratoga*, had worked together. Between November 1942 and September 1943 the Admiralty had 'lent' the carrier *Victorious* to the American Navy in an effort to assist the latter following the losses occasioned to the carriers *Hornet* (sunk) and *Enterprise* (badly damaged) during the Battle of Santa Cruz in the Solomon Islands between 25–27 October 1942. *Victorious* and *Saratoga* formed Task Force 14, which fought in the campaigns in New Georgia under Admiral William F. Halsey. The files pertaining to this deployment can be found in: UK National Archives. ADM 199/534. 'Special operations: reports of proceedings by HM ships and vessels. 1940–1944'.

35. Somerville Desk Diary entry 15 March 1944. In Michael Simpson (ed.), *The Somerville Papers: Selections from the Private and Official Correspondence of Admiral of the Fleet Sir James Somerville, GCB, GBE, DSO* (London: Scolar, 1995), p. 530.

36. John Prados, *Combined Fleet Decoded: The Secret History of American Intelligence and the Japanese Navy in World War II* (New York: Random House, 1995), p. 547.

37. Somerville Desk Diary entry 02 April 1944. In Michael Simpson (ed.), *The Somerville Papers: Selections from the Private and Official Correspondence of Admiral of the Fleet Sir James Somerville, GCB, GBE, DSO* (London: Scolar, 1995), p. 536. The 'doldrums' quote is by Simpson and is on p. 380.

38. Arthur J. Marder, Mark Jacobsen and John Horsefield, *Old Friends New Enemies, the Royal Navy and the Imperial Japanese Navy Volume II: The Pacific War, 1942–1945* (Oxford: Clarendon, 1990), p. 306.

39. Douglas Ford, *Britain's Secret War Against Japan, 1937–1945* (London: Routledge, 2011), p. 139.

40. Arthur J. Marder, Mark Jacobsen and John Horsefield, *Old Friends New Enemies, the Royal Navy and the Imperial Japanese Navy Volume II: The Pacific War, 1942–1945* (Oxford: Clarendon, 1990), pp. 555–6.

41. Somerville Desk Diary entry 12 March 1944. In Michael Simpson (ed.), *The Somerville Papers: Selections from the Private and Official Correspondence of Admiral of the Fleet Sir James Somerville, GCB, GBE, DSO* (London: Scolar, 1995), p. 529.

42. Douglas Ford, *Britain's Secret War Against Japan, 1937–1945* (London: Routledge, 2011), p. 139.

43. Power. Diary entry. 30 May 1944. Quoted in: Arthur J. Marder, Mark Jacobsen and John Horsefield, *Old Friends New Enemies, the Royal Navy and the Imperial Japanese Navy Volume II: The Pacific War, 1942–1945* (Oxford: Clarendon, 1990), p. 291.

44. Part of the solution to this was the mobilization of womanpower: 'The extent of the mobilization of women which followed was far greater than that which had taken place in Britain in the First World War and far exceeded the use of womanpower in other nations involved in the Second World War. By September 1943 some 7,258,000 women, or 46 per cent of those between the ages of 14 and 59, were engaged in some form of national service. Virtually all able-bodied single women between the ages of 18 and 40 (90 per cent), as well as most of those in this age group who were married but had no children (80 per cent), were involved in the war effort. By the middle of 1943 women comprised 35.4 per cent of the labour force in the vital engineering industry.' Harold L. Smith, 'The Womanpower Problem in Britain during the Second World War', in *The Historical Journal*, Vol. 27, No. 4, December 1984, p. 934.

45. Somerville Desk Diary entry 11 April 1944. In Michael Simpson (ed.), *The Somerville Papers: Selections from the Private and Official Correspondence of Admiral of the Fleet Sir James Somerville, GCB, GBE, DSO* (London: Scolar, 1995), p. 542.

46. UK National Archives. WO 203/4621. 'Operation "Cockpit" Air Bombardment of Sabang 19 April 1944: Operation Order and Reports'. May 1944. This section is based on these reports unless otherwise stated.

47. Stuart Eadon (ed.), *Kamikaze: The Story of the British Pacific Fleet* (Bristol: Crecy, 1995), p. 126.

48. Somerville Desk Diary entry 16 April 1944. In Michael Simpson (ed.), *The Somerville Papers: Selections from the Private and Official Correspondence of Admiral of the Fleet Sir James Somerville, GCB, GBE, DSO* (London: Scolar, 1995), p. 544.

49. Somerville Desk Diary entry 17 April 1944. In Michael Simpson (ed.), *The Somerville Papers: Selections from the Private and Official Correspondence of Admiral of the Fleet Sir James Somerville, GCB, GBE, DSO* (London: Scolar, 1995), p. 544.

50. Somerville Desk Diary entry 17 April 1944. In Michael Simpson (ed.), *The Somerville Papers: Selections from the Private and Official Correspondence of Admiral of the Fleet Sir James Somerville, GCB, GBE, DSO* (London: Scolar, 1995), p. 545.

51. Somerville Desk Diary entry 18 April 1944. In Michael Simpson (ed.), *The Somerville Papers: Selections from the Private and Official Correspondence of Admiral of the Fleet Sir James Somerville, GCB, GBE, DSO* (London: Scolar, 1995), p. 545.

52. The maximum bomb load of the Barracuda was circa 2,000lb; reducing it obviously increased the aircraft's range. Matthew Willis, *The Fairey Barracuda* (Petersfield: MMP, 2016).

53. S. D. Waters, *The Royal New Zealand Navy* (Wellington: War History Branch Department of Internal Affairs, 1956), p. 358.

54. Prime Minister to First Lord and First Sea Lord. 29 April 1944. Winston S. Churchill, *The Second World War Volume V: Closing the Ring* (London: Reprint Society, 1954), p. 543. Sabang was about 600 miles from Singapore.

55. Somerville Desk Diary entry 24 April 1944. In Michael Simpson (ed.), *The Somerville Papers: Selections from the Private and Official Correspondence of Admiral of the Fleet Sir James Somerville, GCB, GBE, DSO* (London: Scolar, 1995), p. 547.

56. Donald Macintyre, *Fighting Admiral: The life of Admiral of the Fleet Sir James Somerville* (London: Evans Brothers, 1961), p. 249.

57. David Wragg, *The Escort Carrier in the Second World War: Combustible, Vulnerable, Expendable!* (Barnsley: Pen & Sword, 2005), p. 157.

58. Somerville Desk Diary entry 24 April 1944. In Michael Simpson (ed.), *The Somerville Papers: Selections from the Private and Official Correspondence of Admiral of the Fleet Sir James Somerville, GCB, GBE, DSO* (London: Scolar, 1995), p. 547.

59. Somerville Desk Diary entry 21 April 1944. In Michael Simpson (ed.), *The Somerville Papers: Selections from the Private and Official Correspondence of Admiral of the Fleet Sir James Somerville, GCB, GBE, DSO* (London: Scolar, 1995), p. 547. See: UK National Archives. WO 203/4767. 'Operation "Transom" Air bombardment of Sourabaya: planning and operational orders: report of operation'. June 1944.

60. Arthur J. Marder, Mark Jacobsen and John Horsefield, *Old Friends New Enemies, the Royal Navy and the Imperial Japanese Navy Volume II: The Pacific War, 1942–1945* (Oxford: Clarendon, 1990), p. 309. Somerville Desk Diary entry 22 April 1944. In Michael Simpson (ed.), *The Somerville Papers: Selections from the Private and Official Correspondence of Admiral of the Fleet Sir James Somerville, GCB, GBE, DSO* (London: Scolar, 1995), p. 547.

61. Somerville Desk Diary entry 22 April 1944. In Michael Simpson (ed.), *The Somerville Papers: Selections from the Private and Official Correspondence of Admiral of the Fleet Sir James Somerville, GCB, GBE, DSO* (London: Scolar, 1995), p. 547.

62. Lester Abbey, *Iowa Class Battleships* (Barnsley: Seaforth, 2012), p. 6.

63. Somerville Desk Diary entry 22 April 1944. In Michael Simpson (ed.), *The Somerville Papers: Selections from the Private and Official Correspondence of Admiral of the Fleet Sir James Somerville, GCB, GBE, DSO* (London: Scolar, 1995), p. 547.

64. See: http://www.historicalrfa.org/

65. Vice-Admiral Eastern Fleet – War Diary – January to April 1944. Available at: https://www.naval-history.net/xDKWD-EF1943Dec-Apr1944.htm

66. 'Report of Senior U.S. Naval Liaison Officer with British Eastern Fleet on Strike on Surabaya by Force 66 on 17 May 1944', p. 8. Available at: http://www.armouredcarriers.com/-liaison-report
67. Somerville Desk Diary entries 16–17 May 1944. In Michael Simpson (ed.), *The Somerville Papers: Selections from the Private and Official Correspondence of Admiral of the Fleet Sir James Somerville, GCB, GBE, DSO* (London: Scolar, 1995), pp. 555–6.
68. Somerville to General MacArthur, circa 19 May 1944. In Michael Simpson (ed.), *The Somerville Papers: Selections from the Private and Official Correspondence of Admiral of the Fleet Sir James Somerville, GCB, GBE, DSO* (London: Scolar, 1995), p. 558.
69. Clark G. Reynolds, *The Fast Carriers: The Forging of an Air Navy* (Annapolis, MD: Naval Institute Press, 2013), p. 311.
70. Somerville to General MacArthur, circa 19 May 1944. In Michael Simpson (ed.), *The Somerville Papers: Selections from the Private and Official Correspondence of Admiral of the Fleet Sir James Somerville, GCB, GBE, DSO* (London: Scolar, 1995), p. 558.
71. 'Ten per cent of the Japanese high octane gasoline supply was destroyed.' United States Navy, Carrier Air Group 12 (CVG-12) USN Air 1207 October 1945. 'This History records the activity of CVG-12 whilst embarked in The USS Saratoga (CV-3) and the USS Randolph (CV-15)', p. 10. Available at: http://www.missingaircrew.com/pdf/vf12history.pdf
72. Somerville Desk Diary entry 17 May 1944. In Michael Simpson (ed.), *The Somerville Papers: Selections from the Private and Official Correspondence of Admiral of the Fleet Sir James Somerville, GCB, GBE, DSO* (London: Scolar, 1995), p. 556. The damage inflicted was compounded later that night when seven B-24 Liberator bombers of the 380th Bombardment Group (Heavy) of the 5th Air Force (but attached to the RAAF), based at Corunna Downs Airfield north of Perth, Australia, made a follow-up attack. They dropped 'demolition bombs which added to the fires and destruction left by the carrier force earlier in the day'. George Odgers, *Australia in the War of 1939–1945 Series Three Air Volume II: Air War against Japan 1943–1945* (Canberra: Australian War Memorial, 1968), p. 230. See also: Maurer Maurer (ed.), *Air Force Combat Units of World War II* (Washington DC: Office of Air Force History, 1983), p. 267.
73. Somerville Desk Diary entry 17 May 1944. In Michael Simpson (ed.), *The Somerville Papers: Selections from the Private and Official Correspondence of Admiral of the Fleet Sir James Somerville, GCB, GBE, DSO* (London: Scolar, 1995), p. 556.
74. Michael Simpson (ed.), *The Somerville Papers: Selections from the Private and Official Correspondence of Admiral of the Fleet Sir James Somerville, GCB, GBE, DSO* (London: Scolar, 1995), pp. 378–9.
75. Somerville to General MacArthur, circa 19 May 1944. In Michael Simpson (ed.), *The Somerville Papers: Selections from the Private and Official Correspondence of Admiral of the Fleet Sir James Somerville, GCB, GBE, DSO* (London: Scolar, 1995), p. 558.
76. Somerville to General MacArthur, circa 19 May 1944. In Michael Simpson (ed.), *The Somerville Papers: Selections from the Private and Official Correspondence of Admiral of the Fleet Sir James Somerville, GCB, GBE, DSO* (London: Scolar, 1995), p. 558.
77. Somerville Desk Diary entry 20 May 1944. In Michael Simpson (ed.), *The Somerville Papers: Selections from the Private and Official Correspondence of Admiral of the Fleet Sir James Somerville, GCB, GBE, DSO* (London: Scolar, 1995), p. 559.
78. Somerville Desk Diary entry 28 May 1944. In Michael Simpson (ed.), *The Somerville Papers: Selections from the Private and Official Correspondence of Admiral of the Fleet Sir James Somerville, GCB, GBE, DSO* (London: Scolar, 1995), p. 561.

79. David Wragg, *The Escort Carrier in the Second World War: Combustible, Vulnerable, Expendable!* (Barnsley: Pen & Sword, 2005), p. 157.
80. Somerville Desk Diary entry 12 June 1944. In Michael Simpson (ed.), *The Somerville Papers: Selections from the Private and Official Correspondence of Admiral of the Fleet Sir James Somerville, GCB, GBE, DSO* (London: Scolar, 1995), p. 564.
81. UK National Archives. ADM 223/629. 'Operation Councillor'. 1944. This section is based on these reports unless otherwise stated.
82. Somerville Desk Diary entry 19 June 1944. In Michael Simpson (ed.), *The Somerville Papers: Selections from the Private and Official Correspondence of Admiral of the Fleet Sir James Somerville, GCB, GBE, DSO* (London: Scolar, 1995), p. 565. David Hobbs, *The British Pacific Fleet: The Royal Navy's Most Powerful Strike Force* (Barnsley: Seaforth, 2011), p. 49.
83. Somerville Desk Diary entry 30 May 1944. In Michael Simpson (ed.), *The Somerville Papers: Selections from the Private and Official Correspondence of Admiral of the Fleet Sir James Somerville, GCB, GBE, DSO* (London: Scolar, 1995), p. 561.
84. Somerville Desk Diary entry 23 June 1944. In Michael Simpson (ed.), *The Somerville Papers: Selections from the Private and Official Correspondence of Admiral of the Fleet Sir James Somerville, GCB, GBE, DSO* (London: Scolar, 1995), p. 566.
85. Somerville Desk Diary entry 22 June 1944. In Michael Simpson (ed.), *The Somerville Papers: Selections from the Private and Official Correspondence of Admiral of the Fleet Sir James Somerville, GCB, GBE, DSO* (London: Scolar, 1995), pp. 565–6. David Hobbs, *The British Pacific Fleet: The Royal Navy's Most Powerful Strike Force* (Barnsley: Seaforth, 2011), p. 50.
86. Somerville Desk Diary entry 23 June 1944. In Michael Simpson (ed.), *The Somerville Papers: Selections from the Private and Official Correspondence of Admiral of the Fleet Sir James Somerville, GCB, GBE, DSO* (London: Scolar, 1995), p. 566.
87. Somerville Desk Diary entry 7 July 1944. In Michael Simpson (ed.), *The Somerville Papers: Selections from the Private and Official Correspondence of Admiral of the Fleet Sir James Somerville, GCB, GBE, DSO* (London: Scolar, 1995), p. 570.
88. UK National Archives. WO 203/4622. 'Operation "Crimson" surface bombardment of Sabang 25 July 1944: Operation Orders and Reports'. August 1944. This section is based on these reports unless otherwise stated.
89. Somerville Desk Diary entry 25 July 1944. In Michael Simpson (ed.), *The Somerville Papers: Selections from the Private and Official Correspondence of Admiral of the Fleet Sir James Somerville, GCB, GBE, DSO* (London: Scolar, 1995), p. 575.
90. The official Allied reporting name for the Mitsubishi A6M Zero.
91. Dated 25 July 1944 to his wife. In Michael Simpson (ed.), *The Somerville Papers: Selections from the Private and Official Correspondence of Admiral of the Fleet Sir James Somerville, GCB, GBE, DSO* (London: Scolar, 1995), pp. 577–8.
92. Trumbull Higgins, *Winston Churchill and the Second Front, 1940–1943* (New York: Oxford University Press, 1957), p. 200. Though this book is a study of the Allied decision to invade North Africa in 1942, rather than to make an early direct assault on Nazi forces across the English Channel, the point made has wider applicability.
93. Clark G. Reynolds, *The Fast Carriers: The Forging of an Air Navy* (Annapolis, MD: Naval Institute Press, 2013), p. 193.
94. Samuel Eliot Morison, *History of United States Naval Operations in World War II Volume 8: New Guinea and the Marianas March 1944 – August 1944* (Boston, MA: Little, Brown, 1953), pp. 152–3. Toshiyuki Yokoi, 'Thoughts on Japan's Naval Defeat' in

David C. Evans (ed.), *The Japanese Navy in World War II: In the Words of Former Japanese Naval Officers* (Annapolis, MD: Naval Institute Press, 1986), p. 515. See also: William T. Y'Blood, *Red Sun Setting: The Battle of the Philippine Sea* (Annapolis, MD: Naval Institute Press, 1981); Mark Stille, *The Philippine Sea 1944: The Last Great Carrier Battle* (Oxford: Osprey, 2017).

95. Samuel Eliot Morison, *History of United States Naval Operations in World War II Volume 8: New Guinea and the Marianas, March 1944–August 1944* (Boston, MA: Little, Brown, 1953), p. 34.

96. Wesley Frank Craven and James Lea Gate, *The Army Air Forces in World War II, Volume Four: The Pacific, Guadalcanal to Saipan August 1943 to July 1944* (Washington DC: Office of Air Force History, 1983), p. 587.

97. George C. Kenney, *General Kenney Reports: A Personal History of the Pacific War* (New York: Duell, Sloan and Pearce, 1949), pp. 380–1.

98. Samuel Eliot Morison, *History of United States Naval Operations in World War II Volume 8: New Guinea and the Marianas, March 1944–August 1944* (Boston, MA: Little, Brown, 1953), p. 36. The shortage of aircraft also bedevilled the Japanese Army's Operation U-Go, an attack on Assam in India of early March 1944. This was a major offensive that involved the Allied Fourteenth Army in desperate fighting at Kohima and Imphal and which did not end until July 1944. According to Japanese officers: 'In the fall of 1942 the enemy air force gradually took the offensive in Burma and showed signs of growing rapidly. In contrast, Japanese air power in Burma had dwindled. There had been a considerable force, with the 5th Air Division as the main body. However, with the aggravation of the war situation in the Southeast Pacific area, the 12th Air Brigade (1st and 11th Air Regiments) was transferred to the Southeast Pacific in January 1943 and the 14th Air Regiment was transferred there in February of the same year. This caused a gradual deceleration of air operations against eastern India and Kunming. With enemy air attacks directed mainly on military establishments in Rangoon, Toungoo, Mandalay and Maymyo, the air defense of strategic points in Burma became a matter of grave concern to the Japanese army.' Headquarters United States Army Japan, *Japanese Monograph No. 134: Burma Operations Record; 15th Army Operations in Imphal Area and Withdrawal to Northern Burma* (No Place: Office of the Chief of Military History Department of the Army, 1957), p. 5.

99. Dated 25 July 1944 to his wife. In Michael Simpson (ed.), *The Somerville Papers: Selections from the Private and Official Correspondence of Admiral of the Fleet Sir James Somerville, GCB, GBE, DSO* (London: Scolar, 1995), p. 577.

Chapter 13

1. With apologies to Richard Hough.

2. Viscount Cunningham of Hyndhope, *A Sailor's Odyssey: The Autobiography of Admiral of the Fleet Viscount Cunningham of Hyndhope* (New York: Dutton, 1951), p. 601.

3. Arthur J. Marder, Mark Jacobsen and John Horsefield, *Old Friends New Enemies, the Royal Navy and the Imperial Japanese Navy Volume II: The Pacific War, 1942–1945* (Oxford: Clarendon, 1990), p. 313. n. 14.

4. Arthur J. Marder, Mark Jacobsen and John Horsefield, *Old Friends New Enemies, the Royal Navy and the Imperial Japanese Navy Volume II: The Pacific War, 1942–1945* (Oxford: Clarendon, 1990), p. 314. Somerville to Fraser. 6 May 1944. In Michael Simpson (ed.), *The Somerville Papers: Selections from the Private and Official Correspondence of Admiral of the Fleet Sir James Somerville, GCB, GBE, DSO* (London: Scolar, 1995), p. 551.

5. Prime Minister to First Lord and First Sea Lord. 29 April 1944. Winston S. Churchill, *The Second World War Volume V: Closing the Ring* (London: Reprint Society, 1954), p. 543.
6. Viscount Cunningham of Hyndhope, *A Sailor's Odyssey: The Autobiography of Admiral of the Fleet Viscount Cunningham of Hyndhope* (New York: Dutton, 1951), p. 601.
7. Churchill to Alexander and Cunningham. 27 May 1944. Cited in: Arthur J. Marder, Mark Jacobsen and John Horsefield, *Old Friends New Enemies, the Royal Navy and the Imperial Japanese Navy Volume II: The Pacific War, 1942–1945* (Oxford: Clarendon, 1990), p. 323.
8. Winston S. Churchill, *The Second World War Volume V: Closing the Ring* (London: Reprint Society, 1954), p. 76.
9. Prime Minister to Viceroy of India. 24 August 1943. In: Winston S. Churchill, *The Second World War Volume V: Closing the Ring* (London: Reprint Society, 1954), p. 87.
10. Quoted in: Philip Ziegler, *Mountbatten: The Official Biography* (London: Collins, 1985), p. 260.
11. T. O. Smith, *Britain and the Origins of the Vietnam War: UK policy in Indo-China, 1943–50* (New York: Palgrave Macmillan, 2007), p. 22.
12. Winston S. Churchill, *The Second World War Volume VI: Triumph and Tragedy* (London: Reprint Society, 1956), p. 130.
13. Mountbatten, a great-grandson of Queen Victoria, had five given names: Louis Francis Albert Victor Nicholas. However, as Ziegler points out, 'with a perversity characteristic of the British upper classes at the time the child was never called any of these. A nickname was *de rigueur* and the Queen [Victoria] suggested Nicky. This served for a while but caused confusion amid the plethora of Nickies at the Russian court and recourse was had to Dicky, or, more frequently, Dickie. Dickie he remained for the rest of his life.' Philip Ziegler, *Mountbatten: The Official Biography* (London: Collins, 1985), p. 25.
14. To his wife. 30 September 1943. In Michael Simpson (ed.), *The Somerville Papers: Selections from the Private and Official Correspondence of Admiral of the Fleet Sir James Somerville, GCB, GBE, DSO* (London: Scolar, 1995), p. 476.
15. To his wife. 29 October 1943. In Michael Simpson (ed.), *The Somerville Papers: Selections from the Private and Official Correspondence of Admiral of the Fleet Sir James Somerville, GCB, GBE, DSO* (London: Scolar, 1995), p. 482.
16. Michael Simpson (ed.), *The Somerville Papers: Selections from the Private and Official Correspondence of Admiral of the Fleet Sir James Somerville, GCB, GBE, DSO* (London: Scolar, 1995), p. 368.
17. Arthur J. Marder, Mark Jacobsen and John Horsefield, *Old Friends New Enemies, the Royal Navy and the Imperial Japanese Navy Volume II: The Pacific War, 1942–1945* (Oxford: Clarendon, 1990), p. 327.
18. 'As Chief of Combined Operations, Lord Louis has shown rare powers of organization and resourcefulness. He is what – pedants notwithstanding – I will venture to call "a complete triphibian", that is to say, a creature equally at home in three elements – earth, air and water – and also well accustomed to fire.' From a speech of 31 August 1943. In: Winston S. Churchill, *The Second World War Volume V: Closing the Ring* (London: Reprint Society, 1954), p. 108.
19. Churchill to Mountbatten. 10 January 1944. UK National Archives. PREM 3/147/7. 'Buccaneer Operation (Andaman Islands)' November 1943-January 1944.
20. Jonathan Templin Ritter, *Stilwell and Mountbatten in Burma: Allies at War, 1943–1944* (Denton, TX: University of North Texas, 2017), p. 112.
21. Jonathan Templin Ritter, *Stilwell and Mountbatten in Burma: Allies at War, 1943–1944* (Denton, TX: University of North Texas, 2017), p. 112. McLynn argues that 'almost all

British politicians and generals by now regarded Burma as an expensive waste of time and Chiang as a waste of space'. Frank McLynn, *The Burma Campaign: Disaster Into Triumph 1942–45* (New Haven, CT: Yale University, 2011), p. 245.

22. Charles F. Romanus and Riley Sunderland, *United States Army in World War II: China-Burma-India Theater Stilwell's Command Problems* (Washington DC: Center of Military History United States Army, 1987), p. 171.

23. Charles F. Romanus and Riley Sunderland, *United States Army in World War II: China-Burma-India Theater Stilwell's Command Problems* (Washington DC: Center of Military History United States Army, 1987), p. 171.

24. David Fraser, *Alanbrooke* (Feltham: Hamlyn, 1983), p. 410.

25. Martin Gilbert, *Road to Victory: Winston S. Churchill 1941–1945* (London: Minerva, 1989), pp. 604, 654.

26. For Culverin see: Office of the Combined Chiefs of Staff, *Sextant Conference November-December 1943: Papers and Minutes of Meetings* (Washington DC: Office of the Combined Chiefs of Staff, 1943), p. 418.

27. Winston S. Churchill, *The Second World War Volume V: Closing the Ring* (London: Reprint Society, 1954), p. 326.

28. Winston S. Churchill, *The Second World War Volume V: Closing the Ring* (London: Reprint Society, 1954), p. 326.

29. Quoted in: Philip Ziegler, *Mountbatten: The Official Biography* (London: Collins, 1985), p. 266.

30. Quoted in: David Fraser, *Alanbrooke* (Feltham: Hamlyn, 1983), p. 410.

31. Quoted in: David Fraser, *Alanbrooke* (Feltham: Hamlyn, 1983), p. 411.

32. Diary entry. 18 August 1943. Aboard *Queen Mary.* In: Arthur Bryant, *The Turn of the Tide 1939–1943: A Study based on the Diaries and Autobiographical Notes of Field Marshal The Viscount Alanbrooke* (London: Collins, 1957), p. 694.

33. Grace Person Hayes, *The History of the Joint Chiefs of Staff in World War II: The War Against Japan* (Annapolis, MD: Naval Institute Press, 1982), p. 456.

34. Charles F. Brower, *Defeating Japan: The Joint Chiefs of Staff and Strategy in the Pacific War 1943–1945* (New York: Palgrave Macmillan, 2012), p. 57. He had actually first proposed landing there in April 1943 as opposed to fighting in Burma which would be like 'munching a porcupine quill by quill'. Brooke to Montgomery. 12 April 1943. In: Arthur Bryant, *The Turn of the Tide 1939–1943: A Study based on the Diaries and Autobiographical Notes of Field Marshal The Viscount Alanbrooke* (London: Collins, 1957), p. 603.

35. Minutes of First Meeting of the President and Prime Minister with the Combined Chiefs of Staff. 19 August 1943. Quoted in: Martin Gilbert, *Road to Victory: Winston S. Churchill 1941–1945* (London: Minerva, 1989), p. 478.

36. Diary entry. 28 October 1943. In: Brian Bond (ed.), *Chief of Staff: The Diaries of Lieutenant-General Sir Henry Pownall. Volume Two 1940–1944* (Hamden, CT: Archon, 1974), p. 116.

37. From a speech at the Lord Mayor's Mansion House luncheon, 11 November 1942. https://www.theguardian.com/theguardian/2009/nov/11/churchill-blood-sweat-tears

38. The term originated, I think, with Benjamin Disraeli, who almost used it at a speech in the Free Trade Hall, Manchester, on 3 April 1878. In criticizing his Liberal opponents' policy and attitude towards India, Disraeli argued that it had been proven with 'mathematical demonstration to be the most costly jewel in the Crown of England'. See: W. F. Moneypenny and George E. Buckle, *The Life of Benjamin Disraeli: Earl of Beaconsfield.* Six Vols (New York: MacMillan, 1920) Vol. IX, pp. 191–2; Sneh Mahajan, *British Foreign Policy 1874–1914: The Role of India* (London: Routledge, 2002), p. 34.

39. His attitude is well summed up in a letter he wrote to his wife on 1 February 1945 from Malta: 'I have had for some time a feeling of despair about the British connection with India and still more about what will happen if it is suddenly broken. Meanwhile we are holding on to this vast Empire, from which we get nothing, amid the increasing criticism and abuse of the world and our own people and increasing hatred of the Indian population, who receive constant and deadly propaganda to which we can make no reply. However out of my shadows has come a renewed resolve to go fighting on as long as possible and to make sure the Flag is not let down while I am at the wheel.' In: Mary Soames (ed.), *Speaking for Themselves: The Personal Letters of Winston and Clementine Churchill* (London: Black Swan, 1999), p. 512.

40. In: Arthur Bryant, *Triumph in the West, 1943–1946: Based on the Diaries and Autobiographical Notes of Field Marshal The Viscount Alanbrooke* (London: Collins, 1959), pp. 154–5.

41. Jonathan Templin Ritter, *Stilwell and Mountbatten in Burma: Allies at War, 1943–1944* (Denton, TX: University of North Texas, 2017), p. 112.

42. Roosevelt to Churchill. 24 February 1944. Quoted in: Winston S. Churchill, *The Second World War Volume V: Closing the Ring* (London: Reprint Society, 1954), p. 445.

43. Churchill to Roosevelt. 25 February 1944. Quoted in: Arthur J. Marder, Mark Jacobsen and John Horsefield, *Old Friends New Enemies, the Royal Navy and the Imperial Japanese Navy Volume II: The Pacific War, 1942–1945* (Oxford: Clarendon, 1990), p. 297.

44. Minute by Brigadier Ian Jacob. 17 February 1944. UK National Archives. PREM 3/148/4. 'Strategy in S.E. Asia Command – Culverin Operation (Sumatra) (Axiom papers)'. February–March 1944.

45. Diary Entry. 3 March 1944. In: Arthur Bryant, *Triumph in the West, 1943–1946: Based on the Diaries and Autobiographical Notes of Field Marshal The Viscount Alanbrooke* (London: Collins, 1959), p. 161.

46. David Fraser, *Alanbrooke* (Feltham: Hamlyn, 1983), p. 417.

47. For Ismay see: Alex Danchev, 'Waltzing with Winston: Civil-Military Relations in Britain in the Second World War', in *War in History*, Vol. 2, No. 2, July 1995, p. 214.

48. General Ismay to the Prime Minister. 4 March 1944. Quoted in: Arthur Bryant, *Triumph in the West, 1943–1946: Based on the Diaries and Autobiographical Notes of Field Marshal The Viscount Alanbrooke* (London: Collins, 1959), p. 161.

49. Diary entry. 8 May 1944. Quoted in: David Fraser, *Alanbrooke* (Feltham: Hamlyn, 1983), p. 413.

50. Winston S. Churchill, *The Second World War Volume V: Closing the Ring* (London: Reprint Society, 1954), p. 447.

51. Winston S. Churchill, *The Second World War Volume V: Closing the Ring* (London: Reprint Society, 1954), p. 446.

52. Prime Minister to President Roosevelt. 10 March 1944. Quoted in: Winston S. Churchill, *The Second World War Volume V: Closing the Ring* (London: Reprint Society, 1954), p. 447.

53. Winston S. Churchill, *The Second World War Volume V: Closing the Ring* (London: Reprint Society, 1954), p. 448.

54. Prime Minister to First Sea Lord, CIGS (Chief of the Imperial General Staff) and CAS (Chief of the Air Staff). 20 March 1944. Quoted in: Winston S. Churchill, *The Second World War Volume V: Closing the Ring* (London: Reprint Society, 1954), p. 448.

55. Nicholas Evan Sarantakes, 'One Last Crusade: The British Pacific Fleet and Its Impact on the Anglo-American Alliance', in *The English Historical Review*, Vol. 121, No. 491, April 2006, p. 429.

56. 'Minute from WSC to the Chiefs of Staff marked "Secret"'. 20 Mar 1944. The Chartwell Papers at Churchill Archives Centre, Cambridge. CHAR 20: Official: Prime Minister, 1940–1945. CHAR 20/188A/64–68.
57. Diary entry. 20 March. In: Alex Danchev and Daniel Todman (eds), *War Diaries 1939–1945: Field Marshal Lord Alanbrooke* (London: Weidenfield & Nicolson, 2015) Kindle edition. Loc. 12197.
58. Diary entry. 21 March. In: Alex Danchev and Daniel Todman (eds), *War Diaries 1939–1945: Field Marshal Lord Alanbrooke* (London: Weidenfield & Nicolson, 2015) Kindle edition. Loc. 12197–12202.
59. 'Minute from Chiefs of Staff to WSC marked "Private and Top Secret."' 28 March 1944. The Chartwell Papers at Churchill Archives Centre, Cambridge. CHAR 20: Official: Prime Minister, 1940–1945. CHAR 20/188B/84–88.
60. Field Marshal Sir William Slim, *Defeat into Victory* (London: Reprint Society, 1957), p. 281.
61. Louis Allen, *Burma: The Longest War 1941–1945* (London: Phoenix, 1998), p. 633.
62. Arthur J. Marder, Mark Jacobsen and John Horsefield, *Old Friends New Enemies, the Royal Navy and the Imperial Japanese Navy Volume II: The Pacific War, 1942–1945* (Oxford: Clarendon, 1990), p. 299.
63. Gordon L. Rottman, *Landing Ship, Tank (LST) 1942–2002* (Oxford: Osprey, 2005). Tristan Lovering (ed.), *Amphibious Assault: Manoeuvre from the Sea From Gallipoli to the Gulf – A Definitive Analysis* (Woodbridge: Seafarer, 2005).
64. Prime Minister to President Roosevelt. Top Secret and Personal. 4 April 1944. In: Warren F. Kimball (ed.), *Churchill & Roosevelt: The Complete Correspondence Volume III: Alliance Declining February 1944-April 1945* (London: Collins, 1984), pp. 76–7.
65. From the President for the Former Naval Person [Churchill]. 13 April 1944. Personal and Secret. In: Warren F. Kimball (ed.), *Churchill & Roosevelt: The Complete Correspondence Volume III: Alliance Declining February 1944-April 1945* (London: Collins, 1984), p. 89.
66. Churchill to Ismay. 5 May 1944. Quoted in: Martin Gilbert, *Road to Victory: Winston S. Churchill 1941–1945* (London: Minerva, 1989), p. 757. The shortage of LSTs and the perceived rationing of them by the United States in the Mediterranean context, also earned the ire of Brooke. He recorded on 11 April how 'history' would '. . . never forgive them for bargaining equipment against strategy and for trying to blackmail us . . . by holding a pistol of withdrawing craft at our heads . . .'. Quoted in: David Fraser, *Alanbrooke* (Feltham: Hamlyn, 1983), p. 410.
67. For the relationship between the two, see: D. M. Horner, 'Blamey and MacArthur: The Problem of Coalition Warfare', in William M. Leary (ed.), *We Shall Return!: MacArthur's Commanders and the Defeat of Japan, 1942–1945* (Lexington, KY: University Press of Kentucky, 2004), pp. 23–59.
68. Major D. M. Horner, 'The Military Aspects of Curtin's 1944 Overseas Visit', in *Defence Force Journal*, No. 49, November/December 1984, pp. 22–3.
69. Major D. M. Horner, 'The Military Aspects of Curtin's 1944 Overseas Visit', in *Defence Force Journal*, No. 49, November/December 1984, p. 23.
70. Diary Entry. 18 May. Arthur Bryant, *Triumph in the West, 1943–1946: Based on the Diaries and Autobiographical Notes of Field Marshal The Viscount Alanbrooke* (London: Collins, 1959), p. 192.
71. Chiefs of Staff Memorandum to Churchill, 22 May 1944. UK National Archives. PREM 3/160/4. 'The "Middle" Strategy'. May-June 1944.

72. Diary entry. 21 March. In: Alex Danchev and Daniel Todman (eds), *War Diaries 1939–1945: Field Marshal Lord Alanbrooke* (London: Weidenfield & Nicolson, 2015) Kindle edition. Loc. 12549.

73. Ed Cray, *General of the Army: George C Marshall, Soldier and Statesman* (New York: Cooper Square, 2000), p. 458.

74. Anthony Tucker-Jones, *Operation Dragoon: The Liberation of Southern France, 1944* (Barnsley: Pen & Sword, 2009).

75. Diary entry. 14 June 1944. In: Alex Danchev and Daniel Todman (eds), *War Diaries 1939–1945: Field Marshal Lord Alanbrooke* (London: Weidenfield & Nicolson, 2015) Kindle edition. Loc. 12733.

76. Grace Person Hayes, *The History of the Joint Chiefs of Staff in World War II: The War Against Japan* (Annapolis, MD: Naval Institute Press, 1982), p. 631.

77. The title was coined by William Manchester. William Manchester, *American Caesar: Douglas Macarthur, 1880–1964* (Boston, MA: Little, Brown, 1978).

78. MacArthur to King. 5 August 1944. Quoted in: Grace Person Hayes, *The History of the Joint Chiefs of Staff in World War II: The War Against Japan* (Annapolis, MD: Naval Institute Press, 1982), p. 632.

79. MacArthur to Marshall. 10 August 1944. Quoted in: Grace Person Hayes, *The History of the Joint Chiefs of Staff in World War II: The War Against Japan* (Annapolis, MD: Naval Institute Press, 1982), p. 633. See also: Forrest C. Pogue, *George C Marshall: Organizer of Victory 1943–1945* (New York: Viking, 1973), pp. 452–3. When the possibility of the British Pacific Fleet coming under his command, on the terms stated, was later mooted MacArthur was all for it.

80. Viscount Cunningham of Hyndhope, *A Sailor's Odyssey: The Autobiography of Admiral of the Fleet Viscount Cunningham of Hyndhope* (New York: Dutton, 1951), p. 598.

81. Diary Entry. 6 July 1944. In: Earl of Avon, *The Memoirs of Anthony Eden, Earl of Avon: The Reckoning* (Boston: Houghton Mifflin, 1965), p. 462.

82. Diary entry. 6 July 1944. In: Alex Danchev and Daniel Todman (eds), *War Diaries 1939–1945: Field Marshal Lord Alanbrooke* (London: Weidenfield & Nicolson, 2015) Kindle edition. Loc. 12915.

83. Diary entry. 14 July 1944. In Michael Simpson (ed.), *The Cunningham Papers: Selections from the private and official Correspondence of Admiral of the Fleet Viscount Cunningham of Hyndhope . . . Volume II: The Triumph of Allied Sea Power 1942–1946* (Aldershot; Ashgate, 2006), p. 320.

84. Diary entry. 14 July 1944. In Michael Simpson (ed.), *The Cunningham Papers: Selections from the private and official Correspondence of Admiral of the Fleet Viscount Cunningham of Hyndhope . . . Volume II: The Triumph of Allied Sea Power 1942–1946* (Aldershot; Ashgate, 2006), p. 320. See also: Major D. M. Horner, 'The Military Aspects of Curtin's 1944 Overseas Visit', in *Defence Force Journal*, No. 49, November/December 1984, pp. 23–4.

85. Diary Entry. 14 July 1944. In: Earl of Avon, *The Memoirs of Anthony Eden, Earl of Avon: The Reckoning* (Boston: Houghton Mifflin, 1965), p. 536.

86. Diary entry. 14 July 1944. In: Alex Danchev and Daniel Todman (eds), *War Diaries 1939–1945: Field Marshal Lord Alanbrooke* (London: Weidenfield & Nicolson, 2015) Kindle edition. Loc. 12984.

87. Quoted in: John Prados, *Storm Over Leyte: The Philippine Invasion and the Destruction of the Japanese Navy* (New York: NAL Caliber, 2016), p. 16.

88. Diary entry. 20 July 1944. In: Alex Danchev and Daniel Todman (eds), *War Diaries 1939–1945: Field Marshal Lord Alanbrooke* (London: Weidenfield & Nicolson, 2015) Kindle edition. Loc. 13055.

89. Martin Gilbert, *Road to Victory: Winston S. Churchill 1941–1945* (London: Minerva, 1989), p. 865.

90. Diary entry. 4 August 1944. In: Alex Danchev and Daniel Todman (eds), *War Diaries 1939–1945: Field Marshal Lord Alanbrooke* (London: Weidenfield & Nicolson, 2015) Kindle edition. Loc. 13143. Also: Philip Ziegler, *Mountbatten: The Official Biography* (London: Collins, 1985), p. 281.

91. Diary entry. 8 August 1944. In: Alex Danchev and Daniel Todman (eds), *War Diaries 1939–1945: Field Marshal Lord Alanbrooke* (London: Weidenfield & Nicolson, 2015) Kindle edition. Locs. 13169–13174. Fraser, Brooke's biographer, expertly summarizes Churchill's position: 'Churchill wanted a British offensive, with British forces, in a British theatre of operations, supported from British bases. He wished, with these forces, to liberate British possessions or protected states. He did not relish sending large forces of all three services to act as an adjunct, possibly not even a very welcome and certainly not a vital adjunct, to great American forces in a great American campaign. Churchill believed that we should operate from our main Imperial base, India and should be seen in South East Asia as liberators not auxiliaries.' David Fraser, *Alanbrooke* (Feltham: Hamlyn, 1983), p. 413.

92. Diary entry. 8 August 1944. In Michael Simpson (ed.), *The Cunningham Papers: Selections from the private and official Correspondence of Admiral of the Fleet Viscount Cunningham of Hyndhope . . . Volume II: The Triumph of Allied Sea Power 1942–1946* (Aldershot; Ashgate, 2006), p. 321.

93. UK National Archives. CAB 79/79/5. 'Strategy for the War against Japan'. 8 August 1944, p. 3.

94. UK National Archives. CAB 79/79/5. 'Strategy for the War against Japan'. 8 August 1944, p. 1.

95. UK National Archives. CAB 79/79/5. 'Strategy for the War against Japan'. 8 August 1944, p. 4.

96. Diary entry. 9 August 1944. In: Alex Danchev and Daniel Todman (eds), *War Diaries 1939–1945: Field Marshal Lord Alanbrooke* (London: Weidenfield & Nicolson, 2015) Kindle edition. Loc. 13179.

97. Diary entry. 9 August 1944. In: Alex Danchev and Daniel Todman (eds), *War Diaries 1939–1945: Field Marshal Lord Alanbrooke* (London: Weidenfield & Nicolson, 2015) Kindle edition. Loc. 13185.

98. Field Marshal Sir William Slim, *Defeat into Victory* (London: Reprint Society, 1957), p. 341.

99. UK National Archives. CAB 79/79/9. 'Strategy for the War against Japan'. 9 August 1944, p. 1.

100. UK National Archives. CAB 79/79/9. 'Strategy for the War against Japan'. 9 August 1944, p. 1.

101. UK National Archives. CAB 79/79/9. 'Strategy for the War against Japan'. 9 August 1944, p. 2.

102. Prime Minister to President Roosevelt. Personal and Top Secret. 10 August 1944. In: Warren F. Kimball (ed.), *Churchill & Roosevelt: The Complete Correspondence Volume III: Alliance Declining February 1944–April 1945* (London: Collins, 1984), pp. 271–2.

103. Diary entry. 22 August 1944. In Michael Simpson (ed.), *The Somerville Papers: Selections from the Private and Official Correspondence of Admiral of the Fleet Sir James Somerville, GCB, GBE, DSO* (London: Scolar, 1995), p. 583.
104. Diary entry. 24 August 1944. In Michael Simpson (ed.), *The Somerville Papers: Selections from the Private and Official Correspondence of Admiral of the Fleet Sir James Somerville, GCB, GBE, DSO* (London: Scolar, 1995), p. 584.
105. Diary entry. 4 September 1944. In: Alex Danchev and Daniel Todman (eds), *War Diaries 1939–1945: Field Marshal Lord Alanbrooke* (London: Weidenfield & Nicolson, 2015) Kindle edition. Loc. 13363.
106. Prime Minister's Personal Minute. Top secret. 9 September 1944. Quoted in: Martin Gilbert, *Road to Victory: Winston S. Churchill 1941–1945* (London: Minerva, 1989), p. 948.
107. Diary entry. 9 September 1944. [aboard] *Queen Mary*. In: Alex Danchev and Daniel Todman (eds), *War Diaries 1939–1945: Field Marshal Lord Alanbrooke* (London: Weidenfield & Nicolson, 2015) Kindle edition. Locs. 13412–13417.
108. Diary entry. 10 September 1944. In: Alex Danchev and Daniel Todman (eds), *War Diaries 1939–1945: Field Marshal Lord Alanbrooke* (London: Weidenfield & Nicolson, 2015) Kindle edition. Loc. 13422.
109. Winston S. Churchill, *The Second World War Volume VI: Triumph and Tragedy* (London: Reprint Society, 1956), p. 132.
110. Winston S. Churchill, *The Second World War Volume VI: Triumph and Tragedy* (London: Reprint Society, 1956), pp. 134–5. The official record has the exchange thus: 'The offer he, the Prime Minister, now wished to make, was for the British Main Fleet to take part in the main operations against Japan under United States Supreme Command. THE PRESIDENT said that the offer was accepted on the largest possible scale.' Minutes of the First Plenary Meeting . . . 13 September 1944. In: *Papers and Minutes of Meetings: Octagon Conference and Minutes of Combined Chiefs of Staff Meetings in London, June 1944* (Washington DC: Office, US Secretary of the Combined Chiefs Of Staff, 1944), p. 238.
111. Diary entry. 10 August 1944. Michael Simpson (ed.), *The Cunningham Papers: Selections from the private and official Correspondence of Admiral of the Fleet Viscount Cunningham of Hyndhope . . . Volume II: The Triumph of Allied Sea Power 1942–1946* (Aldershot; Ashgate, 2006), p. 322.
112. Winston S. Churchill, *The Second World War Volume VI: Triumph and Tragedy* (London: Reprint Society, 1956), p. 136. The official record has the exchange thus: 'THE PRIME MINISTER said that the offer had been made and asked if it was accepted. THE PRESIDENT replied in the affirmative.' Minutes of the First Plenary Meeting . . . 13 September 1944. In: *Papers and Minutes of Meetings: Octagon Conference and Minutes of Combined Chiefs of Staff Meetings in London, June 1944* (Washington DC: Office, US Secretary of the Combined Chiefs Of Staff, 1944), p. 241.
113. Forrest C. Pogue, *George C Marshall: Organizer of Victory 1943–1945* (New York: Viking, 1973), p. 453.
114. Thomas B. Buell, *Master of Seapower: A Biography of Fleet Admiral Ernest J King* (Annapolis, MD: Naval Institute Press, 2012), p. 444.
115. Diary Entry. 14 September. In: Alex Danchev and Daniel Todman (eds), *War Diaries 1939–1945: Field Marshal Lord Alanbrooke* (London: Weidenfield & Nicolson, 2015) Kindle edition. Loc. 13475.

116. Diary entry. 14 September 1944. Michael Simpson (ed.), *The Cunningham Papers: Selections from the private and official Correspondence of Admiral of the Fleet Viscount Cunningham of Hyndhope . . . Volume II: The Triumph of Allied Sea Power 1942–1946* (Aldershot; Ashgate, 2006), p. 160. See also: Michael A. Simpson, *A Life of Admiral of the Fleet Andrew Cunningham: A Twentieth-century Naval Leader* (London: Frank Cass, 2004), p. 201.

117. Thomas B. Buell, *Master of Seapower: A Biography of Fleet Admiral Ernest J King* (Annapolis, MD: Naval Institute Press, 2012), p. 444.

118. Dracula replaced Vanguard, the latter being originally planned for autumn 1944.

119. Combined Chiefs of Staff Directive to Supreme Allied Commander, Southeast Asia Command. 22 September 1944. In: *Papers and Minutes of Meetings: Octagon Conference and Minutes of Combined Chiefs of Staff Meetings in London, June 1944* (Washington DC: Office, US Secretary of the Combined Chiefs Of Staff, 1944), p. 47. The Allied plan to recapture Burma (Operation Capital) called for the Fourteenth Army to advance southeast and capture Mandalay. Meanwhile in northern Burma a Chinese Expeditionary Force would reopen the Burma Road then advance to Mandalay as well. Both these advances to take place by mid-February 1945 during the dry season. If additional resources were available, then Mountbatten would use them to launch Operation Dracula. If not, then the Fourteenth Army would continue to attack southwards and take Rangoon before the monsoon began in May.

120. H. P. Willmott, *Graveyard of a Dozen Schemes: British Naval Planning and the War against Japan 1943–1945* (Annapolis, MD: Naval Institute Press, 1996), p. 19.

121. See: Thomas Hall, '"Mere Drops in the Ocean": The Politics and Planning of the Contribution of the British Commonwealth to the Final Defeat of Japan, 1944–45', in *Diplomacy & Statecraft*, Vol. 16, Issue 1, 2005, pp. 93–115. John Winant, the US Ambassador in London, had argued: 'If we allow the British to limit their active participation to recapture areas that are to their selfish interests alone and not participate in smashing the war machine of Japan . . . we will create in the United States a hatred for Great Britain that will make for schisms in the postwar years that will defeat everything that men have died for in this war.' John Winant to Harry Hopkins, 1 September 1944. Quoted in: Nicholas E. Sarantakes, 'The Short but Brilliant Life of the British Pacific Fleet', in *Joint Force Quarterly (JFQ)*, Issue 40, 1st Quarter 2006, p. 86.

122. Warren F. Kimball (ed.), *Churchill & Roosevelt: The Complete Correspondence Volume III: Alliance Declining February 1944–April 1945* (London: Collins, 1984), p. 318.

123. Michael A Simpson, *A Life of Admiral of the Fleet Andrew Cunningham: A Twentieth-century Naval Leader* (London: Frank Cass, 2004), p. 159. According to his autobiography, he and the Admiralty had been preparing for this eventuality for some time. 'I was wholeheartedly in favour of sending the fleet to join with the American fleet in active operations. The Chiefs of Staff also agreed, for it seemed about the only force that could be spared. For some reason which I never really understood the Prime Minister did not at first agree. . . . It was not until some months later that the Prime Minister was eventually brought round, as I felt quite sure he would be, to agreeing that the fleet should join the Americans in the Pacific. Meanwhile the Admiralty went steadily on with their preparations.' Viscount Cunningham of Hyndhope, *A Sailor's Odyssey: The Autobiography of Admiral of the Fleet Viscount Cunningham of Hyndhope* (New York: Dutton, 1951), p. 598.

124. There are a multitude of variations on the theme of 'sausages' and 'law' and what Bismarck is supposed to have said. There is, in fact, no evidence that he actually said it at all.

Chapter 14

1. Diary entry. 3 August 1944. In Michael Simpson (ed.), *The Somerville Papers: Selections from the Private and Official Correspondence of Admiral of the Fleet Sir James Somerville, GCB, GBE, DSO* (London: Scolar, 1995), p. 581.
2. Geoff Spooner, *Admiralty Floating Dock 26: A First Hand Account of the Sinking.* Available at: https://www.divesrilanka.com/DSTrincoAFD23.html
3. The anti-torpedo protection of the *King George V* class battleships involved using a triple 'sandwich' arrangement of void spaces with a central fuel bunker. As the fuel oil was used it was replaced with seawater to maintain the level of protection. There was some inevitable mixing and contamination of fuel with sea water, but light fuel oil of Admiralty quality could be burned with about 11 per cent of sea water without loss of efficiency. The problem was the usage of lower-quality fuel oil, of necessity as the war progressed and the consequent increase in seawater contamination and thus loss of efficiency. See: Alan Raven and John Roberts, *British Battleships of World War Two: The Development and Technical History of the Royal Navy's Battleships and Battlecruisers from 1911 to 1946* (Annapolis, MD: Naval Institute Press, 1977), p. 403. C. J. Gray and W. Kilner, 'Sea Water Contamination of Boiler Fuel and its Effects', in *Transactions of the Institute of Marine Engineers*, 1948, Vol. LX, No. 2, p. 43.
4. Henry 'Hank' Adlam, *The Disastrous Fall and Triumphant Rise of the Fleet Air Arm from 1912 to 1945* (Barnsley: Pen & Sword, 2014), p. 155.
5. Robert J. Cressman, *The Official Chronology of the U.S. Navy in World War II* (Annapolis, MD: Naval Institute Press, 2000). Available online at: http://www.ibiblio.org/hyperwar/USN/USN-Chron/
6. *Sea Rover* arrived safely at Exmouth Gulf on 1 September.
7. Viscount Cunningham of Hyndhope, *A Sailor's Odyssey: The Autobiography of Admiral of the Fleet Viscount Cunningham of Hyndhope* (New York: Dutton, 1951), p. 608.
8. Michael Simpson, *A Life of Admiral of the Fleet Andrew Cunningham: A Twentieth-Century Naval Leader* (London: Frank Cass, 2004), p. 165.
9. Henry 'Hank' Hedlam, *On and Off the Flight Deck: Reflections of a Naval Fighter Pilot in World War II. Book 1: The Years 1941–1948* (Barnsley: Pen & Sword, 2007) Kindle edition. Locs. 2581–2587.
10. UK National Archives. WO 203/4982. 'Operation "Light" to carry out a fighter sweep over airfields in the Medan, Balawan Deli areas and a photographic reconnaissance of the Pangkalan Susu area'. September 1944. Unless otherwise stated, this is the source for this section.
11. Henry 'Hank' Hedlam, *On and Off the Flight Deck: Reflections of a Naval Fighter Pilot in World War II. Book 1: The Years 1941–1948* (Barnsley: Pen & Sword, 2007) Kindle edition. Locs. 2587–2592.
12. J. Jongejans, *Land En Volk Van Atjeh: Vroeger En Nu* (Baarn: Hollandia, 1939), pp. 38–9. Guus Veenendaal, 'De locomotief van de moderniteit: Aanleg van het net van spoor- en tramwegen', in Wim Ravesteijn and J. H. Kop (eds), *Bouwen in de archipel; Burgerlijke Openbare Werken in Nederlands-Indië en Indonesië 1800–2000* (Zutphen: Walburg, 2004), pp. 82–3. See also: http://searail.malayanrailways.com/PJKA/Atjeh%20Tram/AT.htm
13. Dunstan Hadley, *Barracuda Pilot* (Shrewsbury: Airlife, 1992), p. 156.
14. Dunstan Hadley, *Barracuda Pilot* (Shrewsbury: Airlife, 1992), p. 160.
15. Captain Eric M. Brown, *Duels in the Sky: World War II Naval Aircraft in Combat* (Shrewsbury: Airlife, 1989), p. 147. For Brown see: https://www.theguardian.com/uk-news/2016/feb/21/royal-navy-most-decorated-pilot-dies-eric-winkle-brown

16. For the photo-reconnaissance version of the Hellcat see: Cory Graff, *F6F Hellcat at War* (Minneapolis, MN: Zenith, 2009), p. 124.

17. Dunstan Hadley, *Barracuda Pilot* (Shrewsbury: Airlife, 1992), p. 162.

18. Henry 'Hank' Hedlam, *On and Off the Flight Deck: Reflections of a Naval Fighter Pilot in World War II. Book 1: The Years 1041–1948* (Barnsley: Pen & Sword, 2007) Kindle edition. Loc. 2624.

19. UK National Archives. WO 203/4983. 'Operation "Millet" Units of Eastern Fleet including Battleships and Carriers operating in Nicobar area'. October–November 1944. Unless otherwise stated, this is the source for this section.

20. Sanat Kaul, *Andaman and Nicobar Islands: India's Untapped Strategic Assets* (New Delhi: Pentagon, 2015), p. 38. Special Correspondent, 'Nicobar as an IAF Base in the Indian Ocean: Strategic Asset or Liability?' in *Indian Defence Review*, Vol. 31.4, October–December 2016. Available online at: http://www.indiandefencereview.com/news/nicobar-as-an-iaf-base-in-the-indian-ocean-strategic-asset-or-liability/

21. It was intercepted by the US. Commodore Richard W Bates USN (Ret), *The Battle for Leyte Gulf October 1944: Strategical and Tactical Analysis Volume II: Operations from 0719 October 17th until October 20th (D-Day)* (Newport, RI: US Naval War College, 1955), p. 72.

22. Henry 'Hank' Hedlam, *On and Off the Flight Deck: Reflections of a Naval Fighter Pilot in World War II. Book 1: The Years 1941–1948* (Barnsley: Pen & Sword, 2007) Kindle edition. Locs. 2651–2657.

23. Henry 'Hank' Hedlam, *On and Off the Flight Deck: Reflections of a Naval Fighter Pilot in World War II. Book 1: The Years 1941–1948* (Barnsley: Pen & Sword, 2007) Kindle edition. Loc. 2673.

24. Commodore Richard W. Bates USN (Ret), *The Battle for Leyte Gulf October 1944: Strategical and Tactical Analysis Volume II: Operations from 0719 October 17th until October 20th (D-Day)* (Newport, RI: US Naval War College, 1955), p. 72.

25. Henry 'Hank' Hedlam, *On and Off the Flight Deck: Reflections of a Naval Fighter Pilot in World War II. Book 1: The Years 1941–1948* (Barnsley: Pen & Sword, 2007) Kindle edition. Loc. 2679.

26. Henry 'Hank' Hedlam, *On and Off the Flight Deck: Reflections of a Naval Fighter Pilot in World War II. Book 1: The Years 1941–1948* (Barnsley: Pen & Sword, 2007) Kindle edition. Loc. 2679.

27. Commodore Richard W. Bates USN (Ret), *The Battle for Leyte Gulf October 1944: Strategical and Tactical Analysis Volume II: Operations from 0719 October 17th until October 20th (D-Day)* (Newport, RI: US Naval War College, 1955), p. 206.

28. For a history of the aircraft see: John Stanaway, *Nakajima Ki.43 'Hayabusa:' Allied Code Name 'Oscar'* (Bennington, VT; Merriam, 2006).

29. Ikuhiko Hata, Yasuho Izawa and Christopher Shores, *Japanese Army Fighter Aces 1931–45* (Mechanicsburg, PA: Stackpole, 2012), p. 60.

30. Signals quoted in: Commodore Richard W. Bates USN (Ret), *The Battle for Leyte Gulf October 1944: Strategical and Tactical Analysis Volume II: Operations from 0719 October 17th until October 20th (D-Day)* (Newport, RI: US Naval War College, 1955), pp. 330, 365.

31. Vice Admiral The Earl Mountbatten of Burma, *Report to the Combined Chiefs of Staff by the Supreme Allied Commander South-East Asia 1943–1945* (New Delhi: English Book Store, 1960), pp. 89–90. Commodore Richard W. Bates USN (Ret), *The Battle for Leyte Gulf October 1944: Strategical and Tactical Analysis Volume II: Operations from 0719 October 17th until October 20th (D-Day)* (Newport, RI: US Naval War College, 1955), p. 72.

32. Thomas J. Cutler, *The Battle of Leyte Gulf 23–26 October 1944* (Annapolis, MD: Naval Institute Press, 1994), p. i.

33. Albert C. Wedemeyer, *Wedemeyer Reports!* (New York: Henry Holt, 1958), p. 132. Wedemeyer was referring to the Mediterranean Theatre.

34. There is still a good deal of debate around the merits or otherwise of the Barracuda and its subsequent place in aviation history. Willis states that it '. . . stands among the most reviled aircraft of the Second World War'. Matthew Willis, *The Fairey Barracuda* (Petersfield: MMP, 2016), p. i. His book explores the matter.

35. A point specifically mentioned by Hadley in relation to the attack on Sigli. Dunstan Hadley, *Barracuda Pilot* (Shrewsbury: Airlife, 1992), p. 160.

36. Minutes of Joint Chiefs of Staff Meeting September 15 1944. In: Richardson Dougall, Arthur G. Kogan, Richard S. Patterson and Irving L Thomson (eds), *Foreign Relations of the United States: Conference at Quebec 1944* (Washington DC: United States Government Printing Office, 1972), p. 352.

37. David Hobbs, *British Aircraft Carriers: Design, Development & Service Histories* (Barnsley: Seaforth, 2013), p. 95.

38. Henry 'Hank' Hedlam, *On and Off the Flight Deck: Reflections of a Naval Fighter Pilot in World War II. Book 1: The Years 1941–1948* (Barnsley: Pen & Sword, 2007) Kindle edition. Loc. 2733.

39. The phrase is by Rear Admiral Frederic S Withington. He went on to say: 'The surest way to produce that hole is still with our most potent weapons, the torpedo and the mine.' Quoted in: Gilford G. Quarles, 'The Modern Torpedo: A Case Study In Systems Engineering', in *Journal of the American Society for Naval Engineers*, Vol. 68, Issue 4, November 1956, p. 801.

40. The final confirmation, if one were needed, that the battleships' demise was complete had come on 24 October 1944 with the destruction of the *Musashi*. Aircraft from the carriers *Essex, Intrepid, Lexington, Franklin, Enterprise* and *Cabot* fulfilled Yamamoto's prophecy concerning super-battleships: 'The fiercest serpent may be overcome by a swarm of ants.' (Evan Thomas, *Sea of Thunder: Four Commanders and the Last Great Naval Campaign 1941–1945* (New York: Simon & Schuster, 2006), p. 25). That *Musashi* and her sister *Yamato* were 'the largest and, in many respects, the most powerful warships in the world' was not known at the time. Indeed the 1946 report by the US Naval Technical Mission to Japan stated that 'an almost complete lack of authentic information existed . . . intelligence reports estimated the displacement of *Yamato* as 45,000 tons standard, although prisoner-of-war reports gave vague indications of a much larger ship'. (US Naval Technical Mission to Japan, *Reports of Damage to Japanese Warships – Article 2: Yamato (BB), Musashi (BB), Taiho (CV), Shinano (CV)* (San Francisco, CA; US Naval Technical Mission to Japan, 1946), pp. 1, 5). As noted, Yamamoto had not been impressed with them: 'These ships [*Yamato* and *Musashi*] are like elaborate religious scrolls which old people hang up in their homes . . . These battleships will be as useful in modern warfare as a Samurai sword.' (John Deane Potter, *Admiral of the Pacific: The Life of Yamamoto* (London: Heinemann, 1965), p. 30). Having been struck by somewhere between ten and twenty aerial torpedoes and about the same number of bombs, *Musashi* '. . . disappeared into the ocean to the sound of a deafening roar . . .' (Akira Yoshimura and Vincent Murphy (trans.), *Battleship Musashi: The Making and Sinking of the World's Biggest Battleship* (Tokyo: Kodansha, 1999), p. 172.)

41. UK National Archives. ADM 1/29992. 'Awards to 5 officers and men of FAA squadrons from HM Ships Indomitable and Victorious for services in attacks on shipping and shore

installations in Sumatra Aug 1944 (Operation BANQUET)'. 1944. Major R. C Hay, 'Report of Wing Leader, No. 47 Naval Fighter Wing'. 27 August 1944.

42. Michael Whitby, *Navy Blue Fighter Pilot: The Wartime Naval Aviation Career of Lieutenant Don Sheppard, Canada's only Corsair Ace: Episode Two: Strike and Strike Again.* Available online at: http://www.vintagewings.ca/VintageNews/Stories/tabid/116/articleType/ArticleView/articleId/471/Navy-Blue-Fighter-Pilot-Episode-Two.aspx

43. Vice Admiral The Earl Mountbatten of Burma, *Report to the Combined Chiefs of Staff by the Supreme Allied Commander South-East Asia 1943–1945* (New Delhi: English Book Store, 1960), pp. 90, 92.

44. Philip Ziegler, *Mountbatten: The Official Biography* (London: Collins, 1985), p. 285.

45. *The Navy List . . . April 1945: Volume II*, p. 908.

46. Sir Philip Vian, *Action This Day: A War Memoir* (London: Frederick Muller, 1960), p. 100. He went on to say: '. . . this deficiency was in part repaired by the unparalleled generosity of Rear Admiral Clement Moody, who lent me his own Chief Staff Officer'.

47. The index of his autobiography contains twenty entries for Vian, whilst Moody is mentioned not at all. Viscount Cunningham of Hyndhope, *A Sailor's Odyssey: The Autobiography of Admiral of the Fleet Viscount Cunningham of Hyndhope* (New York: Dutton, 1951), pp. 698, 708.

48. Somerville, by then ensconced in Washington as head of the British Admiralty Delegation, wrote to Fraser apropos the remark: 'I can of course quite appreciate the circumstances under which this remark was made and that in itself it was only intended to suggest that we have to gain experience of the special conditions which apply in the Pacific. I feel, however, it might be desirable to pass the word round that care should be taken to avoid any suggestion that our ships are green or that any experience they require for operating in the Pacific cannot be acquired in a very short space of time.' Letter from Somerville to Fraser. 2 April 1945. Quoted in: Jon Robb-Webb, *The British Pacific Fleet: Experience and Legacy, 1944–50* (London: Routledge, 2016), p. 71.

49. For example; Captain Edward 'Eddie' Ewen, the former commander of *Independence* who had extensive experience of carrier aviation, was the senior US Naval Liaison Officer attached to Vian's command. He reported that 'suggestions were seldom well received' by Vian and 'often ignored or occasionally acted upon at some later date after having been initially disapproved. Station keeping by carriers and rotation of the axis into the wind were two important examples which were constantly ignored until after written comments had been submitted.' 'Report of the British Pacific Fleet in Support of the Okinawa Campaign, 23 April 1945' by Captain E. C. Ewen, Senior US Naval Liaison Officer BPF. Quoted in: Jon Robb-Webb, *The British Pacific Fleet: Experience and Legacy, 1944–50* (London: Routledge, 2016), p. 126. Having said that, Vian is supposed to have been unpopular with his own command as well. Adlam christened him a 'penguin' (unable to fly) and was highly critical of his abilities. See: Chapter 7, 'Penguinisms', in: Henry 'Hank' Adlam, *The Disastrous Fall and Triumphant Rise of the Fleet Air Arm from 1912 to 1945* (Barnsley: Pen & Sword, 2014).

50. David McCullough, *John Adams* (New York: Simon & Schuster, 2001), p. 144.

Chapter 15

1. The matter is investigated thoroughly in 'Appendix 8: Japanese Radar at Midway', of Jonathan Parshall and Anthony Tully, *Shattered Sword: The Untold Story of the Battle of Midway* (Dulles, VA; Potomac, 2005) pp. 497–8. It was a deficiency soon to be made

good to a certain extent: 'Anyone inclined to laugh off Japanese radar is a likely candidate for trouble. Such is the sobering implication of recent discoveries.' Anon., 'The Menace of Japanese Radar', in *Combat Information Center*, Vol. 1, No. 8, 25 October 1944. p. 24 (*Combat Information Center* (*CIC*) was a confidential magazine published monthly by the Chief of Naval Operations for the information of those 'whose duties are connected with the tactical use and operation of electronic and associated equipment').

2. Keith Kyle, *Suez: Britain's End of Empire in the Middle East* (London: I B Taurus, 2011), p. 136. According to Smith, Mountbatten was 'ruthless . . . in challenging or silencing anyone prepared to question his skilfully tailored version of events.' Adrian Smith, *Mountbatten: Apprentice War Lord* (London: I B Taurus, 2010), p. 307.

3. Ray Murphy, *Last Viceroy: The Life and Times of Rear-Admiral The Earl Mountbatten of Burma* (London; Jarrolds, 1949) p. 168.

4. Letter to his wife, 25 June 1944. In Michael Simpson (ed.), *The Somerville Papers: Selections from the Private and Official Correspondence of Admiral of the Fleet Sir James Somerville, GCB, GBE, DSO* (London: Scolar, 1995), p. 568.

5. Philip Ziegler, *Mountbatten: The Official Biography* (London; Collins, 1985), p. 235.

6. From a 1956 interview between Roskill and Power. Quoted in Stephen Roskill, *Churchill and the Admirals* (Barnsley: Pen & Sword, 2004), p. 260.

7. Eisenhower knew MacArthur of old, and when asked to comment on what kind of man he was, answered: 'You will notice that our communiques . . . go out from AFHQ [Allied Force Headquarters]. In the South West Pacific, on the other hand, communiques are issued as from General MacArthur's Headquarters. That is the kind of man he is.' Eisenhower on MacArthur. 1 March 1944. Quoted in Philip Ziegler, *Mountbatten: The Official Biography* (London: Collins, 1985), p. 255.

8. Roosevelt's anti-colonialist views were strongly held, and Churchill's remark about not having 'become the King's First Minister in order to preside over the liquidation of the British Empire' was made in response to an accusation concerning his alleged (mis)interpretation of the Atlantic Charter. See Foster Rhea Dulles and Gerald E. Ridinger, 'The Anti-Colonial Policies of Franklin D Roosevelt', in *Political Science Quarterly*, Vol. 70, No. 1, March 1955, pp. 8–9. For the Charter see: https://history.state.gov/milestones/1937-1945/atlantic-conf

9. Sir Philip Vian, *Action This Day: A War Memoir* (London: Frederick Muller, 1960) p. 196.

10. BPF aircraft sank three destroyers and damaged a number of others. Nicholas E. Sarantakes, 'The Short but Brilliant Life of the British Pacific Fleet', in *Joint Force Quarterly* (*JFQ*), Issue 40, 1st Quarter 2006, p. 90.

11. Entry by Somerville in the British Admiralty Delegation Desk Diary concerning a meeting with James Forrestal, Secretary of the Navy 1944–1947. 6 November 1944. In Michael Simpson (ed.), *The Somerville Papers: Selections from the Private and Official Correspondence of Admiral of the Fleet Sir James Somerville, GCB, GBE, DSO* (London: Scolar, 1995), p. 607.

Index